British and American
UTOPIAN LITERATURE
1516–1975

an annotated bibliography

A
Reference
Publication
in
Science Fiction

Lloyd W. Currey
David G. Hartwell
Editors

British and American
UTOPIAN LITERATURE
1516–1975

an annotated bibliography

LYMAN TOWER SARGENT

G.K.HALL&CO.

70 LINCOLN STREET, BOSTON, MASS.

Library of Congress Cataloging in Publication Data

Sargent, Lyman Tower, 1940–
  British and American utopian literature, 1516–1975.

  (A Reference publication in science fiction)
  Includes indexes.
  1. English literature — Bibliography. 2. Utopias — Bibliography. 3.
American Literature — Bibliography. 4. Science fiction, English — Bibliography. 5. Science fiction, American — Bibliography. I. Title. II. Series.
Z2014.U84S27 [PR149.U8] 016.823'.008'0372 78–11086 ISBN 0-8161-
8243-4

This publication is printed on permanent/durable acid-free paper
MANUFACTURED IN THE UNITED STATES OF AMERICA

Contents

Preface

About seven years ago I began a study of the political ideas in utopian literature in English. This seemed a reasonable project since I could find no bibliography that listed more than some 400 titles in all languages. But when I checked further I found first that no two bibliographies were the same and second that they were all remarkably incomplete. I then undertook to develop a bibliography, still expecting it to be no larger than a few hundred titles. This volume is the result, and I know that it is far from complete.

Over seven years one develops an incredible number of debts, and I wish to give my heartfelt thanks to the following people for titles of books, help in finding them, and moral support. Without some of them this project would never have been started. Without all of them it would never have reached this stage. Gorman Beauchamp, I. F. Clarke, L. W. Currey, Robert Fogarty, Arthur O. Lewis, George Locke, R. D. Mullen, Glenn Negley, Joel Nydahl, Robert Plank, J. G. A. Pocock, Carolyn Rhodes, John Rockey, Kenneth Roemer, Angele B. Samaan, David Samuelson, Mulford Q. Sibley, Milton Spahn, Darko Suvin, Roy A. Swanson, Leslie Kay Swigart, and Stuart Teitler. I am also greatly in the debt of many librarians at the University of Missouri-St. Louis, the British Museum, the Library of Congress, the New York Public Library, The Widener Library at Harvard University, Duke University Library, the Newberry Library, the Bodleian Library, Cambridge University Library, London University Library, the London Library, the London School of Economics Library, and the National Library of Scotland. I also wish to thank a number of research assistants who helped over the years, particularly, Linda Lewis, Marie Casey, and Roy Billington. Finally those who typed various parts of the manuscript deserve particular praise. Brenda King, Marie Casey, Linda Lewis, Teresa Murphy, Jeanine O'Brien, Greta Corkhill, and Linn Woodward-Myrick have been burdened with my poor handwriting and with keeping this project going. I thank them all.

Of course, I am responsible for all the errors of omission and commission that undoubtedly exist.

Introduction

Utopian literature is, in seeming contradiction, one of the most studied and most neglected genres of literature. There are hundreds of works that analyze some aspect of the genre and dozens that purport to survey it all. But the bases of good scholarship, definition and bibliography, have been singularly absent.

My own case is instructive. Having been interested in utopianism for a number of years, I decided to undertake a study of the utopian novel in English and prepared to spend a sabbatical year in the British Museum (now British Library) reading the few hundred titles that I had not already read during summers spent in the Library of Congress. I rapidly concluded that I had no good basis for deciding among borderline cases and could find little or no help in the studies of utopias, most of which assumed that we all knew what we were talking about and that there was no such thing as a borderline case. Therefore, I undertook to write an article, originally for my own use, trying to provide some means of discrimination among the rapidly lengthening list of possible utopias.[1]

A bit earlier I had discovered science fiction and found a tremendous number of works that made the problem of definition philosophically more complicated, since it raised the problem of intention, and extended the list of possible works enormously. In order to avoid carrying this story to inordinate lengths, suffice it to say that the bibliography began to take on enormous proportions in comparison to the usual list of English utopias. As a result I was finally persuaded to consider publishing an annotated version of what had originally been intended as a useful checklist for myself and others working in the field. The bibliography that follows is the result.

THE PROBLEMS OF DEFINITION

Before looking at the specific characteristics of this bibliography, it is essential to indicate the problems faced in trying to define the genre. Any definition must be usable as a discriminating tool in the analysis of a body of literature. Too many scholars simply ignore the problem or pretend it goes away by considering only the "mainstream" of the genre and ignoring the vast bulk of the literature; thus, unfortunately, most scholars who have attempted to define utopian literature have not been familiar with more than the "mainstream." They have, therefore, tended to produce definitions that are of no use to someone trying to decide if a particular work is a utopia or not.

This situation has arisen from three main problems. First, there is Sir Thomas More's original use of the word. Second, there is the usage that confuses utopian literature, utopian thought, and utopian communities. Third, there is the problem of form versus purpose or intention. If more were needed, one might also mention the effect of the derogatory connotations of utopianism in popular usage and the influence of Karl Mannheim's concept of the utopian mentality. These have both led to further uncertainty regarding the characteristics of the literary genre.

The word *utopia,* as coined by More, means *nowhere* and implies nothing relevant to the quality of that nowhere. It could be good or bad. It could include the various discussions of heaven that are sometimes called utopias — such as Elisabeth S. (Phelps) Ward's *The Gates Ajar* (1868), *Beyond the Gates* (1883), and *The Gates Between* (1887). It could include the Tarzan stories; Tolkien; H. Rider Haggard; *The Battle of Dorking* and its progeny; and, in fact, all presentation, in any form and for any purpose, of places that do not exist.[2] Unfortunately some bibliographers have not resisted the temptation to use the term in this way. But even More clearly meant more by it than that, and further analysis of the words he employed can be helpful.

Topia comes from the Greek word *topos* or *place*. "U" is the equivalent of *"ou,"* meaning *no* or *not;* or we can follow Mumford and say that *"u"* is to include both *"ou"* and *"eu"* (*good*), since More was also making a pun on *eutopia (good place).*[3] Others have analogously adopted the word *dystopia* or *bad place.* (A variety of alternative terms has been used to describe this latter category and its sub-types, but dystopia is most nearly parallel to the earlier forms. Of the alternate terms, I believe that anti-utopia, which has gained a large following, should be reserved for that large class of works, both fictional and expository, which are directed against utopia and utopian thought.[4]) Neither eutopia or dystopia directly refers to the existence or non-existence of the place. For example, St. Augustines's *De Civitate Dei,* which supposedly refers to an existent good place, could be included as an eutopia. And of course Hell is the archetypal dystopia. Perhaps this point should be stressed: neither eutopia or dystopia in any way assert non-existence. It is partially for this reason that we often use the term utopian to refer to communitarian experiments; they all have been attempts to move from utopia to eutopia; from nowhere to the good place. But we have also transferred More's pun into our own usage; we read both utopia and eutopia as a good, non-existing place and dystopia as a bad, non-existing place. The pun and More's use of irony and satire in the *Utopia* express his ambivalence, and we have transferred his ambivalence into our usage: utopian also means overly idealistic and unrealistic; it is a term used to dismiss an unacceptable idea.[5]

Finally, it should be remembered that in addition to the various prefixes "u," "eu," and "dys," — the word *topos,* or *place,* is an important part of the terminology. *Topos* implies that the utopia must be located spatially and temporally; even though nowhere, it must have some place. This is, of course, a device for imparting reality, making it seem possible rather than impossible. In general, the voyage — whether through space or time — has been the device used for locating these existing utopias.[6] Quite a number of works having no specified location, notably Plato's *Republic,* have been labelled utopian. It may at least be argued that such labelling is wrong. Concern with both parts of the original word should help avoid many such problems.

After all this, there seem to be three useful terms. Utopia may be used as the general term covering all the various classes of utopian literature. Eutopia — although the word has unfortunately fallen out of favor — or the positive utopia refers to presentations of good places. Dystopia or the negative utopia refers to presentations of bad places. The satirical utopia refers to works where the satire is the focus of the work. The archetypal example is, of course, Samuel Butler's *Erewhon* (1872).

But unfortunately we still do not have adequate criteria for saying whether any given book is a utopia, let alone a specific type of utopia. Therefore, we must turn to the second major problem — the confusion of utopian thought, utopian literature, and the utopian communities. Utopianism does clearly include three separate activities. There is the creation of utopian communities, communitarian experiments, communes, or what have you; utopian thought; and the writing of utopias. The communal movement has two connections with the rest of utopianism. First, many were founded on ideas from utopian writings, notably those based on the works of Fourier, Cabet, and Owen. Secondly, most of them have been attempts to create ideal, or at least significantly better, societies.

The second thread, utopian thought, is more difficult to characterize. Although the phrase is fairly common, it is rarely, if ever, defined. Frank E. Manuel once contrasted utopias and utopian thought on the basis of the form used in portraying the optimum society: the former being a "description, a dramatic narrative portrayal," with the latter based more on exposition and argument.[7] While I find such a division tempting since it would be a useful way to separate types of utopian writings, I am afraid it is inadequate.

There has sprung from Mannheim and others a literature which is concerned with the social, psychological, and religious dimensions of utopianism and does not address itself directly to the question of the good society. These are not simply scholarly works about utopia. They are concerned with exploring the strain of utopianism in man — some see man as he who creates utopias.[8] This concern with man's social dreams, of which utopia is but one expression, must be encompassed within utopian thought; therefore, Manuel's distinction is inadequate.[9] Utopian thought can best be seen as concerned with utopia as a social force rather than as an aspect of literature or history or political philosophy. If the distinction Manuel has in mind is worth making, some better way will have to be found to do it.

This brings me to the third problem — the confusion of form and purpose. Although not peculiar to the utopian genre, this problem poses particular difficulties in a consideration of the genre, if a utopia can take any form, we would have to include virtually all works of political philosophy, most suggestions for reform, and perhaps even all attempts at city planning. This can be seen not only in the inclusion in bibliographies of utopias of such works as Filmer's *Patriarcha,* Hobbes' *Leviathan,* Kropotkin's *Mutual Aid,* and Rousseau's *Contrat social,*[10] but also in some of the definitions of utopia found in the critical literature.

These definitions demonstrate the crux of the matter, and they need to be looked at carefully. Voigt says that utopias are "...idealistic pictures of other worlds...."[11] Hertzler defines them by identifying a "distinctive characteristic" of More's *Utopia,* saying "...More depicted a perfect, and perhaps unrealizable, society, located in nowhere, purged of the shortcomings, the wastes, and the confusion of our own time and living in perfect adjustment, full of happiness and contentment."[12] Also basing his definition on More, Patrick says:

> ...a utopia conforms to certain basic features of More's Libellus, which gave the genre its name. A utopia should describe in a variety of aspects and with some consistency an imaginary state or society which is regarded as better, in some respects at least, than the one in which its author lives. He does not ordinarily claim that the fictitious society and its people are perfect in all respects and that he is propounding a total ideal or model to strive toward or imitate: most utopias are presented not as models of unrealistic perfection but as alternatives to the familiar, as norms by which to judge existing societies, as exercises in extrapolation to discover the social and other implications of realizing certain theories, principles and projects.[13]

In two special issues of journals devoted to utopianism in literature, we are provided with a number of different, and mutually exclusive definitions of utopia that reflect some of the problems that I have indicated. Among those that bother to define, and most don't,[14] some insist that the utopian society must be perfect and *therefore* unrealizable. One goes so far as to say that "Utopia is a place where everybody lives happily ever after...."[15] which certainly does not reflect the reality of utopian literature. People do not "live happily ever after" even in More's *Utopia.* Perfection is not a characteristic of utopias, and it is doubtful if it ever has been.[16] It is unfortunate that this type of definition is still being used and demonstrates the need for a discussion of the problems of definition. In the same issue, a discussion of dystopia insists that a defining characteristic of the dystopian genre must be a warning to the reader that something must, and by implication, can be done in the present to avoid the future.[17] Even though it seems fairly clear that most dystopias do do this, using the intentions of the author as a defining characteristic of a genre would probably lead to an intolerable situation, but is, at the minimum, insufficient and misleading.[18]

The central difficulty is that students of the genre have assumed perfection and this has led to the continued misrepresentation of utopianism. In recent scholarship, the first, rather crude, formulation of the position was by Judith N. Shklar.[19] A much more sophisticated version has been published by Elisabeth Hansot.[20] In both versions the assumption is made that the utopia is first presented as a model of perfection to be held up to the present world, a model within which there is no change, no history. Shklar then goes on to argue that the utopian tradition ended when works of this sort were no longer written. Hansot argues that there was a shift to the presentation of progress. In both cases they fail to appreciate the complexity of the tradition.

Most works of this sort go wrong in two ways. First, they limit themselves to a very few of the appropriate books, the "great books" of utopianism, and ignore over a thousand minor works. Secondly, they tend to impose their model on the works involved rather than allow the complexity of the works to show through.

Regarding the first point, it must be said that the great books never represent a tradition, but certain weaknesses in the available scholarly apparatus have made it difficult to deal adequately with anything but the great works.

The second point is more complicated and more open to debate. Shklar characterizes utopias as follows:

> ...utopia was a model, an ideal pattern that invited contemplation and judgement but did not entail any other activity.[21]
> ...utopia, the moralist's artifact, is of necessity a changeless harmonious whole, in which a shared recognition of truth united all the citizens.[22]

Hansot, by contrast, distinguishes between two utopian traditions, the classical and the modern. The former is characterized in approximately the same way Shklar describes all utopias, but the distinction between the two types of utopias is basic. She writes,

> Among the characteristics that distinguish classical from modern utopian ideals, a most important feature of the classical utopian ideal is that its existence does not *directly* depend on a particular form of social organization but hinges rather upon the existence of a suprasensible reality.

> The social organization itself contains 'secondary' or supporting ideas that emphasize a facet or make concrete some of the implications of the primary transcendent ideal. They are 'secondary' ideals because their existence as virtues in the utopian universe depends upon a primary set of ideals that reflect the ends men should pursue. Typically, the classical utopia's emphasis is on the primary ideal, which transcends the utopia proper and under which the secondary ideal can be subsumed.
>
> The modern utopia, by contrast, has only one ideal, which is directly dependent on the utopian social organization. The ideal is 'social' because both the necessary and sufficient conditions for understanding the activities of a modern utopian citizen can be found in the arrangement of utopian society which determine the ways in which men will interact. Indeed, it is difficult to distinguish the ideal activity of a modern utopia from the social organization within which it takes place.[23]

While it is true that Hansot shows that to some extent different modes of social theorizing exist in different periods of history (it would be more startling if they did not differ), she has, I believe, mis-ascribed the change, although in a much more subtle way than has Shklar, who probably would deny the name utopia to the modern works.

There are three basic elements to any such analysis and a number of side issues. The three basic issues are the existence and nature of the distinction made by Hansot, the assumptions regarding human nature held by writers of utopias, and their attitude toward change. The latter two are often closely related and tied to the former.

Although it would be fairly easy to quibble with the evidence on any of these points by producing utopias from one period that fit the model of the other,[24] I shall instead argue that a different interpretation altogether makes more sense. No matter how you view a utopia, unless the author was writing purely for his own intellectual pleasure (a case that might be made regarding More), he is likely to make certain assumptions regarding change. First, even if he were not aware of prior social change and did not depict change within his utopia and did not say much about how his utopia was to be achieved, he must have assumed that change is possible or the utopia would be the most sterile of intellectual exercises. And although many people today see utopias in this light, it is difficult to believe that most authors of utopias could have viewed their efforts in this way. And even though the author fails to picture a changing society, that is no reason to assume he rules out change. In most cases the utopias are pictured at a moment in time, often, but not always, with a history (i.e. prior change). The society is pictured as stable, not unchanging. I am not arguing that there are no utopias that present pictures of unchanging perfection; I am merely stating that it is not a valid generalization about the genre. More makes a bad model because his society is one of the least changing. Plato, whether or not he intended to write a utopia, clearly allows for change both in the development of the ideal polis and in its inevitable collapse. Even if the polis presented is the Form of the polis, man is capable of only a momentary glimpse of the Forms; he cannot build a lasting model of them from the obdurate materials with which he has to work.

In some ways More makes the case even more strongly; his utopians are hedged about with innumerable restrictions. One gets the impression that given a moment's relaxation, the whole edifice will collapse. The currently accepted interpretation of *Utopia* that argues that the Utopians are essentially Christians and intended as a contrast to the Christianity of Europe still must recognize that the practice of the utopians, however widely the ideals are shared, is achieved ultimately by force. *Utopia* is a strong argument for the deterrent theory of punishment.

While not wanting to overemphasize the negative assumptions regarding human nature in the classical utopians, it is essential that we clearly recognize that they are not models of perfect social orders. On this, of course, Hansot agrees. But the classical utopias are, I am convinced, also more complex than she is willing to accept. Clearly one would expect that the "primary ideal," as she calls it, would be the emphasis of the classical utopians. The significance of religion throughout the entire period should make this clear. But to go from this to the statement that "The changelessness of utopian society [Plato] is, part of its transcendence..."[25] is simply wrong. For Plato, as she indicates, changelessness is an attribute of perfection, but, as she notes but does not recognize, Plato is talking about gods not men or states when he says this.[26]

The modern utopia also has this same ambivalence to change. Most modern utopias do not have a transcendental ideal, although one might quibble a bit about what constitutes such an ideal to a modern writer. They also have, or at least had until post-World War I, much more faith in the human being.[27] But the ambivalence is still there; the utopia is often motivated by horror at contemporary conditions and faith in the possibility of radical change.[28] Some take the easy way out and assume that progress or evolutionary change will sooner or later produce eutopia, or, if only people listen, eutopia can be easily achieved. But a substantial number (probably a majority) believe that at some state a violent revolution will be essential. Here the utopian is suggesting the need for extreme, probably violent, change to bring about a healthy and relatively stable society, but not an unchanging one. Wells puts the point nicely in *Men Like Gods* (1922), a eutopia achieved through violence, where he compares the society to a mill-race that looks immobile, but is in fact moving with incredible swiftness.[29] It is stable but hardly unchanging.

Among the recent[30] definitions of utopia, the one already alluded to by Darko Suvin is by far the best. He defines utopia as:

> The verbal construction of a particular quasi-human community where
> sociopolitical institutions, norms and individual relationships are or-

ganized according to a more perfect principle than in the author's community, this construction being based on estrangement arising out of an alternative historical hypothesis.[31]

The only weakness in Suvin's definition is that, to be made useful, it needs some further comment and exemplification which he does not sufficiently provide; moreover, Suvin misses an important point that Patrick makes when Patrick says "a Utopia should describe in a variety of aspects and with some consistency an imaginary state or society." Each utopia describes fairly completely an imaginary society.

Too many works that are sometimes thought of as utopias actually fail to provide sufficient material for an analysis. Short stories almost always are too slight for an analysis of the society presented in them. Three recently republished stories illustrate the problem neatly. Among other works in *American Utopias; Selected Short Fiction* (1971) are "An Allegorical Description of a Certain Island and Its Inhabitants" (1790); A Vision of Bangor in the Twentieth Century" (1848) by Edward Kent; and "The Midas Plague" (1954) by Frederik Pohl. The first can be included only because the "certain island" is part of the territory of the King of Utopia; there simply is no description of social institutions at all. The second is almost as destitute of such information. It does describe an architecturally transformed city and mentions briefly such matters as the role of women, temperance, the abolition of slavery, and the basis of the economy. There is enough to identify it as a utopia, but it is questionable whether it is an eutopia or a dystopia. There is simply not enough detail to know what is happening. In contrast, by focusing more on specific aspects of society, Pohl's "The Midas Plague" provides a short story that makes it possible to say a great deal about the society. But because there is a focus and because it illuminates only the economic system and those other sectors directly connected to it, the analyst is still left in doubt regarding many important points.

The problem, though, is not just found in short stories; many novels which present imaginary societies present similar difficulties. For example, *Kennaquhair; A Narrative of Utopian Travel* (1872) by Theophilus McCrib, B.A. (pseud.) presents a subterranean world peopled by characters from fiction. It certainly is a nowhere, but there is no discernible society. Virtually all imaginary war novels do the same thing; they include virtually no social description at all.[32] Finally, much science fiction presents overwhelming changes in technology but only suggests the social changes connected with the technological changes. For example, Bob Shaw's *One Million Tomorrows* (1970) presents a world in which men can become immortal only by becoming impotent, while women can become immortal and keep their normal sex life; with few exceptions, however, the only social changes seen are those directly connected to sexual relations. It is utopia, but there simply is not enough social detail for an analyst to say much of anything about it.

Thus, there is a general form for the term utopia as a literary genre. It refers to works which describe an imaginary society in some detail. Obviously the completeness will vary. Some centuries stressed certain aspects of society and neglected others, and some authors are concerned with certain parts of society more than others. But it must be a society — a condition in which there is human (or some equivalent) interaction in a number of different forms and in which human beings (or their equivalent) express themselves in a variety of ways.

It would be nice to be able to say with Schomann that "A utopia is a literary product of fantasy, which desires to show humanity the way to the betterment of its political, moral and social condition,"[33] and that therefore anything using the expository form would be excluded, but I find after much consideration that no such simple line can be drawn. To cite but one example, Edgar Chambless' *Roadtown* (1910) is written as an essay, but presents a society that can only be called a utopia. There are quite a few others that fall into this category. But it is a mistake to *automatically* include all forms. Some criteria must be established and rigorously applied, but particularly rigorously to expository forms. Utopia is primarily a type of prose fiction.

As Negley warns us, "The determination of whether a particular work is 'utopian' is admittedly somewhat arbitrary; any attempt at a precise definition would surely do violence to the latitude of idealization and expression which is the very essence of utopian thought."[34] And although many writers have contended wrongly that the basic lineaments of utopian society are unchanging,[35] we must recognize that its literary form has changed. For example, before the 1940s almost no one would have said that science fiction was part of utopian literature. Today the utopian novel exists almost solely as a sub-type of science fiction.[36]

There has been considerable recent discussion regarding the relationship between utopia and science fiction, trying to establish once and for all which is a sub-species of the other or whether they are related at all.[37] Obviously this is not the place to attempt to settle such a controversy, even assuming that it could be settled, but equally obviously the problem does add another complication to any attempt to define utopia.

Under such conditions, it seems a bit foolhardy to forge ahead, but it has to be done. The mess is so overwhelming that no analysis of utopian literature that hopes to deal with anything other than the commonly accepted "mainstream" can avoid it. I believe that the nature of the task dictates a twofold approach — definition and organization.

To reiterate some of the arguments advanced previously, a utopia must contain a fairly detailed description of a social system that is nonexistent but located in time and space. At least one of the foci of the work must be such a description. It may be provided as a background, as in many current works of science fiction, or it can be the central focus of the work. But it has to be there. And for the general term utopia, this characterization is probably sufficient. It eliminates many of the works that clutter up the bibliographies of utopias. Very few reform tracts present more than a very limited view of society. And of course virtually all city plans and the like would be excluded. Although there would still be problems with individual works, they would be reduced.

But too much still remains that is questionable, and some attempt at classification helps. There are three simple categories — the eutopia or positive utopia, the dystopia or negative utopia, and the satirical utopia. They all raise the problem of intention, but it can be dealt with somewhat as follows. The questions that must be answered are (1) Did the author intend to produce a utopia? (2) Did he in fact do so even if his intention was to write something else? (3) Assuming yes to one or two, does the work describe a good place or a bad place? (satire will be discussed shortly). Yet, this is not as simple as it sounds. I admit that B. F. Skinner sees the society in *Walden Two* as a good one, but on first reading I did not and I am still ambivalent. Many of my students view the world of Edward Bellamy's *Looking Backward* with horror, even though Bellamy clearly thought it was good. And, of course, many writers contemporary with Bellamy saw his society as a dystopia.[38] Of course when an author says that to him this work is good or bad, that settles the question for the analyst. In such a case, the fact that the analyst disagrees is irrelevant, but the examples used illustrate just how difficult it will be to decide in cases where there is no clear indication from the author.

In order to answer these questions we have recourse to the traditional evidences of literary scholarship — the internal evidence of the work and other material by and about the author. And we have our own highly personal reaction which we hold in abeyance until we have exhausted the other material, but which we cannot forget entirely in answering question three.

The satirical utopia is a more complicated proposition because most utopias contain some element of satire.[39] Taking *Erewhon* as the best known case, one can see that a satirical utopia is basically a description of a nonexistent place, the major focus of which is satire. The point here is that the satire is the major focus; if it is merely a secondary or tertiary focus in a description of a good or bad nonexistent place, the work would be placed in one of the previous two categories.

All works that present nonexistent societies can be put in one of these categories, but it will be useful to illustrate the discriminating nature of the tool. as a first example, there is *The Lord of the Rings*. Clearly it presents a nonexistent place located in space and time, but it is still not a utopia. It does not present at any point, although I expect some dispute on this, a fairly detailed description of a society in a variety of its aspects. I would make the same case against *The Wizard of Oz*.[40] The Robinsonades present a similar problem.

Often classified as utopias, they are bound together primarily by the island motif and the solitary or nearly solitary existence of the protagonist. Obviously, such presentation precludes a description of a society, and they are therefore at best peripheral to the utopian genre.[41]

A different type of problem is posed by Isaac Asimov's *Foundation* trilogy. Although it is clearly a utopia in the general sense of a nonexistent society located in space and time, I cannot see any way of putting a good-bad label on the place except by my personal reaction, which is highly ambivalent. Asimov's presentation of an evolving society over vast time periods means that one's judgment must vary depending on the period described. It is a utopia, but it is not either a eutopia or a dystopia.

It can be argued that science fiction produces this type of problem quite frequently. Whatever we label these works — be it utopias, social science fiction, or tales of the future — they are part of the utopian tradition since they do present fairly detailed descriptions of nonexistent social systems. Even though the utopian elements are rarely the primary focus of the work, they are often a secondary focus. Much science fiction presents utopias and dystopias with a fairly rare eutopia. This is where the question of intent is shown to confuse rather than help. The science fiction writer is often not primarily concerned with the utopia he is presenting, but he does still present one. Thus unless the purely formal characteristics of the genre are stressed, most contemporary utopias would be lost.

NOTES

1. "Utopia — The Problem of Definition," *Extrapolation,* 16 (May 1975), 137–148. Sections of this article are used as a basis for the definitional parts of this chapter. I have corrected a number of errors that appeared in the published version, and I have brought it up to date.

2. Among the types of works included in bibliographies of utopias or definitions of utopian literature are the following: the positive utopia or eutopia, the negative utopia or dystopia, the satirical utopia, the utopia of the mind, myths of an earthly paradise, *Insulae fortunatae,* imaginary voyages, Robinsonades, Atlantis legends, science fiction, fantasy, fairy tales, instructions to princes, works of political philosophy, speculations on the nature of heaven, Oriental tales, tales of the future, novels of spiritualism or psychical research, stories about early man, imaginary wars, allegory, satire, romance, adventure stories, and disaster stories.

3. Lewis Mumford, "Utopia, The City and The Machine," in Frank E. Manuel (ed.) *Utopias and Utopian Thought* (Boston: Beacon Press, 1966), p. 8.

4. Here I would include, on the fictional side, anti-Bellamy writings and those written against other utopists. For a discussion of anti-utopianism in general, see George Kateb, *Utopia and Its Enemies.* New York: The Free Press of Glencoe, 1963.

5. For a brief treatment of some further difficulties with the way utopia has been used, see Harry Levin, "Some Paradoxes of Utopia," in his *The Myth of the*

Golden Age in the Renaissance (Bloomington: Indiana University Press, 1969), pp. 187–193.

6. See, for example, Geoffroy Atkinson, *The Extraordinary Voyage in French Literature Before 1700.* New York: Columbia University Press, 1920; Atkinson, *The Extraordinary Voyage in French Literature from 1700 to 1720.* Paris: Edouard Champion, 1922; and Philip Babcock Gove, *The Imaginary Voyage in Prose Fiction.* London: The Holland Press, 1961.

7. "Introduction," in Manuel, p. vii.

8. See, for example, Frederick L. Polak, *The Image of the Future; Enlightening the Past, Orientating the Present, Forecasting the Future,* 2 Vols. New York: Oceana, 1961.

9. This type of utopian thought is a major strain in Manuel's *Utopias and Utopian Thought,* with essays by Eliade, Polak, and Tillich, among others, representing this approach.

10. These examples are taken from Wilder Bentley, *The Communication of Utopian Thought: Its History, Forms, and Use,* Volume 1, *Bibliography* (San Francisco: San Francisco State College Bookstore, 1959), pp. 9, 20; and W. J. Lang, "Utopias," unpublished bibliography in the Harvard University Library, pp. 1–2.

11. Andreas Voigt, *Die sozialen Utopien* (Leipzig: G. J. Goschen'sche Verlagshandlung, 1906), p. 1.

12. Joyce Oramel Hertzler, *The History of Utopian Thought* (New York: Macmillan, 1923), pp. 1–2.

13. J. Max Patrick, "Introduction," R. W. Gibson and J. Max Patrick; "Utopias and Dystopias, 1500–1750," Section IX of R. W. Gibson (comp.) *St. Thomas More: A Preliminary Bibliography of the Works and Moreana to the Year 1750* (New Haven: Yale University Press, 1961), p. 293.

14. In the December 1973 issue of *Comparative Literature Studies,* devoted to "Utopian Social Thought in Literature and the Social Sciences, only my article, on "Women in Utopia," mentions the problem of definition.

15. David Ketterer, "Utopian Fantasy as Millenial Motive and Science-Fictional Motif," *Studies in the Literary Imagination,* 6 (Fall 1973), 81. The editor, Jack I. Biles, takes the same position in his "Editor's Comments." Different positions are taken by Robert M. Philmus, who refers to utopias as being "more or less ideal," and Darko Suvin, who refers to "a more perfect principle than in the author's community." Philmus, "The Language of Utopia," p. 62; Suvin, "Defining the Literary Genre of Utopia: Some Historical Semantics, Some Genology, A Proposal and A Plea," p. 132.

16. For evidence on this point, see my "A Note on the Other Side of Human Nature in the Utopian Novel," *Political Theory,* 3 (February 1975), 88–97.

17. Robert O. Evans, "The *Nouveau Roman,* Russian Dystopias, and Anthony Burgess," *Studies in the Literary Imagination* 6 (Fall 1973), 33.

18. Suvin, p. 142.

19. Judith N. Shklar, *After Utopia; The Decline of Political Faith.* Princeton: Princeton University Press, 1957; and Shklar, "The Political Theory of Utopia: From Melancholy to Nostalgia," in Manuel (ed.) *op. cit.,* pp. 101–115.

20. Elisabeth Hansot, *Perfection and Progress: Two Modes of Utopian Thought.* Cambridge: The MIT Press, 1974.

21. Shklar, "The Political Theory of Utopia," *op. cit.,* p. 105.

22. *Ibid.*

23. Hansot, *op. cit.,* p. 11.

24. To buttress the quibble slightly, I would argue, although I'm sure Hansot would disagree, that the following modern utopias fit her classical model: [John Macmillan Brown], *Limanora; The Island of Progress* by Godfrey Sweven (pseud.) (1903); Austen Tappen Wright, *Islandia* (1942); and Aldous Huxley *Island* (1962).

25. Hansot, p. 28.

26. Plato, *Republic ii.* 380ᵉ - 381ᶜ . . . Quoted by Hansot in Cornford's translation, *Ibid.*

27. The emergence of the dystopia as the dominant mode of utopianism is a result of this change. But there have been positive utopias published in virtually every year of the twentieth century and this mode seems to be reemerging as the dominant one.

28. For an analysis of some of the difficulties that this combination poses, see Sargent, "Human Nature and the Radical Vision," *Nomos XVII: Human Nature in Politics. Yearbook of the American Society of Political and Legal Philosophy* (New York: New York University Press, 1977), pp. 250–261.

29. H. G. Wells, *Men Like Gods* (New York: Grosset & Dunlap, 1922), p. 171.

30. See, in addition to those discussed in this article, Alexandre Cioranescu, *L'Avenir du passé; Utopie et littérature.* Paris: Gallimard, 1972; Hans Jürgen Krysmanski, *Die Utopische Methode; Eine Literatur und wissenssozologische Untersuchung deutscher Utopischer Romane des 20. Jahrhunderts.* Cologne: Westdeutscher Verlag, 1963; *Dortmunder Schriften zur Sozialforschung* Bd. 21; Hubertus Schulte Herbrüggen, *Utopie und Anti-Utopie; von der Strueckturanalyse zur Strukturtypologie.* Bochum-Langendreer: H. Pöppinghaus, 1960; *Beitrage zur englischen Philologie,* No. 43; and Renato Poggioli, *Definizione dell'utopia; e, Morte del sense della tragedia; due saggi di critica delle idee* [Pisa:] Nistri-Lischi, [1964].

31. Suvin, p. 132.

32. See I. F. Clarke, *Voices Prophesying War 1763-1984.* London: Oxford University Press, 1966.

33. Emilie Schomann, *Franzosische Utopisten und ihr Frauenideal* (Berlin: Verlag von Emil Felber, 1911), p. 7.

34. Glenn Negley, "Introduction," *Utopia Collection of the Duke University Library* (Durham: Friends of the Duke University Library, 1965), p. ii.

35. See, for example, Mumford, *op. cit.,* pp. 3–24; Ralf Dahrendorf, "Out of Utopia: Toward a Reorientation of Sociological Analysis," *American Journal of Sociology,* 64 (September 1958), pp. 115–127; and the essays already referred to in the special issue of *Studies in the Literary Imagination.*

36. For a brief consideration of some of this literature, see Sargent, "Utopia and Dystopia in Contemporary Science Fiction," *The Futurist* (June 1972), pp. 93–98; and Sargent "Images of the Future in Science Fiction, Paper presented before the American Political Science Association, 1974.

37. See Ketterer, pp. 82–85; and Suvin, p. 144 for opposing points of view.

38. See, for example, Richard Michaelis, *Looking Further Forward* (1890); Arthur Dudley Vinton, *Looking Further Backward* (1890); and J. W. Roberts, *Looking Within* (1893).

39. See the discussion in Robert C. Elliott, *The Shape of Utopia; Studies in a Literary Genre.* Chicago: University of Chicago Press, 1970.

40. But against this see S. J. Sackett, "Utopia of Oz," *The Georgia Review,* 14 (Fall 1960), pp. 275–291; and Edward Wagenknecht, *Utopia Americana.* Seattle: University of Washington Bookstore, 1929.

41. But see, Fritz Brüggemann, *Utopie und Robinsonade; Untersuchungun zu Schnabels Insel Felsenburg (1731–1743)*, volume 8 of *Forschungen zur neueren Literaturgeschichte,* (ed.) Franz Muncker. Weimar: Alexander Duncker, 1914.

How To Use the Bibliography

The bibliography is divided into three major sections:
1. An annotated chronological list of utopias in English, 1516–1975;
2. A list of secondary works on utopian literature;
3. Author and title indexes to the chronological list.

In the chronological list the complete citation is given for the first edition whenever possible. A symbol is given that locates the library or libraries in which I actually saw the book (A location list follows these notes.) Where no symbol is given, the book is usually in my personal collection, and I did not see it elsewhere. No symbols are given for journals since they are fairly easily located through the *Union List of Serials*.

No bibliography is complete and this is no exception. The short fiction included is selected to represent the range of such material. The book length material is fairly complete within the terms of my definition. The greatest area of disagreement among scholars trying to classify utopias centers on lost race works. I have included few of these titles, since in most cases the utopia is not a central part of the work but merely a setting for adventure and romance.

In a few cases, an entry includes the statement "not located." The source of my reference is given, and I would appreciate help in locating these. In a few cases the book may never have existed or may not now exist. And from past experience, many of them may not be utopias. In two cases individuals who have seen the books have provided annotations, and they are included in the main listing.

The secondary list is not restricted to materials related to British and American utopias but is meant to be more generally useful. I have seen most, but not all, of these items. If I have not seen them, I have verified the citation in at least two reputable sources. Understandably there are still errors, and I would appreciate any corrections. A bibliography is a tool to be used and it can be constantly improved by its users. Corrections and additions to this bibliography will be published from time to time in *Alternative Futures: The Journal of Utopian Studies*.

Location Symbols

C	Cambridge University, England
CLU	University of California, Los Angeles
CNoS	San Fernando Valley State College, Northbridge
CSmH	Huntington Library
CSt	Stanford University
CU	University of California, Berkeley
CU-Riv	University of California, Riverside
CaBViPA	Provincial Archives, Library, Victoria
CaOKQ	Queen's University, Kingston
CaOTP	Toronto Public Library
CaOTU	University of Toronto
CoDU	University of Denver
CoFS	Colorado State University, Fort Collins
CoU	University of Colorado
CtY	Yale University
CtY-M	Yale University, Medical Library
DL	U.S. Department of Labor Library
DLC	Library of Congress
DeGE	Eleutherian Mills Historical Library
FTaSU	Florida State University, Tallahassee
GU	University of Georgia
ICarbS	Southern Illinois University, Carbondale
ICJ	John Crerar Library
ICN	Newberry Library, Chicago
ICRL	Center for Research Libraries, Chicago
ICU	University of Chicago
IEdS	Southern Illinois University, Edwardsville
IEN	Northwestern University
IHi	Illinois State Historical Library
IU	University of Illinois

IaU	University of Iowa
InU	Indiana University
KU	Kansas University
KyU	University of Kentucky
L	British Library (formerly British Museum)
LLL	London Library
LSE	London School of Economics
LU	London University
LUG	London University, Goldsmith's Library
MB	Boston Public Library
MH	Harvard University
MiEM	Michigan State University, East Lansing
MiU	University of Michigan
MoK	University of Missouri — Kansas City
MoSW	Washington University, St. Louis
MoU	University of Missouri — Columbia
MoU-St	University of Missouri — St. Louis
N	New York State Library, Albany
NIC	Cornell University
NN	New York Public Library
NNC	Columbia University
NcD	Duke University
NjP	Princeton University
NjR	Rutger's University
O	Bodleian Library, Oxford University
OCl	Cleveland Public Library
ODW	Ohio Wesleyan University
OFH	Rutherford B. Hayes Library
OO	Oberlin College
OU	Ohio State University
OrU	University of Oregon
PSt	Pennsylvania State University
PU	University of Pennsylvania
RPB	Brown University
STC	*Short Title Catalog*
TxU	University of Texas
UU	University of Utah
ViU	University of Virginia
WA	Wright, Lyle H., *American Fiction*
WHi	Wisconsin Historical Society
WaE	Everett Public Library

Chronological List of
Utopian Literature, 1516–1975

nd.   **Albertson, Garrett V.** *A Visit to Mars.* Chicago: Moody Press. **MoU-St**
Detailed eutopia — stress on religion. Technology. Struggle of good and evil. Probably published about 1945–1950.

nd.   **Burroughs, S. M.** *A Strange Dream.* London: np. **LSE**
England transformed by the single tax.

nd.   **Cole, Clara Gilbert.** *The Castle in the Air or The Might-Be Land.* London: Dreadnought Press.
1920's? Communist eutopia.

nd.   **[Crandall, E.E.]** *The Marvelous Isles of the Western Sea.* Np: np. **DLC**
Pure, simple Christianity informing an advanced, democratic eutopia. Story of conflict over monetary policy — paper money must be backed by gold or silver.

nd.   *Popery in A.D. 1900,* by One J. M. London: Seeley
Dystopia, success of the Papacy in England by 1900.

[1516]   **[More, St. Sir Thomas.]** *Libellus vere aureus nec minus salutaris quam festivus de optimo reip[ublicae] statu, deq[ue] noua Insula Vtopia* [Louvain:] Arte Theodorice Martini. **C**
The classic work. Known as *The Utopia.*

1579   *A Pleasant Dialogue betweene a Lady called Listra, and a Pilgrim. Concerning the gouernment and common weale of the great province of Crangalor.* Signed T. N. London: John Charlewood. **CSmH STC 18335+**
Small town of good Christians. Emphasis on piety, equity, honesty. Has a godly prince, humble nobility, obedient citizens and a good clergy. See also 1579 *The Second Part. . . .*

[1579]   *The second part of the painefull Iorney of the poore Pylgrime into Asia, and the straynge woonders that he sawe: Both delectable*

and profytable, in sequell of the lytle Dialogue, betweene Lady Lystra, and the same Pilgrime, 1579. Signed T. N. London: John Charlewood. **CSmH STC 18335 + +**
Continuation of 1579 *A Pleasant Dialogue. . . .*

1580 **[Lupton, Thomas].** *Siuqila. Too Good, to be true: Omen. Though so at a vewe, Yet all that I tolde you, Is true, I upholde you: Now Cease to aske why For I can not lye. Herein is shewed by waye of Dialogue, the wonderfull maners of the people of Mauqsun, with other talke not frivolous.* London: Henrie Bynneman. [*Siuquila* — variant spelling.] **L**
Standard Christian eutopia, very similar to the *Utopia.* Emphasis on hierarchical nature of society and the responsibility of the superior for the inferior. Very strong emphasis on purity and obedience of women. Stresses quick and sure punishment as the means of social control. See also 1581 Lupton.

1581 **Lupton, Thomas.** *The Second part and Knitting up of the Boke entituled Too good to be true. Wherein is continued the discourse of the wonderfull Lawes, commendable customes, and strange manners of the people of Mauqsun.* London: Printed by Henry Binneman. **L**
Continuation of 1580 [Lupton]. Anti-Roman Catholic. Emphasis on landlord-tenant relations.

1583 **Stubbes, Phillip.** *The Anatomie of Abuses: Contayning a Discoverie or Briefe Summarie of such Notable Vices and Imperfections, as now raigne in many Christian Countreyes of the Worlde: but (especiallie) in a verie famous ISLANDE called AILGNA: Together, with most fearefull Examples of Gods Iudgements, executed upon the wicked for the same, aswell in AILGNA of late, as in other places, elsewhere. Verie Godly, to be read of all true Christians euerie where: but most needefull to be regarded in ENGLANDE.* **O**
Satire on England using the imaginary country approach. See also 1583 Stubbes. *The Second part. . . .*

[1583] **Stubbes, Phillip.** *The Second part of the Anatomie of Abuses, conteining The display of Corruptions, with a perfect description of such imperfections, blemishes and abuses, as now reigning in euerie degree, require reformation for feare of Gods vengeance to be powred upon the people and countrie, without speedie repentance and conuersion unto God: made dialogwise by Phillip Stubbs.* London: Printed by R. W. For William Wright. **L**
Continuation of 1583 Stubbes. *The Anatomie of Abuses.*

[1590] **Sidney, Sir Philip.** *The Countesse of Pembrokes Arcadia.* London: William Ponsonbie. **L**

Arcadian, sentimental eutopia with the emphasis on romance and knightly virtue.

1605   **[Hall, Joseph.]** *The Discovery of a New World or A Description of the South Indies, Hetherto Unknowne,* by an English Mercury (pseud.). [London:] imprinted by G. Eld for Ed. Blount and W. Barrett, 1609. *Mundus Alter et Idem.* London: H. Lownes. 1669 edition entitled *Psittacorum Regio. The Land of Parrots: Or, The She-lands. With a Description of other strange adjacent Countries, in the Dominions of Prince Del' Amour, Not hitherto found in any Geographical Map.* **L, ICN**

Satire — new world is divided into states of Tenter-belly, with its provinces of Eat-allia (Gluttonia) and Drinke-allia (Quaffonia), Shee-landt or Womandecoia, with its provinces of Tattlingen, Scoldonna, Blubberick, Giggot-tangir, Cocka-trixia, Shrewes-bourg, and Blackswanstack (Modestiana), Fooliana, and Theeve-ingen, with its provinces of Robbers-waldt and Liegerdemaine.

1611   **Shakespeare, William.** *The Tempest.*

Includes a very brief description of the Golden Age.

1621   **[Burton, Robert.]** ["An Utopia of Mine Owne"], "Democritus Iunior to the Reader," in his *The Anatomy of Melancholy, What It Is. With All the Kindes, Causes, Symptomes, Prognostickes, and Severall Cures of It. In Three Maine Partitions with thier seuereii Sectionsn Membnd Subsections. Philosophically, Medicinally, Historically, Opened and Cut Up,* by Democritus Iunior (pseud.) (Oxford: Printed by Iohn Lichfield and Iames Short, for Henry Cripps, 1621), pp. 56–61. **O**

A formal, conservative eutopian fragment.

1626   **Bacon, Francis.** *New Atlantis,* a work unfinished added to *Sylva sylvarium or a Naturall History. In ten centuries.* [London:] J. H. for W. Lee. **L**

Christian eutopia, with emphasis on a traditional paternal family system and science. Gave rise to many continuations.

1638   **[Godwin, Francis.]** *The Man in the Moone; or A Discourse of a Voyage Thither,* by Domingo Gonsales (pseud.). London: Printed by John Norton. Also available in *The Harleian Miscellany,* Vol. 8, pp. 344–361.

Eutopia brought about largely through the innate disposition of the people. Land provides plenty without labor.

1640   **Brome, Richard.** *The Antipodes; A Comedie.* London: Printed by J. Okes, for Francis Constable. **L**

Play first performed in 1638. Comedy of reversal — women rule men, people rule magistrates.

1641   **[Plattes, Gabriel.]** *A Description of the famous Kingdom of Macaria; showing its excellent government, wherein the inhabi-*

tants live in great prosperity, health, and happiness; the King obeyed, the nobles honoured, and all good men respected; vice punished, and virtue rewarded. An Example to Other Nations: In a Dialogue between a Scholar and a Traveller. London: Printed for Francis Constable. Also available in The Harleian Miscellany, Vol. 1, pp. 580–585. **L**

> Traditionally attributed to Samuel A. Hartlib. See Charles Webster, "The Authorship and Significance of Macaria," Past and Present, No. 56 (August 1972), pp. 34–48 for the new attribution. A short dialogue covering economic organization, religion, and some governmental organization. Monarchy with power in a grand or general council or parliament and five under-councils. Government revenues are derived largely from the king's lands.

1648 **[Gott, Samuel.]** Novae Solymae. Libri Sex. Londini: Typis Joannis Legati. Second edition: **[Gott, Samuel.]** Nova Solyma. The Ideal City; or Jerusalem Regained, edited by Rev. Walter Begley. 2 Vols. London: John Murray, 1902. **L**

> Emphasis on family and education for developing good citizens. Jews had been converted. Annual elections. Class distinctions.

[1649] **[Chamberlen, Peter.]** The Poore Mans Advocate, or England's Samaritan. Powring Oyle and Vyne into the wounds of the Nation. By making the present Provision for the Souldier and the Poor, by reconciling all Parties. By paying all Arreares to the Parliament Army. All publique Debts, and all the late Kings, Queenes, and Princes Debts due before Session. London: Printed for Giles Calvert. **L**

> Better society brought about by nationalizing all unused lands and mines and the remains of the estates of the king, the bishops, etc. Provide work for the poor.

1652 **Winstanley, Gerrard.** The Law of Freedom in a Platform: Or, True Magistracy Restored. Humbly presented to Oliver Cromwel, General of the Common-wealths Army in England, Scotland, and Ireland. And to all Englishmen my brethren whether in Church-fellowship, or not in Church-fellowship, both sorts walking as they conceive according to the Order of The Gospel: and from them to all the Nations in the World. Wherein is Declared, What is Kingly Government, and what is Commonwealth Government. London: Printed for the author. **L**

> Classic Digger tract — includes detailed social reform.

1655 **[Cavendish, Margaret.] Lady M[argaret] of Newcastle.** "The Inventory of Judgements Commonwealth, the Author cares not in what World it is established," in her The Worlds Olio (London: Printed for J. Martin Allestrye, 1655), pp. 205–212. **L**

Instructions to princes. Lists a short series of specific reforms.

1656   **Harrington, James.** *The Common-wealth of Oceana.* London: Printed by J. Streater for Livewell Chapman. **DLC**
Classic work on the reform of England.

1659   **Baxter, Richard.** *A Holy Commonwealth, or Political Aphorisms, Opening the true Principles of Government: For The Healing of the Mistakes, and Resolving the Doubts, that most endanger and trouble ENGLAND at this time: (if yet there may be hope.) And directing the desires of sober Christians that long to see the Kingdoms of this world, become the Kingdoms of the Lord, and of his Christ.* London: Printed for Thomas Underhill and Francis Taylor. **L**
Description of a theocracy based on obligation and consent. Mostly a treatise setting out rules for areas of possible conflict between the pastor and the magistrate.

1659   *Chaos: or, A Discourse, Wherein Is presented to the view of the Magistrate, and all others who shall peruse the same, a Frame of Government by way of a Republique, wherein is little or no danger of miscarriage, if prudently attempted, and thoroughly prosecuted by Authority. Wherein is no difficulty in the Practice, nor obscurity in the Method; But all things plain and easie to the meanest capacity. Here's no hard or strange Names, nor unknown Titles (to amaze the hearers) used, and yet here's a full and absolute Power derivative insensibly from the whole, and yet practically conveyed to the best men: wherein if any shall endeavor a breach, he shall break himself: and if its must be so, that Cats shall provide Supper, here they shall do it suitable to the best Palats, and easie to digest,* by a well-wisher to the Publique Weale (pseud.). London: Printed for Livewel Chapman. **L**
Has been attributed to Peter Chamberlen. Democratic system with annual election to Parliament and with various reforms aimed at establishing more unity. Anti-Roman Catholic.

[1659] **Eliot, John.** *The Christian Commonwealth: or, The Civil Policy of the Rising Kingdom of Jesus Christ.* London: Printed for Livewell Chapman. **L**
Derives government structure from the Bible; particularly *Exodus* 18:25 and *Deuteronomy* 1:15.

[1659] **[Plockhoy, Pieter.]** *A Way Propounded to Make the poor in these and other Nations happy. By bringing together a fit suitable and well qualified people unto one Household-government, or little-Commonwealth, Wherein every one may keep his propriety, and be imployed in some work or other, as he shall be fit, without being oppressed. Being the way not only to rid these and other Nations from idle, evil and disorderly persons, but also from all* *such that have sought and found out many inventions to live upon the labour of others. Whereunto is also annexed an invitation to the Society, or little Common-wealth,* by Peter Cornelius, *Van-Zurik-Zee* (pseud.). London: Printed for G. C. **L**

Pamphlet that formed the basis for the first American Communitarian experiment (1667). Goods not to be held in common. No common religious practices.

1660   *New Atlantis. Begun by the Lord Verulam, Viscount St. Albans: and Continued by R. H. Esquire. Wherein is set forth A Platform of Monarchical Government. With A Pleasant intermixture of divers rare Inventions, and wholsom customs, fit to be introduced into all Kingdoms, States, and Common-Wealths.* London: Printed for John Crooke. **L**

Monarchy with laws that are "...easy, plain, and all writ in our native language...." Religion and education are emphasized. Ten percent of all children are chosen for the church. No poor because all parents must teach their children their trade, and also how to read, shoot and swim.

1660-64   **[Ingelo, Nathaniel.]** *Bentivolo and Urania, in [six] books,* by N.I.D.D. 2 Vols. London: Printed by J. C. for Richard Harriot. **L, LLL**

Allegory — book six describes a Christian eutopia stressing good will to others, self-knowledge, and the other Christian virtues.

1666   **[Cavendish, Margaret.]** Duchess of Newcastle. *The Description of a New World, Called the Blazing World.* Part IV of her *Observations Upon Experimental Philosophy.* London: Printed by J. Maxwell. Separately paged. 1668 edition the first separate publication. **L**

World attached at the Pole. Various animals (bears, foxes, geese, etc.) with human characteristics. Eutopia is a small part of an allegory. Monarchy, religion, few laws.

1668   **[Neville, Henry.]** *The Isle of Pines, or, a late Discovery of a fourth ISLAND near Terra Australis, Incognita, by Henry Cornelius Van Sloetten* (pseud.). *Wherein is contained, A True Relation of certain English persons, who in Queen Elizabeths time, making a Voyage to the East Indies were cast away, and wracked near to the Coast of Terra Australis, Incognita, and all drowned, except one Man and four Women. And now lately Anno Dom. 1667. a Dutch Ship making a Voyage to the East Indies, driven by foul weather there, by chance have found their Posterity, (speaking good English) to amount (as they suppose) to ten or twelve thousand persons. The whole Relation (written, and left by the Man himself a little before his death, and delivered to the Dutch by his Grandchild) Is here annexed with the Longitude and Latitude*

*of the Island, the situation and felicity thereof, with other mat-
ter observable.* London: Printed for Allen Banks and Charles
Harper. Available in *Shorter Novels: Seventeenth Century,*
edited by Philip Henderson (London: J. M. Dent, 1967), pp.
225–243.

> One man and four women shipwrecked on a beautiful island.
> Establish political and religious order based on European
> forms. See also 1669 [Neville].

1669   **[Neville, Henry.]** *A New and Further Discovery of the Isle of Pines
in a Letter from Cornelius Van Sloetten* (pseud.), *A Dutchman,
who first discovered the same in the Year, 1667.* London: Allen
Bankes and Charles Harper. **L**

> Continuation of 1668 [Neville]. Period of "whoredoms,
> incest and adulteries" followed by the imposition of harsh
> laws.

1671   **[Howard, Edward.]** *The Six Days Adventure, or the New Utopia.
A Comedy, as it is acted at his Royal Highness the Duke of
York's Theatre.* London: Tho. Dring. **L**

> Set in Utopia — emphasis on women's rights. Women take
> over the government, but the men all decide to leave and
> women return to previous roles.

1673   **[Head, Richard.]** *The Floating Island, or a New Discovery relating
the strange adventures on a late voyage from Lambethna to Villa
Franca, alias Ramalia, to the Eastward of Terra del Temple,
under Captain Owe-Much describing the Inhabitants, their Religion, Laws and Customs. Published by Frank Careless* (pseud.),
one of the discoverers. London: Np. **L, DLC**

> Borderline — satire on English, particularly London, man-
> ners and customs.

1674   **[Head, Richard.]** *The Western Wonder; or, O Brazeel, an
Inchanted Island discovered; with a Relation of Two Ship-
wracks in a dreadful Sea-storm in that discovery. To which is
added, a Description of a Place, called, Montecapernia, relating
the Nature of the People, their Qualities, Humours, Fashions,
Religion, &c.* London: Printed for N. C. **ICN**

> Satire. Presents a society that is generally bad.

1675   **Barnes, Joshua.** *Gerania: A New Discovery of a Little Sort of People Anciently Discoursed of, called Pygmies. With a lively
Description of their Stature, Habit, Manners, Buildings, Knowledge, and Government, being very delightful and profitable.*
London: Printed by W. G. for Obadia Blagrave. **LLL, O**

> Agrarian, monarchical eutopia.

1675   **[Vairasse D'Allais, Denis.]** *The History of the Sevarites or Seva-
rambi; a Nation Inhabiting Part of the Third Continent, Commonly called, Terrae Australes Incognitae. With an account of*

their admirable government, religious customs and language. Written by one Captain Siden (pseud.), *a worthy person, who together with many others, was cast upon those coasts, and lived many years in that country,* translated by A. Roberts. London: Printed for H. Brome. Part 2 published 1679. **DLC**

> A major work of French utopianism first published in English. Detailed eutopia stressing equality and moderation. New language presented.

1676   *A New Discoverie of an Old Traveller Lately Arrived from Port-Dul, Shewing the Manner of the Country, Fashions of the People, and their Laws. And withal giving an account of the Shifts and Tricks he was Forced to use for the time of his Continuance there.* London: Np. **CtY**

> Borderline — describes a barren but peaceful country living off the bounty of its neighbors.

1682   **S.,J.** *A Discovery of Fonseca In a Voyage to Surranam. The Island so long sought for in the Western Ocean. Inhabited by Women with the Account of their Habits, Customs and Religion. And the Exact Longitude and Latitude of the Place Taken from the Mouth of a Person cast away on the Place in an Hurricane with the Account of their being Cast away.* Dublin: Np. **L**

> No men allowed on the island for any length of time. Male children must leave at an early age. Male visitors must leave at the end of a month.

1686   **D'Urfey, Mr. [Thomas].** *A Common-Wealth of Women. A Play: As it is acted at the Theatre Royal, By their Majesties Servants.* London: Printed for R. Bentley and J. Hindmarsh. **L**

> Standard story of a society of isolated women, in this case ruled by a man-hating woman. Handsome man appears and women revert to traditional roles.

1688   **Behn, Mrs. A[phra].** *Oroonoko: or, The Royal Slave. A True History.* London: Printed for Will Canning. Available in *Shorter Novels: Seventeenth Century,* edited by Philip Henderson (London: J. M. Dent, 1967), pp. 145–224.

> Borderline — stress on naturally good man.

1689   **L'Epy, M. Heliogenes de** (pseud.?). *A Voyage into Tartary. Containing a Curious Description of that Country, with part of Greece and Turkey; the Manners, Opinions, and Religion of the Inhabitants therein; with some other Incidents.* London: Printed by T. Hodgkin. **L**

> Heliopolis — all goods held in common. Men above 30 are enfranchised. No lawyers. New opinions must be approved by a council.

1693   *Antiquity Reviv'd or the Government of a Certain Island Antiently Called Astreada.* London: Np. **L**

Largely a treatise on political philosophy and religion, but also a defense of absolute monarchy based on forcing any disobedient person to be so identified along with all his relatives.

1696   *The Free State of Noland.* London: J. Whitlock. **L**
Detailed administrative and democratic political reform.

1698   *An Essay Concerning Adepts: or, A Resolution of this Inquiry, How it cometh to pass that Adepts, if there are any in the World, are no more Beneficial to Mankind than they have been known hitherto to be, and whether there could be no way to Encourage them to Communicate themselves. With some Resolutions concerning the Principles of the Adeptists; And a Model, Practicable, and Easy, of living in Community,* by a Philadept (pseud.). London: Printed by J. Mayos. **L**
Community on Spartan model after a discussion of the Hermetic tradition. Everyone must be married but live separately. No men and women dancing together; "no range must be allowed on the Subjects of Love, nor drinking." See also 1700 *Annus Sophiae Jubilaeus.*

1700   *Annus Sophiae Jubilaeus, The Sophick Constitution: or, The Evil Customs of the World Reformed. A Dialogue between a Philadept and a Citizen; Concerning The Possibility of the Sophick Transmutation; The Probability that there are Adepts in the World; And, in that Case, the Duties of Adepts and Other Men to each other, and the Advantages that would accrue from the Observation of those Duties. To which is added, A Summary of some Conferences with an Artist.* London: Printed for A. Baldwin. See also 1698 *An Essay Concerning Adepts.* **C**
Discusses regulations that would be established if adepts would cooperate with a good Prince.

1708   *A Voyage to the New Island Fonseca, Near Barbadoes, With some Observations Made in a Cruize among the Leward Islands. In Letters from Two Captains of Turkish Men of War, driven thither in the Year 1707. Translated out of Turkish and French.* London: Np. **ICN**
Two letters — both are imaginary voyages. The first describes Fonseca as a dystopia. The people are dirty, uneducated, drunk, etc.

1713   **[Ward, Edward?].** *A New Voyage to the Island of Fools, Representing the Policy, Government, and Present State of Stultitians,* by A Noble Venetian (pseud.). London: Printed for John Morphew. **O**
Satire on England.

1719   **[Defoe, Daniel.]** *The Farther Adventures of Robinson Crusoe Being the Second and Last Part of His Life, and Strange and Surprizing Accounts of his Travels Round Three Parts of the*

Globe. London: Printed for W. Taylor. **L**
See 1719 [Defoe].

1719   **[Defoe, Daniel.]** *The life and strange surprizing adventures of Robinson Crusoe, of York, Mariner: who lived eight and twenty years all alone on the coast of America, near the mouth of the great river of Oroonoque; having been cast on shore by ship-wreck, where-in all the men perished but himself. With an account of how he was at last as strangely deliver'd by pyrates.* Written by himself. 3 Vols. London: W. Taylor, 1719–1720. **L**
> Although not strictly a utopia gave rise to a whole sub-genre of works dealing with a castaway on an isolated island. Possible to treat it and the sub-genre as an eutopia of solitude. See also 1719 [Defoe, Daniel.] *The Farther. . . .*

1719   **[Evans, Ambrose.]** *The Adventures and Surprizing Deliverances, of James Dubourdieu, and His Wife: Who Were taken by Pyrates, and carried to the Uninhabited-Part of the Isle of Paradise, Containing A Description of that Country, its Laws, Religion, and Customs: Of Their being at last Releas'd; and how they came to Paris, where they are still living. Also, The Adventures of Alexander Vendchurch, Whose Ship's Crew Rebelled against him, and set him on Shore of an Island in the South-Sea, where he liv'd five Years, five Months, and seven Days; and was at last providentially releas'd by a Jamaica Ship.* London: Printed by J. Bettenham. **ICN**
> The two items are bound together but separately paged. The second is a Robinsonade. The first is an eutopia. The people go nude and are very healthy. Stress on reason. No government. Religious.

1720   **[Gildon, Charles** supposed author]. "A Description of New Athens in Terra Australis incognita," by One who resided many years on the Spot (pseud.). [Signed] Maurice Williams, in *Miscellanea Aurea: or the Golden Medley* [attributed to Thomas Killegrew] (London: A. Bettesworth, 1720), pp. 80–118. **DLC**
> No secrecy. Christianity, art, music, compulsory education. Everyone walks rather than riding. No lawyers. A charity system is run on a ward basis by the church.

1726   **[Swift, Jonathan.]** *Travels into several Remote Nations of the World. In Four Parts,* by Lemuel Gulliver (pseud.). London: Printed for Beng. Motte. **DLC**
> Basis of an entire sub-genre of utopias in which the imaginary voyage leads to worlds peopled by beings of different physical characteristics but normally endowed with speech and reason. Many such works include an eutopia. In *Gulliver's Travels* the eutopia is a land of rational horses, the Houyhnhnms.

1727   **Brunt, Captain Samuel.** *A Voyage to Cacklogallinia with a*

Description of the Religion, Policy, Customs and Manners of that Country. London: Printed by J. Watson. Reprinted: New York: The Facsimile Text Society, 1940.

Satire — virtuous chickens had become corrupt and petty. Stress on differences between theory and practice.

1731 **[Stubbes, George.]** *A New Adventure of Telemachus.* London: Printed for W. Wilkins. Parts published in 1724 in *London Journal.* **L**

Continuation of Fenelon's *Les Aventures de Télémaque* (1699) arguing against established churches and for freedom of inquiry.

1737 **[Berington, Simon.]** *The Memoirs of Sig^r Guadentio di Lucca* (pseud.) *taken from his Confession and Examination before the Fathers of the Inquisition at Bologna in Italy. Making a Discovery of an Unknown Country in the Midst of the Vast Deserts of Africa.* London: Printed for T. Cooper. **L**

Social system based on the law "Thou shalt do no wrong to anyone." This avoids legal hairsplitting. Patriarchal political system.

1741 **Hume, David,** "Idea of a Perfect Commonwealth," in his *Essays Moral and Political.* Edinburgh: R. Fleming & A. Alison.

Borderline — partially a commentary on the subject. Includes a few pages of the structure of a republican eutopia designed to correct perceived defects in 1656 Harrington. *The Commonwealth of Oceana.*

1745 **[Kirkby, John.]** *The Capacity and Extent of the Human Understanding; exemplified in the Extraordinary Case of Automathes; a Young Nobleman, Who was accidentally left in his Infancy, upon a desolate Island, and continued Nineteen Years in that solitary State separated from all Human Society. A Narrative Abounding with many Surprizing Occurences both Useful and Entertaining to the Reader.* London: Printed for R. Manby and H. Shute Cox. Originally published in 1736 without the utopian material as *The History of Autonous.* **L, LLL**

Robinsonade. Christian Eutopia called Soteria with a detailed description of church organization.

1754 **[King, William.]** *The Dreamer.* London: Printed for W. Owen. **L**
Largely satire but includes a variety of specific reforms.

1755 *A Voyage to the World in the Centre of the Earth. Giving an account of the manners, customs, laws, government and religion of the inhabitants. Their Persons and Habits described: With several other Particulars. In which is introduced, The History of an Inhabitant of the Air, Written by Himself. With some account of the planetary worlds.* London: Printed for S. Crowder and H. Woodgate. **DLC**

Vegetarian. Rational — all creatures are rational souls; there-fore, there are no extremes of inequality. Strict life — people spend as little time as possible on the needs of nature.

1757   **C., C.** *The Father of the City of Eutopia; or The Surest Road to Riches, Being a Narrative of the remarkable Life and Adventures of an elevated Bear. Delivered under the Similitude of a Dream. Dedicated to the Rt. Hon. Wm. P----, Esq.* London: Printed for J. Cooke. **L**
Allegory using imaginary country approach.

1759   **Goldsmith, Oliver.** "Asem, the Man-Hater; An Eastern Tale." *The Royal Magazine.* Republished in *Essays,* 1765. **L**
World of rational men without vices and how bad it is.

1759   **Johnson, Samuel.** *The Prince of Abissinia. A Tale.* London: R. and J. Dodsley. Also known as *Rasselas* and *The History of Rasselas.* **DLC**
Borderline — Happy Valley — perfect life for children of emperor seems dull to Rasselas, and he explores the world.

1761   **[Wallace, Robert.]** *Various Prospects of Mankind, Nature, and Providence.* London: Printed for A. Millar. **L**
Short sketch of ideal government. Small government that is concerned with establishing and maintaining an equitable economic system. Stress on equality except where inequality is unavoidable.

1762   **[Scott, Mrs. Sarah (Robinson).]** *A Description of Millenium Hall, And the Country Adjacent: Together with the Character of the Inhabitants, And such Historical Anecdotes and Reflections, As May excite in the Reader proper Sentiments of Humanity, and lead the Mind to the Love of Virtue,* by A Gentleman on his Travels (pseud.). London: Printed for J. Newbury. **L, O**
Describes a country estate of celibate women who help support the people of the area, mostly the old women, by providing work and orphans for them to raise. Also, there is an enclosure for deformed people.

1763   *The Reign of George VI 1900–1925.* London: Printed for W. Nicholl. **O**
An enlightened monarch encourages art and literature and builds a city for the nobility and rich commoners to support the arts.

1764   **[Burgh, James.]** *An Account of the First Settlement, Laws, Form of Government, and Police, of the Cessares, a People of South America: In Nine Letters, from Mr. Vander Neck* (pseud.), *one of the Senators of that Nation, to his Friend in Holland.* London: Printed for J. Payne. **L**
A detailed, regimented eutopia. Everyone is expected to be "sober, industrious and peaceable" and anything that would

lead to a different condition is illegal. There are no lawyers, and plain speaking in trials is expected.

1764-65   **[Gentlemen, Francis.]** *A Trip to the Moon. Containing an Account of the Island of Noibla. Its Inhabitants, Religious and Political Customs, Etc.,* by Sir Humphrey Lunatic, Bart. (pseud.). 2 Vols. Vol. I, York: Printed by A. Ward for S. Crowder, *et al.,* 1764. Vol. II, London: Printed for S. Crowder, *et al.,* 1765. Reprinted in *Gulliveriana: I,* edited by Jeanne Welcher and George E. Bush, Jr. (Gainesville, Florida: Scholars' Facsimiles and Reprints, 1970), pp. 97–204.

Simple laws. Head of the family is responsible for the conduct of all family members and must give a weekly account of their activities. Everyone must attend public worship at least once a day. Children are raised by a woman other than the natural mother because she is more likely to be willing to correct the child.

1769   *Private Letters from an American in England to his Friends in America.* London: Printed for J. Almon. 1781 edition entitled *Anticipation, or The Voyage of an American to England in the Year 1899, in a series of letters, humourously describing the supposed situation of this Kingdom at that Period.* London: Printed for W. Lane. **O, L**

England depopulated. The seat of government is in America. England's downfall was largely due to lawyers who were willing to overthrow the law for profit.

1769   **Rationales** (pseud.). "Remarks which are supposed will be made in this Kingdom, by two North American travellers in the year one thousand nine hundred and forty-four." *The Literary Register or Weekly Miscellany* (Newcastle), 1(1769), 98–99. **L, NcD**

Depopulated London. United States supreme.

1778   **Bowman, Hildebrand** (pseud.). *The Travels of Hildebrand Bowman, Esq. into Carnovirria, Taupinieria, Olfactaria and Auditante in New Zealand; in the Island of Bonhommica, and the powerful Kingdom of Luxo-volupte, on the Great Southern Continent.* London: Printed for W. Strahan and T. Cadell. **L**

Gulliver type — Bonhommica is an eutopia of sorts. The people have a sixth sense, conscience.

1778   *A Trip to Melasge; or, Concise Instructions to a Young Gentleman Entering into Life: With Observations on the Genius, Manners, Ton, Opinions, Philosophy, and Morals of the Melasgians.* 2 Vols. London: Printed for B. Law. **ICN**

Intelligence, education, grace, beauty, arcadian land plus graceful architecture.

1782   **[Spence, Thomas.]** *A Supplement to the History of Robinson Crusoe, Being the History of Crusonia, or Robinson Crusoe's*

Island, Down to the Present Time, Copied from a letter sent by Mr. Wishit, Captain of the Good-Intent, to an Intelligent Friend in England, after being in a Storm in May, 1781 driven out of his Course to the Said Island. New edition. Newcastle: T. Saint. Also in Spence's phonetic spelling in the same volume. **L**

Island had developed standard institutions found in Britain at the time, but a revolution had overthrown the system, abolished all landlords, except the local parish, and had established majority rule and a citizen's militia. See also Spence under 1795, 1798, and 1805.

1784   *A Journey lately performed through the Air, in an Aerostatic Globe, commonly called an Air Balloon, from this terraqueous Globe to the Newly Discovered Planet, Georgium Sidus, by Monsieur Vivenair* (pseud.). London: Np. **DeGE**

Satire on the England of George III.

[1785?]   *An Account of Count D'Artois and his Friend's Passage to the Moon, in a Flying Machine, called, an Air Balloon; Which was constructed in France, and from which place they ascended.* Litchfield, Connecticut: Collier and Copp. **DLC**

Probably the earliest U.S. utopia although the utopian elements are limited. The moon is harmonious, peaceful, and so forth.

1785   **Celadon** (pseud.). *The Golden Age: or; Future Glory of North-America Discovered by An Angel to Celadon. In Several Entertaining Visions. Vision I.* Np.: Np. **W1,500**

Vision of the United States as a collection of harmonious ethnic and racial groups each having a separate state.

1785   **[Raspe, Rudolf Erich.]** *Baron Munchausen's Narrative of His Marvellous Travels and Campaigns In Russia. Humbly Dedicated and Recommended to Country Gentlemen; and, if they please, to be repeated as Their Own, After a Hunt, at Horse Races, In Watering-Places, and Other Such Polite Assemblies; Round the Bottle and Fire-Side.* Oxford: Printed for the Editors.

First edition, a 45-page pamphlet, was published at Oxford in English. There have been innumerable editions, under many different titles, and in many languages. Some include utopian elements.

1789   *Plan for a Free Community upon the Coast of Africa, Under the Protection of Great Britain; But Intirely Independent of all European Laws and Governments. With an Invitation, under certain Conditions, to all Persons desirous of partaking the Benefits thereof.* London: Printed by R. Hindmarsh. Signed by August Nordenskjold, Charles Bernhard Wadstrom, Colburn Barrell, and Johan Gottfried Simpson. **L**

Borderline — proposal for a community with a constitution and organization of government. Swedenborgian.

1789   **[Thomson, William.]** *Mammuth; or, Human Nature Displayed on a Grand Scale: In a Tour with the Tinkers, into the Inland Parts of Africa,* by The Man in the Moon (pseud.). 2 Vols. London: Printed for J. Murray. Reprinted in *Gulliveriana: IV,* edited by Jeanne Welcher and George E. Bush, Jr. (Delmar, New York: Scholars' Facsimiles and Reprints, 1973), pp. 229–384.

Anti-technology — better to use nature than the best mechanical contrivances. Reason, learning, good repute, and nobility are the bases for government. Euthanasia is allowed for the old of good character.

1790   "An Allegorical Description of a certain Island and its Inhabitants." *The Massachusetts Magazine.* Reprinted: *American Utopias,* edited by Arthur O. Lewis, Jr. New York: Arno Press and *The New York Times,* 1971.

Allegory using utopian imagery.

[1790?]   *A True and Faithful Account of the Island of Veritas; Together with the Forms of Their Liturgy; and a Full Relation of the Religious Opinions of the Veritasians, as Delivered in Several Sermons Just Published in Veritas,* by Jasper Richardson (pseud.). London: Printed for C. Stalker. **MH**

Mostly a defense of Unitarianism with detailed forms of their religious services. Eutopia is based on religion, reason, and virtue.

1793   **Aratus** (pseud.). *A Voyage to the Moon; Strongly Recommended to all Lovers of Real Freedom.* London: Author. **L**

Dystopia on the moon — allegory about contemporary England.

1795   **Hodgson, William.** *The Commonwealth of Reason.* London: Printed for the author. **L**

Borderline — essay including an outline of a new government and a proposed constitution.

1795   **[Northmore, Thomas.].** *Memoirs of Planetes, or a Sketch of the Laws and Manners of Makar,* by Phileleutherus Devoniensis (pseud.). London: Printed by Vaughan Griffiths. **L**

Detailed constitution of thirty-one articles.

1795   **[Spence, Thomas.]** *Description of Spensonia.* London: Hive of Liberty. **L**

Earliest version of Spence's cooperative commonwealth. See also Spence 1782, 1798, and 1805.

1796   **Gulliver, Lemuel, Jr.** (pseud.). *Modern Gulliver's Travels. Lilliput: Being a New Journey to that Celebrated Island. Containing a Faithful Account of the Manners, Character, Customs, Reli-*

gion, Laws, Politics, Revenue, Taxes, Learning, General Progress in Arts and Sciences, Dress, Amusements, and Gallantry of Those Famous Little People. From the Year 1702 (When They Were First Discovered and Visited by Captain Lemuel Gulliver, The Father of the Compiler of this Work), to the Present Aera 1796. London: Printed for T. Chapman. Sometimes ascribed to H. Whitmore. **L**

Satire on contemporary English life. Extensive invented language.

1798   *Human Vicissitudes; or, Travels into Unexplored Regions.* 2 Vols. London: Printed for G. G. and J. Robinson. **MH, NjP**

Borderline — imaginary voyage describing an essentially feudal system that is far from perfect but presents a number of improvements, primarily in education.

1798   **Spence, T[homas].** *The Constitution of a Perfect Commonwealth. Being the French Constitution of 1794. Amended and rendered entirely conformable to the Rights of Man.* London: Author. 1801 edition entitled *The Constitution of Spensonia A Country in Fairyland Situated Between Utopia and Oceana Brought from Thence by Captain Swallow (i.e. Thomas Spence).* **L**

Detailed eutopia — another version of Spence's cooperative commonwealth. See also Spence 1782, 1795, and 1805.

[18--]   **Webster, R. M.** *One Wise Rich Man. A Parable. Owe No Man Anything But To Love One Another.* Np: Np. **ICU**

Eutopia — cooperative commonwealth brought about by a rich man. Based on the principles in the title.

[1802]   *Bruce's Voyage to Naples, and Journey Up Mount Vesuvius; giving an account of the Strange Disaster Which Happened on His Arrival at the Summit: The Discovery of the Central World; with the Laws, Customs, and Manners of that Nation, described; their swift and Peculiar Mode of Travelling; the Wonderful Riches, Virtue, and Knowledge, the Inhabitants possess; the Author's Travels in that Country; and the Friendly Reception he met with from its Sovereign and His People.* London: Printed by S. Fisher. **O**

Communal eutopia. Vegetarian.

1802   *Equality, A History of Lithconia* [by James Reynolds?]. Philadelphia: The Prime Press, 1947. Originally published in *The Temple of Reason.* **W1,920a**

Probably the first complete utopia published in the United States. No money, land is held in common and labor is required from all until 50. No towns — houses are spread over the entire country. Everyone over 15 has a separate apartment and keeps it even if married. Gerontocracy. Deist.

Every male over 18 is provided with arms — must know how to use them.

[c1805]   **[Spence, Thomas.]** *The receipt to make a millenium or happy world.* 4th ed. single sheet. Also entitled *Something to a Purpose.* **LLL, LSE**

Extract from his *Constitution.* See also Spence 1782, 1795, and 1798.

1811   **Lawrence, James.** *The Empire of the Nairs; or, The Rights of Women. An Eutopian Romance.* 4 Vols. in 2. London: Printed for T. Hookhan, Jun. and E. T. Hookhan. **L**

Originally published in German in 1801 but best known in this edition. English author. Presented as a picture of equality for women, it is more a sexual fantasy. Men are completely free from any duties except warfare. Free love. Women are rulers.

1813   **Fowler, Geor[ge].** *A Flight to the Moon; or, The Vision of Randalthus.* Baltimore: A. Miltenberger. **W1,997**

Equality has brought about similar stature and appearance. Pure, moderate people who eschew philosophy because it is confusing. Obey "the simple impulse of nature" rather than laws. Second eutopia in a dream — innocence, purity, bliss. Third similar eutopia is in the interior of the sun.

1813   **[Owen, Robert.]** *A New View of Society; or, Essays on the principle of the foundation of the human character, and the application of the principle to practice. By one of His Majesty's justices of the peace for the county of Lanark.* London: Printed for Cadell and Davies, by R. Taylor and Company. **DLC**

Not strictly a utopia, but basic to the development of British and American utopianism.

1816   **Evans, Thomas.** *Christian Policy; The Salvation of the Empire. Being a Clear and Concise Examination into the Causes that have Produced the Impending, Unavoidable National Bankruptcy; And the Effects that must ensue, unless averted by the Adoption of this only real and Desireable Remedy, Which Would Elevate These Realms to a Pitch of Greatness Hitherto Unattained By any Nation that ever Existed.* London: Printed for the Author. **L, LSE**

All land made public. Evans was a close associate of Spence. See also 1818 [Evans?].

1817   **[Erskine, Thomas.]** *Armata, A Fragment.* London: John Murray. **L**

Parallel history of England. Emphasis on gradual change. See also 1817 [Erskine].

1817   **[Erskine, Thomas.]** *The Second Part of Armata.* London: John Murray. **L**

Continuation of 1817 [Erskine]. Emphasizes bad side of Armata.

1817 **Shelley, Percy Bysshe.** "The Revolt of Islam. A Poem in Twelve Cantos."

Poem. Includes eutopia.

1818 **[Evans, Thomas?]** *Christian Policy in Full Practice Among the People of Harmony, A Town in the State of Pennsylvania, North America; As Described in Melish's Travels through the United States, and Birkbeck's Notes on a Journey in America. To which are subjoined, a Concise View of the Spencean System of Agrarian Fellowship, and some Observations on the manifest Similarity between the Principles of that System and of the truly Fraternal and Christianly Establishment of the Harmonists,* by A Spencean Philanthropist (pseud.). London: Hay and Turner. **LUG**

Christian, all land and other major goods public. Written constitution. Politically divided into small parishes or districts.

1818 **[Kelsall, Charles?]** *Constantine and Eugene, or an Evening at Mount Vernon. A Political Dialogue,* by Junius Secundus (pseud.). Brussels: Printed for the author, by P. J. DeMat. **L**

Detailed legal system with some political material.

1819 **[Clopper, Jonas.]** *Fragments of the History of Bawlfredonia: Containing an Account of the Discovery and Settlement, of that Great Southern Continent; and of the Formation and Progress of the Bawlfredonian Commonwealth,* by Herman Thwackius (pseud.). Translated from the original Bawlfredonian Manuscript, into the French language, by Monsieur Traducteur and Rendered into English, by a citizen of America. [Baltimore?:] Printed for the American Booksellers. **L, W1,551**

Satire on American history using utopian form.

1820 **[Ellis, Mr. (pseud.?).]** *New Britain. A Narrative of a Journey, by Mr. Ellis, To a Country So Called By Its Inhabitants, Discovered in the Vast Plain of the Missouri, in North America, and Inhabited by a People of British Origin, Who Live Under an Equitable System of Society, Productive of Peculiar Independence and Happiness. Also, some account of Their Constitution, Laws, Institutions, Customs and Philosophical Opinions: Together With a Brief Sketch of Their History from the Time of Their Departure from Great Britain.* London: Printed for W. Simpkin and R. Marshall. **L**

Detailed eutopia emphasizing small town democracy.

1820 **[Symmes, John Cleves?]** *Symzonia; A Voyage of Discovery,* by Captain Adam Seaborn (pseud.). New York: Printed by J. Seymour. Reprinted: Gainesville, Florida: Scholars' Facsimiles and

Reprints, 1965. Almost universally attributed to Symmes but seriously questioned by a recent scholar — see "The Authorship of Symzonia," *Science-Fiction Studies* 3 (March 1976), pp. 98–99. **W1,2326**
> Land in the center of the earth. A society ruled by the Good, the Wise, and the Useful. The dull, the indolent, and the selfish had been driven out.

1821   **Shelley, Percy Bysshe.** "Epipsychidion."
> Love poem — describes an island lover's eutopia.

1822   **Brown, Charles Brockden,** "The Paradise of Women, From 'Alciun,' " in William Dunlap, *Memoirs of Charles Brockden Brown, The American Novelist. Author of Wieland, Ormond, Arthur Mervyn, &c. With Selections from his Original Letters, and Miscellaneous Writings* (London: Printed for Henry Colburn and Co., 1822, pp. 247–308. **L**
> Written 1798. Complete equality. No marriage.

1824   **[Banim, John.]** *Revelations of the Dead-Alive.* London: W. Simpkin and R. Marshall. **L**
> Satire set in 2083 — primarily concerned with improvements in taste, art, etc.

1824   **[Morgan, John Minter.]** *Hampden in the Nineteenth Century; or, Colloquies on the Errors and Improvement of Society.* 2 Vols. London: Edward Moxon. **L**
> Vol. 1 includes a cooperative eutopia among the remnants of the Incas.

1824   **[Stirrat, David.]** *A Treatise on Political Economy: or the true principles of political economy in the form of a romaunt, for the more pleasing accommodation of readers; Explained in a series of letters to Aristippus, from Aristander, perceived in a deep vision. The subject is presumed to be considered upon strict philosophical, mathematical, and geometrical principles.* Baltimore: Printed for the editor. **NN**
> Technologically advanced. City in a series of levels, working from storehouses, to homes for workers, to higher levels for higher occupations. Concerned with sinking fund.

1825   *Gulliver's Last Voyage, Describing Ballymugland, or the Floating Island.* 2nd edition. London: William Cole. **IU**
> Utopian satire.

1825   **[Trotter, John.]** *Travels in Phrenologasto,* by Don Jose Balscopo (pseud.). Translated from the Italian [written in English]. Calcutta: Samuel Smith. 1829 edition London: Saunders and Otley has pseudonym Gio[vanni] Battista Balscopo. **L, CtY-M**
> Society based on phrenology which ensures that the right person is in the right job.

1825   *The Vision of Hades, or the Region Inhabited by the Departed Spirits of the Blessed. With Cursory Notes, Theological and Metaphysical. To which is now added the Vision of Noos.* London: Printed for G. B. Whittaker. **L**
>Entirely concerned with religion, but the utopian form is used.

1826   **Morgan, John Minter.** *Revolt of the Bees.* London: Longman, Rees, Orme, Brown, and Green. **L**
>Better society possible through the application of Christianity and reason. Anti-capitalist.

1826   **[Paulding, James Kirke.]** "The Man Machine, or the Pupil of 'Circumstances,' " in his *The Merry Tales of the Three Wise Men of Gotham* (New York: G. and C. Carvill, 1826), pp. 21–142. **L, W1, 2015**
>Anti-Robert Owen — uses dystopian form.

1827   **[Tucker, George.]** *A Voyage to the Moon: With Some Account of the Manners and Customs, Science and Philosophy, of the People of Morosofia, and Other Lunarians,* by Joseph Atterley (pseud.). New York: Elam Bliss, **W1, 2611**
>Mostly satire. Eutopia, called Okalbia, in which people limit family size to means.

1827   **[Webb, Jane.]** *The Mummy! A Tale of the Twenty-second Century.* 3 Vols. London: Henry Colburn. **L**
>Much technical advance. Female absolute monarch. The Roman Catholic church is the established church. Universal education had led to simple speaking by upper classes and affected speech by the lower classes.

1828   **[Disraeli, Benjamin.]** *The Voyage of Captain Popanilla.* London: Henry Colburn. **L**
>Imaginary voyage to contemporary England (heavily satirized). Starts from a South Seas Island eutopia.

1828   **Edmonds, T[homas] R[owe].** *Practical Moral and Political Economy; or, the Government, Religion, and Institutions, Most Conducive to Individual Happiness and To National Power.* London: Effingham Wilson. **DLC**
>Includes a short section on the founding of a utopia.

1828   *The History of Bullanabee and Clinkataboo, Two Recently Discovered Islands in the Pacific.* London: Printed for Longman, Rees, Orme, Brown and Green. **L**
>South Seas Island eutopia. Loses eutopian qualities by the end of the book.

1828   **[Sanford, Ezekial.]** *The Humours of Eutopia. A Tale of Colonial Times,* by An Eutopian (pseud.). 2 Vols. Philadelphia: Carey, Lea and Carey. **W1, 2278**
>Includes a small section on a religious community.

1830   **Brothers, [Richard].** *The New Covenant Between God and His People; or, The Hebrew Constitution and Charter, with the Statutes and Ordinances, the Laws and Regulations, and Commands and Covenants,* by the late Mr. Brothers. London: Printed by A. Snell for Mr. Finleyson. **NN, L**
        Very detailed constitution.

1830   **Gulliver, Lemuel, Jr.** (pseud.). *Sequel to Gulliver's Travels. An Eulogy.* London: J. Jaques. **L**
        Discourse on religion presented as a sequel to the Yahoo section of *Gulliver's Travels.*

1830   **San Blas, Caesario, Bachelor** (pseud.). *A Voyage to the Island of Philosophers. Part First, Containing an account of the Island and its Inhabitants, together with the Incidents which occurred there, during the sojourn of the Writer.* Np: np. **W1, 2275**
        Satire on the Stoics.

1831   **Gray, John.** *The Social System: A Treatise on the Principle of Exchange.* Edinburgh: William Tait. Reprinted: New York: Augustus M. Kelley, 1973. **DLC**
        Includes a chapter detailing a new economic system.

1832   **Thimbleby, J.** *Monadelphia; or, The Formation of a New System of Society, without the intervention of a Circulating Medium.* Barnet: Printed for the Author, and W. Baldoc, and W. Ford. **L**
        Mostly an essay, but the conclusion shows an eutopia. Monadelphia means a single brotherhood. There is no money and no individual property. All goods are freely taken to and from a central warehouse.

1833   **Etzler, J[ohn] A[dolphus].** *The Paradise within Reach of All Men, without Labour, by Powers of Nature and Machinery.* 2 Parts. Pittsburgh: Etzler and Reinhold. **L, DLC**
        The basic work of Etzler's many depicting eutopia through technology. See also Etzler 1841, 1843, and 1844 (2).

1835   **Bolokitten, Oliver, Esq.** (pseud.). *A Sojourn in the City of Amalgamation in the Year of Our Lord 19--.* New York: Author. **W1, 333**
        Racist dystopia.

1835   **[Cooper, James Fenimore.]** *The Monikins.* 2 Vols. Philadelphia: Carey, Lea and Blanchard. **W1, 647**
        Eutopian satire using a society of monkeys to satirize human foibles.

1836   **[Griffith, Mary.]** "Three Hundred Years Hence," in her *Camperdown; or, News from Our Neighborhood: Being Sketches,* by the Author of "Our Neighborhood" (pseud.) (Philadelphia: Carey, Lea and Blanchard, 1836), pp. 9–92. Reprinted under the title of the utopia. Philadelphia: Prime Press, 1950, and in *American Utopias,* edited by Arthur O. Lewis, Jr. New York:

Arno Press and *The New York Times,* 1971. **W1, 1071**
A strict, reformed society brought about by the economic equality of women.

1836 **Tarascon, Louis Anastasius.** *L... A... T... to his fellow citizens of the United States of America; and Through Their Medium, To All His Other Human Beings on Earth, Not Any Where Else!* New York: H. D. Robinson, 1837. Reprinted: *Magazine of History with Notes and Queries,* No. 148 (1929), pp. 5–42. **NN, L**
Argues that a commune should be founded and presents detailed regulations of life in the commune.

1837 **Fox, Lady Mary,** ed. [written by]. *Account of an Expedition to the Interior of New Holland.* London: Richard Bentley. 1860 edition entitled *The Southlanders.* **L, MoU-St**
A detailed system of political reform.

1837 **[Williams, R. F.]** *Eureka: A Prophecy of the Future.* 3 Vols. in 1. London: Longman, Rees, Orme, Brown, Green, and Longman. **L**
Mostly adventure, but volume two includes a description of a number of fictional countries, including one with some eutopian elements named Athenia where goods are distributed on the basis of contributions to the country. England has degenerated. Anti-Irish.

1838 **Bower, Samuel.** *A Sequel to the Peopling of Utopia; or, the Sufficiency of Socialism for Human Happiness: Being a Further Comparison of the Social and Radical Schemes.* Bradford: Printed for C. Wilkinson. **L**
Short sequel to a political pamphlet, *The Peopling of Utopia,* both of which detail the advantages of communal life. *A Sequel* is presented as an eutopia.

1838 **Cooper, Robert.** *A Contrast between the new moral world and the old immoral world. A Lecture Delivered in the Social Institution, Salford.* Manchester: Published by A. Heywood, Printed for William Chapwick. **L**
Depicts eutopia based on the ideas of Robert Owen.

1838 **Prospero, Peter, L.L.D.** (pseud.?). "The Atlantis: A Southern World, — Or a Wonderful Continent, — Discovered in the Great Southern Ocean, and Supposed to be The Atlantis of Plato, or The Terra Australis Incognita of Dr. Swift, During a Voyage Conducted by Alonzo Pinzon Commander of The American Metal Ship Astrea." *The American Museum of Science, Literature and the Arts,* 1 (September-December), 42–65, 222–255, 321–341, 421–446.
Country where the great men of the past live and converse.

1838 **[Walker, Richard.]** *Oxford in 1888, A Fragmentary Dream,* by a Sub-Utopian (pseud.). *Published from the Original MS. by the*

editor, R. P. (pseud.). Oxford: Henry Slatter. **L**
A dream of a future Oxford, complete with town plans.

1840s   **Goodwyn, Burmby.** "The Book of Platonopolis," in *The Communist Chronicle* [Lost?]. Mentioned in Thomas Frost, *Forty Years Recollections; Literary and Political* (London: Sampson Low, Searle and Rivington, 1880), p. 61. **L, DLC**

1840   **Hake, William Augustus Gordon.** *Society Organized. An Allegory: Part I* [no more published]. London: Sherwood. **O, L.**
Poem with notes — vague utopia. Cooperation of elites, masses, and scientists.

1840-41   **[Bray, John Francis.]** *A Voyage from Utopia to Several Unknown Regions of the World,* by Yarbjf (pseud.), edited by M. F. Lloyd-Prichard. London: Lawrence and Wishart, 1957. **MoU-St**
First publication of a book written in 1840–1841. Satire on contemporary nations.

1841   **Etzler, J[ohn] A[dolphus].** *The New World or Mechanical System, To Perform the Labours of Man and Beast by Inanimate Powers, That Cost Nothing, for Producing and Preparing the Substances of Life.* Philadelphia: C. F. Stollmeyer. **L**
One of Etzler's pictures of eutopia through technology. See also Etzler 1833, 1843, and 1844 (2).

1842   **Savage, Timothy** (pseud?). *The Amazonian Republic Recently Discovered in the Interior of Peru,* by Ex-Midshipman Timothy Savage, B. C. New York: Samuel Colman. **L, W1, 2315**
A developed country with the government the same as the United States. Effeminate men. Some material on a new religion.

[1842?]   *The Scheme of Universal Brotherhood; or the Christian System of Mutual Assistance. Proposing A System of Society, Natural In Its Construction, Easy In Its Application, Interfering With No Sect In Religion, Or Party In Politics, And Insuring the Happiness and Innocence of All Mankind. Compiled from the Works of Celebrated Authors.* London: Watson. **L**
Eutopia with extraordinary detail on all aspects of life including such things as detailed descriptions of horses, dress, and amusements. Women are physically and mentally inferior. No marriage. Sexual freedom.

1843   **[Etzler, John Adolphus.]** *Dialogue on Etzler's Paradize Between Messrs. Clear, Flat, Dunce, and Grudge.* London: James B. O'Brien. **IEN**
One of Etzler's pictures of eutopia through technology. See also Etzler 1833, 1841, and 1844 (2).

1844   **Etzler, John A[dolphus].** *Emigration to the Tropical World, for the*

Melioration of all Classes of People of all Nations. Surrey: The Concordium. **L**

One of Etzler's pictures of eutopia through technology. See also Etzler 1833, 1841, and 1843.

1844   **Etzler, J[ohn] A[dolphus].** *Two Visions of J. A. Etzler, (Author of the Paradise Within the Reach of All Men, By Powers of Nature and Machinery, and Other Writings Connected Therewith.) A Revelation of Futurity.* Surrey: The Concordium. **ICN**

One of Etzler's pictures of eutopia through technology. See also Etzler 1833, 1841, and 1843.

1845   **[Judd, Sylvester.]** Margaret: A Tale of the Real and the Ideal, Blight and Bloom; Including Sketches of a Place not Before Described, Called Mons Christi. Boston: Jordan and Wiley. Revised edition, 2 Vols. Boston: Phillips, Sampson and Company, 1851. **MoU-St, W1, 1512**

Small town Christian eutopia.

1845   *1945: A Vision.* London: Francis and John Rivington. **C**

Eutopia of restored religion.

1846   *Henry Russell; or, The Year of Our Lord Two Thousand.* New York: William H. Graham. **W1, 1155**

Future eutopia — begins in a commune based loosely on Fourier but ends by being established worldwide.

1846   **Melville, Herman.** *Typee.* London: John Murray.

South Seas Island eutopia.

1847   **[Cooper, James Fenimore.]** *The Crater; or, Vulcan's Peak. A Tale of the Pacific.* 2 Vols. New York: Burgess, Stringer and Company. English edition entitled *Mark's Reef; or, The Crater. A Tale of the Pacific.* 3 Vols. London: Richard Bentley. **L, W1, 588**

Mostly a dull adventure story, but includes a conservative eutopia.

1847   **Jerrold, Douglas.** *The Chronicles of Clovernook; With Some Account of The Hermit of Bellyfulle.* London: Punch Office. **IU**

Humor. Describes an eutopia of simplicity and no government or laws. A life based on morality and kindness.

1848   **[Appleton, Jane Sophia].** "Sequel to the Vision of Bangor in the Twentieth Century," in *Voices from the Kenduskeag* (Bangor: David Bugbee, 1848), pp. 243–265. Reprinted: *American Utopias,* edited by Arthur O. Lewis, Jr. New York: Arno Press and *The New York Times,* 1971. **W1, 39, MoU-St**

Sequel to 1848 [Kent] on women's rights.

1848   **Forrest, Henry J.** *A Dream of Reform.* London: John Chapman. **L**

Reform tract using the utopian form.

1848   *The Island of Liberty; or, Equality and Community,* by the Author

of "Theodore" (pseud.). London: Joseph Masters. **L**
Novel presenting the development and failure of a communal experiment.

1848   **[Kent, Edward].** "A Vision of Bangor in the Twentieth Century," in *Voices from the Kenduskeag* (Bangor: David Bugbee, 1848), pp. 61–73. Reprinted: *American Utopias,* edited by Arthur O. Lewis, Jr. New York: Arno Press and *The New York Times,* 1971. **W1, 39, MoU-St**
See also 1848 [Appleton]. No slavery, temperance, traditional sex-roles. No writing.

1848   **Rowcraft, Charles.** *The Triumph of Women; A Christmas Story.* London: Parry and Company. **NN, L**
Ideal planet without women but an earth woman's attraction proves too strong for a visitor from that planet.

1848   **Wood, George.** *Peter Schlemihl in America.* Philadelphia: Carey and Hart. **W1, 2753**
Mostly social commentary but includes some discussion of fictional communal experiments.

[1849]   **Buckingham, James S[ilk].** *National Evils and Practical Remedies, with the Plan of a Model Town.* London: Peter Jackson, Late Fisher, Son and Company. **L, DLC**
Proposes a communal experiment and gives detailed plans.

1849   **[Peck, George Washington.]** *Aurifodina; or, Adventures in the Gold Region* by Cantell A. Bigly (pseud.). New York: Baker and Scribner. **W1, 2030**
City of gold in California where gold is treated as a common stone. Religious. Hereditary monarchy. Common law.

1849   **Poe, Edgar Allan.** "Mellonta Tauta." *Godey's Lady's Book,* 38 (February), 133–138.
Satire on the future. Technological advance but individualism and democracy are gone.

1850   *Hints From Utopian Schools on Prefects. Being Two Addresses Delivered by the Warden of a New Collegiate School in that Happy Land.* Oxford: John Henry Parker. **L**
Two addresses by the head of a school in Utopia on the duties of Prefects.

1852   **Hawthorne, Nathaniel.** *The Blithedale Romance.* Boston: Ticknor, Reed and Fields. **W2, 1134**
Classic novel on Brook Farm.

1852   **Payne, A. R. Middletoun.** *The Geral-Milco; or The Narrative of a Residence in a Brazilian Valley of the Sierra-Paricis.* New York: Charles B. Norton. 1854 edition entitled *Rambles in Brazil.* **DLC**
Incas as eutopia.

1853 *A Few Things Worth Knowing About the Heretofore Unexplored Country of Theopolis.* London: Hope and Company. **O**
> Utopia Christiana is the name of one country. Detailed eutopia stressing church reform.

1854 **Pemberton, Robert.** *The Happy Colony.* London: Saunders and Otley. **L**
> An eutopia designed to be founded in New Zealand and based on a reformed educational system.

1855 **Corvaja, Baron Joseph.** *Perpetual Peace to the Machine by the Universal Millenium, or The Sovereign Bankocracy, and the Grand Social Ledger of Mankind.* London: Author. **LSE**
> A series of letters to Robert Owen. Reform of savings banks — more money made available to the community.

1855 **Owen, Robert.** *The Inauguration of the Millenium May 14th 1855. Being the report of two public meetings with an introduction.* London: J. Clayton and Son. **IU**
> Speeches by Owen describing the Millenium State.

1855 **[Whiting, Sydney.]** *Heliondé; or, Adventures in the Sun.* London: Chapman and Hall. **L**
> Religious eutopia. Money replaced by good sayings, the worth of which are judged by the shopkeeper. Language is "composed of groups of musical notes; and rhythm imparts all the variety of meaning."

[c1856] **[Gazlay, Allen W.]** *Races of Mankind; With Travels in Grubland,* by Cephas Broadluck (pseud.). Cincinnati: Longley Bros. **W2, 991**
> Satire on the United States, particularly on slavery.

1856 **[Howard, Charles F.]** *Olympus.* London: Simpkin, Marshall and Company. **MiU**
> Eutopia of reason and intellect among immortal spirits. Serves primarily as an excuse for discussion of various topics.

1856 **Moore, David A.** *The Age of Progress; or, A Panorama of Time. In Four Visions.* New York: Sheldon, Blakeman and Company. **DLC**
> New society brought about through education and Christianity. Limit on income. Detailed world constitution.

1858 **Wood, George.** *Future Life; or, Scenes in Another World.* New York: Derby and Jackson. 1869 edition entitled *The Gates Wide Open.* Boston: Lee and Shepard. **L, W2, 2786**
> Heaven but presented as an eutopia of beauty, art, etc.

1859 **Lang, Herrmann.** *The Air Battle: A Vision of the Future.* London: William Penney. Reprinted: London: Cornmarket Reprints, 1972.

Mostly science and adventure. World power held by black nations.

1860   **[Andrews, William S.?]** *Constitution or Organic Basis of the Pantarchy,* by Andrusius, *Pantarch* (pseud.). New York: Baker and Godwin. **LUG**

Detailed constitution of the new spiritual government of the world.

1860   **Lookup, Alexander** (pseud.?). *Excelsior; or, The Heir Apparent. Showing the Adventures of a Promising and Wealthy Young Man, and His Devoted Friends; and Presenting Entwined with the varying story, the Key to a Diamond United States, or a Vitally Consolidated Republic, A Perfect Union, Otherwise Kingdom of Heaven. Likewise Giving, in Picturesque Dramatic Dialogue, the Notorious Actions and Secret Lives of Two Celebrated Dictators of Party and Leaders in Political Conventions. The Whole Embodied in A Thrilling and Exquisite Poetical Romance.* New York: Kennedy. **DLC**

Mostly on current evils, but includes a minimal utopia.

1860   **Lookup, Alex[ander]** (pseud.?). *The Road Made Plain to Fortune for the Million: or, The Popular Pioneer to Universal Prosperity.* ed. Thos. Ward, M.D. New York: Kennedy. **DLC**

"Politics is divulged in the light of God as the craft of the Devil, and the opposite of a useful science." Bring about change by refusing to pay rents.

1860   **Lookup, Alexander** (pseud.?). *The Soldier of the People; or, The World's Deliverer. A Romance.* New York: Kennedy. **DLC**

Millennium.

1860   **[Nichols, Thomas Low.]** *Esperanza. My Journey Thither and What I Found There.* Cincinnati: Valentine Nicholson. **W2, 872**

A communal system, spiritualism, privacy, and free love with little sex are the bases of this eutopia.

1861   **[Vickers, John.]** *The New Koran of the Pacifican Friendhood: or, Text-book of Turkish Reformers, in the Teaching and Example of Their Esteemed Master, Jaido Morata* (pseud.). London: George Manwaring. 1874 edition entitled *The New Koran; or, Federan Monitor....* **L, OC1**

In form of a holy book — conservative eutopia.

1862   *The Times No. 55,567, Thursday, May 1, 1962.* **L**

Satire.

1864   **[Blanchard, Calvin.]** *The Art of Real Pleasure: That New Pleasure, for which An Imperial Reward Was Offered.* New York: Calvin Blanchard. Reprinted: New York: Arno Press and *The New York Times,* 1971.

First United States free-love eutopia. Pleasure oriented

society with a government whose "sole business" is to *"satis-fy all human desires."*

Currency represents useful production. No freedom to pollute or live in poverty.

1864   *The History of a Voyage to the Moon; with an Account of the Adventurers' Sub-Sequent Discoveries. An Exhumed Narrative Supposed to Have Been Ejected from a Lunar Volcano,* by Stephen Howard (pseud.) and Carl Geister (pseud.), edited by Chrysostom Trueman (pseud.). London: Lockwood. **L, CtY**

Eutopia with a simple language, private property, and no corruption. Emphasis on moderation.

1865   "A Glimpse of Utopia." *The Eclectic and Congregational Review,* n.s. 9 (October), 344–358.

The Pentateuch as utopia.

1866   "Heliomanes" (pseud.). *A Journey to the Sun.* London: James Cornish. **L**

Utopian satire. For example, it is the tradition to elect men whose hat is biggest and legislative decisions are made by the throw of the dice.

1866   *The Monk of the Mountains; or, A Description of the Joys of Paradise: Being the Life and Wonderful Experiences of an Aged Hermit, Who Was Taken by His Deceased Friend to the First Heaven, and There Shown the Beauties and Happiness of the Spirit Land; with the Destiny and Condition of the Nations of the Earth for One Hundred Years to Come,* by The Hermit Himself (pseud.). Indianapolis: Downey and Brouse. **W2, 1729a**

Mostly heaven, but includes a projection of a future world society.

1867   **Hale, Edward Everett.** "My Visit to Sybaris." *Atlantic Monthly,* 20 (July), 63–81.

A quiet eutopia of gentle, good-humored people. Includes a variety of miscellaneous reforms.

1868   *The Philosophers of Foufouville,* by Radical Freelance, Esq. (pseud.). New York: G. W. Carleton. **W2, 953**

Satire on Fourier.

1869   **[Bassett, Edward Barnard.]** *The Model Town; or, The Right and Progressive Organization of the Production of Material and Moral Wealth.* Cambridge: Printed for the Author. **DLC**

Christian community with private property. Emphasis on education.

1869   **Stoddard, C. W.** "Utopia." *Overland Monthly,* 2 (June), 506–507.

Poem — South Seas Island eutopia.

1870   **Cridge, Annie Denton.** *Man's Rights; or, How Would You Like It?*

Comprising Dreams. Boston: William Denton. **W2, 658**
Sex-role reversal satire.

1870   **Holcombe, William H., M.D.** *In Both Worlds.* Philadelphia: J. B.
Lippincott. **W2, 1222**
World of spirits between earth and heaven as eutopia. Not
perfect; there are still evil spirits.

1870   "A Railway in Utopia." *Hours at Home,* 10 (February), 370–375.
Short sketch about an ideal railroad.

1871   **[Bulwer-Lytton, Edward.]** *The Coming Race.* Edinburgh: William
Blackwood. **L**
Classic utopia in the center of the earth. Highly rational
winged people illustrating the strengths and weaknesses of
reason.

1871   **[Hale, Edward Everett.]** *Ten Times One is Ten: The Possible Reformation. A Story in Nine Chapters,* by Colonel Frederic Ingham
(pseud.). Boston: Roberts Brothers. **W2, 1060**
Christian eutopia brought about by the each one teach one
method.

1871   "The Travels and Adventures of a Philosopher in the Famous
Empire of Hulee. From an Old MS., A.D. 2070." *Fraser's
Magazine,* n.s. 3 (June), 703–717.
Satire — Anti-socialist. Eugenics. State takes all money.
Technology.

1872   **Brown, Fred H.** "What John Smith Saw in the Moon; A Christmas
Story for Parties Who were Children Twenty years ago," in his
One Dollar's Worth ([Chicago:] Np., 1893), pp. 5–44. Originally
published in *The Workingman's Advocate.* **W3, 707**
Technologically advanced. No money.

1872   **Butler, Samuel.** *Erewhon; or, Over the Range.* London: Trübner.
DLC
The classic utopian satire. See also 1901 Butler, *Erewhon
Revisited.*

1872   **Elder, Cyrus.** *Dream of a Free-Trade Paradise.* Philadelphia: Published for the Industrial League by Henry Carey Baird. Reprinted in: *American Utopias,* edited by Arthur O. Lewis, Jr.
New York: Arno Press and *The New York Times, 1971.*
Country of laissez faire.

1872   "If I Were Dictator." *St. Paul's Magazine,* 11 (November),
593–624.
Satire, but includes reform proposals.

1872   **Landis, S[imon] M[ohler].** *An entirely new feature of a thrilling
new novel! Entitled, the Social War of the Year 1900; or, The
Conspirators and Lovers! A Lesson for Saints and Sinners.*
Philadelphia: Landis Publishing Company. **DLC, W2, 1503**

Emphasis is on conspiracy and revolt, but provides an authoritarian constitution.

1872 **[Mackay, Charles.]** *Baron Grimbosh, Doctor of Philosophy and sometime Governor of Barataria. A Record of his Experience, Written by Himself in Exile, and Published by Authority.* London: Tinsley. **L**
Satire.

[1872] **An Octogenarian** (pseud.). *The British Federal Empire. A Speech Delivered in a Certain Year of the Twentieth Century, in a Certain City of the Empire.* London: Charles H. Clarke. **L**
Improved British Empire.

1872-73 **Authwise, Eugene.** "Ultrawa." *The Overland Monthly,* 9–11 (July 1872-November), pp. 176–182, 468–478, 551–563, 71–81, 173–183, 266–279, 372–381, 468–476, 9–20, 259–66, 369–380, 464–474.
Hidden village of forty families. No formal government but informally led by the eldest man and woman.

1873 **Aermont, Paul** (pseud.). *A Narrative of the Travels and Adventures of Paul Aermont Among the Planets.* Boston: Rand, Avery. **DLC**
A variety of societies are depicted. These include one religious eutopia and a number of physically ideal eutopias.

1873 **[Dudgeon, Robert Ellis.]** *Colymbia.* London: Trubner and Company. **L**
A mixture of satire and reform located under water.

1873 **[Lumley, Benjamin.]** *Another World; or, Fragments from the Star City of Montalluyah,* by Hermes (pseud.). Third edition. London: Samuel Tinsley. 1st edition 1873. **L**
Eutopia based on the correct cultivation of character.

1873 **Maitland, Edward.** *By and By; An Historical Romance of the Future.* 3 Vols. London: Richard Bentley and Son. **L, DLC**
Mostly adventure, but includes some descriptions of a better society.

1873 **[Murray, Grenville.]** "Franklin Bacon's Republic: Diary of an Inventor." *Cornhill's Magazine,* 27 (May), 562–580.
Satire on the founding of an island community.

1873 **[Thomas, Bertha.]** "A Vision of Communism." *Cornhill's Magazine,* 28 (September), 300–310.
Anti-Communist story.

1874 **[Blair, Andrew.]** *Annals of the Twenty-ninth Century; or, The Autobiography of the Tenth President of the World-Republic.* 3 Vols. London: Samuel Tinsley. **L**
Mostly science, but a beautiful eutopia of reason is vaguely described.

1874   **[Collins, J.L.]** *Queen Krinaleen's Plagues; or, How a Simple People Were Destroyed. A Discourse in the Twenty-Second Century,* by Jonquil (pseud.). New York: American News Co. **W2, 601**
        Fall of America due to women's fashions.

1874   **Howland, Marie.** *Papa's Own Girl.* New York: John P. Jewett. **W2, 1290**
        Includes a description of a commune being established and the ideas behind it.

1874   *The Last Inca; or, The Story of Tupac Amāru.* 3 Vols. London: Tinsley Bros. **CtY**
        Last Chapter is an Incan socialist eutopia.

1874   **[Mortimer, Edward James.]** *Transmigration,* by Mortimer Collins (pseud.). 3 Vols. London: Hurst and Blackett. **PU**
        Eutopia on Mars in volume 2. No money. Perfect climate. Village life — Arcadian.

1875   **[Clemens, Samuel.]** "The Curious Republic of Gondour," by Mark Twain (pseud.). *Atlantic Monthly,* 36 (October), 461–463.
        Satire (?) proposing additional votes based on education and wealth.

1875   **[Davis, Ellis James?]** *Etymonia.* London: Samuel Tinsley. **L**
        Eutopia founded by a geometrician. Detailed.

1875   **[Davis, Ellis James.]** *Pyrna: A Commune; or, Under the Ice.* London: Bickers and Son. **L**
        Eutopia located inside a glacier in Switzerland. Emphasis on educational system. Highly refined — "looked upon eating as a disagreeable necessity. . . ."

[1875] *In the Future: A Sketch in Ten Chapters.* [Hampstead:] Printed by G. S. Jealous. **L**
        Starts as an eutopia. London with broad, straight, clean streets, and good housing. But gradually reveals that this is the result of authoritarianism. The utopia is a very dull place.

1876   **Collens, T. Wharton.** *The Eden of Labor; or, The Christian Utopia.* Philadelphia: Henry Carey Baird. **L**
        Borderline— an essay on how society could be changed by Christian faith and the detailed application of the labor theory of value.

1876   **Richardson, Benjamin Ward.** *Hygeia: A City of Health.* London: Macmillan. **L**
        Address to the Health Department of the Social Science Congress describing the healthy city of the future.

1876   **Wells, David A[mes].** *Robinson Crusoe's Money; or the Remarkable Financial Fortunes and Misfortunes of a Remote Island Community.* New York: Harper and Brothers. **W3, 5858**
        Imaginary country — argument against Greenbacks.

1877   **[Mallock, William Hurrell.]** *The New Republic or Culture, Faith and Philosophy in an English Country House.* 2 Vols. London: Chatto and Windus. **L**
    Utopia constructed over a country weekend. Much discussion, little detail.

1877   **Masquerier, Lewis.** *Sociology; or, The Reconstruction of Society, Government, and Property, Upon the Principles of the Equality, the Perpetuity, and the Individuality of the Private Ownership of Life, Person, Government, Homestead and the Whole Product of Labor, by Organizing All Nations into Townships of Self-Governing Homestead Democracies — Self-Employed in Farming and Mechanism, Giving All the Liberty and Happiness to be Found on Earth.* New York: The Author. Reprinted: Westport, Connecticut: Greenwood Press, 1970 — includes separately published *Appendix,* 1884. Largely published originally in the *Boston Investigator.* **DLC**
    Equality of the sexes. All land held in trust by the government. Atheist. Includes a model constitution.

1878   **Wright, Henry.** *Mental Travels in Imagined Lands.* London: Trübner Company. **L**
    Travels through Labourland, Fortuneland, and Nomunniburgh (the utopia). In Nomunniburgh education is the basis of all political advancement. Sex education. Major recreation is work. Only good literature, etc. is available. All basic goods and services provided.

1879   **[Watson, H. C. M.]** *Erchomenon; or, The Republic of Materialism.* London: Sampson Low, Marston, Searle, and Rivington. **L**
    Eutopia 600 years in the future in which everyone lives in cities, there is a religion of humanity based on Auguste Comte, and children are raised by women other than their own mother.

[188?]   **Cowan, Frank.** *Revi-Lona; A Romance of Love in a Marvelous Land.* [Greensburgh, Pennsylvania: Tribune Press.] Wright says about 1890. **MoU-St, W3, 1224**
    Communal utopia but without love.

1880   **Dooner, P[ierton] W.** *Last Days of the Republic.* San Francisco: Alta California Publishing Company. **MoU-St, W3, 1583, DLC**
    Yellow war dystopia — China conquers United States.

1880   **[Gaston, Henry A.]** *Mars Revealed; or, Seven Days in the Spirit World: Containing an account of the spirit's trip to Mars, and his return to earth. What he saw and heard on Mars. With Vivid and Thrilling Descriptions of Its Majestic Scenery; Its Mountains, Its Mines; Its Valleys, Rivers, Lakes, and Seas; Its People, Temples of Learning, Worship, Religion, Music, Manners, Customs, Laws; Its Highly Cultivated and Productive Lands, To-*

*gether With Its Beautiful Parks, and Its Delightful Paradise.
Being a work full of diamonds of thought, and of absorbing
interest. A thrilling poem, in beautiful prose,* by A Spirit Yet in
the Flesh (pseud.). San Francisco: Published for the writer, by
A. L. Bancroft and Company. **W3, 2133**
> Spiritualism. Children taught politeness and grace and obe-
> dience to their elders. Useful knowledge is emphasized.

1880   **Greg, Percy.** *Across the Zodiac; The Story of a Wrecked Record.* 2
Vols. London: Trübner. Reprinted: Westport, Connecticut:
Hyperion Press, 1974. **L**
> Racist, socialist, sexist, technological society.

1880   **Pratt, Parley Parker.** *The Angel of the Prairies; A Dream of the
Future.* Salt Lake City: Deseret News Printing and Publishing
Establishment. **MoU-St**
> Mormon tract presenting future eutopia.

1881   **Balch, William S.** *A Peculiar People; or, Reality in Romance.*
Chicago: Henry A. Sumner and Company. **MoU-St**
> Religious Eutopia.

1881   **Hartshorne, Henry.** *1931; A Glance at the Twentieth Century.*
Philadelphia: E. Claxton. **L**
> Written as a projection. Technology, general enlightenment,
> democratization.

1881   **Hay, William Delisle.** *Three Hundred Years Hence; or, A Voice
from Posterity.* London: Newman. **L**
> Racist, socialist, sexist, technological society.

1882   **Besant, Sir Walter.** *The Revolt of Man,* new edition. London:
Chatto and Windus, 1896. **L, MoU-St**
> Sex-role reversal.

1882   **Fitch, Thomas and Anna M. Fitch.** *Better Days; or, a Millionaire
of To-morrow.* San Francisco: Better Days Publishing Company, 1891. **MoU-St, W3, 1882, DLC**
> Transformation of a city by one rich man.

1882   **Green, Nunsowe** (pseud.). *A Thousand Years Hence, Being Personal Experiences.* London: Sampson Low, Marston, Searle and
Rivington. **L**
> Equality for women except that the state intervenes to ensure
> suitable marriages. Many technical advances. Mormon
> church the largest.

1882   **Trollope, Anthony.** *The Fixed Period.* 2 Volumes. London: William Blackwood and Sons. Originally published in *Blackwood's
Magazine.* **L**
> Borderline — society established with a fixed period for life
> (voluntary). Problems as first people reach that age.

1882   **[Welch, Edgar L.]** *The Monster Municipality; or, Gog and Magog*

Reformed. A Dream, by Grip (pseud.). London: Sampson Low, Marston, Searle and Rivington. **L**

Anti-democratic diatribe in the form of a dystopia.

1882   **[Wood, Mrs. J.]** *Pantaletta: A Romance of Sheheland.* New York: American News Company. **W3, 6064**

Sex-role reversal.

1883   **[Baker, William Elliott Smith.]** *The Battle of Coney Island; or Free Trade Overthrown. A Scrap of History Written in 1900,* by An Eye Witness (pseud.). Philadelphia: J. A. Wagenseller. **W3, 238**

Free trade brings depression — overthrown.

1883   *The Battle of the Moy or How Ireland Gained Her Independence 1892–1894.* Boston: Lee and Shepard. **L**

Borderline — successful Irish revolution. New government established modeled on the United States.

1883   **Centennius, Ralph** (pseud.). *The Dominion in 1983.* Peterborough, Ontario: Toker and Comapny. **L**

Canada as eutopia in 1983. No taxes. Only 15, unpaid M.P.s. Private charity.

1883   **Lach-Szyrma, Rev. W[ladjslaw] S[omerville].** *Aleriel: or, A Voyage to Other Worlds.* London: Wyman. **L**

Mostly science fiction but minimal utopian elements.

1883   "The Last Voyage of Lemuel Gulliver." *The World* (December), 5–41 (entire issue).

Journey to the Isle of Moralia; Satire on contemporary England.

1883   **[Macnie, John.]** *The Diothas; or, A Far Look Ahead,* by Ismar Thiusen (pseud.). New York: G. P. Putnam's Sons. Also entitled *A Far Look Ahead; or, The Diothas.* **W3, 3556**

A pre-Bellamy book that is similar to Bellamy except for a great emphasis on custom.

1883   **Schellhous, E. J.** *The New Republic. Founded on the Inalienable Rights of Man, and Containing the Outlines of Such a Government as the Patriot Fathers Contemplated and Formulated in the Declaration of Independence, When Struggling for Liberty.* San Francisco: Bacon and Company. **DLC**

Borderline — essay. Stress on popular government, votes for women, publicly owned utilities and limitations on corporations.

1883   **Sumner, William Graham.** "The Cooperative Commonwealth," in his *The Forgotten Man and Other Essays,* edited by Albert Galloway (New Haven: Yale University Press, 1918), pp. 441–462. **L**

Anti-commune.

1883   **[Welch, Edgar L.]** *Politics and Life in Mars: A Story of a Neigh-*

boring Planet. London: Sampson Low, Marston, Searle and Rivington. **L**
Satire on contemporary England.

1884 **[Allen, Charles G. B.]** "The Child of the Phalanstery," by J. Arbuthnot Wilson (pseud.). *Belgravia,* 54 (August), 163–176.
Anti-Fourier.

1884 **Bellamy, Charles J.** *The Way Out. Suggestions for Social Reform.* New York: G. P. Putnam's Sons. **L**
Reform tract that uses the utopian form.

1884 **[Brookfield, Arthur].** *Simiocracy; A Fragment from Future History.* Edinburgh: William Blackwood. **L**
Satire — monkeys take over England.

1884 **Cridge, Alfred Denton.** *Utopia; or, The History of an Extinct Planet.* Oakland: Winchester and Pew, printers. **W3, 1296**
Small communities (100-300 families) that own the industries of the town. National clearing house where all accounts are balanced every six months. Detailed constitution. Ends negatively — the planet's ecology was destroyed.

1884 *Darkness and Dawn; The Peaceful Birth of a New Age.* London: Kegan Paul, Trench and Company. Sometimes attributed to C. Wise. **L**
Christian cooperative commonwealth.

[1884] *England in 1910.* London: Willing and Company. Also published as *Glasgow in 1910.* Glasgow: Macrone and Company. **L**
Short history of transformed society — technological advance, no paupers, no compulsory education.

1884 **Gronlund, Lawrence.** *The Coöperative Commonwealth in its Outlines. An Exposition of Modern Socialism.* Boston: Lee and Shepard. Reprinted: Cambridge, Massachusetts: Belknap Press, 1965.
Detailed essay — picture of a functioning cooperative society.

1884 **[Ouseley, Rev. Gideon Jasper Richard.]** *Palingenesia; or, The Earth's New Birth,* by Theosopho and Ellora (pseud.). Glasgow: Hay Nisbet. **L**
Mysticism— theocracy. Extremely detailed eutopian (including diagrams and lists of plants) picture of City Four Square.

1884 *The Socialist Revolution of 1888,* by An Eye-Witness (pseud.). London: Harrison and Sons. **L**
Anti-socialist dystopia.

1884 **Truman, O. H.** *The Conquest: A Story of the Past, Present, and Future, Real and Ideal.* Monticello, Iowa: O. H. Truman. **DLC**
Religious transformation achieves eutopia.

1885 **Casey, James.** *A New Moral World, and a New State of Society.*

Providence, Rhode Island: Author. **RPB**
Picture of an Owenite society.

1885   **[Coverdale, Henry Standish]** pseud.). *The Fall of the Great Republic.* Boston: Roberts Brothers. [Added title page adds *(1885–88)* New York: 1895.] **DLC, W3, 1222**
Standard anti-socialist dystopia.

1885   **[Coxe, Edward D.]** *The Fool Killer,* by A. Fugitive (pseud.). Chicago: American Publishers' Association. **DLC**
Detailed eutopia stressing cleanliness, honesty, high technology, workers and capitalists working together.

1885   **Jeffries, Richard.** *After London; or, Wild England.* London: Cassell and Company. **L, MoU-St**
Return to barbarianism produces eutopia.

1885   *A Radical Nightmare or, England Forty Years Hence,* by An Ex M.P. (pseud.). London: Field and Tuer. **L**
Anti-socialist dystopia.

1885   **Shelhamer, Miss M. T.** *Life and Labor in the Spirit World. Being a Description of the Localities, Employments, Surroundings, and Conditions in the Spheres.* Boston: Colby and Rich. **MoU-St**
Spiritualism. Detailed eutopia — spirit life as eutopia. Equality of the sexes. No strife. Learning.

1885   **Strachey. [John] S[aint] L[oe].** *The Great Bread Riots and What Came of Fair Trade.* Bristol: J. W. Arrowsmith. **DLC**
Protective tariff produces dystopia.

1885   **Tuckwell, Rev. W.** *The New Utopia, or England in 1985. A Lecture delivered in the Town Hall, Birmingham, on Sunday February 8th, 1885.* Birmingham: Birmingham Sunday Lecture Society. **L**
Village society. Trained farmers. All land owned by the state and rented to farmers based on their qualifications.

1885   **[Van Deusen, Alonzo.]** *Rational Communism. The Present and the Future Republic of North America,* by A Capitalist (pseud.). New York: The Social Science Publishing Company. **L, MoU-St**
All works of strictly public character owned by the government. Small communities. Very detailed.

1886   **[Allen, Henry Francis.]** *The Key of Industrial Co-operative Government,* by Pruning Knife (pseud.). St. Louis: The Author. **DLC, W3, 74**
Detailed exposition of cooperative system. See also 1891 [Allen.]

[1886]   *Among the Têtchas of Central Asia.* London: Southern Publishing Company. **DLC**
Satire on matriarchal society.

1886   **[Bridge, James Howard.]** *A Fortnight in Heaven; An Unconven-*

tional Romance, by Harold Brydges (pseud.). New York: Henry Holt and Company. **L, W3, 667**
> Jupiter — identical with earth except giants. Appears perfect on the surface but flaws are revealed. Socialist society, good on the surface, is corrupt.

[1886]   **Carne-Ross, Joseph, M.D.,** ed. [written by]. *Quintura; Its Singular People and Remarkable Customs.* London: Joseph and Robert Maxwell. **CtY**
> Rational, egalitarian eutopia that has gone too far and rejected emotion.

1886   **[Fayette, John B.]** *Voices from Many Hill Tops, Echoes from Many Valleys, or the Experiences of Spirits Eon and Eona, In Earth Life and Spirit Spheres, In Ages Past, In the Long, Long Ago, And their Many Incarnations in Earth Life, And On Other Worlds, Given Through the Sun Angels' Order of Light.* Springfield, Massachusetts: Press Springfield Printing Comapny. **DLC**
> Mostly set in the past, but includes a number of eutopias on various planets. E.g. one is a primitive Eden called Harmona. Spiritualism.

1886   **Innominatus** (pseud.). *In the Light of the Twentieth Century.* London: John Hodges. **L**
> Authoritarian dystopia. Charity illegal.

1886   **Lee, Thomas,** ed. [written by] *Falsiver's Travels. The Remarkable Adventures of John Falsiver* (pseud.), *Seaman, at the North Pole and in the Interior of the Earth with a description of the wonderful people and the things discovered there.* [London:] np. **L**
> Mostly adventure, but some social.

1886   **Parnell, John.** *Cromwell the Third: or The Jubilee of Liberty. A Letter Written by Julius Boanerges to His Son.* London: Author. **L**
> Set. A.D. 1951. Authoritarian dystopia.

1886   **[Roe, William James.]** *Inquirendo Island,* by Hudor Genone (pseud.). New York: G. P. Putnam's Sons. **MoU-St, W3, 4633**
> Satire on religion. mathematics is the religion.

[1886]   **Watlock, W. A.** *The Next 'Ninety-three; or, crown, commune and colony. Told in a citizen's diary.* London: The Leadenhall Press. **L**
> Anti-socialist dystopia.

1886-87   **Morris, William.** "A Dream of John Ball." *Commonweal.* First published in book form. London: Reeves and Turner, 1888.
> Not strictly a utopia but includes some descriptions that are utopian. See also 1890 Morris.

1887   **Dodd, Anna Bowman.** *The Republic of the Future; or, Socialism A*

Reality. New York: Cassell and Company. **W3 1557**
Anti-socialist dystopia.

1887 **[Hudson, W. H.]** *A Crystal Age.* . . London: T. F. Unwin. **DLC**
Future Arcadian society organized in large families. Detailed picture of the society.

1887 *The Island of Anarchy. A Fragment of History in the 20th Century,* by E. W. Reading: Miss Langley, Lovejoy's Library. **MH, NcD, LSE**
Anarchist commune — eutopia.

1887 **[Lach-Szyrma, Wladjslaw Somerville.]** "Letters from the Planets," by Our Roving Correspondent (pseud.) signed Alerial (pseud.) (1887-93), in *Worlds Apart,* edited by George Locke (London: Cornmarket Reprints, 1972), pp. 1-26. Originally published in *Cassell's Family Magazine.*
October 1887 — Venus as an Athenian democracy.

1887 *Man Abroad; A Yarn of Some Other Century.* New York: G. W. Dillingham. Reprinted: Boston: Gregg Press, 1976. **W3, 3594**
Mostly satire, but describes a community based on the principles, somewhat modified, of Henry George.

1887 **[Roe, William James.]** *Bellona's Husband,* by Hudor Genone (pseud.). Philadelphia: J. B. Lippincott. **W3, 4631**
Set on Mars — satire.

1887 **[Von Swartwout, William H.]** *Declaration of Principles and Proclamations of Emancipation.* London: Columbia University Press, Also entitled *Truthology with.* . . . **L**
See 1893 Von Swartwout. See also Von Swartwout, 1890, 1892-1893, 1894 (3).

1888 **Batchelor, John M.** *A Strange People.* New York: J. Ogilvie.
Lost race utopia — atheists and anarchists.

1888 **Bellamy, Edward.** *Looking Backward: 2000-1887.* Boston: Ticknor and Company. **W3, 460**
The classic American eutopia.

1888 **Clapperton, J[ane] H[ume.]** *Margaret Dunmore: or A Socialist Home.* London: Swan Sonnenschein. **L, LLL**
Story of a successful commune.

1888 **Leonhart, Rudolph.** *The Treasure of Montezuma.* Canton, Ohio: Cassidy. **MoU-St, W3, 3282**
Better society brought about by a man of wealth.

1888 **[Nicholson, Joseph Shield.]** *Thoth; A Romance.* London: William Blackwood and Sons. **L, DLC**
Rule by reason alone — result mixed. Genetics. Scientifically advanced. Hatred of women.

1888 **Richardson, Benjamin Ward.** *The Son of a Star; A Romance of the Second Century.* 3 Vols. London: Longmans, Green. Also pub-

lished in an abridged one volume edition. The utopia was published separately in 1897 as *At Noviomagus: A Tribute of Affection to the Late Sir Benjamin Ward Richardson Fifteen Years Lord High President of the Noviomagians, 1881–1896.* London: Chiswick Press. **O, MH**
Satire of reversal.

1889   **Bellamy, Charles J.** *An Experiment in Marriage. A Romance.* Albany, New York: Albany Publishing Company. **W3, 453, L**
Successful experiment in free love.

1889   **Bellamy, Edward.** "To Whom This May Come." *Harper's New Monthly Magazine,* 78 (February), 458–466. Reprinted: *American Utopias,* edited by Arthur O. Lewis, Jr. New York: Arno Press and *The New York Times,* 1971.
ESP brings self-knowledge and empathy.

1889   **Bunce, Oliver Bell.** "The City Beautiful," in his *The Story of Happinolande and Other Legends* (New York: D. Appleton, 1889), pp. 98–140. **W3, 775**
Eutopia through neatness.

1889   **Bunce, Oliver Bell.** "The Story of Happinolande," in his *The Story of Happinolande and Other Legends* (New York: D. Appleton, 1889), pp. 5–67. **W3, 775**
Anti-egalitarian.

1889   **Clark, Francis E[dward].** *The Mossback Correspondence Together With Mr. Mossback's Views on Certain Practical Subjects, with a Short Account of His Visit to Utopia* [pp. 175–185]. Boston: D. Lothrop. **DLC, MoU-St**
Religion, wisest man chosen for office. "...in utopia it is the custom to put the best construction upon every action."

1889   **[Clemens, Samuel L.]** *A Connecticut Yankee in King Arthur's Court,* by Mark Twain (pseud.). New York: Charles L. Webster
Borderline — failed attempt to build a democratic, technological society in the time of Arthur.

[1889]   **Corbett, Mrs. George.** *New Amazonia; a Foretaste of the Future.* London: Tower **L**
Feminist eutopia.

1889   **Dalton, Henry Robert S[amuel].** *Lesbia Newman.* London: George Redway. **L**
Rights of women. Training so they can exercise them. Roman Catholic church allows priestesses.

1889   **[De Medici, Charles.]** *Two Lunatics; A Remarkable Story,* by One of Them (pseud.). New York: Oxford Publishing Company. **CSmH**
Eutopia that rejects equality in favor of equity. Encourages genius, talent and skill of all sorts.

[1889]   **Fraser, Joseph,** ed. [written by]. *Melbourne and Mars; My Myste-*
             rious Life on Two Planets. Extracts from the Diary of a Mel-
             bourne Merchant. Melbourne: E. W. Cole.
             Detailed eutopia based on abundance. No money. Electricity
             does almost all the work.

1889   **Griffin, C. S.** *Nationalism.* Boston: C. S. Griffin. **DLC**
             Eutopia based on 1887 Gronlund and 1888 Bellamy.

1889   **Heywood, D. Herbert.** *The Twentieth Century. A Prophecy of the*
             Coming Age. Boston: F. B. Heywood, 2000. **DLC, W3, 2658**
             Something of a ghost. All that exists is a prospectus for a
             book that appears never to have been published. Prospectus
             indicates it would have been an utopia.

1889   **[Lane, Mary E. (Bradley).]** *Mizora: A Prophecy. A Mss. Found*
             Among the Private Papers of the Princess Vera Zarovitch
             (pseud.); *Being a true and faithful account of her Journey to the*
             Interior of the Earth, with a careful description of the Country
             and its Inhabitants, their Customs, Manners and Government.
             Written by Herself. New York: G. W. Dillingham. First pub-
             lished in Cincinnati *Commercial* 1880–1881. **W3, 3203**
             Feminist eutopia.

1889   **Maccoll, Hugh.** *Mr. Stranger's Sealed Packet.* London: Chatto and
             Windus. **L, LLL**
             Set on Mars. Mostly adventure. Technologically based abun-
             dance. Equality. Socialism.

1889   **Murray, G. G. A.** *Gobi or Shamo; A Story of Three Songs.*
             London: Longmans, Green and Company. **MoU-St**
             Athenian society that has gained control over nature. Similar
             to 1871 Bulwer-Lytton.

1889   **[Sears, Alfred.]** *The Lost Inca; A Tale of Discovery in the Vale of*
             the Inti-Mayu, by the Inca-Pancho-Ozollo (pseud.). New York:
             Cassell. **MoU-St**
             Lost Incan society with advanced technology presented as an
             eutopia.

1889   **Stockton, Frank R[ichard].** *The Great War Syndicate.* New York:
             P. F. Collier. **L, W3, 5239**
             Establishment of a syndicate to run future wars.

1889   **Vogel, Sir Julius.** *Anno Domini 2000; or, Woman's Destiny.* Lon-
             don: Hutchinson. **L**
             Sexual equality.

1889   **Yelverton, Christopher.** *Oneiros or Some Questions of the Day.*
             London: Kegan Paul, Trench and Company. **ICU**
             Authoritarian system for the benefit of the lower classes —
             good society results.

[189?]   **Bevington, L[ouisa] S[arah].** *Common-Sense Country.* London:

James Tochatti, "Liberty" Press. Liberty Pamphlets. **NcD**
Anarchist socialist eutopia.

1890   **[Bachelder, John.]** *A.D. 2050. Electrical Development at Atlantis,* by A Former Resident of "The Hub." San Francisco: The Bancroft Company. **W3, 194**
Bellamy's society not working smoothly so some emigrate and form a capitalist (much reformed) eutopia.

1890   **Berwick, Edward.** "Farming in the Year 2000, A.D." *Overland Monthly,* 2nd series, 15 (June), 263–273.
Filling in a gap in 1888 Bellamy.

[1890]   **Booth, General [William].** *In Darkest England and The Way Out.* London: International Headquarters of the Salvation Army. **L**
Mostly a reform scheme centered on the Salvation Army, but includes the transformation of society through a series of city and farm colonies.

1890   **Cromie, Robert.** *A Plunge into Space.* London: Frederick Warne. **L**
Mars technically and aesthetically advanced. Older culture, less passion, less government.

1890   **Dail, C. C.** *Willmoth, The Wanderer; or The Man From Saturn.* [Atchison, Kansas: Haskill Printing Company]. **W3, 1370**
Vegetarian, polygamous. A form of ESP means that no one has evil thoughts.

1890   **De Bernardi, G. B.** *Trials and Triumphs of Labor. The Needle's Eye of Legal Tender Money.* Marshall, Missouri: Capitol Parlor Print. 1894 edition has subtitle, *The Text Book of the Labor Exchange.* **MoU-St**
Labor exchange brings eutopia.

1890   **[Donnelly, Ignatius.]** *Caesar's Column: A Story of the Twentieth Century,* by Edmund Boisgilbert, M.D. (pseud.). Chicago: F. J. Schulte and Company. New edition edited by Walter B. Rideout. Cambridge, Massachusetts: Belknap Press, 1960. **MoU-St, W3, 1579**
Largely social catastrophe novel, but includes a populist eutopia at the end.

1890   **Fuller, Lieut. Alvarado M.** *A.D. 2000.* Chicago: Laird and Lee. **L, MoU-St**
Detailed political and economic reform. Little social change.

1890   **Gilpin, William.** *The Cosmopolitan Railway. Compacting and Fusing Together All the World's Continents.* San Francisco: The History Company. **ICU, MoU-St**
Borderline — railroad around the world will transform the world.

[1890]   **Grove, W.** *The Wreck of a World.* 6th edition. London: Digby and

Long, Publishers. First edition 1890. **L**
Pan-Britannic Confederation.

1890   **[Herbert, Auberon].** "An English Tax-Day, June 15, 1927." *The Free Life,* 1 (July 11), 41–42; 1 (July 18), 47–48; 1 (July 25), 53–54; 1 (August 1), 59–60. **L(Col.)**
Individualist eutopia — taxes are freely given, not imposed.

1890   **Leggett, M[ortimer] D[ormer].** *A Dream of a Modest Prophet.* Philadelphia: J. B. Lippincott. **L, W3, 3268**
Set on Mars, which is like Earth but advanced. Religion as a way of life.

1890   **Longley, Alcander.** *What is Communism? A Narrative of the Relief Community. Common Property, United Labor, and Equal Rights to All, Will Immediately Displace all the Poverty, Vice and Crime of Society, and Secure to Eyerybody* [sic.] *The Greatest Plenty Purity and Peace.* St. Louis: Altruist Community. **WHi**
Founding and development of a commune.

1890   **Michaelis, Richard.** *Looking Further Forward.* Chicago: Rand McNally. Reprinted: Arno Press and *The New York Times,* 1971. Also entitled, *Looking Forward* and *A Sequel to Looking Backward or Looking Further Forward.* **W3, 3717**
Anti-Bellamy.

[1890]   **[Miller, George Noyes.]** *The Strike of a Sex. A Novel,* by ? (pseud.). New York: G. W. Dillingham. **W3, 3735**
Women go on strike. See also [1891] Miller.

1890   **Morris, William.** *News from Nowhere or an Epic of Rest; Being Some Chapters from a Utopian Romance.* Boston: Roberts Bros. **DLC, NcD**
Agrarian socialist eutopia. See also 1886–1887 Morris.

[1890]   **[Norton, Rev. Philip.]** *Sub Sole or Under the Sun. Missionary Adventures in the Great Sahara,* by the Right Reverend Artegall Smith, D.D. (pseud.). London: James Nisbet. **CU**
Lost race — eutopia of science and technology.

1890   **Petzler, John.** *Life in Utopia; Being a Faithful and Accurate Description of the Institutions that Regulate Labour, Art, Science, Agriculture, Education, Habitation, Matrimony, Law, Government, and Religion in this Delightful Region of Human Imagination.* London: Authors' Cooperative Publishing Company. **L**
Fairly standard socialist eutopia.

1890   **Pittock, Mrs. M.A.** *The God of Civilization. A Romance.* Chicago: Eureka Pub. Co. **DLC**
Borderline — mostly a romantic adventure tale, but includes description of a South Seas island utopia.

1890   **[Porter, Linn Boyd.]** *Speaking of Ellen,* by Albert Ross (pseud.). New York: G. W. Dillingham. 1903 edition entitled *Riverfall.* **W3, 4325**
    Pro-Bellamy eutopia. Brought about by activist women.

1890   **Salisbury, H[enry] B[arnard].** *The Birth of Freedom; A Socialist Novel.* New York: Humboldt Publishing Company. Also published in *The Nationalist,* 1890–1891. Also entitled *Miss Worden's Hero.* **L**
    Standard socialist eutopia — stress on revolution.

1890   **Satterlee, W. W.** *Looking Backward; and What I Saw.* 2nd edition. [Minneapolis: Harrison and Smith]. Reprinted: New York: Arno Press and *The New York Times,* 1971.
    Written against Bellamy and George.

1890   **Schindler, Solomon.** "Dr. Leete's Letter to Julian West." *The Nationalist,* 3 (September), 81–86.
    Pro-1888 Bellamy.

1890   **Stone, Mrs. C. H.** *One of "Berrian's" Novels.* New York: Welch, Fracker Company. **W3, 5264**
    Berrian was the great novelist of Bellamy's future.

1890   **Vinton, Arthur Dudley.** *Looking Further Backward. Being a Series of Lectures Delivered to the Freshman Class at Shawmut College, by Professor Won Lung Li (Successor of Professor Julian West), Mandarin of the Second Rank of the Golden Dragon and Chief of the Historical Section of the Colleges in the North-Eastern Division of the Chinese Province of North America. Now, For the First Time, Collected, Edited and Condensed.* Albany, New York: Albany Book Company. **W3, 5697**
    Anti-Bellamy dystopia.

1890   **[Von Swartwout, William H.]** *The World's Crisis and the Only Way Out. The Olombia Commonwealth Jubilee Proclamation and Declaration of Independence No. 2.* New York: New Columbia University Press. **L**
    See 1893 Von Swartwout. See also Von Swartwout 1887, 1892–1893, 1894 (3).

1890   **[Watson, Henry Crocker Marriott.]** *The Decline and Fall of the British Empire; or, The Witches Cavern.* London: Trischler.
    Socialism, and a lack of religion and authority cause the collapse of Britain.

1890   **[Worley, Frederick U.]** *Three Thousand Dollars a Year. Moving Forward; or, How We Got There. The Complete Liberation of All the People. Abridged from the Advance Sheets of a History of Industrial and Governmental Reforms in the United States, To Be Published in the Year 2001,* by Benefice (pseud.). Washington: [J. P. Wright, printer]. **DLC, W3, 6111**
    Cooperative system.

1891   **[Allen, Henry Francis.]** *A Strange Voyage. A Revision of The Key of Industrial Cooperative Government. An Interesting and Instructive Description of Life on Planet Venus,* by Pruning Knife (pseud.). St. Louis: Monitor Publishing Company. **DLC, W3, 75**
              See 1886 [Allen.]

1891   **[Barlow, James William.]** *History of a World of Immortals Without a God: Translated from an Unpublished Manuscript in the Library of a Continental University,* by Antares Skorpios (pseud.). Dublin: William McGee. 1909 edition entitled *The Immortals' Great Quest.* Author's name sometimes given incorrectly as Jane Barlow. **O, L**
              Cyclical life — grow old, grow young, grow old again. Society based on this fact. No reproduction. No death from natural causes.

1891   **Bigg, [Henry Robert] Heather.** *Human Republic.* London: David Stott. **L**
              Interior of the human body; emphasis is on interdependence and equality.

1891   **Fiske, Amos K[idder].** *Beyond the Bourn. Reports of a Traveller Returned from "The Undiscovered Country."* New York: Fords, Howard and Hulbert. **MoU-St, W3, 1875**
              Eutopia of perfected human beings after death.

1891   **Fitzporter, J[ohn] L.** *My Vacation; or, The Millennium.* St. Louis: np. **W3, 1883**
              Venus — vegetarian, spiritualist. Detailed reform.

[1891]   **Folingsby, Kenneth.** *Meda. A Tale of the Future.* [Glasgow:] Printed for Private Circulation. **L**
              World of fantastic intelligence. Man has passed beyond the need to eat. Monarchy because every society needs central focus.

[1891]   **Geissler, L[udwig] A.** *Looking Beyond. A Sequel to "Looking Backward," by Edward Bellamy, and An Answer To "Looking Further Forward," by Richard Michaelis.* New Orleans: L. Graham and Son. **W3, 2145**
              Pro-Bellamy eutopia.

[1891]   **Gould, F. J.** *The Agnostic Island.* London: Watts. **L**
              Agnostic eutopia — religious toleration.

1891   **Heuston, B[enjamin] F.** *The Rice Mills of Port Mystery.* Chicago: Charles H. Kerr. Unity Library No. 8. **DLC, MoU-St**
              Borderline — novel arguing for free trade. In almost all bibliographies the author's name is misspelled as Houston.

1891   **Jerome, Jerome K.,** "The New Utopia," in his *Diary of a Pil-*

grimage (And Six Essays). (New York: Henry Holt), pp. 337–60. **DLC**
Equality achieved by limiting those better than the average.

1891   **Leland, Samuel Phelps.** *Peculiar People.* Cleveland: Aust and Clark. **W3, 3273**
Anti-commune.

1891   **Middleton, William.** *An Account of an Extraordinary Living Hidden City in Central Africa and Gatherings from South Africa.* London: King, Sell, and Railton.
Mostly non-fiction but includes a section entitled "A Living Hidden City in South Africa" that describes a democratic lost race. Population control. Sexual equality and free love.

[1891]   **Miller, George Noyes.** *After the Strike of a Sex; or, Zugassent's Discovery with the Oneida Community, and the Perfectionists of Oneida and Wallingford.* London: William Reeves. Bellamy Library No. 26.
Exposition of Noyes' system. See also [1890] Miller.

1891   **Norton, Seymour F.** *Ten Men of Money Island.* London: William Reeves, [1895] The Bellamy Library No. 27. Part published as newspaper articles in 1879. **L**
United States author. Eutopia brought about through tax reform.

1891   **Ramsey, Milton W.** *Six Thousand Years Hence.* Minneapolis: Press of Alfred Roper. **W3, 4420**
Visit to the sun — finds various vaguely described eutopias. Returns to earth 6,000 years later — finds a society with a large population functioning well. Technology. Careful job placement.

1891   **[Rickett, Joseph Compton.]** *The Christ That Is To Be. A Latter-Day Romance.* London: Chapman and Hall. **L**
England in small communities with a powerful guild system. The Second Coming is ignored and rejected.

1891   **Simpson, William.** *The Man From Mars. His Morals, Politics and Religion. 3rd edition. Revised and Enlarged by an Extended Preface and a Chapter on Woman Suffrage.* San Francisco: Press of E. D. Beattie, 1900. 1st edition published under the pseudonym Thomas Blot. **W3, 4949**
Christianity and socialism combined.

1891   **Thomas Chauncey.** *The Crystal Button or, Adventures of Paul Prognosis in the Forty-Ninth Century,* edited by George Houghton. Boston: Houghton, Mifflin. **W3, 5430**
Written 1872–1878. Scientific advance. Emphasis on how eutopia was achieved.

1891   **[Walker, Samuel.]** *The Reign of Selfishness. A Story of Concen-*

trated Wealth. New York: M. K. Pelletreau. 1899 edition entitled *Dry Bread.* **W3, 5716**
Authoritarian, capitalist dystopia.

1891 **Z., X. Y.** (pseud.). *The Vril Staff.* London: David Stott. **L**
Compare to 1871 [Bulwer-Lytton.] A man invents something like Vril and forces world change.

1891 **Andrew, J. O.** "Looking Forward." *Belford's Monthly* (April), 181–190.
Anti-feminist.

1892 **[Armstrong, Charles Wicksteed.]** *The Yorl of the Northmen; or, the Fate of the English Race; Being the Romance of a Monarchical Utopia,* by Charles Strongi'th'arm (pseud.). London: Reeves and Turner. **L**
Feudal eutopia.

1892 **Beard, Dan[iel Carter].** "Moonblight," in his *Moonblight and Six Feet of Romance* (New York: Charles L. Webster, 1892), pp. 17–197. **W3, 428, DLC, MoU-St**
Man can see the true character of people; reforms a small mining area.

1892 **Bennett, Arthur.** *The Dream of an Englishman.* London: Simpkin, Marshall, Hamilton, Kent and Company. **L**
World federation.

1892 **Bradshaw, William R[ichard].** *The Goddess of Atvatabar; Being the History of the Discovery of the Interior World and Conquest of Atvatabar.* New York: J. F. Douthitt. **W3, 648, MoU-St**
Borderline — romance and adventure. Religion based on the "...worship of the human soul under a thousand forms...." Hopeless love the ideal.

1892 **Braine, Robert D.** *Messages from Mars; by the Aid of the Telescope Plant.* New York: J. S. Ogilvie. **L**
Science and technology brings eutopia. Government by the most intelligent.

1892 **Chavannes, Albert.** *The Future Commonwealth, or What Samuel Balcom Saw in Socioland.* New York: True Nationalist Publishing Company. **DLC**
See also 1895 Chavannes. Eutopia in Africa based on the ideas of Herbert Spencer.

1892 **Clarke, General F. M.** *A Maiden of Mars.* Chicago: Charles H. Sergel and Company. **DLC**
E.S.P. Abundance. Technologically advanced. Spiritualism.

1892 **Cowdon, James Seldon.** *Pantocracy or The Reign of Justice.* Washington, D.C.: Author. **DLC**
Detailed reform proposed through third political party.

· 1892 **[Crocker, Samuel.]** *That Island; A Political Romance,* by Theodore

Oceanic Islet (pseud.). Kansas City, Missouri: Press of the Sidney F. Woody Printing Company. **W3, 1304**
Detailed eutopia with many specific reforms.

[1892] **Crusoe, Robinson** (pseud.). *Looking Upwards; or, Nothing New. The Up Grade: From Henry George Past Edward Bellamy on to Higher Intelligences.* 2 Parts. Auckland, New Zealand: H. Brett. Only one part published. **L**
Pamphlet — nationalize land and industry.

1892 **Daniel, Charles [S.].** *Ai. A Social Vision.* Philadelphia: Miller Publication Company. **L, W3, 1389**
Reform through cooperation, Christianity and brotherhood.

1892 **Donnelly, Ignatius.** *The Golden Bottle; or, The Story of Ephraim Benezet of Kansas.* New York: D. D. Merrill Company. **MoU-St, DLC, W3, 1581**
Preface says, ''...it is intended to explain and defend, in the thin disguise of a story, some of the new ideas put forth by the People's Party....'' Man gets a bottle that can produce gold. After a great struggle with vested interests, he is able to establish an eutopia on the basis of cooperation, free medical care, owner-occupied homes, cheap governmentally owned transportation, and the eight-hour day.

[1892] **Everett, Henry L[exington].** *The People's Program; The Twentieth Century is Theirs. A Romance of the Expectations of the Present Generation.* New York: Workmen's Publishing Company. **DLC, W3 1780**
Detailed labor colony scheme.

1892 **Grimshaw, Robert.** *Fifty Years Hence; or, What May Be in 1943: A Prophecy Supposed to Be Based on Scientific Deductions by an Improved Graphical Method.* New York: Practical Publishing Company. **W3, 2288**
Detailed description of the Electrical Age. Bathing is compulsory.

1892 **Harben, William.** ''In the Year Ten Thousand.'' *Arena,* 6 (November), 743–749.
Sketch of a much advanced people. Vegetarian. No government.

1892 **[Hearn, Mary Ann.]** *1900? A Forecast and a Story,* by Marianne Farningham (pseud.). London: James Clarke. **MoU-St, L**
Establishment of a successful religious commune.

[1892] **Herbert, William** (pseud?). *The World Grown Young: Being a Brief Record of Reforms Carried Out From 1894–1914 By the Late Mr. Philip Adams Millionaire and Philanthropist.* London: W. H. Allen. **L**
Eutopia including almost all the standard reforms of the day.

[1892]   **[Hume, Ferguson Wright.]** *The Island of Fantasy; A Romance,* by Fergus Hume (pseud.). 3 Vols. London: Griffith Farran and Company. **L, MoU-St**
Greek arcadian eutopia.

1892   **Hythloday Junior** (pseud.). "Warrington: As It Might Be," in *Warrington: As It Was, As It Is, and As It Might Be* (Warrington: "Sunrise" Publishing Co., 1892), pp. 167–230. Originally published in *Sunrise.* **O**
City of Warrington as an eutopia 30 years in the future. Cleaned up. Technology. Brought about by municipal ownership of utilities and then industries.

1892   **[Moore, M. Louise.]** *Al-Modad; or, Life Scenes Beyond the Polar Circumflex. A Religio-Scientific Solution of the Problems of Present and Future Life,* by An Untrammeled Free-Thinker (pseud.). Shell Bank, Cameron Parish, Louisiana: M. L. Moore and M. Beauchamp. **W3, 3817**
Includes detailed eutopia with an emphasis on education.

[1892]   **[Morris, Alfred.]** *Looking Ahead! A Tale of Adventure.* London: Henry. **L**
Failure of a socialist revolution and the beginning of a new feudal system.

1892   **Schwahn, John George.** *The Tableau; or, Heaven As a Republic.* Los Angeles: Franklin. **W3, 4821**
Allegory — history of the world builds to a future eutopia based on reason.

1892   **Stockwell, Lucius A.** *The Earthquake; A Story of To-Day.* Indianapolis: Nonconformist Publishing Company. **MoU-St**
Mostly a condemnation of capitalism from a populist perspective, but includes a short description of desirable reforms and procedures for achieving them.

1892   **Tibbles, T. H. [and Elia M. Peattie].** *The American Peasant; A Timely Allegory,* by T. H. Tibbles and Another (pseud.). Indianapolis: Vincent Brothers Publishing Company. Name is usually given as Beattie. **DLC**
Temperate continent in the Arctic. Christian. Few laws — equality more important than laws. United States as dystopia.

1892   **Tincker, Mary Agnes.** *San Salvador.* Boston: Houghton Mifflin. **W3, 5500**
Christian, aristocratic eutopia in a hidden valley.

1892-93   **Von Swartwout, Dr. William H.** *Olombia or The New Political Economy.* Revised edition. Volume 1. New York: New Columbia University Press. **L**
See 1893 Von Swartwout. See also Von Swartwout 1887, 1890, 1894 (3).

1893   *The Beginning. A Romance of Chicago As It Might Be.* Chicago: Charles H. Kerr. **IHi**
> Better public education and estate taxes bring eutopia to Chicago.

1893   **Bramston, M[ary].** "The Island of Progress," in her *The Wild Lass of Estmere and Other Stories* (London: Seeley and Co., 1893), pp. 227–274. **L**
> Set 500 years in the future. Equality, science and technology. Highly refined. Placid.

1893   **Brooks, Byron A[lden].** *Earth Revisited.* Boston: Arena Publishing Company. **W3, 681**
> Technology, cooperation and no idleness. Four hour work day. Moral training.

1893   **Brown, Fred H.** "A Message from the Stars," in his *One Dollar's Worth.* ([Chicago:] Np., 1893), pp. 129–169. **W3, 707**
> Religious, technological.

[1893]   **Dick, Mr.** (pseud.). *James Ingleton: The History of a Social State A.D. 2000.* London: James Blackwood. **L**
> Revolt against a standard socialist dystopia.

[1893]   *"Englands Downfall" or, The Last Great Revolution,* by An Ex-Revolutionist (pseud.). London: Digby, Long and Company. **L**
> Set in 1930. Anti-socialist dystopia.

1893   **Hawthorne, Julian.** "June, 1993." *Cosmopolitan Magazine,* 14 (1893), pp. 450–458.
> Technology. Anti-urban.

1893   **Hayes, Frederick W[illiam].** *The Great Revolution of 1905; or, The Story of the Phalanx.* London: Robert Forder. Also published as *State Industrialism: The Story of the Phalanx.* London: William Reeves, 1893. Bellamy Library No. 34. **L**
> Standard socialist eutopia of the Bellamy type. Traces out the development to eutopia.

1893   **[Jones, Alice Ilgenfritz and Ella Merchant.]** *Unveiling a Parallel: A Romance,* by Two Women of the West (pseud.). Boston: Arena Publishing Company. **W3, 5627**
> Eutopia stressing equality between the sexes.

1893   **Leonhart, Rudolph.** *Either, Or.* Canton, Ohio: Roller Printing Company. **W3, 3281, MoU-St**
> Satire on United States — cooperative eutopia at the end.

[1893]   **L'Estrange, Henry.** *Platonia; A Tale of Other Worlds.* Bristol: J. W. Arrowsmith. **L**
> An unknown, small planet nearer than Mars. Its capital is Campanella. Private enterprise but protected by the state. Stress on gradual reform.

1893   **Miller, Joaquin.** *The Building of the City Beautiful.* Cambridge,

Massachusetts: Stone and Kimball. **W3, 3737, L**
Religion. Rural or small town utopia.

1893   **Moffat, W. Graham and John White.** *What's the World Coming To? A Novel of the Twenty-First Century, Founded on the Fads, Facts, and Fiction of the Nineteenth.* London: Elliot Stock. **L**
Society within the world of 1888 Bellamy with all the fads of the late Nineteenth Century practiced.

[1893]   **Olerich, Henry.** *A Cityless and Countryless World: An Outline of Practical Co-operative Individualism.* Holstein, Iowa: Gilmore and Olerich. Reprinted: Arno Press and *The New York Times,* 1971. **W3, 4030**
Detailed description of a complete society without traditional city-country divisions or families. See also 1915 Olerich and 1923 Olerich.

1893   **Pearson, Charles H[enry].** *National Life and Character. A Forecast.* London: Macmillan. **DLC**
Anti-socialist and racist. General decay.

1893   **Roberts, J. W.** *Looking Within. The Misleading Tendencies of "Looking Backward" Made Manifest.* New York: A. S. Barnes. **MoU-St, W3, 4568**
Anti-Bellamy.

1893   **Rogers, [John Rankin].** *The Graftons; or, Looking Forward. A Story of Pioneer Life,* by S. L. Rogers (pseud.). Chicago: Milton George. **W3, 4639**
Populist eutopia. Also published under author's real name as *Looking Forward; or, The Story of an American Farm* (1898).

1893   **Russell, A[ddison] P[eale].** *Sub-Coelum; A Sky-Built Human World.* Boston: Houghton, Mifflin. **W3, 4720**
Emphasis on self-control, moderation — people don't even snore.

1893   **Swift, Morrison I.** *A League of Justice or Is It Right To Rob Robbers?* Boston: The Commonwealth Society. **L**
League of men who take from the rich and give to the poor gradually transform society. See also 1903 Swift.

1893   **Von Swartwout, William H.** *Olombia or Utopia Made Practical.* New York: New Columbia University Press. **L**
Eutopia brought about by abolishing money. Can be done by simply changing the name of the country. Detailed system. See also Von Swartwout 1887, 1890, 1892–1893, 1894 (3).

1894   **Astor, John Jacob.** *A Journey in Other Worlds; A Romance of the Future.* New York: D. Appleton. **MoU-St, W3, 148**
Eutopia in which electricity does all the work.

[1894]   **Barnett, Rev. Canon [Samuel Augustus].** *The Ideal City.* Bristol: Arrowsmith. **O, L**
          Stress on variety but no very rich or poor. Religion, education.

1894   **Browne, Walter.** *"2894" or, The Fossil Man (A Mid-Winter Night's Dream).* New York: G. W. Dillingham. **W3, 731 (NA)**
          Sex-role reversal. Technology.

1894   **Crawford, T. C.** *A Man and His Soul; An Occult Romance of Washington Life.* New York: Charles B. Reed. **MoU-St**
          Detailed eutopia — stress on training for public life.

[1894]   **Giles, Fayette Stratton.** *Shadows Before or a Century Onward.* New York: Humboldt Publishing Company. No. 57 of *The Twentieth Century Library.* **L**
          Presented as a prediction. No religion. Doctors paid to prevent disease, and they are not paid when their patients are sick. Capitalist.

1894   **Gillette, King Camp.** *Human Drift.* Boston: New Era Publishing Company. **DLC**
          Eutopia brought about by the foundation of a gigantic corporation which gradually absorbs the whole world economy. See also 1910 Gillette.

[1894]   **Harben, Will N[athaniel].** *The Land of the Changing Sun.* New York: Merriam Company. **W3, 2447**
          Authoritarian utopia.

[1894]   **Hertzka, Dr. Theodor.** *A Visit to Freeland, or The New Paradise Regained.* London: William Reeves and The British Freeland Association. The Bellamy Library No. 21. **L, NN**
          Appears to have been originally published in English. Portrait of Hertzka's proposed Freeland colony.

1894   **[Hird, James Dennis.]** *Toddle Island. Being the Diary of Lord Bottsford.* London: Richard Bentley. **L**
          Satire — Erewhonian in character, but suggests a cooperative system.

1894   **Howells, William Dean.** *A Traveler from Altruria.* New York: Harper and Bros. **W3, 2833**
          This and its sequel (see 1907 Howells) depict first the troubles of the contemporary United States and then an arcadia.

1894   **Knapp, Adeline.** "One Thousand Dollars a Day," in her *One Thousand Dollars a Day. Studies in Practical Economics.* (Boston: Arena, 1894), pp. 11–41. **MoU-St**
          Everyone quits work when they are all given $1,000 a day. Disaster followed by the voluntary establishment of a labor exchange.

1894 **Lazarus, Henry,** ed. [written by]. *The English Revolution of the 20th Century; A Prospective History.* London: T. Fisher Unwin. **L**
  Mostly criticism of contemporary society from the perspective of a future eutopia.

1894 **McIver, G.** *Neuroomia: A New Continent. A Manuscript delivered by the Deep.* London: Swan Sonnenschein. **L**
  Mostly adventure, but includes detailed reform.

1894 **Pomeroy, William C.** *The Lords of Misrule; A Tale of Gods and of Men.* Chicago: Laird and Lee. **DLC**
  Series of future dystopias.

1894 **Pope, Gustavus W., M.D.** *Journey to Mars. The Wonderful World: Its Beauty and Splendor; Its Mighty Races and Kingdoms; Its Final Doom. Romances of the Planets.* No. 1. New York: G. W. Dillingham. Reprinted: Westport, Connecticut: Hyperion Press, 1974. **MoU-St, W3, 4304**
  Linear city, 2,000 miles long, 20 miles wide.

1894 **Rosewater, Frank.** *'96; A Romance of Utopia, Presenting a Solution to the Labor Problem, A New God and a New Religion.* Omaha: The Utopia Company (c. 1893). **W3, 4683**
  Labor theory of value institutionalized.

1894 **Schindler, Solomon.** *Young West; A Sequel to Edward Bellamy's Celebrated Novel, "Looking Backward."* Boston: Arena Publishing Company. **MoU-St, W3, 4812**
  Education in Bellamy's world.

1894 **Stead, William T[homas].** *If Christ Came to Chicago! A Plea for the Union of All Who Love in the Service of All Who Suffer.* London: Review of Reviews. **L**
  Religious, cooperative eutopia. See **Edward E[verett] Hale,** *If Jesus Came to Boston,* Boston: J. Stilman Smith, 1894 (W3, 2381); and **M. W. Howard,** *If Christ Came to Congress,* Washington, D.C.: Author, 1894.

[1894] **Thomson, William.** *A Prospectus of Socialism; or, A Glimpse of the Millenium, Showing Its Plan and Working Arrangements and How It May Be Brought About.* London: W. Reeves. **ICN**
  Detailed description of a socialist eutopia.

1894 **Tucker, Horace.** *The New Arcadia; An Australian Story.* London: Swan Sonnenschein. **L**
  Story of a commune.

1894 **Von Swartwout, [William H.],** ed. *The Olombia Commonwealth Hercules,* Volume 1, No. 1. New York and London. **L**
  See 1893 Von Swartwout. See also Von Swartwout 1887, 1890, 1892–1893.

1894 **Von Swartwout, William H.** *Olombia Manifesto or Solution of the*

Social and Financial Problem. Addressed to the Congress and People of the U.S.A. and of the Whole World. New York: New Columbia University Press. **L**

> See 1893 Von Swartwout. See also Von Swartwout 1887, 1890, 1892–1893.

1894   **Von Swartwout, William H.** *An Open Letter to the Committee of Constitutional Convention at Albany, State of New York.* [New York: New Columbia University Press.] **L**

> See 1893 Von Swartwout. See also Von Swartwout 1887, 1890, 1892–1893.

1895   **Aikin, Charles.** *Forty Years With the Damned; or, Life Inside the Earth.* [Evanston, Illinois: Regan Printing House.] **DLC**

> Racist. Perfect life without social institutions.

1895   **Bishop, W. H.** *The Garden of Eden, U.S.A. A Very Possible Story.* Chicago: Charles H. Kerr. **W3, 533**

> Usually ascribed to William Henry Bishop; there is some evidence that this is incorrect. Wright says William Henry Bishop 1843-   . Emphasis on equality, particularly between men and women. Author believes his Eden is possible.

1895   **Chavannes, Albert.** *In Brighter Climes, Or Life in Socioland. A Realistic Novel.* Knoxville, Tennessee: Chavannes and Company. **W3, 1000, DLC**

> Continuation of 1892 Chavannes.

1895   **Davenport, Benjamin Rush.** *Uncle Sam's Cabins. A Story of American Life Looking Forward a Century.* New York: The Mascot Publishing Company. **DLC**

> Emphasis is on problems and transition, but reforms are spelled out.

1895   "The Discovery of Altruria. Narrative of Sir Robert Horton," [by John Brisbane Walker?]. *The Cosmopolitan,* 20 (November), 85–93.

> Introduction to 1895–1896, "A Brief History of Altruria."

1895   **[Fitzpatrick, Ernest Hugh.]** *The Marshall Duke of Denver or The Labor Revolution of 1920. A Novel,* by Hugo Barnaby (pseud.). Chicago: Donohue and Henneberry Company. **OFH**

> Mostly on revolution, but some reform.

1895   **Haedicke, Paul.** *The Equalities of Para-Para, Written from the Dictation of George Rambler, M.D., F.R.G.S.* Chicago: The Schuldt-Gathmann Company. **L**

> Satire. Country in which everyone is made equal in all things by disfiguring the favored. E.g., all are bald.

1895   **Holford, Castello N.** *Aristopia; A Romance-History of the New World.* Boston: Arena Publishing Company. **W3, 2701**

> Based on 1516 More.

[1895?]   **[Howard, Albert Waldo.]** *The Milltillionaire,* by M. Auberré Hovorrè (pseud.). [Boston: np.] **W3, 2796**
Rational, scientific, statist eutopia.

1895   **[Jones, George C. G.]** *The Outlaws of the Air,* by George Griffith (pseud.). London: Tower Publishing Company. **L, LLL, MH, MoU-St**
Two chapters describe two eutopias — both stress personal freedom.

1895   **Mears, A[melia] Garland.** *Mercia, The Astronomer Royal: A Romance.* London: Simpkin, Marshall, Hamilton, Kent and Company. **L, NcD**
Better life for women in 2002.

1895   **Mitchell, Professor W[illis].** *The Inhabitants of Mars. Their Manners and Advancement in Civilization and Their Opinion of Us.* Malden, Massachusetts: C. E. Spofford and Company (c. 1894). **W3, 3788**
Physical perfection. ESP. Technologically advanced.

1895   **Nisbet, Hume.** *The Great Secret. A Tale of To-morrow.* London: F. V. White **L, LLL**
Mostly adventure, but includes a eutopia of rest and almost static perfection.

1895   **Phelps, Corwin.** *An Ideal Republic or Way Out of the Fog.* Chicago: W. L. Reynolds. (*American Politics,* No. 10, February 1896).
Reformed capitalism — limit on wealth.

[1895]   **Smith, Titus K[eiper].** *Altruria.* New York: Altruria Publishing Company. Reprinted: Arno Press and *The New York Times,* 1971. **W3, 5061**
Christian commune spreads around United States.

[1895]   **Southwick, E. B.** *The Better World.* New York: Truth Seeker Publishing Company. **W3, 5079, DLC**
Extraordinarily detailed eutopia.

1895   **Welcome, S. Byron.** *From Earth's Center. A Polar Gateway Message.* Chicago: Charles H. Kerr (c. 1894). **DLC**
Capitalist eutopia.

1895   **Wells, H. G.** *The Time Machine.* London: William Heinemann.
Gradual development of two classes, the Eloi and the Morlocks, who are the final stages of the bourgeoisie and the proletariat respectively.

1895   **Wheeler, David Hilton.** *Our Industrial Utopia and Its Unhappy Citizens.* Chicago: A. C. McClurg and Company. **L**
Borderline — essay arguing that the United States is currently an eutopia although more free competition would make things even better.

1895 **Wilkes, A. B.** *The Great Social Boycott; or, Society Readjusted and the Causes Leading to its Establishment. This is a small Picture Gallery and your portrait hangs in it.* Brownwood, Texas: Author. **W3, 5973, DLC**
  A viceless world in 1905 brought about by the women refusing to have anything to do with men who were in any way touched by vice.

1895 **Williams, Frederic Condé,** ed. [written by]. *"Utopia" The Story of a Strange Experience.* Cambridge: Metcalfe and Company. *The Cambridge Christmas Annual 1895.* **O**
  Arcadia.

1895-96 "A Brief History of Altruria. Narrative of Sir Robert Horton," [by John Brisbane Walker?]. *The Cosmopolitan,* 20 (December 1895, January, February, March 1896), 218-224, 321-325, 437-441, 545-547.
  Eutopia through moderation.

1896 **Acworth, Andrew.** *A New Eden.* London: Ward and Lock. **L**
  Set in 2096. Mankind has degenerated mentally and lost the science and technology of the past. There is a small quasi-anarchist enclave ruled by custom where man is starting over.

1896 **Cowan, James.** *Daybreak, A Romance of an Old World.* New York: George H. Richmond. Reprinted: New York: Arno Press and *The New York Times,* 1971. **MoU-St, W3, 1225**
  Set on Mars. Suburban eutopia.

1896 **[Emmens, Stephen H.]** *The Sixteenth Amendment,* by Plain Citizen (pseud.). New York: G. W. Dillingham. **DLC**
  Founding of the Legion of Labor — similar to Bellamy's Industrial Army.

1896 **Flürscheim, Michael.** *The Real History of Money Island.* London: Brotherhood Publishing Company. **IU**
  Monetary reform brings eutopia.

1896 **Galier, W. H.** *A Visit to Blestland.* London: Gay and Bird. **L**
  Cooperative system.

1896 **Giles, Fayette Stratton.** *The Industrial Army.* New York: Baker and Taylor. **DLC**
  Detailed exposition of Bellamy's Industrial Army.

1896 **Glyn, [Alice] Coralie.** *A Woman of Tomorrow: A Tale of the Twentieth Century.* 2nd edition. [London:] Women's Printing Society. 1st edition, 1896.
  Eutopia of equality in 10 years.

1896 **Lockwood, Ingersoll.** *1900; or, The Last President.* New York: American News Company. **W3, 3378**
  Election of Bryan causes collapse of American system.

1896 **[McCoy, John.]** *A Prophetic Romance; Mars to Earth,* by The

Lord Commissioner (pseud.). Boston: Arena Publishing Company. **W3, 3489**
> Eutopia brought about by votes for women. Rule by those especially trained for job, but elected. All laws must be approved by the people.

1896   *Man or Dollar, Which? A Novel,* by A Newspaper Man (pseud.). Chicago: Charles H. Kerr. **DLC**
> Eugenics. Eutopia brought about by general strike. Standard socialist eutopia.

1896   **Marwick, Edward.** *The City of Gold; A Tale of Sport, Travel and Adventure in the Heart of the Dark Continent.* London: Tower Publishing Company. **MoU-St**
> Lost race utopia. Matriarchy. Equality.

1896   **Sheldon, Charles M.** *In His Steps. "What Would Jesus Do?"* Chicago: Advance Publishing Company. **W3, 4892**
> World changed by each person asking the question in the title before acting.

1896   **Stump, D. L.** *From World to World. A Novel.* Asbury, Missouri: World to World Publishing Company. **W3, 5310**
> Cooperative system. No money. Detailed eutopia.

1896   **Swan, H[erbert] E.** *It Might Be: A Story of the Future Progress of the Sciences, The Wonderful Advancement in the Methods of Government and the Happy State of the People.* Stafford, Kansas: H. E. Swan. **W3, 5334**
> Machine-governed eutopia.

1896   **Thorne, Gerald.** *Heaven on Earth.* New York: Lovell Brothers. **NcD**
> Commune — Christian socialism.

1897   **Adams, Frederick Upham.** *President John Smith; The Story of a Peaceful Revolution.* Chicago: Charles H. Kerr and Company (c. 1896). Reprinted: New York: Arno Press and *The New York Times,* 1971. **MoU-St**
> Direct democracy. Socialist eutopia.

1897   **Bellamy, Edward.** *Equality.* New York: D. Appleton, **W3, 459, MoU-St**
> Expansion of ideas found in 1888 Bellamy.

[1897]   **Bellsmith, H[enry] W[entworth].** *Henry Cadavere; A Study of Life and Work.* New York: Commonwealth Company. **W3, 468**
> Story of a commune.

[1897?]   **Berens, Lewis H., and Ignatius Singer.** *The Story of My Dictatorship; The Taxation of Land Values Clearly Explained.* New and unabridged edition. London: Land Values Publishing Department, [1910]. **L**
> Single tax.

1897   **[Brown, John Macmillan.]** *Riallaro; The Archepelago of Exiles,* by Godfrey Sweven (pseud.). New York: G. P. Putnam's Sons, 1901. **NcD, L**
Detailed eutopia stressing the overcoming of man's physical limitations. See also 1903 [Brown].

[1897]   **[Caryl, Charles W.]** *New Era. Presenting the Plans for the New Era Union To Help Develop and Utilize the Best Resources of this Country. Also to Employ the Best Skill There is Available. To Realize the Highest Degree of Prosperity for All Who Will Help To Attain It. Based on Practical and Successful Business Methods.* Denver: Author. Reprinted: New York: Arno Press and *The New York Times,* 1971.
New Era Union will provide capital so that workers can buy their own mines, etc. Union makes a profit. Detailed eutopia.

1897   **Flood, Jno. [John] H[eber], Jr.** *The Great Seven — The Greater Nine; A Story for the People.* Chicago: W. B. Conkey. **W3, 1932**
Struggle against monopolies is successful.

1897   **[Galloway, James M.]** *John Harvey. A Tale of the Twentieth Century,* by Anon Moore (pseud.). Chicago: Charles H. Kerr (c. 1896). **MoU-St, W3, 2092, DLC**
Socialist eutopia.

[1897]   **Hendow, Z. S.** *The Future Power; or, the Great Revolution of 190–.* Westminster: Roxburghe Press. **L**
Mostly on revolution. Fairly standard socialist eutopia sketched in. Women not financially dependent on husbands.

1897   **Lathrop, George Parsons.** "In the Deep of Time." *English Illustrated Magazine,* 16–17 (March, April), 679–693, 81–91.
Authoritarian eutopia.

1897   **Little, William.** *A Visit to Topos, and how the science of heredity is practiced there.* Ballerat, Australia: Berry, Anderson. **NN**
Eugenic eutopia.

[1897]   **Morris, Henry O.** *Waiting for the Signal.* Chicago: The Schulte Publishing Company. **W3, 3844**
Mostly story of a revolution, but includes a new constitution.

[1897]   **Munro, John.** *A Trip to Venus.* London: Jarrold **UU**
Eutopia on Venus. Arcadian, small-town. Abundance.

[1897]   **Orpen, Mrs. [Adela E.].** *Perfection City.* London: Hutchinson. **L, MoU-St**
Novel about a commune.

[1897]   **Owen, Albert Kimsey.** *A Dream of an Ideal City.* Revised edition. London: Murdock and Company. **DLC, ICJ**
Dream of the Topoblampo Commune before its foundation.

1897   *Posterity; Its Verdicts and Its Methods or Democracy A.D. 2100.*

London: Williams and Norgate. **L**
Eugenic legislation. Against equality.

1897   **Windsor, William.** *Loma; A Citizen of Venus.* St. Paul: Windsor and Lewis. **W3, 6026, L**
Venus — phrenology. Women more equal. Free love, with the emphasis on love.

1898   **Athey, Henry, and A. Herbert Bowers.** *With Gyves of Gold. A Novel.* New York: G. W. Dillingham. **W3, 165**
Anti-egalitarian, capitalist eutopia. Telepathy.

1898   **Augustinus** (pseud.). *Two Brothers: A Story of the Twentieth Century.* Cardiff: Printed by Chapple and Kemp. **L**
Roman Catholic vs. materialism. Armageddon. See also 1899 Augustinus (pseud.).

1898   **Bellamy, Edward.** "The Blindman's World," in his *The Blindman's World and Other Stories* Boston: Houghton, Mifflin, 1898), pp. 1–29. **W3, 456, MoU-St**
Eutopia based on foreknowledge about one's own life.

1898   **Buchanan, Robert.** *The Rev. Annabel Lee. A Tale of To-morrow.* London: C. Arthur Pearson. **L**
Utopia in physical sense — scientific, without religion. Religious revival overcomes too great dependence on reason.

1898   **[Clarke, Frances H.]** *The Co-opolitan; A Story of the Co-operative Commonwealth of Idaho,* by Zebina Forbush (pseud.). Chicago: Charles H. Kerr. **DLC**
Cooperative eutopia — detailed.

1898   **Craig, Alexander.** *Ionia; Land of Wise Men and Fair Women.* Chicago: E. A. Weeks. **W3, 1242**
Detailed eutopia. All land owned by the municipality; mixture of public and private ownership. Little government.

1898   **Drane, Augusta Theodosia (Mother Francis Raphael, O.S.D.).** *The New Utopia.* London: Catholic Truth Society. Originally published in *The Irish Monthly.* **L**
Community founded by a monastery — good physical surroundings, prohibition, and Roman Catholic education.

1898   **Farnell, George.** *Rev. Josiah Hilton. The Apostle of the New Age.* Providence: Journal of Commerce Company, Printers and Publishers. **W3, 1800**
How to establish an economy based on labor notes.

1898   **Graves, C[harles] L. and E[dward] V. Lucas.** *The War of. the Wenuses.* Bristol: Arrowsmith (Arrowsmith's Bristol Library Vol. 78). **L**
Satire — invasion of women from Venus.

1898   **[Greener, William O.]** *The Warstock; A Tale of Tomorrow,* by Wirt Gerrare (pseud.). London: W. W. Greener. **L**
Borderline — mostly adventure. Concern with patent rights.

1898   **Hix, J. Emile.** *Can a Man Live Forever?* Chciago: Western news
        Company. **DLC, OU**
        Answers the question, yes. Use only distilled water. Replace
        blood with a substitute. Result is eutopia of eternal life.

1898   **Howard, E[benezer].** *To-Morrow: A Peaceful Path to Real
        Reform.* London: Swan Sonnenschein. **L**
        Borderline — essay, but describes a suburban eutopia that
        unites town and country. Basis for the Garden City
        movement.

1898   **Miller, William Amos.** *The* [*My* on cover] *Sovereign Guide; A Tale
        of Eden.* Los Angeles: Geo. Rice & Sons. **W3, 3750**
        Short description of Eden as eutopia. Includes class and labor
        system. Monarchy. Religious.

1898   **Odell, S. W.** *The Last War or The Triumph of the English Tongue.
        A Story of the Twenty-Sixth Century, Compiled from the Offi-
        cial Notes of Newman, Reporter to the President of the United
        States.* Chicago: Charles H. Kerr. **DLC**
        White Anglo-Saxons against a Holy Empire (composed of
        Islam, Catholicism, and Buddhism). Mostly on war.

[1898] **[Rehm, Warren S.]** *The Practical City. A Future City Romance; or
        A Study in Environment,* by Omen Nemo (pseud.). Lancaster,
        Pennsylvania: Lancaster County Magazine. **W3, 4503, DLC**
        Detailed, authoritarian eutopia.

[1898] **[Reynolds, Walter Doty.]** *Mr. Jonnemacher's Machine. The Port to
        which we drifted,* by Lord Prime Esq. (pseud.). Librarian to the
        State Library of Pennsylvania A.D. MMXVI. Philadelphia;
        Knickerbocker Book Company. **W3, 4524**
        Anti-technology, Machines put people out of work, must be
        destroyed.

1898   *The Rise and Fall of the United States; A Leaf from History, A.D.
        2060,* by A Diplomat (pseud.). New York: F. Tennyson Neely.
        NN, MoU-St
        Borderline — future collapse of United States after revolution
        against the plutocracy.

1898   **Sullivan, J[ames] W[illiam].** "A Modern Coöperative Colony (A
        Whimsey)," in his *So The World Goes* (Chicago: Charles H.
        Kerr, 1898), pp. 213–33. **W3, 5317**
        Commune — detailed.

[1898] **Waterloo, Stanley.** *Armageddon. A Tale of Love, War, and Inven-
        tion.* Chicago: Rand, McNally. **MoU-St, W3, 5815, DLC**
        United States and Great Britain against Europe.

1898   **[Wellmen, Bert J.]** *The Legal Revolution of 1902,* by A Law-
        abiding Revolutionist (pseud.). Chicago: Charles H. Kerr.
        (c. 1897). Reprinted: New York: Arno Press and *The New York*

Times, 1971 [Incorrectly attributed to William Stanley Child.]
Populist eutopia.

1898 **Wooldridge, C. W., M.D.** *"The Kingdom of Heaven is at Hand".
A Text Book of the Better Civilization Within Reach, Which Is
Identical with the Kingdom of Heaven as it Was Proclaimed by
Jesus of Nazareth.* Chicago: Charles H. Kerr. **IU**
Religious version of the cooperative commonwealth.

1899 **Adolph, Mrs. Anna.** *Arqtiq; A Study of the Marvels at the North
Pole.* Np: Author. **W3, 30, DLC**
Eutopia at North Pole. Idealized people. Equality of the
sexes.

1899 **Augustinus** (pseud.). *Paul Rees: A Story of the Coming Reformation.* London: Simpkin, Marshall, Hamilton, Kent & Company. **L**
England declines due to laws passed against Roman Catholics. See also 1898 Augustinus (pseud.).

1899 **Bird, Arthur.** *Looking Forward; A Dream of the United States of
the Americas in 1999.* [Utica, New York: Press of L. C. Childs &
Son]. Reprinted: New York: Arno Press and *The New York
Times,* 1971. **MoU-St**
Manifest destiny. Racist. Highly moral tone — cursing out-
lawed.

1899 **Bond, Daniel.** *Uncle Sam in Business.* Chicago: Charles H. Kerr.
Unity Library No. 92. **DLC**
Populist eutopia.

1899 **Brady, Adhemer.** *The Mathematics of Labor.* Chicago: Charles H.
Kerr. **WiH**
Includes eutopia which incorporates his detailed laws of eco-
nomics.

1899 **Dake, Charles Romyn.** *A Strange Discovery.* New York: H. Ingalls
Kimball. **L, MoU-St**
Continuation of Poe's *Narrative of Arthur Gordon Pym.*
Eutopia near South Pole. Society controlled best by "prop-
erly educated feeling" rather than reason.

1899 **D'Argenteuil, Paul.** *The Trembling Borealis.* London: F. Tennyson
Neely. **MoU-St**
Dystopian allegory — plutocracy.

1899 **Fishbough, William.** *The End of the Ages; with Forecasts of the
approaching Political, Social and Religious Reconstruction of
AMERICA AND THE WORLD.* New York: Continental Publishing Company. **ICRL**
Eutopia based on grand harmonies of love, etc.

1899 **Franklin, A[braham] B[enjamin].** *The Light of Reason. Showing
The First Step The Nation Should Take Toward A Social Order*

Based On Justice. Chicago: Charles H. Kerr. **ICRL**
Socialist eutopia.

1899   **Griggs, Sutton E[lbert].** *Imperium in Imperio.* Cincinnati: Editor
Publishing Company. Reprinted 1969. **W3, 2286**
Black enclave in Texas with government parallel to United
States government.

1899   **Hahn, Charles Curtz.** "The Wreck on the South Pole," in his *The
Wreck of the South Pole or the Great Dissembler and Other
Strange Tales* (New York: Street and Smith, 1899), pp.
5-76. **MoU-St**
Detailed eutopia based on ESP.

1899   **Merrill, Albert Adams.** *The Great Awakening; The Story of the
Twenty-second Century.* Boston: George Book Publishing
Company. **MoU-St, W3, 3704**
Colony, called Money Republic, founded in Africa spreads
around the world. Based on equal division of wealth among
all who worked.

1899   **[Michels, Nicholas.]** *The Godhood of Man. His Religious, Political
and Economic Development and the Sources of Social Inequal-
ity,* by Nicolai Mikalowitch (pseud.). Chicago: Author.
W3, 3719
Mostly religion — man in harmony with nature.

1899   **Pereira Mendes, H[enry].** *Looking Ahead; Twentieth Century
Happenings.* New York: F. Tennyson Neely. Reprinted: New
York: Arno Press and *The New York Times,* 1971.
Struggle among all religions for control of holy places. Argu-
ments for each. Decision by a council.

1899   **[Petersilea, Carlyle.]** *The Discovered Country,* by Ernst von
Himmel (pseud.). Boston: Ernst von Himmel Publishing Com-
pany. **W3, 4203**
Heaven as eutopia.

1899   **Stebbing, W[illiam],** ed. [written by]. *Probable Tales.* London:
Longmans, Green. **LLL**
Series of short stories describing countries with one unusual
custom.

1899   **Wells, H. G.** "A Story of The Days To Come," in *Tales of Space
and Time* (London: Macmillan, 1920), pp. 167-324. **MoU**
Trusts. No family life. No rural life. Dystopia.

1899   **Wells, H. G.** *When the Sleeper Wakes.* London: Harper & Bros.
Archetypal Wells dystopia. Class division. Slightly altered
edition published in 1910 entitled *The Sleeper Wakes.*

1899   **Wright, Henry.** *Depopulation: A Romance of the Unlikely.* London: George Allen. **DL, MH**

Borderline — trusts control economy; trusts taken over by government.

[1900]   **Bayne, Charles J.** *The Fall of Utopia.* Boston: Eastern Publishing Company. **W3, 416**
Utopia, seemingly More's, collapses due to indiscriminate immigration.

1900   **Bennett, Arthur.** *The Dream of a Warringtonian.* Warrington: Sunrise Publishing Company. **L**
Town described as a future eutopia. Clean and improved both architecturally and morally. Much control by local government.

1900   **[Caswell, Edward A.]** *Toil and Self,* by Myself and Another (pseud.). Chicago: Rand, McNally and Company. **CU**
Series of future societies, good and bad. Selfishness is the law of life.

1900   **Cole, Robert William.** *The Struggle for Empire; A Story of the Year 2236.* London: Elliot Stock. **L, O**
Triumph of Anglo-Saxons and science. Two classes — intellectuals and menials.

1900   **Drayton, Henry S.,** ed. [written by]. *In Oudemon; Reminiscences of an Unknown People by an Occasional Traveler.* New York: The Grafton Press. **DLC**
Egalitarian, anarchist eutopia.

1900   **Edson, Milan C.** *Solaris Farm; A Story of the Twentieth Century.* Washington, D.C.: Author. **W3, 1702**
Detailed picture of the development of a communal system.

1900   **Ellis, Havelock.** *The Nineteenth Century; A Dialogue in Utopia.* London: Grant Richards. United States edition subtitled: *An Utopian Retrospect.* **L, DLC**
Discussion of the 19th century from the vantage point of a future eutopia.

[1900?]   **Evans, Chris.** *Eurasia.* San Francisco: James H. Barry. **NNC**
Detailed reform.

1900   **[Grigsby, Alcanoan O.]** *Nequa or The Problem of the Ages,* by Jack Adams (pseud.). Topeka, Kansas: Equity Publishing Company. Volume 1 of the Equity Library. **DLC, W3, 2288**
Standard communal eutopia.

1900   **Harney, Gilbert Lane.** *Philoland.* New York: F. Tennyson Neely. **DLC**
Detailed eutopia at center of the earth. Cooperative economic system. Technology.

1900   **Hoskin, Albert A.** *The City Problem.* New York: John B. Alden (c. 1899). **NjP**

Eutopia based on abolishing both city and rural life — even distribution of population.

1900 **James Henry.** "The Great Good Place." *Scribner's Magazine,* 27 (January), 99–112.
Eutopia of rest.

1900 **Lubin, David.** *Let There Be Light; The Story of a Workingmen's Club, Its Search for the Causes of Poverty and Social Inequality, Its Discussions, and Its Plan for the Amelioration of Existing Evils.* New York: G. P. Putnam's Sons. **L, W3, 3417**
Religion will bring about eutopia.

1900 **McMartin, Donald.** *A Leap Into the Future; or How Things Will Be. A Romance of the Year 2000.* Albany, New York: Weed, Parsons. **W3, 3540**
Cover says "A Sequel to Looking Backward." Various reforms.

1900 **Newcomb, Simon.** *His Wisdom, The Defender.* New York: Harper and Bros. **DLC, W3, 3951**
Inventor of airship controls the world, forms one world nation and abolishes war, armies and navies. Allows freedom. He acts as arbitrator in disputes.

1900 **[O'Grady, Standish James.]** *The Queen of the World or, Under the Tyranny,* by Luke Netterville (pseud.). London: Lawrence and Bullen. **L**
Authoritarian dystopia.

1900 **Peck, Bradford.** *The World a Department Store. A Story of Life Under a Coöperative System.* Lewiston, Maine: Bradford Peck. Reprinted: New York: Arno Press and *The New York Times,* 1971. **W3, 4138**
Cooperative Association of America converts nation to cooperative system in twenty-five years.

1900 **Persinger, Clark Edmund.** *Letters from New America; or an Attempt at Practical Socialism.* Chicago: Charles H. Kerr and Company. **ODW**
Detailed socialist eutopia.

[1900] **Rogers, Lebbeus Harding.** *The Kite Trust (A Romance of Wealth).* New York: Kite Trust Publishing Company. **W3, 4640**
Trust becomes world-wide and establishes eutopia.

[1900] **Williams, Frank Purdy.** *Hallie Marshall: A True Daughter of the South.* New York: Abbey Press. **W3, 5986**
Reformed South presented as eutopia — still has slavery.

1900 **Wilson, [John] Grosvenor.** *The Monarchy of Millions; or, The Rise and Fall of the American Empire.* New York: The Neeley Company. **DLC**

Borderline — Emperor controls Americas through wealth. He is overthrown.

1900   **Wright, W[illiam] H[enry].** *The Great Bread Trust.* New York: Abbey Press. **DLC, MoU-St**
Men gain control of wheat and then the world.

1901   **Bennet, Robert Ames.** *Thyra; A Romance of the Polar Pit.* London: Kegan Paul, Trench, Trubner. **L**
Borderline — country based on Norse mythology at North Pole.

1901   **Borders, Joe H.** *The Queen of Appalachia.* New York: Abbey Press. **DLC, KyU**
Mostly adventure. Eutopia is an arcadian monarchy combined with advanced technology.

1901   **Butler, Samuel.** *Erewhon Revisited twenty years later, both by the original discoverer and his son.* London: G. Richards. **DLC**
Continuation of 1872 Butler, stressing religion.

1901   **Frisbie, Henry S[amuel].** *Prophet of the Kingdom.* Washington: The Neale Publishing Company. **DLC**
Single tax.

1901   **Gilman, Bradley.** *Back to the Soil or From Tenement House to Farm Colony. A Circular Solution to an Angular Problem.* Boston: L. C. Page. **DLC**
Eutopia brought about by the establishment of farm colonies.

1901   **Henley, Carra Depuy.** *A Man from Mars.* Los Angeles: Printed by B. R. Baumgardt. **DLC**
Dead go to Mars which is an arcadian eutopia. Very ethereal.

1901   **Kelly, Colonel William.** *The Progressives Abroad.* London: William Reeves. **O**
Detailed eutopia — free medical care, every youth above 14 must be proficient at arms. Many detailed reforms.

1901   **McGrady, Rev. T[homas].** *Beyond the Black Ocean.* Terre Haute, Indiana: Standard Publishing Company. Reprinted: New York: Arno Press and *The New York Times,* 1971. DLC has subtitle: *A Socialist Story.* Chicago: Charles H. Kerr, 1901.
Socialist eutopia.

1901   **Paine, Albert Bigelow.** *The Great White Way: A Record of an Unusual Voyage of Discovery, and Some Romantic Love Affairs Amid Strange Surroundings.* New York: J. F. Taylor. **L, MoU-St**
Eutopia at the South Pole. ESP. No technology and opposed to technological development. Few laws, no money.

1901   **Taylor, William Alexander.** *Intermere.* Columbus, Ohio: Twentieth Century Publishing Company. **DLC**
Atlantis. Pure democracy. Simple life.

1901   **Wells, H. G.** *The First Man in the Moon.* London: George Newnes. **L**
        Classic dystopia. Creatures bred for service to society.

1902   **Cooley, Winnifred Harper.** "A Dream of the Twenty-First Century." *Arena,* 28 (November), 511–516.
        Government ownership of basic resources and utilities brought about by women's votes.

1902   **Devinne, Paul.** *The Day of Prosperity.* London: T. Fisher Unwin. **L**
        Socialist eutopia. Generally equality for the sexes — male and female elected by the same sex for most public offices.

1902   **Perry, James Raymond.** "The Constitution of Carnegia." *North American Review,* 175 (August), 243–253.
        At the age of sixty all property is given to the state and support is provided for life. No military — too expensive.

1902   **Pinkerton, Thomas [A.].** *No Rates and Taxes; A Romance of Five Worlds.* Bristol: J. W. Arrowsmith. **L**
        Man degenerated; women dominant.

1902   **Wilkie, J.** *The Vision of Nehemiah Sintram.* London: Elliot Stock. **L**
        Dystopian satire — evil effects of worshipping money. World ruled by Satan.

1902   **Wooldridge, C[harles] W[illiam].** *Perfecting the Earth: A Piece of Possible History.* Cleveland: Utopia Publishing Company. **DLC, MoU-St**
        Cooperative eutopia.

1903   **[Brown, John Macmillan.]** *Limanora. The Island of Progress,* by Godfrey Sweven (pseud.). London: Putnam's Sons. 2nd edition. London: Humphrey Milford, Oxford University Press, 1931.
        Eutopia devoted to overcoming physicality. See also 1897 [Brown].

1903   **Bunker, Ira S.** *A Thousand Years Hence or Startling Events in the Year A.D. 3000. A Trip to Mars. Incidents by the Way.* Portland, Oregon: Author. **DLC**
        Christian science. Technological advance.

1903   *Christopolis; Life and Amenities in a Land of Garden Cities.* London: S. W. Partridge. **L**
        Based on the ideas of Ebenezer Howard who advocated the development of suburban living. Socialist, Christian eutopia.

1903   **Cook, William Wallace.** *A Round Trip to the Year 2000.* New York: Street and Smith, 1925. Reprinted: Westport, Connecticut: Hyperion Press, 1974.
        Satire — robots, air controlled by trust, assertive women.

1903   **Dague, R[obert] A[ddison].** *Henry Ashton; A thrilling Story of*

How the Famous Co-operative Commonwealth was established in Zanland. Alameda, California. Author. **MoU-St, OrU**
Christian socialism.

1903 **Forrest, Aston.** *The Extraordinary Islanders; Being an Authentic Account of the Cruise of the 'Asphodel,' as Related by Her Owner.* London: R.A. Everett. **L, O**
Gulliver type — three countries: Rectinia (reason), Scrumpolen (art), Melanoon (oratory, religion).

1903 **Gratacap, L[ouis] P[ope],** ed. [written by]. *Certainty of a Future Life in Mars; Being the Posthumous Papers of Bradford Torrey Dodd.* New York: Brentano's. **MoU-St, NcD**
Spirit world but become flesh and blood. Socialist eutopia. Simple life. No sex.

1903 **Griffith, George.** *The Lake of Gold: A Narrative of the Anglo-American Conquest of Europe.* London: F. V. White **L, O**
Power of Money used for good — free trade, trusts abolished, no strikes or lockouts, arbitration, no war.

1903 **Hanvey, Robert.** *Myora; Land of Eternal Sunshine.* Chicago: Gimlin Press. **CU-Riv**
Mars — three races living in harmony.

1903 **Kinkaid, Mary Holland.** *Walda; A Novel.* New York: Harper and Bros. **MoU-St**
Novel of a religious commune.

1903 **Noto, Cosimo, M.D.** *The Ideal City.* New York: Author. **DLC**
Socialist eutopia.

1903 **[O'Neill, Henry J.]** *The Travels of John Wryland* (pseud.); *being an account of His Journey to Tibet, of His Founding a Kingdom on the Island of Palti, and of His War Against the Ne-ar-Bians.* London: International News Company; Allentown, Pennsylvania: Equitable Publishing Company. **L, DLC**
Satire — authoritarian dystopia.

1903 **Sinclair, Upton.** *Prince Hagen; A Drama in Four Acts.* Boston: L. C. Page. First performed in 1909. Later versions differ some. **L**
Financial basis of the world destroyed. Revolt. Based on Wagner.

1903 **Snyder, John.** *The Wind Trust: A Possible Prophecy.* Boston: James H. West Company. **NN**
Anti-trust novel. Revolution.

1903 **Stanley, William F.** *The Case of The. Fox, Being his Prophecies Under Hypnotism of the Period Ending A.D. 1950. A Political Utopia.* London: Truslove and Hanson. **L, MoU-St**
The. is an abbreviation for Theodore. Almost always incor-

rect in bibliographies. Political eutopia — emphasis on administrative and structural changes.

1903   **Swift, Morrison I.** *The Monarch Billionaire.* New York: J. S. Ogilvie. **L**
Conflict between capitalists and idealists. The latter barely win.

1903   **Van Laun, Henri.** *The Gates of Afree A.D. 1928.* London: W. H. White. British libraries list as Laun, Henri Van.
Technology, socialism in Africa.

1904   **Bell, Geo[rge].** *Mr. Oseba's Last Discovery.* Wellington, New Zealand: The New Zealand Times. **L, MoU-St**
Fictionalized account of New Zealand (Zelania) as eutopia.

1904   **Burland, Harris.** *The Princess Thora.* Boston: Little, Brown. 1905 edition *Dr. Silex,* by J.B. Harris-Burland. London: Ward, Lock. **L, MoU-St**
Feudal kingdom at the North Pole.

1904   **Chesterton, G. K.** *The Napoleon of Notting Hill.* London: John Lane. **DLC, NcD**
Return to the medieval ideal of independent villages in London.

1904   **Davis, Capt. Nathan.** *Beulah; or A Parable of Social Regeneration.* Kansas City, Missouri: Press of Hudson-Kimberly Publishing Company. **DLC**
Christian socialism.

1904   **[De Bury, Mme. F. Blaze.]** *The Storm of London; A Social Rhapsody,* by F. Dickberry (pseud.). London: John Long. **L**
Reform through disappearance of clothes.

1904   **Hudson, W[illiam] H[enry].** *Green Mansions.* London: Duckworth. **L, DLC**
Borderline — arcadia.

1904   **Johnson, E. A.** *Light Ahead for the Negroes.* New York: Grafton Press. **ViU**
One hundred years from now — segregated South as eutopia.

1904   **Lloyd, J[ohn] Wm.** *The Dwellers in Vale Sunrise. How They Got Together and Lived Happy Ever After. A Sequel to "The Natural Man" Being an Account of the Tribes of Him.* Westwood, Massachusetts: The Ariel Press. **DLC**
Ideal of Noble Savage. His *The Natural Man; A Romance of the Golden Age,* Newark, New Jersey: Benedict Prieth, 1902 was about one man living in tune with nature. This is about a group living the same way.

1904   **Ross, Olin J.** *The Sky Blue; A Tale of the Iron Horse and of the Coming Civilization.* Columbus, Ohio: Author. **DLC, MoU-St**

World united into a great new civilization by the railroad. Eugenics.

1904   **Wells, H.G.** *The Food of the Gods.* London: Macmillan **L**
New food produces giants who are also of superior intelligence. Conflict. Giants decide to allow little people to live but expect them to die out. Compare the parody, *The Food of the Dogs and What Became of It* (1904) by G[eorge] E[dward] Farrow.

1904   **X** (pseud.). *The Setting Sun. An Ante-Dated Picture for a People.* London: Skeffington and Son. **MoU-St**
Future failure of Britain. Loss of Empire.

1905   **Armour J[ohn] P.** *Edenindia; A Tale of Adventure.* New York: G. W. Dillingham. **DLC**
Eutopia based on model of health — well-balanced, moderation. Few laws, no lawyers. Arbitration to settle disputes.

1905   **Brockhouse, H.** *Hopetown. An industrial town, as it is, and as it might be.* West Bromwich: J. B. Round. **LUG**
Detailed reform. Land public.

1905   **Fry, Lena Jane.** *Other Worlds; A Story Concerning the Wealth Earned by American Citizens and Showing How It Can Be Secured to Them Instead of to the Trusts.* Chicago: Author. **DLC**
Socialist eutopia.

1905   **Harris, Rev. W[illiam] S[huler].** *Life in a Thousand Worlds.* Harrisburg, Pennsylvania: The Minter Company. Reprinted: New York: Arno Press and *The New York Times,* 1971. **MoU-St**
Borderline — brief pictures of various worlds. Anti-capitalist.

1905   **Kernahan, [John] Coulson.** *A World Without a Child; A Story for Women and for Men.* London: Hodder and Stoughton. **L**
No children born. Death of religion. World concerned only with variety and pleasure.

1905   *Laputa Revisited by Gulliver Redivivus* (pseud.) *in 1905.* London: Hirschfeld. **C**
Laputa has degenerated. Standard satire.

1905   **Magnus, Leonard A[rthur].** *A Japanese Utopia.* London: George Routledge & Sons. **L**
No government. Experts exercise minimal authority. Education.

1905   **Marks, William Dennis.** *An Equal Opportunity: A Plea for Individualism.* Philadelphia: Patterson and White. **L**
Equality of opportunity based on athletics and intelligence.

1905   **Middleton, John B.** *The God of this World; A Story for the Times.* London: Kegan Paul, Trench, Trubner. **L**

Mostly on revolution. Creation of an anarchist, socialist, religious eutopia.

1905   **Peterson, E[phraim].** *An Ideal City for an Ideal People.* [Independence, Missouri: Author.] **DLC**
Christian socialism — proposal for a commune.

1905   **Rogers, Bessie Story.** *As It May Be; A Story of the Future.* Boston: Richard G. Badger, The Gorham Press. **MoU-St, DLC**
Great technological advancement — control of weather, personal airplanes, no illness, religious but no churches (praise God everyday and everywhere). Vegetarian, all animals tame.

1905   **Russell, T. Baron.** *A Hundred Years Hence; The Expectations of an Optimist.* London: T. Fisher Unwin. **L**
Eutopia presented as a prediction based on the assumption of moral improvement. Much mechanical.

[1905]   **Spring, Summer** (pseud.). *Backwards and Forwards.* London: V. Glaisher. **L**
Detailed anti-socialist dystopia.

1905   **Wells, H. G.** *A Modern Utopia.* New York: Scribners. **DLC**
Classic world state eutopia.

1906   *Balmanno; The City of Our Quest and Its Social Problems.* Paisly: Alexander Gardner. Sometimes attributed to J. Paton. **L**
Wealthy man decides to use his estate to establish a suburban eutopia. Profit sharing. Religion.

1906   **Burroughs, Joseph Birkbeck, M.D.** *Titan, Son of Saturn. The Coming World Emperor.* Oberlin, Ohio: Emeth Publishers. (c. 1905) **OO**
Moston on Armageddon.

1906   **Casparian, Gregory.** *An Anglo-American Alliance. A Serio-Comic Romance and Forecast of the Future.* Floral Park, New York: Mayflower Presses. **NjP**
Wide variety of reforms.

1906   **Dyvirta, Tems** (pseud.). *London's Transformation; A Suggestive Sketch of Days to Come.* London: King, Sell & Olding. Originally published in *Knowledge and Scientific News.* **C**
Anglo-American alliance. England controlled by American wealth.

1906   **[Ford, Douglas Morey.]** *A Time of Terror. The Story of a Great Revenge (A.D. 1912).* London: Greening & Company. **L, MoU-St**
Dystopia but with eutopian ending. Terror of attacks on law and lawyers.

1906   **[Gull, Cyril Arthur Edward Ranger.]** *Made in His Image,* by Guy Thorne (pseud.). London: Hutchinson and Company. **L, MoU-St**

          Establishment of a slave colony in England — Christianity overcomes it.

1906   **Hillman, H. W.** *Looking Forward; The Phenomenal Progress of Electricity in 1912.* Northampton, Massachusetts: Valley View Publishing Company. **PSt**
          Based on 1888 Bellamy. Eutopia by 1912 by cooperation and electricity.

1906   **Jacob, T. Evan.** "The Burden of Troisilia." *Westminster Review,* 165 (February), 172–190.
          Satire — anti-labor.

1906   **[Jones, George C. G.]** *The Great Weather Syndicate,* by George Griffith (pseud.). London: F. V. White. **L**
          Control of weather for political purposes, then for the good of the world.

1906   **Parry, David M.** *The Scarlet Empire.* Indianapolis: The Bobbs-Merrill Company, **L, DLC, MoU-St**
          Authoritarian dystopia.

1906   **Regnas, C.** *The Land of Nison.* London: C. W. Daniel. **L**
          Nison means no sin. Eutopia of few institutions. Rule of wisdom. Women inferior.

1906   **Smith, W. T. F., M.D.** *The Trust Trusted.* San Francisco: Primo Press. **MoU-St**
          Eutopia brought about by all property being owned by a single combine.

1906   *Star of the Morning; A Chronicle of Karyl the Great and the Revolt of 1920-22.* London: Thomas Burleigh. **L**
          Almost entirely a romance, but an extensive list of detailed reforms is included.

1906   **Wells, H. G.** *In the Days of the Comet.* London: Macmillan. **L**
          Something in the tail of a comet changes all human beings, freeing them from greed, power, and all baser passions.

1907   **Benson, Robert Hugh.** *Lord of the World.* London: Sir Isaac Pitman & Sons Ltd. **L, MoU-St**
          Armageddon after split between secular humanism and the Roman Catholic Church.

[1907]   **Blatchford, Robert.** *The Sorcery Shop; An Impossible Romance.* London: The Clarion Press. **NcD**
          Anarchist eutopia.

1907   **Blyth, James.** *The Tyranny.* London: William Heinemann. **C**
          Tyrant rules Britain. War with Germany leads to mass uprising.

1907   **Dawson, A. J.** *The Message.* London: E. Grant Richards. **L, LLL**
          Germany invades Britain. Britain wins the war after a conver-

sion to Christian duty and the simple life plus alliance with the U.S.

1907   **Firmin, Albert Bancroft.** "The Altrurian Era." *Altruria,* 1 (September), pp. 9–17.
Set in 2007. Series of standard reforms of the time — monopolies taken over by the government, referendum, recall, and initiative, etc.

1907   **Harding, Ellison.** *The Demetrian.* New York: Brentano's. 1908 edition entitled *The Woman Who Vowed.* **L, MoU-St**
Standard collectivist eutopia. Classical Greek culture.

1907   **Howells, William Dean.** *Through the Eye of the Needle; A Romance with an Introduction.* New York: Harper and Bros. **MoU-St**
Sequel to 1894 Howells, describing an arcadian eutopia.

1907   **Hutchinson, Alfred L.** *The Limit of Wealth.* New York: Macmillan. **L**
Limiting wealth the solution to all social problems.

1907   **London, Jack.** *The Iron Heel.* New York: Macmillan. **DLC**
Primarily an anti-capitalist dystopia stressing revolution.

1907   **Lull, Rev. D.** *Celestia.* New York: Reliance Trading Company. **DLC**
Mostly romance but presents the basis of eutopia in religion and education.

1907   **Mastin, John.** *The Immortal Light.* London: Cassell. **L, MoU-St**
Minimal utopian elements — life of a soul in an eutopia.

1907   **Moore, Frank Frankfort.** *The Marriage Lease; The Story of a Social Experiment.* London: Hutchinson. Also entitled *A Trial Marriage.* **L, MoU-St**
Marriage contract for a limited time — failure.

1907   **Newte, Horace W. C.** *The Master Beast; Being a True Account of the Ruthless Tyranny Inflicted on the British People by Socialism A.D. 1888–2020.* London: Rebman Ltd. **L**
Anti-socialist dystopia.

1907   *Proposals for a Voluntary Nobility.* Norwich: Samurai Press. **L**
Development of the idea of the samurai from 1905 Wells.

1907   **Sinclair, Upton.** *The Industrial Republic; A Study of the America Ten Years Hence.* New York: Doubleday, Page & Company.
Socialist eutopia.

1907   **[Smith, Ernest Bramah.]** *What Might Have Been; The Story of a Social War,* by Ernest Bramah (pseud.). London: John Murray. 1909 edition entitled *The Secret of the League; The Story of a Social War.* **L**
Anti-socialist dystopia.

1907   **[Spaulding, Wayland.]** *When Theodore is King. Extracts Taken From a Complete Account of the New Declaration of the Change From the United States of America To the United Kingdom of America and the Establishing of Theodore on the Throne,* by Viter Strikeshoulder (pseud.). New York: Chauncey Holt. **DLC**
        Egalitarian eutopia.

1907   **Straus, Ralph.** *The Dust which is God; An Undimensional Adventure.* [Norwich:] Samurai Press. **L**
        Evolution and religion — minimal utopian elements.

1908   **Agricola** (pseud.). *How England Was Saved; History of the Years 1910–1925.* London: Swan Sonnenschein.
        Series of reforms, particularly in land. Intensive farming, agribusiness. Borderline.

1908   **Coutts, Tristam.** *The Prodigal City.* London: Greening & Company. **L**
        Model town and its failure. Anti-socialist.

1908   **Flecker, James Elroy.** *The Last Generation; A Story of the Future.* London: New Age Press. **L**
        Stopped producing children in order to live better. Horrors of the last generation.

1908   **Hatfield, Richard,** ed. [written by]. *Geyserland; Empiricisms in Social Reform. Being Data and Observations Recorded By the Late Mark Stubble, M.D., Ph.D.* Washington, D.C.: Printed for Richard Hatfield (c. 1907). **MoU-St, DLC**
        No money. All property common. Eugenic legislation. Occupation and status revealed by dress.

1908   **Koebel, W[illiam] H[enry].** *The Singular Republic.* London: Francis Griffiths. **L**
        Failure of a utopian community.

1908   **London, Jack.** "Goliah," in *Revolution and Other Essays* (London: William Heinemann, 1910), pp. 73–116. Reprinted: *Goliah; A Utopian Essay.* Berkeley, California: Thorp Springs Press, [1973].
        Communal eutopia; all labor gradually abolished.

1908   **Martin, Nettie Parrich.** *A Pilgrim's Progress in Other Worlds; Recounting the Wonderful Adventures of Ulysum Storries and His Discovery of the Lost Star "Eden."* Boston: Mayhew Publishing Company **DLC**
        Immature, crude Earthman travels around planets. Spiritualism. Most planets advanced spiritually, and hence socially, beyond Earth. Advance largely due to the improved status for women.

1908   **Maxim, Hudson.** "Man's Machine-Made Millenium,"

Cosmopolitan Magazine, 45 (November), pp. 569–576.
Technological eutopia.

1908   **Mayne, John D.** *The Triumph of Socialism and How It Succeeded.*
London: Swan Sonnenschein. **L**
Anti-socialist dystopia.

1908   **Nichol, Mrs. C.A. Scrymsour.** *The Mystery of the North Pole.*
London: Francis Griffiths. **L**
Christian eutopia at the North Pole.

[1908]   **Omen, Edward.** *Nutopia; or Nineteen-Twenty-One.* London:
Henry J. Drane. **L**
Women rule and improve Britain. All advancement by merit.
Workers get shares in companies until they own them.

1908   **Reeth, Allan.** *Legions of the Dawn.* London: T. Fisher Unwin. **L**
Sex-role reversal.

1908   *The Rev. John Smith Died — and Went to Jupiter via Hell.* New
York: The Juno Society. **NN**
No greed, money, competition, or alcohol. Science. Religion.

1908   **Rice, Harry E.** *Eve and the Evangelist; A Romance of A.D. 2108.*
Boston: the Roxburgh Publishing Company. **NcD, MoU-St**
Brotherhood of Man rules North America. Christianity.
Segregation. All laws passed by initiative and referendum.

1908   **Rosewater, Frank.** *The Making of a Millenium; The Story of a Millenial Realm and Its Law.* Omaha: Century Publishing Com-
pany. **L**
Eutopia named Temploria. New monetary system.

1908   **Sedgwick, Henry Dwight.** "The Coup D'Etat of 1961," in his *The
New American Type and Other Essays* (Boston: Houghton,
Mifflin, 1908), pp. 317–343. Reprinted: *American Utopias,*
edited by Arthur O. Lewis, Jr. New York: Arno Press and *The
New York Times,* 1971.
Capitalist monarchy — satire.

1908   **Steere, C. A.** *When Things Were Doing.* Chicago: Charles H. Kerr
and Company. **DLC**
Socialist eutopia.

1908   **Stevens, Isaac N.** *The Liberators; A Story of Future American
Politics.* New York: B. W. Dodge and Company. **MoU-St, NcD**
Nationalization of utilities and railroads.

1908   **[Stevens, John.]** *The Realm of Light,* by Frank Hatfield (pseud.).
Boston: Reid Publishing Company. **DLC, L**
Socialist eutopia. Religion.

1909   **Alexander, James B.** *The Lunarian Professor and His Remarkable
Revelations Concerning the Earth, the Moon and Mars. Together with an Account of the Cruise of the Sally Ann.* Minneapolis: np.

Instinct to work for community and to respect others. Single tax — fails. Reformed United States system for government — has executive authority; more power to House. Strict control of population.

1909   *An Amazing Revolution and After.* London: George Allen. **L**
Stress on evolution to cooperative eutopia.

1909   **Blanchard, H[enry] Percy.** *After the Cataclysm. A Romance of the Age to Come.* New York: Cochrane Publishing Company. **NcD**
Purified future world of abundance. Little work, little social organization, no sex.

1909   **Brant, John Ira.** *The New Regime, A.D. 2202.* New York: Cochrane Publishing Company. **DLC**
Eutopia brought about by ending competition. Basically uses the Bellamy model.

1909   **Cassius-Minor** (pseud.). *The Finding of Mercia,* with an "Introduction" by H.N. Robbins. London: Kegan Paul, Trench, Trubner. L catalogued under Robbins. C cataloged under title. **L, C**
Detailed eutopia inhabited by Puritans. Austere, devoted Christians — moneyless, state ownership.

1909   **Clarke, Francis H.** *Morgan Rockefeller's Will; A Romance of 1991–2.* Portland, Oregon: Clarke-Cree Publishing Company. **MoU-St, NcD, OrU**
Rockefeller estate (accumulated for five generations) is donated to the government and is controlled by a paternal brotherhood for the good of the people.

1909   **Dixon, Thomas.** *Comrades; A Story of Social Adventure in California.* New York: Doubleday Page. **L**
Standard failure of a commune.

1909   **Everett, Frances.** *John Bull: Socialist.* London: Swan Sonnenschein. **L**
Standard anti-socialist dystopia.

1909   **Forster, E. M.** "The Machine Stops," *Oxford and Cambridge Review,* 8 (Michaelmas term 1909), 83–122.
Dystopia — people become dependent on machine.

1909   **Hamilton, [Mary] Cicely and Christopher St. John.** *How the Vote Was Won.* Chicago: Dramatic Publishing Company, 1910. First performed London 1909. **NcD**
General strike of all women who do not have the means to support themselves — go on relief.

1909   **Kipling, Rudyard.** "With the Night Mail; A Story of 2,000 A.D.," in his *Actions and Reactions* (London: Macmillan, 1909), pp. 111–169.
See 1912 Kipling for development of this story. This serves as an introduction to the latter.

1909 **[Kirwan, Thomas.]** *Reciprocity (Social and Economic) In the Thirtieth Century; The Coming Co-operative Age. A Forecast of the World's Future,* by William Wonder (pseud.). New York: Cochrane Publishing Company (c. 1908). **DLC**
  Socialist eutopia.

1909 **Peterson, E[phraim].** *Redemption.* Independence, Missouri: Author. **DLC, NN**
  Proposal for a commune with a constitution.

1909 **[Phelps, George Hamilton.]** *The New Columbia or the Re-United States,* by Patrick Quinn Tangent (pseud.). Findley, Ohio: New Columbia Publishing Company. **DLC**
  Public ownership. Deport all who won't work. Unite United States and Canada.

1909 **Pressey, Edward Pearson.** *The Vision of New Clairvaux or Ethical Reconstruction through combination of Agriculture and Handicrafts, under Conditions which exercise Emotion, Sentiment and Imagination, with loyalty to a supreme Ideal.* Boston: Sherman, French and Company. **NN**
  Commune modelled on the vision of Bernard of Clairvaux, founder of the Cistercian monastery of Clairvaux.

1909 *Red England; A Tale of the Socialist Terror.* London: John Milne. **L**
  Anti-socialist dystopia.

1909 **Rhodes, H. Henry.** *Where Men Have Walked; A Story of the Lucayos.* Boston: C. M. Clark. **DLC**
  Lost race—cooperative egalitarian eutopia.

1909 **Rock, James.** *Thro' Space.* Boston: New England Druggist Publishing Company. **L**
  All planets are inhabited. Venus an eutopia, but little detail.

1909 **Sedgwick, S[idney] N[ewman].** *The Last Persecution.* London: Grant Richards. **L**
  Successful Chinese invasion of Europe due to falling away from God. Religious revival brings the overthrow of the Chinese.

1909 **[Teed, Cyrus Reed.]** *The Great Red Dragon or the Flaming Red Devil,* by Lord Chester (pseud.). Estero, Fla.: Guiding Star Pub. House (c. 1908). **L, DLC**
  Borderline — Japan and China overrun the earth — Christianity and astrology win.

[1909] **Wilson, Jesse.** *When the Women Reign. 1930.* London: Arthur H. Stockwell. **L**
  Sex-role reversal.

1909 **Wright, Allen Kendrick.** *To the Poles by Airship or Around the*

World Endways. Los Angeles: Baumgardt. **DLC**
Includes eutopia after Armageddon. Science, religion.

1910   **Ashbee, C[harles] R[obert].** *The Building of Thelema*. London: J.M. Dent. **L**
Thelema is the reconstructed city of the dreamers of all times.

1910   **Cecil, Algernon.** "Gulliver Redivivus," in his *Essays in Imitation* (London: John Murray, 1910), pp. 59–128. **L**
Borderline — descendent of Gulliver visits England and Ireland.

1910   **Chambless, Edgar.** *Roadtown*. New York: Roadtown Press. **DLC, MoU-St**
Long, road-like city. Cooperative housework and cooking. Cottage industry — each house has a work room and machines can be purchased or rented.

1910   **Dowding, Henry Wallace (Dunraven).** *The Man From Mars or Service, for Service's Sake*. New York: Cochrane Publishing Company. **DLC**
Detailed eutopia. Constitution. Rational, artistic people.

1910   **[Ford, Douglas Morey.]** *The Raid of Dover: A Romance of the Reign of Woman: A.D. 1940*. London: King, Sell, & Olding. **NcD**
Anti-socialist dystopia.

1910   **Gillette, King Camp.** *World Corporation*. Boston: New England News Company. **DLC**
Form a cooperative to absorb the world's economy and put it on a sound financial basis. See also 1894 Gillette.

1910   **Gratacap, L[ouis] P[ope].** *The Major of New York: A Romance of Days to Come*. New York: G. W. Dillingham. **MoU-St, FTaSU**
A dystopia of corrupt upper classes and irreligious lower classes. Revolution. Religious revival.

1910   **Herbert, Edward G[eisler].** *Newaera. A Socialist Romance, with a Chapter on Vaccination*. London: P. S. King & Son. **L, MoU-St**
Failure of a commune.

1910   **Le Queux, William [Tufnell].** *The Unknown To-morrow; How the Rich Fared at the Hands of the Poor Together with a full account of the Social Revolution in England*. London: F. V. White.**L**
Standard anti-socialist dystopia.

1910   **Markow, Ralston J.** *Startling Statements or the downfall of the Great Republic*. St. Paul, Minnesota: np. **MoU-St**
Mostly criticism of contemporary conditions, but the last section is a detailed authoritarian eutopia (written in 1897) stressing efficiency, training, and administration responsibility with little or no popular participation in government.

1910   **Morris, Gouverneur.** *The Voice in the Rice.* New York: Dodd, Mead (c. 1909). **MoU-St**
Hidden country that maintains the culture of an idealized antebellum South.

1910   **Prince, Edward.** *Wake Up, England! Being the amazing Story of John Bull — Socialist.* Westminster: St. Stephen's Press. **L, NN**
Standard anti-socialist dystopia.

1911   **Dawson, Coningsby.** *The Road to Avalon.* London: Hodder & Stoughton. **L**
Borderline — medieval fantasy. Avalon is an eutopia.

1911   **[Ford, Ford Madox.]** *The Simple Life Limited,* by Daniel Chaucer (pseud.). London: John Lane, The Bodley Head. **DLC**
Novel directed against a utopian community.

1911   **Gilman, Charlotte Perkins.** *Moving the Mountain.* New York: Charlton Company. **KU**
Feminist eutopia.

1911   **[Henham, Ernest George.]** *The Reign of the Saints,* by John Trevena (pseud.). London: Alston Rivers. **DLC, L**
Anti-socialist dystopia.

1911   **[Horner, Jacob W.]** *Military Socialism,* by Dr. Walter Sensney (pseud.). Indianapolis: Author. **DLC**
Authoritarian eutopia.

[1911] *The Laws of Leflo,* by The Author of Miss Molly (pseud.). London: John Ouseley. **L**
Colony — strict laws and their bad effects. Mostly romance.

1911   *Our Sister Republic; A Single Tax Story.* New York: Cochrane Pub. Co. (Sometimes attributed to Jacob W. Horner — doubtful.) **DLC**
Attack on the income tax, and an argument for the single tax.

1911   **Saunders, W. J.** *Kalomera; The Story of a Remarkable Community.* London: Elliot Stock. **DLC**
Communist eutopia.

1911   **Schuette, H. George.** *Athonia or, The Original Four Hundred.* Manitowoc, Wisconsin: The Lakeside Company (c. 1910). **DLC, MoU-St**
Series of eutopias — all fail.

1911   **Swift, Morrison I[saac].** *The Horroboos.* Boston: The Liberty Press. **DLC, MoU-St**
Satire on capital. Anti-capitalist.

1911   **Ward, Captain Will J.** *Shanghaied Socialists: A Romance.* Cardiff: Maritime Review. **L**
A socialist colony is established by capitalists to prove that socialism is unworkable. Anti-socialist.

1911   **Wicks, Mark.** *To Mars Via the Moon; An Astronomical Story.*
        Philadelphia: J. B. Lippincott; London: Seeley & Company. **L**
        Those who die on earth are reincarnated on Mars. Those who
        die on Mars are reincarnated on another planet. Mars is an
        eutopia.

1912   **Benson, Arthur Christopher.** *The Child of the Dawn.* London:
        Smith, Elder and Company. **DLC, OO**
        Heaven as an eutopia. No sex. No property. Religion is perva-
        sive.

1912   **Brinsmade, Herman Hine.** *Utopia Achieved; A Novel of the
        Future.* New York: Broadway Pub. Co. **DLC**
        1960. Single tax. Many reforms, particularly in diet.

1912   **Fendall, Percy.** *Lady Ermyntrude and the Plumber; A Love Tale of
        MCMXX.* London: S. Swift. 1919 edition changes date in title
        to *MCMXXX.* **L**
        Everyone must work. E.g. — monarch is paid by the job for
        ceremonial duties. Queen took in paying guests.

1912   *The Great State; Essays in Construction,* by H. G. Wells, et al.
        London: Harper and Bros. **TxU**
        Number of essays describing aspects of a future eutopia.

1912   **Hile, William H.** *The Ostrich for the Defense.* Boston: Geo. H.
        Ellis Co. **MoU-St, DLC**
        Lost race — cooperative eutopia.

1912   **[House, Edward M.]** *Philip Dru: Administrator. A Story of
        Tomorrow 1920–1935.* New York: B. W. Huebsch. **MoU-St**
        Series of reforms. House was advisor to Woodrow Wilson.

1912   **Kipling, Rudyard.** "As Easy as A.B.C.," in his *A Diversity of
        Creatures* (London: Macmillan, 1917), pp. 1–44. First published
        in the *London Magazine,* March, April 1912.
        World controlled by Aerial Board of Control. People have
        rejected democracy, returned to agriculture. See also 1909
        Kipling.

[1912] **Levy, J[oseph] H[iam].** *An Individualist's Utopia.* London:
        Lawrence Nelson. **O**
        Eugenics, technology and the simple life.

1912   **Lewis, Dewitt F.** *A Trip to the North Pole and Beyond to
        Civilization,* edited and compiled by E. Z. Ernst. Linwood,
        Kansas: Industrial Exchange. **NN**
        Almost all property owned by the Industrial Exchange Asso-
        ciation in order to eliminate wasteful competition.

1912   **[Newman, H. E.]** *The Prophet,* by N (pseud.). New York:
        Broadway Pub. Co. **DLC**
        Anti-socialist dystopia. Religious revival.

[1912] **Pain, Barry.** "The New Gulliver," in his *The New Gulliver and*

Other Stories (London: T. Werner Laurie, [1912]), pp. 3–84. **L**
Two class society — lower class are bred as slaves to the upper class, which is sexless, and stresses moderation and safety.

1913   **Beresford, J[ohn] D[avys].** *Goslings.* London: William Heinemann. Also entitled *A World of Women.* **L, DLC**
Borderline — a plague effects men but not women. Society established based on work — fails. Finally an eutopia is produced, but the author does not describe it.

[1913]   **Burkitt, William T.** *The Coming Day: A Story of Inevitable Social and Industrial Progress.* London: Drane's. **L**
Emphasis on evolution to eutopia through the union movement.

1913   **Chambers, Robert W.** *The Gay Rebellion.* New York: D. Appleton. **L**
Satire on women's rights.

1913   **Dark, Sidney.** *The Man Who Would Not Be King. Being the Adventures of one Fenimore Slavington, who was neither born great nor achieved greatness, but had greatness thrust upon him much to his own discomfort and the discomfort of many others.* London: John Lane, The Bodley Head. **MoU-St**
Socialist dystopia.

1913   **Floyd, Andress.** *My Monks of Vagabondia.* [Union, N.J.:] np. **MoU-St**
Story of a commune that works with tramps, etc.

1913   **Hayes, Jeff W.** *Paradise on Earth.* Portland, Oregon: F. W. Baltor Company. Also entitled *Portland, Oregon A.D. 1999.* **DLC, MoU-St**
Technological wonders.

1913   **Kerr, A[ndrew] W[illiam].** *Space: A Mirage.* Edinburgh: R. Grant and Son. **L**
Eretha — a planet near Sirius. Detailed eutopia stressing religion, the simple life, and the family. Anti-democratic, has a constitutional monarchy. Equality rejected. Property is held privately, but seen as in trust.

[1913]   **Mawson, L. A.** *Methods from Mars.* London: Arthur H. Stockwell. **L**
Detailed eutopia on Mars. No cities — one large garden. No organized religion.

1913   **Pedley, Rev. Hugh.** *Looking Forward. The Strange Experience of the Rev. Fergus McCheyne.* Toronto: William Briggs. **MoU-St, CaOKQ**
United Church of Canada has brought about eutopia.

1913   **Petworth, Algernon.** *The Little Wicket Gate.* London: A. C. Fifield. **L**
        An eutopia with problems, primarily population pressure. Religion. Equality of the sexes — marriage for life.

1913   **Stump, David Leroy.** *The Love of Meltha Laone; or, Beyond the Sun.* Boston: Roxburgh Publishing Company. **DLC**
        Detailed eutopia. No money. "Everybody has all of everything they need and can use and consume...." Stress on the family. Technology. No pets.

[1914]   **[Carrell, Frederic.]** *2010.* London: T. Werner Laurie. **L**
        Mechanical improvement of brains leads to eutopia.

1914   **Chesterton, G. K.** *The Flying Inn.* London: Methuen. **L**
        Humor — Europe part of the Moslem Empire. Effect of the closing of the pubs on the British.

[1914]   **Gubbins, Herbert.** *The Elixir of Life or 2905 A.D. A Novel of the Far Future.* London: Henry J. Drane. **L**
        Contemplative eutopia.

[1914]   **Henry, Dr. W[alter] O.** *Equitania; or, The Land of Equality.* Omaha: Printed by Klapp & Bartlett. **DLC**
        Detailed eutopia. Traditional sex roles. Includes a detailed constitution.

1914   **Neff, M. A.** *Paradise Found.* Cincinnati: Author. **DLC**
        Series of worlds described including two utopias.

1914   **Taber, Albert Ernest.** *Work for All. A Co-operative Commonwealth based on Ruskin's Teaching.* Leeds: Arthur Wigley. **L**
        Cottage industry. Single tax. Little government.

1914   **Wells, H. G.** *The World Set Free; A Story of Mankind.* New York: E. P. Dutton.
        Effect of abundant, cheap energy. Tremendous dislocation followed, in time, by a world-wide eutopia.

1915   **Cannan, Gilbert.** *Windmills; A Book of Fables.* London: Martin Secker. **LU**
        Two utopias — the first starts as a Robinsonade in "Samways Island" but concludes as an eutopia stressing world peace as "Ultimus." The second, "Gynecologia" is a typical sex-role reversal story. Much heavy-handed satire in both.

1915   **England, George Allan.** *The Air Trust.* St. Louis: Phil Wagner. **DLC**
        Trust gains control of the air and enslaves mankind — overthrown.

1915   **Fulton, James A.** *Uncle Sam Banker 1910–1940.* McKeesport, Pennsylvania: Hutchison & Broadbent. **MoU-St**
        A new public banking system brings general prosperity.

1915   **[Gilman, Charlotte Perkins.]** "Herland," *The Forerunner,* 6 (January-December), pp. 12–17, 38–44, 65–72, 94–100, 123–139, 150–155, 181–187, 207–213, 237–243, 265–270, 287–293, 319–325.
Feminist eutopia.

1915   **Higginbottom, W[illiam] Hugh.** *King of Kulturia.* London: The Walter Scott Company. **L**
Satire — attempt to control artistic production. Anti-German.

1915   **[Marshall, Arthur Hammond.]** *Upsidonia,* by Archibald Marshall (pseud.). London: Stanley Paul. **L, MoU-St**
Erewhonian.

1915   **Olerich, Professor Henry.** *Modern Paradise. An Outline or Story of how Some of the Cultured People will probably live, Work and Organize in the Near Future.* Omaha: Equality Pub. Co. **DLC**
Another version of 1893 Olerich. See also 1923 Olerich.

1915   **Stauffer, Mack.** *Humanity and the Mysterious Knight.* Boston: Roxburgh Publishing Company. **DLC**
Battle between labor and capital.

1915   **[Tracy, Roger S.]** *The White Man's Burden, A Satirical Forecast,* by T. Shirby Hodge (pseud.). Boston: Gorham Press. **DLC**
Africa complctely black and Christian. All races advanced except the white. Race war. Anarchism.

1915   **Wallace, Edgar.** *"1925"; The Story of a Fatal Peace.* London: George Newnes.**L**
Problems if Germany is not completely subjugated after the war.

1916   **Chapman, Richard Marvin.** *A Vision of the Future.* New York: The Cosmopolitan Press. **DLC**
Future society based on science and eugenics.

1916   **Dixon, Thomas.** *The Fall of a Nation. A Sequel to the Birth of a Nation.* New York: D. Appleton. **L, MoU-St**
United States defeated by Germany and internal subversion.

1916   **[Gilman, Charlotte Perkins.]** "With Her in Ourland," *The Forerunner,* 7 (January-December), pp. 6–11, 38–44, 67–73, 93–98, 123–128, 152–158, 179–185, 208–213, 237–243, 263–269, 291–297, 318–325.
Continuation of 1915 Gilman "Herland."

1916   **Hughes, Thomas J.** *State Socialism After the War; An Exposition of Complete State Socialism. What It Is: How It Would Work.* Philadelphia: George W. Jacobs and Company. [1919] edition subtitled *A Retrospect of Reconstruction after the War.* Revised edition. Dayton, Ohio: New Era Pub. Co. **DLC**

Detailed exposition of how a system of complete governmental ownership of property, except personal effects, would work.

1916   **Jones, Mrs. Lillian B.** *Five Generations Hence.* Fort Worth, Texas: Dotson-Jones Company. **DLC**
Negroes return to Africa which produces an eutopia in both places.

1916   **Joseph, Gentle** (pseud.). *A Peaceful Revolution.* Bath: Ernest J. Adams. **O**
State controlled economic system. Thorough integration of women into an egalitarian society.

[1916]   **Trygaeus** (pseud.). *The United States of the World; An Utopian Essay towards a Better Ordering of the Affairs of Men.* London: George Routledge & Sons. **O**
Eugenics. World government. Stress on the means of avoiding war.

1916   **Vaughan, H[erbert] M.** *Meleager; A Fantasy.* London: Martin Secker. **L**
Eugenics — defective children killed. Class system. Women have no political rights.

1917   **[Emanuel, Victor Rousseau.]** *The Messiah of the Cylinder,* by Victor Rousseau (pseud.). Chicago: A. C. McClurg. Reprinted: Westport, Connecticut: Hyperion Press, 1974. Also entitled *The Apostle of the Cylinder.*
Scientific dystopia.

1917   **Lucian** (pseud.). *1920; Dips into the Near Future.* 2nd edition. London: Headley Bros. [1918]. Originally published in *The Nation.* **MiU**
Borderline — satire on the possible effects of the attitude that World War I will be of long duration. E.g. — Involuntary euthenasia for the old in order to preserve the food supply. All of life subordinated to the continuing war effort.

1917   **Reynaert, Rev. John Hugh.** *The Eldorado of Socialism, Communism and Anarchism; or a Trip to the Planet Jupiter.* [Orlando, Fla.: Reporter-Star Pub. Co.]. **DLC**
Christian socialism.

1917   **Veiby, John.** *The Utopian Way.* South Bend, Indiana: Author. **DLC, InU**
Religion. Decentralization. See also 1923 Veiby.

1918   **[Bennett, Gertrude.]** "Friend Island," by Francis Stevens (pseud.), *All-Story Weekly,* (September 7). Reprinted: *Under the Moons of Mars,* edited by Sam Moskowitz. (New York: Holt, Rinehart and Winston, 1970), pp. 125–136.
Superiority of women.

1918   **[Draper, Warwick.]** *The Tower,* by Watchman (pseud.). London: Headley Bros. 2nd edition entitled *The New Britain.* **DLC**
Religious revival. Reform of the church followed by a return to a more simple life and craftsmanship.

1918   **Finney, Lewis Erwin.** *Calno, The Super-Man. A Fictional Study of the Antichrist.* Dallas: Ozark Pub. Co. Written in 1914. **MoU-St**
Authoritarian dystopia — antichrist.

1918   **Gregory, Owen.** *Meccania. The Super-State.* London: Methuen. **L, MoU-St**
Authoritarian dystopia — Germany.

1918   **McManus, L.** *The Professor in Erin.* Dublin: M. H. Gill and Son. **IU**
Parallel history — Ireland as an eutopia developed from original Irish roots.

1918   **Mitchell, J. Calvin.** *Excerpts from the Crater of Gold: A Mysterious Manuscript.* Chicago: Crater of Gold Publishing Co.
Includes a description of the future United States where the people vote on a completely new Constitution on a regular basis. If no party wins a majority the old Constitution remains in effect.

1918   **Morrill, Fred B[rown].** *Beyond the Horizon.* New York: Neale Pub. Co. **MoU-St, DLC**
System of voluntary cooperatives — no government. No weapons of destruction — animals no longer are afraid of man. No private property.

[1918]   **Onions, Oliver.** *The New Moon; A Romance of Reconstruction.* London: Hodder and Stoughton. **L, DLC**
Postwar England has almost returned to barbarian state. Stress on romance, but rebuilding of better society also.

1919   **[Bennett, Gertrude.]** *The Heads of Cerberus,* by Francis Stevens (pseud.). Reading, Pennsylvania: Polaris Press, 1952. **IaU**
Authoritarian dystopia.

1919   **Bleackeley, Horace.** *Anymoon.* London: John Lane. **DLC**
Anti-socialist dystopia.

1919   **Bruére, Martha Bensley.** *Mildred Carver, U.S.A.* New York: Macmillan. **DLC**
Universal service produces egalitarian system.

[1919]   **Colwyn, John.** *A City Without a Church.* London: A.H. Stockwell. **C**
Revolution of 1938 leads, after a period without religion, to a realization of a need for religion.

[1919]   **Cournos, John.** *London Under the Bolshevists.* London: Russian Liberation Committee. No. 4 of Russian Liberation Committee

Publications. Reprinted from *The Nineteenth Century.* **L**
Anti-communist dystopia.

1919 **Cram, Ralph.** *Walled Towns.* Boston: Marshall Jones Co. **L**
Medieval eutopia — rural, guild system, crafts.

1919 **Fairfield, Frederick Pease.** *Story of the City of Works; A Community of Peace and Plenty Where Every Man is His Own Policeman. A New Order of Government. Anti-Socialistic. Free Street Cars and Telephones. No Middlemen. No Capitalist Class. All Profit Accrues to Labor. Farm and City Life Conjoined.* Boston: [Author]. **DLC**
Company town as eutopia.

1919 **Guthrie, Kenneth Sylvan.** *A Romance of Two Centuries. A Tale of the Year 2025.* Alpine, New Jersey: The Platonist Press. **L, MoU-St**
Efficiency. Controlled eutopia. Equality.

[1919] **Koepsel, L[ouis] H[erman].** *A Prophecy; The Human Community or The True Social Order.* San Francisco: Human Community. **NN**
Theocratic eutopia. Detailed.

1919 **Marshall, James and Margaret Scott Marshall.** *1960 (A Retrospect).* Los Angeles: J.F. Rowny Press. Also entitled *World of Tomorrow.* **DLC**
Apartheid.

1919 **Muir, Ward.** *"Further East Than Asia." A Romantic Adventure.* London: Simpkin, Marshall, Hamilton, Kent and Co. **MoU-St**
Shangri-la type. Racist.

1919 **Pallen, Conde B[enoist].** *Crucible Island; A Romance, An Adventure and an Experiment.* New York: Manhattanville Press. **NcD, MoU-St**
Anti-socialist dystopia. Shows weaknesses of seemingly good society.

1919 **Rowland, Henry C.** *"Utopia," The Popular Magazine,* 53 (July 20) pp. 1–70. **L, DLC, MH**
Playground for dull, prohibition-ridden U.S.

1919 **Sharp, Evelyn.** *Somewhere in Christendom.* London: George Allen Unwin. **L, MoU-St**
Christian cooperative eutopia.

1919 **Spring, [Henry] Powell.** "Utopia or Common Sense," in his *The Peace Aims of Humanity* (Winter Park, Florida: The Orange Press, 1943), pp. 177–191. Originally published in *Trinity Review* (University of Toronto). Separately published in 1945. **DLC**
Christian. World order.

1920   **Arozin** (pseud.). "A Passing Conversation," *Living Age,* 306 (July), pp. 75–76.
> Based on More.

1920   **Hall, G[ranville] Stanley.** "The Fall of Atlantis," in his *Recreations of a Psychologist* (New York: D. Appleton & Co., 1920), pp. 1–127. **L**
> End of an eutopia through the failure of the people, particularly professional people.

1920   **Hastings, Milo.** *City of Endless Night.* New York: Dodd, Mead. Reprinted: Westport, Connecticut: Hyperion Press, 1974.
> Fascist dystopia.

1920   **Johnston, Mary.** *Sweet Rocket.* London: Constable & Co. **L**
> Religious, agrarian eutopia.

1920   **Lindsay, Vachel.** *The Golden Book of Springfield. Being the Review of a book that will appear in the autumn of the year 2018, and an extended description of Springfield, Illinois, in that year.* New York: Macmillan.
> Mysticism but some on the social system. Drugs. World government.

[1920?]   **Linton, Dr. C.E.** "The Hermit of Chimaso Island," in his *The Earthomotor and Other Stories* (Salem, Oregon: Satesman Pub. Co.) pp. 155–231. Title on spine is *Earthmotor.* **MoU-St, OrU**
> Sketchy technological eutopia.

[1920?]   **Lindon, Dr. C.E.** "Three Weeks Inside the Earth," in his *The Earthomotor and Other Stories* (Salem, Oregon: Statesman Pub. Co.) pp. 101–152. Title on spine is *Earthmotor.* **MoU-St, OrU**
> Sketchy eutopia inside earth — telepathy, no sin, technology.

1920   **Richmond, Sir William Blake.** *Democracy — False or True? A Prologue and Dream.* London: Cecil Palmer. **L**
> Democratic socialism. Decentralization. There are still classes.

1920   **[Rosewater, Frank.]** *Doomed. A Startling Message to the People of our Day, Interwoven in an Antediluvian Romance of Two Old Worlds and Two Young Lovers, by Queen Metel and Prince Loab of Atlo, Re-incarnated in its editors, Marian and Franklin Mayoe* (pseud.). *By the Atlon Calendar, the Year 14,909. by Our Calendar the Year 1920.* New York: Frank Rosewater. **DLC**
> Atlism — everyone must spend their entire income.

1920   **Shanks, Edward.** *The People of the ruins; A Story of the English Revolution and After.* London: W. Collins Sons. **L**
> Strikes cause the downfall of civilization and a return to a more primitive life.

1920   **Unitas** (pseud.). *The Dream City.* London: Simpkin, Marshall, Hamilton, Kent and Company. **L**
Socialist eutopia.

[1921]   **[Beresford, Leslie.]** *The Great Image,* by Pan (pseud.). London: Odhams Press. **L**
Conflict between capitalists and socialists set 100 years in the future. World decimated, then gradually rebuilds.

[1921]   **Bernard, John.** *The New Race of Devils.* London: Anglo-Eastern Pub. Co. **MoU-St**
Dystopia — Germans create supermen.

1921   **Branford, Victor.** *Whitherward? Hell or Eutopia.* London: Williams and Norgate. **MoU**
Regionalism, decentralization.

1921   **Bruce, Stewart E.** *The World in 1931.* New York: F.L. Searl & Co. **DLC**
Standard socialist eutopia.

1921   **Fowler, Horace N. and Samuel, Fowler T.** *The Industrial Public. A Plan of Social Reconstruction in Line with Evolution.* Los Angeles: H.N. Fowler Co. **DLC**
Common ownership frees women from marriage bond.

1921   **Hall, Austin and Homer Eon Flint.** *The Blind Spot.* Philadelphia: Prime Press, 1951. **CoU**
Greatly advanced race spiritually and technically.

1921   **[Howard, Hilda (Glynn).]** *The Writing on the Wall,* by Hilda Glynn-Ward (pseud.). Vancouver: Sun Pub. Co. **NcD**
Dystopia — Chinese immigration leads to domination.

1921   **McDougall, William.** "The Island of Eugenia; The Phantasy of a Foolish Philosopher," *Scribner's Magazine,* 70 (October), pp. 483–491.
Eugenics.

[1921]   **Nedram** (pseud.). *John Sagur.* London: Heath Cranton. **L**
Development of a benevolent dictatorship.

1921   **Roche, Arthur Somers.** *The Day of Faith.* Boston: Little, Brown. **L**
An eutopia where everyone is honest, and there are no police or jails, proves weak and collapses.

[1921]   **Ross, Major-General Charles.** *The Fly-By-Nights.* London: John Murray. **L**
Anti-communist, anti-alien dystopia.

1921   **Shaw, George Bernard.** *Back to Methuselah; A Metabiological Pentateuch.* New York: Brentano's. First performed 1922. **DLC**
Traces history of mankind from prior to Adam to the distant future. Satire.

1921   **Snaith, J[ohn] C[ollins].** *The Council of Seven.* New York: D. Appleton. **DLC**
        Authoritarian dystopia.

1922   **Babcock, George.** *Yezad; A Romance of the Unknown.* Bridgeport, Connecticut: Cooperative Pub. Co. **DLC, MoU**
        A few pages of a martian eutopia.

1922   **Barbor, H[erbert] R.** *Against the Red Sky. Silhouettes of Revolution.* London: C.W. Daniel. **L**
        Story of a future successful revolution bringing about a better society.

1922   **Cummings, Ray.** *The Girl in the Golden Atom.* London: Methuen. **L**
        Gulliver type — world in an atom. Monarchy with advisors (half men and half women). No money.

[1922] **Griffiths, Isabel.** *Three Worlds.* London: Arthur H. Stockwell. **L**
        Heaven, but presented as an eutopia on Jupiter. Little detail.

1922   **Hamada, Nobuya.** *An Ideal World.* Berlin: Carl Heymanns Verlag. **NN**
        Essay, but an eutopia. Free trade, no crime, controlled population. Stress on dedication and leadership of the few best.

1922   **Hamilton, [Mary] Cicely.** *Theodore Savage; A Story of the Past or the Future.* London: Leonard Parsons. Revised edition entitled *Lest ye Die.* **L**
        War and the reaction against it — a vow of ignorance of science.

1922   **Kayser, Martha.** *The Aerial Flight to the Realm of Peace.* St. Louis: Lincoln Press & Pub. Co. **DLC**
        Religion. Equality. Arbitration. Early education is the key.

1922   *1943,* by X (pseud.). New York: Dorrance. **L, MoU-St**
        Satire — all the reformers of the 1920s succeed. Vegetarian, teetotalist, no tobacco. Becomes dictatorship and is finally defeated.

1922   **Schvan, Johan August.** *Towards a New Social Order.* London: George Allen and Unwin. **L**
        Single tax. Absolute freedom of exchange. No monopolies. Many reforms.

1922   **Scrymsour, Ella.** *The Perfect World; A Romance of Strange People and Strange Places.* New York: Frederick A. Stokes Company. **DLC, MoU-St**
        Jupiter — hierarchical but share on a pro rata basis. Custom.

1922   **Wells, H.G.** *Men Like Gods.* New York: Grosset and Dunlap.
        A world composed entirely of the Samurai of 1905 Wells.

1922   **Wright, Allen Kendrick.** *Dalleszona and the Seventh Treasure.* Boston: The Roxburgh Pub. Co. **DLC, NcD, MoU-St**

Pure democracy. Compulsory education. Each person receives a living wage, but must work.

1923   **Ball, Frank P.** *My Wondrous Dream.* New York: Frank P. Ball. **DLC**
Racist utopia based on rigid control of blacks by whites.

[1923] **Broomhead, Reginald.** *A Voice from Mars; Adventure and Romance.* London: Arthur H. Stockwell. **MoU-St**
Mostly adventure, but includes an eutopia on Mars.

[1923] **Campbell, Duncan.** *The Last Millionaire; A Tale of the Old World and the New.* London: Heath Cranton. **L**
Nationalization of land and a limit on income brings an eutopia.

1923   **Clough, Fred M.** *The Golden Age or The Depth of Time.* Boston: The Roxburgh Pub. Co. **DLC**
Science. Reason. Rural life (2-10 acres per home to grow food).

[1923] **Davis, Emry.** *The Bride of Christ. A Message from Jerusalem to the True and Faithful Subjects of Jesus Christ throughout the World.* Jerusalem: Palestine Press. **MH**
Religion — primarily for Baptists. Restore Jerusalem to its former state. Detailed reforms.

1923   **Graham, P[eter] Anderson.** *The Collapse of Homo Sapiens.* London: Putnam. **L, MoU-St**
Barbarianism in two centuries.

1923   **Griesser, Wilhelm.** *The Welcome Island Stories and Laws.* Chicago: Tucker-Kenworthy. **NcD**
Capitalist eutopia.

1923   **Knox, Ronald A.,** ed. [written by]. *Memories of the Future 1915–1972. Written in the Year of Grace, 1988, by Opal, Lady Porstock* (pseud.). London: Methuen. **O**
Utopian satire.

[1923] **Lynch, Colonel Arthur.** *Seraph Wings.* London: John Long, Ltd. **DLC**
Mostly adventure, but includes an eutopia of devolution.

1923   **Marsden, Richard.** "Utopian Conversation." *Germinal,* 1 (July), unpaged.
Short eutopia modeled on 1890 Morris.

1923   **Olerich, Professor Henry.** *The Story of the World a Thousand Years Hence. An Interesting Scientific Forecast of the Important Progressive Changes that Will Likely Take Place On Our Earth During the Next Thousand Years.* Omaha: Olerich Pub. Co. **PSt**
Presented as a forecast. A third version of 1893 Olerich. See also 1915 Olerich.

1923   **[Owen, Harry Collinson.]** *The Battle of London,* by Hugh Addison (pseud.). London: Herbert Jenkins. **L**
Anti-Communist dystopia.

[1923]   **Pauer, Louis.** *The Day of Judgment and the Celestial Missionaries of Life.* [Cleveland: np]. **DLC**
Odd version of a socialist eutopia.

1923   **Pauer, Louis.** *Eurekanian Paternalism. For an economic expedition to explore and exploit Eurekania, the New State in the Realm of Utopia. With Aims and Plans of Providence, final and immediate, for the Development of the Latent Qualities and Resources inherent in Society under Advanced Organization, Production and Distribution through the Administration, eventually, of a Non-Politic, Quasi-Public Economic Institution, which shall be promoted, in the early stages of its development, by a Foundation Society and other Subsidiary Organizations.* Cleveland: np. **DLC**
Odd version of a socialist eutopia.

1923   **Snedden, David.** "Gopher Prairie — A.D. 2000." *School and Society,* 18 (August 25), 211–216.
Education — stress on culture.

[1923]   **[Thompson, Mrs. Harriet Alfarata (Chapman).]** *Idealia; A Utopia Dream; or, Resthaven.* [Albany, New York: printed by J.B. Lyon Co.]. **DLC, MoU-St**
Arcadia.

1923   **Tilden, Freeman.** *Mr. Podd.* New York: Macmillan. **MoU-St**
Commune founded on an island is a failure. Satire on Henry Ford's Peace Ship.

[1923]   *Utopian Jurisprudence,* by A Lawyer (pseud.). London: Arthur H. Stockwell. **L**
Sets out forty essential principles on which to build an eutopia.

1923   **Veiby, John.** *Utopian Essays.* South Bend, Indiana: Author. **InU**
Series of essays on aspects of an eutopian society. See also 1917 Veiby.

1923   *When Woman Rules! A Tale of the First Women's Government,* by A Well-Known Member of Parliament (pseud.). London: John Long. **L, DLC**
Standard anti-woman.

1924   **[Bottomley, Samuel.]** *A Message from "Mars" including The "Martians" Plan for World Peace and Permanent Prosperity Via a New Monetary System.* Providence, Rhode Island: The Martian Pub. Co. **DLC**
Monetary reform — non-fluctuating currency. He also published a *Second* (1925) and a *Third Message from Mars* (1926).

1924 **Collins, Gilbert.** *The Valley of the Eyes Unseen.* New York: Robert M. McBride and Co. **MoU-St**
Lost race utopia — Greek culture.

1924 **Gillette, King C[amp].** *The People's Corporation.* New York: Boni and Liveright. **ICN**
Non-fictional explanation of his ideas for eutopia.

1924 **Harvey, William H[ope].** *Paul's School of Statesmanship.* Chicago: Mundus Pub. Co. **NCD, MoU-St**
Monetary reform — money tied to the amount of goods; it can be constantly in circulation rather than saved.

1924 **Ingram, Kenneth.** *England at the Flood Tide.* London: Damian Press. **L**
Natural aristocracy with checks on the power of the people. Women economically independent.

1924 **Petersen, Rena Oldfield.** *Venus.* Philadelphia: Dorrance & Co. **DLC**
ESP-idyllic society.

1924 **Sanford, Hugh W.** "Idealism and the Ideal State," in his *The Business of Life.* 2 Vols. (New York: Oxford University Press, 1924, Vol. 2, pp. 718–942. **DLC**
Eutopia of eugenics and capitalism.

1924 **Tayler, John Lionel.** *The Last of My Race. A Dream of the Future.* Lincoln, England: J.W. Ruddock & Sons. **L**
Homo Sapiens Varius — a species far above man.

1924 **[Triplett, Henry Franklin.]** *Negrolana,* by Dr. Frank (pseud.). Boston: Christopher Publishing House. **DLC, NcD**
Land founded for freed salves. Single tax. Very strict.

1924 **Wells, H.G.** *The Dream.* New York: Macmillan (c. 1923). **DLC**
The present seen as a dystopia from the perspective of a future eutopia.

1924 **Wilson, David Alec.** *Modern Lilliput: A History of the recent re-discovery of the Lilliput Archipelago, and what has been happening there.* London: C.W. Daniel. **L, DLC, MoU-St**
History of Lilliput after Gulliver.

[1924] **Wright, S[ydney] Fowler.** *The Amphibians. A Romance of 500,000 Years Hence.* London: Merton Press. Also included in 1929, Wright, *The World Below.* **L, O**
Far future; changed race.

[1925] **Coron, Hannah.** *Ten Years Hence?* London: J.M. Ouseley. **L**
Anti-pacifist.

[1925] **Cox, Erle.** *Out of the Silence.* Melbourne: E.A. Vidler. **DLC**
Dystopia of perfected science.

1925 **Craig, Hamilton.** *A Hazard at Hansard.* London: Arthur H. Stockwell. **L**

Cut in government expenditures; return to simpler life.

1925   **Dell, Berenice V.** *The Silent Voice.* Boston: The Four Seas Co. **DLC**
Sex-role reversal in far future.

1925   **Fox, Richard A.** *The People on Other Planets.* Benton Harbor, Michigan: The Walter Southworth Co. **DLC, MoU-St**
Gulliver type.

[1925]   **Madariaga [y Rojo], Salvador de,** ed. [written by]. *The Sacred Giraffe; Being the Second Volume of the Posthumous Works of Julio Arceval* (pseud.). New York: Harper and Bros. Probably written in English. Also published in Spanish 1925. **MoU-St**
Sex-role reversal.

1925   **Richardson, E.** *Neutopia.* London: Simpkin, Marshall, Hamilton, Kent and Company. **L**
Lost race socialist eutopia. Eugenics.

1925   **Rosewater, Frank.** *Easy Millions. A Story of Adventure and the Discovery of How to Make and Keep Everybody Rich.* New York: Frank Rosewater. **NN**
All income must be spent each year. Cooperative system.

1925   **Sieveking, L[ancelot] de Giberne.** *Ultimate Island; A Strange Adventure.* London: George Routledge. **L, MoU-St**
Mostly adventure, but includes an eutopia.

1925   **Williams, Arthur.** *Looking Forward.* Los Angeles: Author. **DLC**
Detailed Cooperative eutopia.

1925   **Willoughby, Frank.** *Through the Needle's Eye; A Narrative of the restoration of the Davidic Kingdom of Israel in Palestine with Jesus Christ as King.* New York: Palestine Press. **DLC**
Millenial — equality, honesty. Climate restored.

1925   **Winship, Glen B[rian].** *Volonor.* New York: Thomas Seltzer. **L**
Free love colony, but women have no status and cannot own property.

1926   **Boswell, Diane.** *Posterity; A Novel.* London: Jonathan Cape. **L**
Good life brought about by a reduction in the birth rate which becomes a required limit. This leads to a mixed result, some good, some bad.

1926   **Chesterton, G.K.** *The Return of Don Quixote.* New York: Dodd, Mead. **DLC**
Return to medieval ideals — craftsmanship, nobility, usufruct.

1926   **George, W.L.** *Children of the Morning.* New York: G.P. Putnam's Sons. **MoU-St**
Similar to 1954 Golding presenting children on an isolated island.

1926   **Glossop, Reginald.** *The Orphans of Space; A Tale of Downfall.* London: G. MacDonald. **L, O**
Yellow Peril and Communism sweep over West. Divine intervention saves the day.

[1926]   **Grant, I[sabell] F[rancis].** *A Candle in the Hills.* London: Hodder and Stoughton. **L**
Communist Britain (dystopia) and a successful revolt against it inspired by a woman.

1926   **Haldane, Charlotte.** *Man's World.* London: Chatto and Windus. **L**
Eugenic dystopia.

1926   **Jacomb, C.E.** *And a New Earth; A Romance.* London: George Routledge. **L, MoU-St**
Borderline — disaster followed by the creation of an eutopia.

1926   **Jaeger, M[uriel].** *The Question Mark.* London: Leonard and Virginia Woolf at the Hogarth Press. **MoU-St, L**
Starts from traditional utopias, but then tries to people them with real people. Ambiguous result. Split between intellectuals and non-intellectuals (known as normals). Much boredom, hero worship.

[1926?]   *A Message to Thee.* np.: np. **NN**
Authoritarian eutopia. Aliens return home. Censorship. No rights without prior training.

1926   **Ridley, F.H.** *The Green Machine.* London: Noel Douglas. **L, MoU-St**
A world of rational ants.

1927   **Barker, Arthur W.** *The Light from Sealonia.* Boston: The Four Seas Co. **DLC, MoU-St**
Racist. Country near North Pole.

1927   **Blakemore, Felix J[ohn].** *The Coming Hour(?).* London: Sands. **L**
Standard anti-socialist dystopia.

1927   **Clark, Cumberland.** *Fairy Tales of Socialism.* London: Wass, Pritchard. **L**
Three stories — "The Fairy Tale of Socialism," "If Bolshevism Comes," and "Bill's Dream" — present socialist societies with terrible conditions resulting from socialism.

1927   **Legge, J[ames] G[ranville].** *The Millenium.* Oxford: Basil Blackwell. **L**
Satire on bureaucracy — overenforcement of a scheme for health improvement. E.g. — too tight shoes are illegal.

1927   **L[ittell], R[obert].** "Things as They Ought to Be." *New Republic,* 49 (February 9), 330–31.
Short satirical sketch of a dull eutopia in 2027.

1927   **Margrie, W[illiam].** *The Story of a Great Experiment. How*

England Produced the First Superman. London: Watts. **L**
Eugenics — women's role only to be mothers of a healthy race.

[1927]   **Maurois, Andre.** *The Next Chapter. The War Against the Moon.* London: Kegan, Paul, Trench, Trubner, & Co. **L**
Control of the world by those who control public opinion.

1927   **Mette, John Allen.** *The Ideal State.* Charleston, South Carolina: Southern Printing and Pub. Co. **DLC**
Poem. Racist, socialist eutopia.

1927   **Montague, C.E.** *Right Off the Map.* London: Chatto and Windus **L, MoU-St**
Recreated British industrial feudalism — dystopia.

1927   **Murray, Rev. William.** *The Messiah. A Problem.* London: Arthur H. Stockwell. **DLC**
Fake messiah (radio) — convinces people to give up competition and stresses quality.

1927   **Ollivant, Alfred.** *To-Morrow; A Romance of the Future.* Garden City: Doubleday, Page & Co. **NcD, MoU-St**
Arcadia — simple life, but with required labor service.

1927   **[Perry, Donald Robert.]** *The Almost Perfect State,* by Don Marquis (pseud.). London: William Heinemann. **L**
Newspaper articles and essays from utopia.

1928   **Belloc, Hilaire.** *But soft — we are observed!* London: Arrowsmith. **DLC, IaU**
Satire — conflict between major political parties of the future, Communists and Anarchists.

[1928]   **Callaghan, Stella.** *Nor Shall My Sword Sleep.* London: Skeffington & Son. **L**
Commune established on an estate.

1928   **Chase, Stuart.** "A Very Private Utopia," *The Nation,* 126 (May 16), 559–562.
Series of reforms.

1928   **Coblentz, Stanton A.** *The Sunken World.* London: Fantasy Books, [1948]. First published in *Amazing.* **L**
Atlantis as eutopia. Greek Democracy. Common property.

1928   **Field, Marlo.** *Astro Bubbles.* Boston: The Four Seas Co. **MoU-St**
Detailed eutopia. Worlds connected in a string at poles. Earth one of the lowest due to the development of science. Spiritually higher world connected at the South Pole. Eden like — eat only fruit, highly refined people. Equality. Ally of nature.

1928   **Gazella, E[dith] V[irginia].** *The Blessing of Azar. A Tale of Dreams and Truth.* Boston: Christopher. **DLC**
Founding of an eutopia.

1928   **Grierson, Francis D.** *Heart of the Moon.* London: Alston Rivers. **L**
Scientific dystopia.

1928   **Howe, Frederic C.** "A Political Utopia," *The Nation,* 127 (August 22), pp. 178–179.
Single tax. Natural aristocracy. Cooperative system.

1928   **Keller, David H.** "The Revolt of the Pedestrians," in *Beyond Time and Space,* edited by August Derleth (New York: Pellegrini and Cudahy, 1950), pp. 347–376.
Pedestrians outlawed. Small group survives and successfully revolts.

1928   **O'Duffy, Eimar.** *The Spacious Adventures of the Man in the Street.* London: Macmillan. **NcD, L, DLC, MoU-St**
Satire — a utopia presented by an anti-utopian.

[1928]   **Symons, J[ohn] H[enry].** *The End of the Marriage Vow.* London: Hutchinson. **L**
All worlds are stages of evolution; earth is on the low end of the scale. Next stage men and women are free and equal. No procreation — no marriage, but love exists.

1928   **Wells, H.G.** *The Open Conspiracy; Blue Prints for a World Revolution.* London: Victor Gollancz. Revised edition entitled *What Are We To Do With Our Lives?* **L, LDC**
Program to bring about an eutopia.

1928   **Younghusband, Sir Francis.** *The Coming Country. A Pre-Vision.* London: John Murray. **L**
Rebirth of England through religion leads to eutopia.

1929   **Bowhay, Bertha Louisa.** *Elenchus Brown, The Story of an Experimental Utopia.* London: H.R. Allenson. **L**
Satire on the failure of a commune.

1929   **Burdekin, Katherine.** *The Rebel Passion.* London: Thornton Butterworth. **DLC**
Traces the history of mankind past the present to a religious, medieval eutopia.

1929   **Clock, Herbert and Eric Boetzel.** *The Light In the Sky.* New York: Coward-McCann. **DLC, MoU-St**
South American Indian eutopia. ESP.

1929   **Cummings, Ray.** *The Man Who Mastered Time.* Chicago: A.C. McClurg. **L**
Time machine story. 6,000 years in the future a class-based dystopia.

1929   **Fuller, Frederick T.** *Beyond the Selvas. A Vision of a Republic That Might Have Been — and Still May Be.* Boston: np. **MoU-St, NcD**
Christian socialism.

1929 **Guest, Ernest.** *At the End of the World: A Vision.* London: Elkin Mathews & Marrot. **L**
  Borderline — world government, search for God.

1929 **Hibbard, Addision.** "Utopia College: A Prospectus," *Outlook and Independent,* 151 (February 27), pp. 323–326, 353–354.
  Description of university education in Utopia. Presents a college and the principles of Utopian education.

1929 **Hodgson, John [Laurence],** ed. [written by]. *The Time-Journey of Dr. Barton: An Engineering and Sociological Forecast based on Present Possibilities.* Eggington, Beds.: John Hodgson. **L, DLC**
  Reason, eugenics, free love. A leisure based eutopia. Mostly technical.

1929 **Macauley, L.** *The Decadence: An Excerpt from "A History of the Triumph and Decay of England," dateable 1949.* London: Watts & Co. **L, NN**
  Argument for free trade.

1929 **[Muir, John R.B.]** *Robinson the Great; A Political Fantasia on the Problems of To-day and the Solutions of To-morrow. Extracted from the works of Solomon Slack, LL.D.,* by An Impenitent Politician (pseud.). London: Christophers. **L, MoU-St**
  Mostly a political novel calling for freeing Parliament from party rule.

1929 **St. Cyr, Emil, M.D.** *Philosophic Tales of the "Arabian Nights." The Three Voyages of Omar and Micromegas.* Chicago: Author's Art Press. **MoU-St**
  Includes an eutopia on Saturn.

1929 **Salisbury, William.** *The Square Heads; the Story of a Socialized State. A Futuristic Novel.* New Rochelle, New York: Independent Pub. Co. **DLC**
  Anti-socialist dystopia. Conformity — must speak in phrases of four syllables and in sentences of equal metric value.

1929 **Sinclair, Upton.** *The Millenium; A Comedy of the Year 2000.* London: T. Werner Laurie. **L, DLC**
  Written in 1907 and lost. Capitalist dystopia.

[1929] **Vaughan, Herbert Millingchamp.** *Nephelococcygia or Letters from Paradise.* Carmarthen: W. Spurell and Son.
  Heaven as an eutopia — even, monastic life. Famous people.

1929 **Wright, Sydney Fowler.** *The World Below.* London: W. Collins Sons. **L, O**
  Part I repeats 1924 Wright *The Amphibians.* The rest is a sequel.

1930 **Baxter, Garrett.** *Bamboa.* [Norfolk, Virginia:] Economic Press. **DLC**

Individualism. Democracy and minimal cooperation. See also 1932 Baxter.

1930   **Bradford, Columbus.** *Terrania; or, The Feminization of the World.* Boston: Christopher Pub. House. **DLC**
Eutopia ruled by women.

1930   **Britton, Lionel [Erskine Nimmo].** *Brain; A Play of the Whole Earth.* London: G. Putnam's Sons. **DLC**
Giant brain built in the Sahara. Comes to control the entire world. Catastrophe. The Brain has a nervous breakdown.

1930   **Guérard, Albert.** "Graphopolis — A Utopia for Literature," *Nineteenth Century,* 108 (August), 255–265.
An eutopia for artists.

1930   **Harris, Frank.** *Pantopia.* New York: The Panurge Press. **MoU-St, IEN**
Natural aristocracy combined with essential equality. Communal economics. Eugenics.

1930   **Jerrold, Douglas.** *Storm Over Europe.* London: Ernest Benn. **L**
History of a small country from monarchy to liberalism to socialism and back to monarchy.

1930   **Schinagel, Gezá.** *Possibilities.* Boston: Meador Pub. Co. **DLC**
Reason. Abundance. Education becomes the main goal in life.

1930   **Sims, Alan.** *Anna Perenna.* London: Chatto and Windus. **L, DLC**
Satire — against both capitalists and workers.

1930   **[Southwold, Stephen.]** *The Seventh Bowl,* by Miles (pseud.). London: Eric Partridge. Also attributed to Francis Marre and to Neil Bell. **L**
Immortality — dystopia.

1930   **Stapledon, [William] Olaf.** *Last and First Men; A Story of the Near and Far Future.* London: Methuen. **L, NcD**
One of Stapledon's visions of the far, far future where man has been replaced by higher species.

1930   **Tillyard, Aelfrida.** *Concrete; A Story of Two Hundred Years Hence.* London: Hutchinson. **L, MH**
Dystopia — reason, communism.

1930   **Vassos, John and Ruth Vassos.** *Ultimo; An Imaginative narration of life under the earth.* New York: E.P. Dutton. **NcD, MoU-St**
New ice age — perfect society under the ice.

1930   **Wells, H.G.** *The Autocracy of Mr. Parham; His Remarkable Adventures in this Changing World.* Garden City: Doubleday, Doran (c. 1929). **DLC**
Fascist dictatorship in Britain.

1931   **Barzevi, A.H. and Marc F. Keller,** eds. [written by]. *Migrants of*

the Stars; Being an Account of the Discovery of the Marvelous Land of Niames, and of the Secrets of its Inhabitants. New York: Classic Press. **MoU-St**
> Two eutopias — isolated eutopia on earth with advanced technology, ESP, etc. and an eutopia on a distant planet Niames. Pictures of a variety of different cultures. Satire.

[1931] **Chilton, H. Herman.** *The Lost Children.* London: Hutchinson. **L**
> Pied Piper of Hamelin — eutopia formed where the children were taken. Simple life — arcadian. Crafts.

1931 **Collier, John.** *No Traveller Returns.* London: White Owl Press. **L**
> Future dystopia brought about by science. All animals are destroyed. Art, music, etc. eliminated.

1931 **Dalton, [Charles] Test.** *The Richest Man on Earth.* New York: Lowe Shearon. **DLC**
> Reformed capitalist eutopia founded in Africa by an American.

[1931] **[Hettinger, John.]** *Our Glorious Future. A Novel in Two Parts. The Miracle Child. The Battle of the Spirits,* by Johnhett (pseud.). London: C.W. Daniel. **L, MoU-St**
> Spiritual World contacts mankind; eutopia results.

1931 **Inge, W. R.** "The Future of the Human Race," Royal Institution of Great Britain, May 29. Pamphlet. **LLL**
> England about 3,000 A.D. Simple life — live in villages and small towns.

1931 **Johnson, Owen [McMahon].** *The Coming of the Amazons; A Sataristic Speculation on the Scientific Future of Civilization.* New York: Longmans, Green. **L**
> Sex-role reversal.

1931 **[Kirk, Mrs. Ellen Warner (Olney).]** *A Woman's Utopia,* by A Daughter of Eve (pseud.). London: Ernest Benn. **L, Pst**
> Two houses in Parliament, men's and women's. Ability and intelligence rewarded. Best salaries for worst work — e.g. mining.

1931 **McKenna, Stephen.** *Beyond Hell.* London: Chapman & Hall.
> Island of convicts. Two experimental societies — before and after revolution.

1931 **Meynell, Laurence.** *Storm Against the Wall.* Philadelphia: J.B. Lippincott. **MoU-St**
> Communist dystopia.

1931 **Schuette, H. George.** *The Grand Mysterious Secret Marriage Temple.* Manitowoc, Wisconsin: np. **DLC**
> Eugenics.

1931 **Wilkins, Hilliard.** *Altrurian Farms.* Washington, D.C.: Employ-

ment Extension Society. **DLC**
Communes in South America.

1932   **Baxter, Garrett.** *Rosma.* [Norfolk, Virginia:] Economic Press. **DLC**
Individualist eutopia. See also 1930 Baxter.

1932   **Blanchard, Charles Elton, M.D.** *A New Day Dawns. A Brief History of the Altruistic Era (1930 to 2162 A.D.) A.F. 200 Writing for Jane Bradshaw* (pseud.). *Historical Section, The National Library Service, Washington, D.C. A Diagnosis and a possible Prognosis of Our Present Social Order.* Youngstown, Ohio: Medical Success Press. **DLC, MoU-St**
Detailed eutopia. Science.

1932   **Coblentz, Stanton A.** *The Planet of Youth.* Los Angeles: Fantasy Pub. Co. **CoU**
Venus where people stay young. Men try to steal secret for earth — fail.

1932   **Croft-Cooke, Rupert.** *Cosmopolis.* London: Jarrolds. **L**
Perfect school — starts eutopia. Fails.

[1932]   **Dyson, S.S.** *The Melting Pot.* Dover, England: Dover Printing & Pub. **L, MoU-St**
Solution for depression — farm colonies.

1932   **Foster, Geo[rge] C.** *Awakening.* London: Chapman and Hall. **DLC**
Borderline — mostly a romance, but includes a few pages describing a conservative eutopia set in 1981. Monarchies have been restored in most of the world. Low taxes. Cars abolished.

1932   **Freese, Stanley.** *The Ten Year Plan; A Dream of 1940.* London: Cecil Palmer. **L**
Decentralization. Town Planning.

1932   **Hoke, Travis.** "Utopia By Thermometer," *North American Review,* 234 (August), 110–116.
Gradual warming of the earth and its social consequences.

1932   **Huxley, Aldous.** *Brave New World.* Garden City: Doubleday, Doran. **DLC**
Classic dystopia — drugs, promiscuity. Authoritarian.

1932   **James, Rowland.** *While England Slept.* London: John Bale, Sons & Danielsson. **L**
Religion. Return to the land.

1932   **[Jenkins, William F.]** "Politics," by Murray Leinster (pseud.), in *Future Tense,* edited by Richard Curtis (New York: Dell, 1968), pp. 138–167. Originally published in *Astounding Stories.*
Anti-pacifist.

1932   **Lawrence, James Cooper.** *The Year of Regeneration; An Impossible Fiction.* New York: Harper & Bros. **L, MoU-St**
Fascist eutopia.

1932   **Leacock, Stephen.** *Afternoons in Utopia; Tales of the New Time.* New York: Dodd, Mead. **L**
Humor — take-off on tales of utopia.

1932   **McCutchen, Duval.** *American Made Young; A Plan for a More Perfect Society.* Philadelphia: Humanities Pub. Co. **DLC**
New Constitution.

1932   **Martin, Prestonia Mann.** *Prohibiting Poverty. Being Suggestions for a Method of Obtaining Economic Security.* Winter Park, Florida: Rollins Press. **L, DLC**
Borderline — essay. Everyone must spend the ages 18-26 in industrial army.

1932   **O'Sheel, Shaemas.** *It Could Never Happen Or the Second American Revolution.* New York: Coventry House. **DLC**
Benevolent dictatorship.

1932   **Palmer, Frederick.** *So a Leader Came.* New York: Ray Long & Richard R. Smith. **L, DLC, NcD, MoU-St**
Period of transition to eutopia needs a strong leader.

1932   **Stapledon, W[illiam] Olaf.** *Last Men in London.* London: Methuen. **L, NcD**
Vintage Stapledon.

1932   **Tillyard, Aelfrida.** *The Approaching Storm.* London: Hutchinson. **L**
Communist dictatorship in Britain.

1932   **Whitham, John W.** *Interworld.* Seattle: Film Row Press. **MoU-St**
Includes an eutopia on Mars.

1932   **Wright, S. Fowler.** *The New Gods Lead.* London: Jarrolds. **L, MoU-St**
Connected stories picture a eugenic dystopia.

1933   **Arlen, Michael.** *Man's Mortality.* London: William Heinemann. **DLC, MoU-St**
Huge trust controls the world — fight for individual liberty.

1933   **[Brash, Margaret M.]** *Unborn Tomorrow,* by John Kendall (pseud.). London: W. Collins & Co. **L**
Anti-Communist dystopia.

1933   **Collier, John.** *Tom's A-Cold.* London: Macmillan. U.S. edition entitled *Full Circle*. **L, MoU-St**
Barbarianism.

1933   **Dearmer, Geoffrey.** *Saint on Holiday.* London: William Heinemann. **L, MoU-St**
Ministry of Grace — consumer advocates, government critics, etc. Gains power.

1933   **Dewey, John.** "Dewey Outlines Utopian Schools," *New York Times,* (April 23), Section 4, p. 7, columns 3–5.
Education in Utopia.

1933   **Gloag, John.** *The New Pleasure.* London: George Allen & Unwin. **DLC**
Enhanced power of smell. Cities gone — replaced by gardens. World unity.

1933   **Herrick, Robert.** *Sometime.* New York: Farrar & Rinehart. **NcD, MoU-St**
Technology. Labor army. Eugenics. Abundance.

1933   **Hilton, James.** *Lost Horizon.* New York: William Morrow & Co. **DLC**
Classic lost race eutopia. Longevity.

1933   **Holtby, Winifred.** *The Astonishing Island; Being a Veracious Record of the Experience Undergone by Robinson Lippingtree Mackintosh from Tristen Da Cunha during an Accidental Visit to an Unknown Territory in the Year of Grace MCMXXX____?* London: Lovat Dickson. **L**
Satire on English customs.

1933   **Hubbard, T[homas] O'B[rian].** *To-Morrow is a New Day.* [Kyrenia, Cyprus?:] np.
Use of an idealistic religious leader by capitalists. New religion founded to free men, but produces an authoritarian dystopia.

1933   **Knowles, W[illiam] P[lenderleith].** *Jim McWhirter.* London: C.W. Daniel. **DLC**
Emphasis on a leader who brings about eutopia, but includes a detailed plan.

[1933]   **Lewis, Henry.** *The Way Out: The Social Revolution in Retrospect. Viewed from A.D. 2050.* London: Elliot Stock. **L**
Socialist eutopia.

1933   **Manning, Laurence.** *The Man Who Awoke.* New York: Ballantine, 1975. Originally published in *Wonder Stories.*
Series of future dystopias; emphasizes dependence on machines.

1933   **Rizk, C.M.** *The Paradise City.* Philadelphia: [Latin Printing Co.]. **NN**
Isolated eutopia in California. Communal. Eugenics. No organized religion.

1933   **Sinclair, Upton.** *I, Governor of California and How I Ended Poverty. A True Story of the Future.* London: T. Werner Laurie. **L**
U.S. title: *I, Candidate for Governor and How I Got Licked.* Sinclair's vision of the future after he has been elected Gov-

ernor of California. Compare his *How I Got Licked and Why* (1935).

1933   **[Southwold, Stephen.]** *Death Rocks the Cradle,* by Paul Martens (pseud.). London: Collins. **L**
Over-concern with health leads to an authoritarian dystopia.

1933   **Wells, H.G.** *The Shape of Things to Come.* New York: Macmillan. **DLC**
Detailed future world state.

1934   **Beard, Charles A.** "The World As I Want It." *Forum,* 91 (June), 332–334.
Workers' republic. Decentralized industry.

[1934]   *The Book of Life.* [Hamilton, Ontario: np.]. **MH**
Government ownership. Religion. Detailed universal language.

1934   **Bradley, Dr. Charles M.** *Me-Phi Bo-Sheth (If The Gods So Decide). An Undated Manuscript.* Chicago: Chicago Printing & Pub. Co. **DLC**
Detailed reform.

1934   **Cooke, David Ewin.** *The History of Lewistonia.* Point Highest: Cooke Pub. Co. **NcD**
Toy city developed by children. Includes a constitution.

1934   **Curtis, Monica.** *Landslide.* London: Victor Gollancz. **L**
Borderline — political novel set in a future political system.

1934   **Dunsany, Lord.** *If I Were Dictator.* London: Methuen. **L**
Satire but includes a series of reforms.

1934   **Ervine, St. John.** *If I Were Dictator.* London: Methuen. **L**
Series of reforms.

1934   **Hathaway, Hanson.** *The Utopians Are Coming; A New Interpretation of Constitutional Americanism.* Hollywood: Cloister Press. **DLC**
Utopian Society of America, Inc. New Monetary system.

1934   **Hoyne, Thomas Temple.** *Intrigue on the Upper Level: A Story of Crime, Love, Adventure and Revolt.* Chicago: Reilly and Lee. **UU, MoU-St**
Rigid class division — employed and unemployed. Luxury and dissipation vs. homelessness. Revolt succeeds. Better society will come.

1934   **Huxley, Julian.** *If I Were Dictator.* London: Methuen. **L, DLC**
Detailed reform. Application of the scientific method to the problems of dictatorship.

1934   **Lemieux, Pierre.** *Universalism, The New Spirit, A Reborn World, Earthly Happiness, The Ideal State!!! A Book dealing with a new social system destined to solve the present irksome problems* *of the world — Peace, disarmament, social improvement, international union and financial recovery.* Montreal: Printed by Standard Sample Card Co. **DLC**

World federalism. Religious cooperation. Regulated economy. One language.

1934 **Mitchell, J[ames] Leslie.** *Gay Hunter.* London: William Heinemann. **L, NcD, MoU-St**

Authoritarian dystopia leads to barbarianism.

1934 **Mosely, Maboth.** *War Upon Women; A Topical Drama.* London: Hutchinson. **L, NN**

Authoritarian dystopia.

1934 **Raglan, Lord.** *If I Were Dictator.* London: Methuen. **L**

A number of reforms.

1934 **Reitmeister, Louis Aaron.** *If Tomorrow Comes.* New York: The Walden Press. **NcD**

Detailed eutopia. No laws. Equality of the sexes. Suburban life.

1934 **Sumner, Park.** *Tomorrow Comes; A Story of Hope.* Akron, Ohio: Artcraft Printing & Pub. Co. **NN**

Cooperative commonwealth based on 1888 Bellamy.

1934 **Webb, Charles T[homas].** *The Kingdom Within; The Relation of Personal Character to the Problems of the World Without.* New York: Macmillan. **DLC**

Borderline — essay, but presents a Christian eutopia.

1934 **Weston, George.** *His First Million Women.* New York: Farrar Rinehart. **DLC**

Humor — all men but one die.

1934 **Whitman, John Pratt.** *Utopia Dawns.* Boston: Utopia Publishing Co. **DLC, NcD, MoU-St**

Mostly a survey of past utopias, but includes a short original eutopia. Communal.

1934 **Yerex, Cuthbert.** *Christopher Brand; Looking Forward.* Los Angeles; Wetzel Pub. Co. **DLC, NcD**

Socialist eutopia. Emphasis is on the struggle for acceptance.

1935 **Bartlett, Vernon.** *If I Were Dictator.* London: Methuen. **L**

Benevolent dictatorship and its failures. Series of reforms.

1935 **Borglum, Gutzon.** "The World As I Want It," *Forum,* 93 (February), 112–113.

Series of reforms.

[1935] **Brockway, [Archibald] Fenner.** *Purple Plague; A Tale of Love and Revolution.* London: Sampson, Low & Marston. **L**

Egalitarian eutopia on a ship.

1935 **Conquest, Joan.** *With the Lid Off.* London: T. Werner Laurie. **L, DLC**
Benevolent dictatorship.

1935 **[Cory, Vivian.]** *Martha Brown M.P.; A Girl of To-Morrow,* by Victoria Cross (pseud.). London: T. Werner Laurie. **L**
Sex-role reversal.

1935 **Frank, Robert.** *Social Integration; A Brief Fictional History of the United States during the Period 1935–1945.* Boston: Christopher Pub. House. **DLC, MoU-St**
Eutopia through unionism.

1935 **[Frazer, James Ian Arbuthot.]** *A Shroud as Well as a Shirt,* by Shamus Frazer (pseud.). London: Chapman & Hall. **L**
Fascist takeover in England.

1935 **Goldsmith, John Francis.** *President Randolph; as I Knew Him. An account of the historic events of the 1950's and 1960's written from the personal experiences of the secretary to the President.* Philadelphia: Dorrance. **MoU-St, DLC**
United Nations of the World — includes constitution.

1935 **Gotthelf, Ezra Gerson.** *The Island of Not-Me. A True Chronicle of the Life of Geoghan Willbe on the Island of Not-Me, preceded by an Account of His Person before His Arrival upon that famous Isle.* New York: Galleon Press. **MoU-St, DLC, NcD**
Satire — dystopia.

1935 **Gresswell, Elsie Kay.** *When Yvonne Was Dictator.* London: John Heritage. **L**
Benevolent dictator.

1935 **Hawkins, Willard E.** *Castaways of Plenty; A Parable of Our Times.* New York: Basic Books. **MoU-St**
Satire on capitalism.

[1935] **[Hunter, Bluebell Matilda.]** *Fraudulent Conversion. A Romance of the Gold Standard,* by George Lancing (pseud.). London: Stanley Paul. **L**
Fight for reform against fascists.

1935 **Lewis, Sinclair.** *It Can't Happen Here.* New York: Doubleday Doran. **DLC**
Fascism in the United States.

1935 **Maxton, James.** *If I Were Dictator.* London: Methuen. **L**
Series of reforms.

1935 **Meyer, John J[oseph].** *Thirteen Seconds that Rocked the World, or the Mentator.* New York: Rae D. Henkle. **NcD, DLC**
ESP.

[1935] **Norman, Alfred.** *The Best Is Yet To Be; A Forecast of the Perfect Social State.* London: James Clarke. **L**
Democratic socialism.

1935   **O'Neill, Joseph.** *Land Under England.* New York: Simon & Schuster. **L, MoU-St**
Fascist dystopia.

1935   **Parker, Joseph W.** *Doctor Crosby's Strange Experience.* Kansas City, Missouri: The Peerage Press. **DLC**
Socialist eutopia.

1935   **Pier, Arthur Stanwood.** *God's Secret.* New York: Charles Scribner's Sons. **DLC**
Life without death. Last chapter describes a very general eutopia of peace and plenty.

1935   **Read, Herbert.** *The Green Child.* London: William Heinemann. **L, MoU-St**
Two imaginary countries. First is located in South America — benevolent dictatorship. Second is under England — mental perfection is the goal.

1935   **Rhondda, Margaret Haig.** "The World As I Want It," *Forum,* 93 (February), 243.
Series of reforms.

1935   **Sheppard, H.R.L.** *If I Were Dictator.* London: Methuen. **L**
Church reform.

1935   **Trevarthan, Hal [Harold] P.** *World D; Being a Brief Account of the Founding of Helioxenon,* edited by J.K. Heydon. New York: Sheed & Ward. **DLC, MoU-St**
Borderline — sphere in the center of the world that will become an eutopia.

1935   **Ward, Richard Heron.** *The Sun Shall Rise.* London: Ivor Nicholson & Watson. **L, DLC**
Fascist dystopia.

1935   **Wilson, Clarence True.** "The World As I Want It." *Forum,* 93 (June), 375.
Series of reforms.

1935   **Wilson, Henry Lovejoy,** "Of Lunar Kingdoms; A Group of Informal Essays." Unpublished doctoral dissertation, State University of Iowa. Published: Caldwell, Idaho: Caxton Printers, 1937.
Series of eutopias.

1935   **[Wybraniec, Peter Frank.]** *Speratia,* by Dr. Raphael W. Leonhart (pseud.). Boston: Meador Pub. Co. **DLC**
Detailed eutopia. Religion. State supervision of all education. Emphasis on vocational education. Candidate for public office must pass examinations. Anti-equalitarian.

1936   **Allen, Henry Ware.** *Prosperity In the Year 2000 A.D. Achieved by Democratic Steps As the natural result of abolishing all taxes upon business, industry, commerce and agriculture, leaving for the necessary expenses of government its natural revenue, eco-*

nomic rent as determined by the site value of land. As presented
in a series of conversations between Justin Waterson, a retired
Chicago merchant, eight-five years of age, and his grandson,
Charles Waterson, aged seventeen. A Challenge to State
Socialism. Boston: Christopher Pub. House. **DLC**
Single Tax.

1936   **Armstrong, C[harles] Wicksteed.** *Paradise Found or Where the Sex
Problem has been solved (A Story from South America).*
London: John Bale, Sons & Danielsson. **L**
Eugenics. Natural position of women — child rearing,
domestic labor. Men — combat, work.

1936   **Balsdon, [John Percy Vyvian] Dacre.** *Sell England?* London: Eyre
and Spottiswoode.
Satire on 20th Century England set in the future.

1936   **[Bayley, Victor.]** *The Machine Stops,* by Wayland Smith (pseud.).
London: Robert Hale.
Disaster dystopia — all metal disintegrates.

1936   **Cunningham, Beall.** *The Wide, White Page.* London: Hutchinson.
L, O
Colony of men in Antarctica. It is harmonious until the first
woman arrives. Men decide to keep the harmony.

1936   **Gorer, Geoffrey.** *Nobody Talks Politics; A Satire with an Appendix
on Our Political Intelligentsia.* London: Michael Joseph. **L**
Dystopia — fascism brought about by lack of concern.

1936   **Herbert, Benson.** *Crisis! 1992.* London: Richards. **L**
World inside a planet — perfect physical surrounding.

1936   **Hill, William Boyle.** *A New Earth and A New Heaven.* London:
Watts & Co. **L**
Two utopias. Hopetown — model town for workers. Cf.
Edward Everett Hale, *How They Lived in Hampton.* Dawn
City — eugenics. Vegetarian. No religion. No money. Health
examination every three months. Standardized dress.

1936   **Jameson, [Margaret] Storm.** *In the Second Year.* London: Cassell.
L
Authoritarian dystopia.

1936   **Lockhart-Mummery, J[ohn] P[ercy].** *After Us; or, The World As It
Might Be.* London: Stanley Paul. **L**
Written as a projection. Eugenics. Chemical food. Anti-
socialist. Technology. Reason.

1936   **Lyons, Edgar Albion.** *The Chosen Race.* [St. Petersburg, Florida:]
The Cavalier Pub. Co. **DLC**
Machine dystopia.

1936   **Macassey, Kenneth.** *Collective Insecurity.* London: Longmans,

Green & Co. **MoU-St**
Dystopian satire on a future German empire.

1936   **Meredith, Edgar.** *Our Stranger; A Kinemato-Romance.* London: Grayson & Grayson. **NcD, L, MoU-St**
Two utopias — far future a Stapledonian vision. 1970's — communal eutopia.

1936   **Nelson, Albert D.** *America Betrayed; Save the Nation.* Los Angeles: Suttonhouse. **DLC**
Anti-Japanese dystopia.

1936   **Nicolaides, Nicholas.** *At the Dawn of the Millenium; A Scientific and Philosophical Treatise for the Advancement of Knowledge and the Promotion of World Peace.* San Diego: City Printing Co. **DLC, NcD**
Short future eutopia — world-wide, universal language, rural, detached houses, machinery.

1936   **Palmer, John [Horsley].** *The Hesperides; A Looking-Glass Fugue.* London: Martin Secker & Warburg. **L, MoU-St**
Dystopia. Art and imagination discouraged. No emotions. Eating and sleeping completely private, considered impolite.

1936   **[Samuels, Philip Francis.]** *Bensalem and New Jerusalem,* by Samuels-Bacon (pseud.). Boston: Samuels-Bacon Pub. Co. **L, DLC**
Continuation of New Atlantis. Conservative. Christian. Political representation by trade or profession.

1936   **Sinclair, Upton.** *Co-op. A Novel of Living: Together.* London: T. Werner Laurie. **L**
Cooperative system. Consensus.

1936   **Van Polen, Herman.** *The Master Plan: Government Without Taxation.* Boston: Christopher Pub. Co. **MoU-St**
One corporation takes over the assets of the United States and brings eutopia.

1936   **Wolf, Howard.** *Greener Pastures; A Fable of Past, Present and Future.* Caldwell, Idaho: The Caxton Printers. **NcD**
Satire — God has illusions of grandeur, thinks he's F.D.R.

1937   **Allott, Kenneth and Stephen Tait.** *The Rhubarb Tree.* London: The Cresset Press. **DLC**
Fascist dystopia.

1937   **Constantine, Murray** (pseud.). *Swastika Night.* London: Victor Gollancz. **L**
500 years of Nazi rule.

1937   **Green, A. Romney.** *To-morrow's Art and Recreation.* London: Vanguard Press. **LSE**
Return to handicrafts. Minimum Wage.

1937   **[Jaffe, Hyman.]** *Abdera and the Revolt of the Asses,* by Alterego (pseud.). New York: Clarion Pub. Co. **DLC**
Satire using the imaginary country approach.

1937   **McCrea, Paul.** "Utopia and/or Bust," *Nation's Business,* 25 (August), 15–17, 62, 66, 68, 70.
Satire — business collapses when everyone is given gold. No one will work.

1937   **Pritcher, Jacob Leon.** *A Love Starved World.* Los Angeles: The Yale Pub. Co. **DLC**
Emphasis on good medical care, healthy sex life. Eugenics.

1937   **Serly, Ludovicus Textoris.** *Stop! ...Distracted People! Two Mirrors of the Future. Romantic Double Utopia.* New York: Bookcraft. [Stamped above publisher's name: Published by L.T. Serly]. **DLC**
Small town and rural eutopia after disastrous earthquakes.

1937   **[Smith, David Eugene.]** *Every Man a Millionaire; A Balloon Trip in the Mathematical Stratosphere of Social Relations.* New York: Scripta Mathematica. **NcD**
Mathematician brings rational eutopia.

1937   **Stapledon, [William] Olaf.** *Star-Maker.* London: Methuen. **DLC, L**
Classic Stapledon.

1937   **[Warde, Beatrice.]** *The Shelter in Bedlam,* by Paul Beaujon (pscud.). Privately printed. Also entitled *Peace Under Earth; Dialogues from the Year 1946.* **DLC, L**
Dystopia — everyone living in bomb shelters.

[1938]   **Anson, August.** *When Woman Reigns.* Oxford: Pen-in-Hand Pub. Co. **L**
Sex-role reversal.

1938   **DeForest, Eleanor.** *Armageddon; A Tale of the Anti-Christ.* Grand Rapids, Michigan: Wm. B. Eerdmans Publishing Co. **MoU-St**
Dystopia — stress on struggle of good and evil.

1938   **Desmond, Shaw.** *World-Birth.* London: Methuen. **DLC**
Education. Cooperative system — production for use, not profit.

1938   **Lewis, C.S.** *Out of the Silent Planet.* London: The Bodley Head. **L**
First of trilogy on struggle between good and evil. Presents an eutopia as a sub-theme.

1938   **Macowan, Norman.** *Glorious Morning; A Play in Three Acts.* London: Victor Gollancz. **L**
Authoritarian dystopia.

1938   **Marvell, Andrew.** *Minimum Man or Time To Be Gone.* London: Victor Gollancz. **L, MoU-St**
Fascist dystopia.

1938 **Morris, M[artha] Marlowe and Laura B. Speer.** *No Borderland.* Dallas: Mathis, Van Nort. **DLC, NcD**
  Atlantis — agrarian, tribal, spiritualist eutopia.

1938 **Watts, Newman.** *The Man Who Could Not Sin.* New York: Fleming H. Revell. Also entitled *The Man Who Did Not Sin.* **L, DLC, MoU-St**
  Christ on the throne as the world ruler.

1938 **Williams, Robert Moore.** "Flight of the Dawn Stars," in *A Treasury of Science Fiction,* edited by Groff Conklin (New York: Crown, 1948), pp. 358–369. **DLC**
  Future Eden.

1938 **Wright, S[ydney] Fowler.** *The Adventure of Wyndham Smith.* London: Herbert Jenkins. **L**
  Machine dystopia.

1939 **Buckle, Richard.** *John Innocent at Oxford.* London: Chatto and Windus. **DLC**
  Adventures in a reformed Oxford (no industry, no suburbs) that has replaced London as the center of English life.

1939 **Churchill, A.T.** *The New Industrial Dawn.* Seattle: Press of Lowman and Hanford Co. **DLC**
  Abundance through State Capitalism. Meritocracy.

1939 **Hamilton, Patrick.** *Impromptu in Moribundia.* London: Constable and Co. **L**
  Satire — caste system.

1939 **Meredith, James Creed.** *The Rainbow in the Valley.* Dublin: Brown and Nolan. **MoU-St**
  Mars as eutopia. Stories on the solutions to the problems of nationalism.

1939 **St. John, Arthur.** *Why Not Now? A Britiish Islander's Dream.* London: C.W. Daniel. **L, MoU-St**
  More simple life, stressing neighborhoods.

1939 **Sullivan, Philip A[loysius].** *Man Finds the Way.* New York: Margent Press. **DLC, MoU-St**
  Religion. United States of the World. National Peace Institute — educate for peace.

1939 **Todd, Ruthven.** *Over the Mountain.* London: George G. Harrap. **L, DLC**
  Authoritarian dystopia.

1939 **Wells, H.G.** *The Holy Terror.* New York: Simon and Schuster. **DLC**
  Problems of leadership — unusual man who leads man toward a good life also develops dictatorial tendencies.

1939 **Whitehouse, J[ohn] Howard.** *Visit to Utopia.* Oxford: Oxford Uni-

versity Press. **L**
    Short talk — naive eutopia.

[194–]   **Cramer, John D.** *The Trumpet.* London: Silk and Terry.
    Machine perfection eutopia is really dystopia.

1940   **Auden, W. H.** "The Unknown Citizen."
    Borderline — poem. Dystopia.

[1940]   **Brown, Douglas and Christopher Serpell.** *Loss of Eden.* London:
    Faber and Faber. Also entitled *If Hitler Comes.* **L**
    Dystopia — Germany wins World War II.

1940   **Cruso, Solomon.** *Messiah on the Horizon. Romance? Novel?*
    Revelation? Prophecy? Reality? New York: Audubon Pub.
    Co. **MoU-St**
    End of the white race. Better society brought about by Orientals and Jews.

1940   **Denturk, Henry C[ornelius].** *Vision of a State of Rightness on a*
    Spiritual Foundation. A Short Outline of Government Whereby
    All Men Have the Same Rights and Privileges With the Capi-
    talistic System Abolished. Huntington, New York: Author. **DLC**
    Religion. Communal eutopia.

1940   **Gieske, Herman Everett.** *Utopia, Inc.* New York: Fortuny's. **DLC,**
    NcD, MoU-St
    Capitalist, scientific eutopia. Stress on battle with Communism.

1940   **Gilbert, J[ohn] W[ilmer].** *The Marsian.* New York: Fortuny's.
    DLC
    Detailed egalitarian eutopia.

1940   **Glenn, Geo[rge] A[lan], M.D.** *When Loneliness Comes.* Denver:
    Author. **MoU-St, DLC, ICRL**
    Lost race eutopia. Emphasis on sexual activity as essential to health.

1940   **Gloag, John.** *Manna.* London: Cassell and Co. **L**
    Manna (a plant that provides complete nourishment) grows
    wild. A reformation of social and political institutions begins
    and is suppressed. Manna is destroyed by governments.

1940   **Hicks, Granville with Richard M. Bennett.** *The First to Awaken.*
    New York: Modern Age Books. **MoSW**
    Socialist eutopia.

1940   **Kühnelt-Leddihn, Erik Von and Christiane Von.** *Moscow 1979.*
    London: Sheed & Ward. **L, DLC**
    Anti-Communist dystopia.

1940   **Langner, Lawrence and Armine Marshall.** *Suzanna and the Elders;*
    An American Comedy. New York: Random House. **DLC**
    Failure of a commune.

1940   **O'Den, Daniel.** *Crimson Courage.* London: Frederick Muller. **L**
        Authoritarian dystopia.

1940   **Smart, Charles Allen.** *Rosscommon.* New York: Random House.
        NcD
        Commune.

1940   **Unwin, J.D.** *Hopousia; or The Sexual and Economic Foundations
        of a New Society.* London: George Allen and Unwin. [Published
        posthumously — written 1935–36]. **L, DLC**
        Detailed eutopia — emphasis on sexual and economic
        foundations.

1941   **Alington, Adrian [Richard].** *Sanity Island.* London: Chatto and
        Windus. **L, MoU-St**
        Satire — humorous rearmament.

[1941] **Beresford, J[ohn] D[avys].** *A Common Enemy.* London: Hutchin-
        son. **L, MoU-St**
        Disaster followed by a socialist eutopia.

[1941] **Beresford, J[ohn] D[avys].** *"What Dreams May Come...."* Lon-
        don: Hutchinson. **L**
        Communal eutopia. Significant changes in man's physical
        characteristics.

1941   **Jameson, Malcolm.** *Tarnished Utopia.* New York: Galaxy, 1956.
        Galaxy Science Fiction Novel No. 27. **MoU-St**
        Authoritarian dystopia.

1941   **Twiford, William Richard.** *Sown in the Darkness A.D. 2,000.* New
        York: Orlin Tremaine. **DLC**
        Racist, anti-communist. Struggle between whites and col-
        oreds. Whites win, enforce segregation. Includes an appendix
        describing a new currency and the possibilities of technology.

1941   **Walton, Nathan.** *Utopia Right Around the Corner. Non-Factual.
        A Story of Fiction Told As If It Were Factual.* Long Beach: H.J.
        Kemp Co. **DLC**
        Social scientists bring about eutopia — abolish politicians.
        Scientific administration.

1941   **Williamson, Jack.** "Breakdown," in his *People Machines,* (New
        York: Ace, 1971), pp. 154–187. Originally published in *Astound-
        ing.*
        Dystopia — union domination.

1941   **Wilson, Philip Whitewell.** *Newtopia; The World We Want.* New
        York: Charles Scribner's Sons. **L, MoU-St**
        Common sense, the common man, home, family and the New
        Deal.

1942   **Davenport, Basil.** *An Introduction to Islandia: its history, customs,
        laws, language, and geography as prepared by Basil Davenport
        from "Islandia: History and Description" by Jean Perrier, first*

French Consul to Islandia, and translated by John Lang, first American Consul. With Maps drawn by John Lang. Toronto: Farrar and Rinehart. **DLC**
Materials supplemental and introductory to 1942 Wright.

1942   **Hall, Hal [Harold Curtis].** *The Great Conflict.* Los Angeles: Printed by the Haynes Corp. **DLC**
New Deal becomes eutopia.

1942   **Jameson, [Margaret] Storm.** *Then We Shall Hear Singing; A Fantasy in C Major.* London: Cassell. **L**
Fascist dystopia.

[1942?]   **Johnson, Frank R.** *Is This Utopia? A Plan of Life in the Post-War World.* Manchester: Perry Brothers Ltd.
Detailed plan for a new economic system.

1942   **Loomis, Noel.** *City of Glass.* New York: Columbia Publishers, 1955. **MoU-St**
Authoritarian dystopia.

1942   **Morton, H[enry Canova] V[ollom].** *I, James Blunt.* London: Methuen. **DLC**
Dystopia — Germany wins World War II.

1942   **Posnack, E[manuel] Robert.** *The 21st Century Sizes Us Up.* np.: np. **DLC**
Introduction to 1946 Posnack.

1942   **Sackville-West, Victoria Mary.** *Grand Canyon.* London: Michael Joseph. **L, DLC**
Dystopia — Germany wins World War II.

1942   **Samuel, Viscount [Herbert Louis].** *An Unknown Land.* London: George Allen and Unwin. **NcD, MoU-St**
New Atlantis. Science. Health.

1942   **Stapledon, [William] Olaf.** *Darkness and the Light.* London: Methuen. **L**
Two alternative future histories, good and bad.

1942   **Van Dalsem, Newton.** *History of the Utopian Society of America; An Authentic Account of Its Origin and Development Up to 1942.* Los Angeles: The Utopian Society. Parts originally published in *The Roman Forum* in 1939 as "Utopias, Past and Present." **DLC**
Detailed reform.

1942   **Wright, Austin Tappan.** *Islandia.* New York: Rinehart and Co. **DLC**
Classic agrarian eutopia. See also 1942 Davenport and 1969 Saxton.

1943   **Dardenelle, Louise.** *World Without Raiment. A Fantasy.* New York: Valiant Press. **DLC, MoU-St**
Nudist eutopia.

[1943]   **Finigan, G. Lysaght.** *Anno Domini 1963.* Liverpool: Direct Publicity Co. **LSE**
        Many reforms.

1943   **Fuller, Ralph.** *The Future Revealed in the Wisdom of Chiska Ru.* Vancouver: Atlas Printers. **CaBViPA**
        Cooperative eutopia.

1943   **Hawkin[s], Martin.** *When Adolf Came.* London: Jarrold's Ltd. **DLC**
        Germany wins, but the English fight on.

1943   **Kearney, [Elfric Wells] Chalmers.** *Erōne.* Guildford, England: Biddles Ltd. **L**
        Detailed eutopia — many technical advances, based on love and cooperation.

1943   **Lewis, C.S.** *Perelandra.* London: The Bodley Head. **L**
        Re-enactment of Adam and Eve myth on Venus — no Fall.

1943   **Maugham, Robin [Robert Cecil Romer].** *The 1946 Ms.* London: War Facts Press. **L, DLC, LSE**
        Fascist dystopia.

1943   **Zahn, Oswald Francis.** *Let's Triumverate or Man, Government and Happiness. A Philosophy of Man and a World-Wide Government Founded Upon Laws of Nature.* San Diego: Author. **DLC**
        Detailed eutopia based on truth.

1943   **Zori, Henri.** *America's Sin Offering; The Budget Balancer.* Boston: Bruce Humphries. **DLC**
        Virtually incomprehensible — authoritarian.

[1944]   **Ardrey, Robert.** *Worlds Beginning.* New York: Duell, Sloan and Pearce. **L**
        Democratic control of individual corporations.

1944   **[Baruch, Hugo Cyril K.]** *Common Sense. Is It Wrong To Be Right? Is It Right To Be Wrong?,* by Jack Bilbo (pseud.). London: Modern Art Gallery, Ltd. **L**
        Borderline — anti-capitalist essay, but it does present some elements of an eutopia.

[1944]   **Beresford, J[ohn] D[avys] and Esme Wynne-Tyson.** *The Riddle of the Tower.* London: Hutchinson. **MH**
        Series of past societies. Anti-utopian.

1944   **Gallego, S[erapio] G[onzalez].** *John Smith, Emperor.* St. Paul: Guild Press. **MoU-St, DLC**
        Authoritarian eutopia. Everything immoral (e.g. divorce) is illegal.

1944   **Gunn, Neil M.** *The Green Isle of the Great Deep.* London: Faber and Faber. Reprinted: [London:] Souvenir Press, 1975. **L**

Heaven as an authoritarian dystopia. Takeover by those attempting to achieve social perfection while God is busy meditating.

1944   **Hughes. W.J. Keith.** *That Would Be Living; A New Outlet for Capital and Character.* Vol. 1 of his *Invitation to Life.* Aldham, Essex: Mundist Press. **L, DLC**
Detailed reforms.

1944   **Kerr, Frank R[obinson].** *Days After Tomorrow; A Voice from 2000 A.D.* Melbourne: Robertson and Mullens. **NN**
World Parliament. Science. Religion.

1944   **King-Hall, Lou.** *Fly Envious Time.* London: Peter Davies. **L**
1979 — Science, eugenics, control. 1999 — World War III.

1944   **Lessner, Erwin [Christian].** *Phantom Victory; The Fourth Reich 1945–1960.* New York: G.P. Putnam's Sons. **DLC**
German officers form underground after defeat. Conquer world.

[1944]   **Mannin, Ethel Edith.** *Bread and Roses; An Utopian Survey and Blue-print.* London: McDonald and Co. **NcD**
Detailed eutopia based on freedom, equality and brotherhood. No central government or state. Equal distribution of goods.

[1944]   **[Milkomane, George Alexis Milkomanovich.]** *Peace in Nobody's Time,* by George Borodin (pseud.). London: Hutchinson. **L**
Satire — socialist dictatorship.

1944   **Stapledon, [William] Olaf.** *Old Man in New World.* London: George Allen & Unwin. **L**
Standard socialist eutopia encouraging diversity and individuality. Doubts expressed at the end — leaders attempt to manipulate the population.

1944   **Vigers, Daphne.** *Atlantis Rising.* London: Andrew Dakers. **DLC**
Detailed eutopia — stress on cooperation and education.

1945   **[Blair, Eric.]** *Animal Farm; A Fairy Story,* by George Orwell (pseud.). London: Secker & Warburg.
Classic story of totalitarianism.

1945   **Dwiggins, W[illiam] A[ddison].** *Millenium 1.* New York: Knopf. **DLC**
Machines revolt; man struggles to regain control.

[1945]   **Erdahl, Silvert.** *The Devil's Altar Boy.* Washington, D.C.: Capitol Hill Press. **MoU-St**
Eutopian allegory — Germans and Japanese had won World War II and produced a second Dark Ages.

1945   **Lewis, C.S.** *That Hideous Strength, A Modern Fairy Tale for Grown Ups.* London: John Lane. Also entitled *The Tortured Planet.*

Final volume of a trilogy of struggle between the forces of good and evil. Good wins.

1945 **McElhiney, Gaile Churchill.** *Into the Dawn.* Los Angeles: Del Vorsa. **DLC**
Eutopia for the spiritually advanced on an isolated island.

1945 **[Rogers, Frederick Rand.]** *Prelude to Peace,* by Count Sussicran Etoxinod (pseud.). Cupertino, California: North American Physical Fitness Institute Bulletin 10. **DLC**
Unification under one world leader chosen by the best educators, who, with priests, are ineligible. One language, one religion. No competition.

1945 **Scott, F[rancis] R[eginald].** *"Mural,"* in his *Overture* (Toronto: Ryerson Press, 1945), pp. 59–60. **L**
Poem — utopian satire. Pictures perfect world through science, but tone is satirical.

1945 **Weaver, Wertie Clarice.** *The Valley of the Poor.* Los Angeles: Wetzel Pub. Co. **MoU-St**
Science cures racial prejudice and brings eutopia.

1945 **Weiss, Jiri.** *The Lost Government; or, Do You Like It? A Fairy Tale for Grown-ups.* London: Nicholson & Watson. **L**
Government in exile returns; people have taken over. Government leaves.

[1946] **Chetwynd, Bridget.** *Future Imperfect.* London: Hutchinson. **L**
Sex-role reversal.

1946 **Ernst, Morris L.** *Utopia 1976.* New York: Rinehart & Co.
Borderline — prophecy of the future which is a detailed eutopia.

1946 **Gross, Werter L[ivingston].** *The Golden Recovery revealing a streamlined cooperative Economic System compiled from the best authorities of the World, both ancient and modern.* [Hollywood: Murray & Gee]. **DLC**
Hero is black. Commune on Owenite principles.

1946 **Hine, Muriel.** *The Island Forbidden to Man.* London: Hodder and Stoughton. **MoU-St**
Island inhabited only by women. Feminist eutopia for a time.

1946 **Joseph, Marie G[ertrude] Holmes.** *Balance the Universe or The Heavenly Abode.* New York: Hobson Brook Press. **DLC**
Weird, but an eutopia.

1946 **Martin, Peter.** *Summer in 3000. Not a prophecy — A parable.* London: Quality Press. **L**
ESP. Eugenics. Totally artificial world.

[1946] **Mottram, R[alph] H[ale].** *Visit of the Princess; A Romance of the Nineteen-sixties.* London: Hutchinson & Co. **L, DLC, MoU-St**
Romance set in a dull, egalitarian dystopia.

1946   **Posnack, Emanuel R[obert].** *The 21st Century Looks Back.* New York: The William-Frederick Press. **DLC**
        Reformed capitalist eutopia.

1946   **Rand, Ayn.** *Anthem.* Los Angeles: Pamphleteers. **DLC, MoU-St**
        Written in 1937. Authoritarian dystopia. Sketches of an individualist eutopia.

1946   **Wolf, Frederick Ellsworth.** *God's Fool!* Wellesley, Mass.: New Age Publications. **DLC, MoU-St**
        Mother and son leave the Amana Colony to experience the life of the world. Experience poverty, war, America's rejection of God. Return to Amana.

1947   **De Chair, Somerset.** *The Teetotalitarian State.* London: Falcon Press. **L**
        Humor — coming of British socialism — nothing changes.

1947   **Heard, H[enry] F[itzgerald].** *Doppelgangers; An Episode of the Fourth, The Psychological, Revolution 1997.* New York: Vanguard Press. **L**
        Dystopia — an eutopia supposed to be brought about by new advances in psychology, turns sour and becomes an authoritarian dystopia based on the same discoveries.

1947   **Keppel-Jones, Arthur.** *When Smuts Goes. A History of South Africa from 1952 to 2010, first published in 2015.* London: Victor Gollancz. **DLC, NcD**
        Barbarianism.

1947   **Kuttner, Henry.** *Fury.* New York: Grosset & Dunlap, 1950. Originally published under pseudonym Lawrence O'Donnell. **IaU**
        Future on Venus of a degenerated mankind living in safety and the successful struggle to re-vitalize the people.

1947   **Matthews, Carleton.** *Flight to Utopia.* Trenton, New Jersey: Mount Eyre Pub. Co. **NcD, MoK, MoU-St**
        Detailed eutopia — no money, labor is the medium of exchange. Evolution to utopia in 25 years.

1947   **Nabokov, Vladimir.** *Bend Sinister.* New York: Holt. **DLC**
        Authoritarian dystopian setting.

1947   **Neville, Derek.** *Bright Morrow.* London: John Crowther.
        Future conflict between democratic societies and communists. Projection of better society.

1947   **Pedroso, Felix and Elizabeth Pedroso.** *The World The World Wants (A Sociocratic Order).* Sao Paulo, Brazil: np. **DLC**
        Capitalist eutopia — one world corporation.

1947   **Staniland, Meaburn.** *Back to the Future.* London: Nicholas Vane. **L**
        Authoritarian, bureaucratic dystopia.

1947   **[Van Zeller, Claude Hubert.]** *The End, A Projection, Not a Prophecy.* London: Douglas Organ. **L**
    Set in 2045 at the end of 100 years of peace. Coming of Christ.

1947   **Williamson, Jack.** "The Equalizer," in his *The Pandora Effect* (New York: Ace, 1969), pp. 127–189.
    Eutopia of abundant power — agrarian, anarchist.

1947   *"Worlds to Watch and Ward," in The Quest for Utopia; An Anthology of Imaginary Societies,* edited by Glenn Negley and J. Max Patrick (New York: Henry Schumann, 1952), pp. 592–599.
    Rule of law, democratic socialism.

1948   **[Burton, Elizabeth.]** *The Roaring Dove,* by Susan Kerby (pseud.). New York: Dodd, Mead. **TxU**
    Satire — anti-socialist.

1948   **Colvin, Ian.** *Domesday Village.* London: Falcon Press. **L**
    Agrarian eutopia.

1948   **De Camp, L. Sprague and Fletcher Pratt.** *The Carnelian Cube; A Humorous Fantasy.* New York: Gnome Press. **DLC**
    Series of worlds — satire.

1948   **De Camp, L. Sprague.** "The Stolen Dormouse," in his *Divide and Rule* (Reading, Pennsylvania: Fantasy Press, 1948), pp. 139–231. **DLC**
    Future dystopia — feudalism based on corporations.

1948   **Green, Henry.** *Concluding.* London: Hogarth Press. **MoU-St**
    Authoritarian dystopia.

1948   **Groom, [Arthur John] Pelham.** *The Purple Twilight.* London: T. Werner Laurie. **L**
    Mars dwindling due to an anti-marriage ideology that saw marriage as being only to man's advantage.

1948   **Heinlein, Robert A.** *Beyond This Horizon.* Reading, Pennsylvania: Fantasy Press. **DLC**
    Conflict over eugenic planning.

1948   **Huxley, Aldous.** *Ape and Essence.* New York: Harper. **DLC**
    Dystopia of post-atomic war.

1948   **Laski, Marghanita.** *Tory Heaven; or Thunder on the Right.* London: Cresset Press. **L**
    Satire — class society.

1948   **Lister, Stephen** (pseud.). *Hail Bolonia!* London: Peter Davies. **L, MoU-St**
    Satire — attempts to modernize an agrarian eutopia.

1948   **Liston, Edward.** *The Bowl of Light.* New York: Coward-McCann. **L, WaE**

Lost race eutopia — advanced, rational people.

[1948]   **Richards, R.P.J.** *The Blonde Goddess.* London: Ken-Pax Pub. Co. **MoU-St**
Two eutopias — one a Shangri-la type, the other set in the near future presents many reforms.

1948   **Skinner, B.F.** *Walden Two.* New York: Macmillan. **DLC**
Eutopia through behavioral engineering.

1948   **Szilard, Leo.** "The Mark Gable Foundation," in his *The Voice of the Dolphin and Other Stories* (New York: Simon and Schuster, 1961), pp. 89–102. **MoU-St**
Freezing becomes a fad and threatens to destroy civilization.

1948   **Whiteside, Edward.** *A Warning From Mars.* New York: Interplanetary Publications. **MoU-St**
Dystopia — attack on welfare and big government.

1949   **[Blair, Eric.]** *1984,* by George Orwell (pseud.). London: Secker & Warburg. **DLC**
Classic totalitarian dystopia — repressive.

1949   **[Eldershaw, Flora Sydney Patricia and Marjoria Faith Barnard.]** *Tomorrow and Tomorrow,* by M. Barnard Eldershaw (pseud.). London: Phoenix Press. **LLL**
Public opinion sampling used to limit liberty.

1949   **Graves, Robert.** *Watch the North Wind Rise.* New York: Creative Age Press. Also entitled *Seven Days in New Crete.* London: Cassell. **L, NN**
World of witches and warlocks ruled by the White Goddess. Future medieval eutopia.

1949   **Jameson, [Margaret] Storm.** *The Moment of Truth.* London: Macmillan. **MoSW**
Dystopia — England under Communism.

1949   **[Jenkins, William F.]** *The Last Space Ship,* by Murray Leinster (pseud.). New York: Frederick Fell. **NcD**
Authoritarian dystopia — technology that allows government to punish selected individuals at a distance leads to universal tyranny. Emphasis on successful revolt.

1949   **McCarthy, Mary [Theresa].** *The Oasis.* New York: Random House. Also entitled *Source of Embarrassment.* **DLC**
Story of a commune and its problems.

1949   **Short, Gertrude.** *A Visitor from Venus.* New York: William-Frederick Press. **DLC, NcD**
Plea for a political and religious role for women.

1949   **Stanley, A[lfred] M[ortimer].** *Tomorrow's Yesterday.* Philadelphia: Dorrance and Co. **DLC, MoU-St**
Sex-role reversal. Eugenics. Socialist system. Degenerated physically but advanced mentally.

1949   **Stewart, George.** *Earth Abides.* New York: Random House. **DLC**
        Destruction and re-birth of civilization.

1949   **Sutton, Paralee Sweeten.** *White City.* Palo Alto, California:
        Palopress. **DLC**
        Communal eutopia located in Antarctica. ESP.

1949   **Walsh, Chad.** *Early Christians of the 21st Century.* New York:
        Harper & Bros. **L**
        Effect of rejuvenated Christianity.

1949   **Williamson, Jack.** *The Humanoids.* New York: Simon and
        Schuster. Based on his "With Folded Hands," *Astounding
        Science Fiction* (c. 1947). **DLC**
        Dystopia — perfected humanoids take over from men.

[1950's   **Haldane, J.B.S.** *The Man With Two Memories.* London: Merlin
written in]   Press, 1976.
        Published posthumously from an unfinished manuscript.
        Detailed eutopia.

1950   **Asimov, Isaac.** *Pebble in the Sky.* Garden City: Doubleday. **DLC**
        Dystopia — earthlings are inferior members of a repressive
        galactic civilization.

1950   **Bair, Patrick.** *Faster! Faster!* New York: Viking Press. **CoDU**
        Class based dystopia located on a constantly travelling train.

1950   **Barber, Elsie Oakes.** *Hunt for Heaven.* New York: Macmillan.
        DLC
        Novel about a commune.

1950   **Capon, Paul.** *The Other Side of the Sun.* London: William Heine-
        mann. **DLC**
        Detailed eutopia based on custom. Advanced technology
        came slowly; society had time to adjust.

1950   **[Klass, Philip].** "Null-P," by William Tenn (pseud.). in his *The
        Wooden Star* (New York: Ballantine, 1968), pp. 57–73. Originally
        published in *Worlds Beyond.*
        Post atomic war satire — absolute average becomes the goal.
        Overthrown by intelligent dogs.

1950   **Leiber, Fritz.** "Coming Attraction," in *the Best of Fritz Leiber*
        (Garden City: Nelson Doubleday, 1974), pp. 101–114.
        Post-atomic war United States. Vicious violent society.
        Women must wear masks — face too sexual.

1950   **Leiber, Fritz.** *Gather Darkness.* New York: Pellegrini & Cudahy.
        DLC
        Religious dystopia. Priests work in twos so they can spy on
        each other. Rigid class system. Control by keeping the major-
        ity in ignorance.

1950   **McCabe, Joseph.** *The Next 50 Years; A Forecast of the Trium-*

*phant Progress of the Race in the Next Half-Century: 1950-
1999.* Girard, Kansas: Haldeman-Julius Publications.
> Presented as a forecast. Detailed eutopia based on the
> assumption of the end of war and the scientific management
> of the economy.

1950   **Ryves, T.E.** *Bandersnatch.* London: The Grey Walls Press. **L,
MoU-St**
> Authoritarian dystopia.

1950   **Wiley, Ray H.** *On The Trail of 1960; A Utopian Novel.* New York:
Exposition Press. **DLC, MoU-St**
> Standard communal eutopia.

1951   **Asimov, Isaac.** *The Stars, Like Dust.* Garden City: Doubleday.
Also entitled *The Rebellious Stars.* **DLC**
> Rebellion against various autocrats — the goal is democracy.

1951   **[Cove, Joseph Walter.]** *Late Final* by Lewis Gibbs (pseud.).
London: J.M. Dent. **L**
> Barbarianism.

1951   **Fennessy, J.C.** *The Sonnet in the Bottle.* London: Herbert Jenkins.
MoU-St
> Lost race — Incan society as eutopia.

1951   **Gray, Curme.** *Murder in Millenium VI.* Chicago: Shasta. **L, DLC**
> Science fiction detective story set in a matriarchy 6000 years
> in the future.

1951   **Hazlitt, Henry.** *The Great Idea.* New York: Appleton-Century-
Crofts. Also entitled *Time Will Run Back.* **DLC, L**
> Anti-communist dystopia.

1951   **[Klass, Philip.]** "Venus is a Man's World," by William Tenn
(pseud.), in his *The Square Root of Man* (New York: Ballantine,
1968), pp. 145–169.
> Contrasts the frontier world of Venus with an Earth ruled by
> women. Men cannot vote or hold public office. Done to avoid
> war.

1951   **Kornbluth, C.M.** "The Marching Morons," in *The Science Fiction
Hall of Fame,* edited by Ben Bova. 2 Vols. in 3 (Garden City:
Doubleday & Co., 1973), Vol. 2A, pp. 204–232. Originally pub-
lished in *Galaxy.*
> High birth rate of lower classes produces a nation of morons.

1951   **Matthews, Ronald.** *Red Sky at Night.* London: Hollis & Carter.
DLC
> Communist dystopia overcome by religion. Stress on the
> battle.

1951   **Michaud, A[lfred] C[harles].** *Our Coming World.* Philadelphia:
World Publication Press. **DLC, MoU-St**

Detailed eutopia located on Mars. Technologically advanced. Extreme emphasis on cleanliness. Intensive agriculture.

1951   **Mittelhölzer, Edgar [Austin].** *Shadows Move Among Them.* London: Peter Nevill. **L**
Dystopia — authoritarian. Nightmare quality.

1951   **Rayer, F[rancis] G[eorge].** *Tomorrow Sometimes Comes.* London: Home & Van Thal. **L, MoU-St**
Mostly adventure and catastrophe — post atomic war barbarianism.

1951   **Russell, Eric Frank.** "...And Then There Were None," in *The Science Fiction Hall of Fame,* edited by Ben Bova. 2 Vols. in 3 (Garden City: Doubleday & Co., 1973), Vol. 2A, pp. 275–341. Originally published in *Analog.*
Anarchist eutopia. See 1962 Russell.

1951   **Tucker, [Arthur] Wilson.** *City in the Sea.* New York: Rinehart. **L**
Redevelopment of civilization after a catastrophe.

1951   **Wylie, Philip.** *The Disappearance.* New York: Holt, Rinehart. **DLC**
Sexes disappear from each other; two single sex societies.

1952   **Anderson, Poul.** *Vault of the Ages.* Philadelphia: Winston. **DLC**
Barbarianism.

1952   **Barnhouse, Perl T.** *My Journeys With Astargo; A tale of past, present and future.* Denver: Bell Publications. **MoU-St**
Includes an authoritarian eutopia.

1952   **Berry, Bryan.** *Born in Captivity.* London: Hamilton & Co. **CoFS**
Authoritarian dystopia.

1952   **Bradbury, Ray.** "The Pedestrian," in his *Twice Twenty-Two* (Garden City: Doubleday & Co., 1966), pp. 16–20. Originally published in the *Magazine of Fantasy and Science Fiction.*
Pedestrian arrested and committed by automated police for walking at night rather than staying in watching T.V.

1952   **Caldwell, Taylor.** *The Devil's Advocate.* New York: Crown. **DLC**
Authoritarian dystopia.

1952   **[Campbell, William Edward March.]** *October Island* by William March (pseud.). London: Victor Gollancz. **L**
South Sea island eutopia.

1952   **Capon, Paul.** *The Other Half of the Planet; A Sequel to "The Other Side of the Sun."* London: William Heinemann. **L**
Authoritarian dystopia.

1952   **Frankau, Pamela.** *The Offshore Light.* London: William Heinemann. U.S. edition under pseudonym Eliot Naylor. **L, DLC**
Eutopia. Simple, ordered life and craftsmanship. No money. Authoritarian.

1952   **Norburn, Hope Robertson.** *Lord Lollypop; A Timely Allegory.*
        New York: Exposition Press. **DLC, NcD**
        Based on 1949 Orwell. Opposed to utopianism and anti-
        communist.

1952   **Roach, Rev. Thomas E.** *Samson.* Boston: Meador. **DLC**
        Borderline — black establishes a benevolent dictatorship in
        the U.S.

1952   **Sheckley, Robert.** "Cost of Living," in his *Untouched by Human
        Hands* (New York: Ballantine, 1954), pp. 12–23. Originally pub-
        lished in *Galaxy.*
        People go in debt for consumer goods — may sign over chil-
        dren's, grandchildren's, etc. earnings for their lifetime to
        credit agency.

1952   **Slater, Henry J.** *The Smashed World.* London: Jarrolds. **L**
        Borderline — population composed of reincarnated greats
        from the past.

1952   **Vonnegut, Kurt, Jr.** *Player Piano.* New York: Holt, Rinehart &
        Winston. Also entitled *Utopia 14.*
        Machine dystopia. Engineers control. Huge unemployed
        population.

1952   **[Wall, John W.]** *The Sound of His Horn* by Sarban (pseud.). Lon-
        don: Peter Davies. **L**
        Success of Hitler — 102 years into the Reich. Breeding
        humans for blood sport.

1952   **Ward, Julian.** *We Died in Bond Street.* London: Hodder & Stough-
        ton.
        Abortive revolt trying to establish a dictatorship.

1952   **Wolfe, Bernard.** *Limbo.* New York: Random House. Also entitled
        Limbo '90. **L, DLC, NcD**
        Amputeeism a way of life.

1953   **Anderson, Poul,** "Sam Hall," in *The Liberated Future,* edited by
        Robert Hoskins (Greenwich, Connecticut: Fawcett, 1974), pp.
        13–51. Originally published in *Astounding.*
        Authoritarian dystopia — control by computers.

1953   **Bouic, Frederic Vernon.** *Good-bye White Man; A Novel of A.D.
        2711.* New York: Exposition Press. **DLC**
        Overthrow of the white race. World empire. E.S.P.
        Christianity.

1953   **Bradbury, Ray.** *Fahrenheit 451.* New York: Ballantine. **DLC**
        Authoritarian, anti-intellectual dystopia.

1953   **Clarke, Arthur C.** *Against the Fall of Night.* New York: Gnome
        Press. Another version entitled *The City and The Stars.* **DLC**
        City utopia that has stagnated regains contact with a rural,
        telepathic utopia that has also stagnated. Cross-fertilization.

1953   **Frankau, Gilbert.** *Unborn Tomorrow. A Last Story.* London: MacDonald. **L**
World in the 50th century which has become entirely Roman Catholic and monarchical. Monopolies. Chivalry.

[1953]   **Harness, Charles Leonard.** *Flight into Yesterday.* New York: Bouregy and Curl. Also entitled *The Paradox Man.* **DLC**
Authoritarian dystopia.

1953   **Heinlein, Robert A.** *Revolt in 2100; The Prophets and the Triumph of Reason Over Superstition.* Chicago: Shasta Publisher. **DLC**
Authoritarian dystopia.

1953   **Karp, David.** *One.* New York: Vanguard. Also entitled *Escape to Nowhere.* **DLC**
Authoritarian dystopia — very similar to 1949 Orwell.

1953   **Kornbluth, C.M.** *The Syndic.* Garden City: Doubleday. **DLC**
Dystopia — militaristic government from the U.S. driven to Ireland. Western U.S. is mob controlled. Eastern U.S. is permissive.

1953   **Leiber, Fritz.** "The Big Holiday," in *The Best of Fritz Leiber* (Garden City: Nelson Doubleday, 1974), pp. 165–172. Originally published in the *Magazine of Fantasy and Science Fiction.*
There is one holiday each year lasting three days and stressing friendship, love, laziness, fun, and joy. No one can be concerned with money, success, hurry, worry, and glamour.

1953   **Leiber, Fritz.** *The Green Millenium.* New York: Abelard-Shuman. **L**
U.S. ruled by the Federal Bureau of Loyalty and Fun, Inc. Sadism.

1953   **Lorraine, Paul.** *Dark Boundaries.* London: Curtis Warren. **GU**
World divided into Normals and Intelligentsia.

1953   **[MacGregor, James Murdoch.]** *World Out of Mind* by J.T. McIntosh (pseud.). Garden City: Doubleday. **DLC**
Whole social and political system based on IQ tests.

1953   **Melville, John.** *Populism (U & I).* The Hague: W.P. Van Stockhum & Zoon. **L**
Majority rule on all questions. World government.

1953   **[Norway, Nevil Shute.]** *In the Wet,* by Nevil Shute (pseud.). London: William Heinemann. **ICU, NN**
Future of the Commonwealth. Britain poor, becoming depopulated, and socialist. Australia, Canada, and New Zealand rich, growing and capitalist.

1953   **Pangborn, Edgar.** *West of the Sun.* Garden City: Doubleday. **NN, DLC**
Borderline — founding of new planet. Integration of alien and human. Ideal small community.

1953   **Pohl, Frederik and C.M. Kornbluth.** *The Space Merchants.* New York: Ballantine. Also entitled *Gravy Planet.* **DLC**
Advertising dystopia.

1953   **Richter, Conrad.** "Sinister Journey," *The Saturday Evening Post Stories 1953* (New York: Random House, 1953), pp. 213–228.
Dystopia of perfect life. Dull, controlled, boring. Equality as dystopia.

1953   **Stanford, J[ohn] K[eith].** *Full Moon at Sweetenham; A Nightmare.* London: Faber & Faber. **DLC**
Bookmaker government.

1953   **Swain, Dwight V.** *The Transposed Man.* New York: Ace. **O**
Man is the flaw in robot-like perfection.

1953   **Vonnegut, Kurt, Jr.,** "Tomorrow and Tomorrow and Tomorrow," in his *Welcome to the Monkey House* (New York: Dell, 1970), pp. 293–308. Originally published in *Galaxy* as "The Big Trip Up Yonder."
Overpopulation dystopia.

1953   **Waugh, Evelyn.** *Love Among the Ruins; A Romance of the Near Future.* London: Chapman and Hall. **L**
Dreary, dingy life in the welfare state. Reformatories the best place to live.

1953   **Yorke, Preston.** *Space-Time Task Force.* London: Hector Kelly. **L**
Earth is divided into two societies, the Primitives (contemporary man) and one based on specialized, synthetic human beings.

1954   **Asimov, Isaac.** *The Caves of Steel.* Garden City: Doubleday. **DLC**
Dystopia — overpopulation.

1954   **[Aycock, Roger Dee.]** *An Earth Gone Mad* by Roger Dee (pseud.). New York: Ace. **DLC**
Dystopia — mental submission to an authoritarian cult.

1954   **Bacas, Paul E[dmond].** *Thirty Years to Win.* Rindge, New Hampshire: Richard R. Smith. **DLC**
Detailed eutopia — nationalist.

1954   **Budrys, Algis.** *False Night.* New York: Lion Books. Longer version published 1961 as *Some Will Not Die.* **DLC**
Barbarianism.

[1954]   **Campbell, H.J.** *Once Upon a Space.* London: Panther. **O**
Authoritarian dystopia — people degenerate.

1954   **Crossen, Kendall Foster.** *Year of Consent.* New York: Dell. **Dc**
Social engineering dystopia.

1954   **Crowcroft, Peter.** *Fallen Sky.* London: Peter Nevill. **L**
Barbarianism.

1954   **De Wohl, Louis.** *The Second Conquest.* Philadelphia: J.B. Lippincott. **MoU**
Advanced civilization on Mars.

1954   **Even, James Eugène.** *Another World.* Boston: Meador Pub. Co. **DLC, MoU-St**
Rational, scientific, authoritarian eutopia.

1954   **Golding, William.** *Lord of the Flies.* London: Faber & Faber. **DLC**
Civilization is only a veneer. Children left alone revert to a violent, primitive existence.

1954   **Johns, Willy.** *The Fabulous Journey of Hieronymous Meeker.* Boston: Little, Brown. **NcD**
Gulliver type. One eutopia — constant change.

1954   **Kimball, Harold C[live].** *The Story of Sourwegia; A Newly Discovered Continent-Island in the Pacific.* Salt Lake City: Author. **DLC**
Every wife has three husbands (connubial, domestic, and business manager.) Improved sense of smell.

1954   **[Kuttner, Henry] and C.L. Moore.** *Beyond Earth's Gates,* by Lewis Padgett (pseud.) and C.L. Moore. New York: Ace.
Authoritarian dystopia.

[1954] **MacDonald, John D.** "Spectator Sport," in *Strange Adventures in Science Fiction,* edited by Groff Conklin (London: Grayson & Grayson, [1954], pp. 99–105. **L**
Permanent feelies the reward in life. Lobotomies for everyone.

1954   **MacGregor, Geddes.** *From a Christian Ghetto; Letters of Ghostly Wit, Written A.D. 2453.* London: Longmans, Green. **L**
Dystopia — anti-religion, anti-intellectual, authoritarian.

1954   **Mead, Shepherd.** *The Big Ball of Wax; A Story of Tomorrow's Happy World.* New York: Simon & Schuster. **DLC**
Advertising dystopia.

1954   **Morrison, D. A. C.** "Another Antigone," in *A.D. 2500; The Observer Prize Stories 1954* (London: William Heinemann, 1955), pp. 96–106.
Dystopia — love, poetry, art, etc. abolished.

1954   **Oliver, Chad.** "Rite of Passage," *Astounding Science Fiction* 53 (April), 49–86.
Two societies, one technological, one rejects technology.

1954   **Pohl, Frederik.** "The Midas Plague," in *The Science Fiction Hall of Fame,* edited by Ben Bova. 2 Vols. in 3 (Garden City: Doubleday & Co., 1973), Vol. 2B, pp. 259–312. Originally published in *Galaxy.*
Consumer dystopia — poor must consume; rich allowed to consume less.

1954   **Pohl, Frederik and C.M. Kornbluth.** *Search the Sky.* Harmondworth: Penguin. **DLC**
        Degeneration of the human race.

1954   **Rymer, G.A.** "The Atavists," in *A.D. 2500; The Observer Prize Stories 1954* (London: William Heinemann, 1955), pp. 131–143. **L**
        Dystopia, degenerated world of morons. No sex. T.V. or sports all day.

1954   **Sheckley, Robert.** "The Academy," *If, Worlds of Science Fiction* 4 (August), 45–62.
        Society organized around Sanity Meters. The Academy provides alternative to psychosurgery — drug induced dreams.

1954   **Sheckley, Robert.** "Skulking Permit," in his *Citizen in Space* (New York: Ballantine, 1955), pp. 154–180.
        Agrarian eutopia wants to be civilized so they appointed a criminal — he fails.

[1954] **[Tubb, E.C.]** *Enterprise 2115,* by Charles Grey (pseud.). London: Merit Books. **L**
        Computer dystopia.

1954   **Vidal, Gore.** *Messiah.* New York: Dutton. **DLC**
        Religious dystopia.

[1954] **Wilson, Hardy.** *Kurrajong. Sit-Look-See.* Kew, Melbourne: Author. **NN**
        New Capital city of Australia designed to amalgamate the best of the Eastern and Western cultures.

1955   **Aldiss, Brian W.** "Panel Game," in his *Space, Time and Nathaniel* (London: New English Library, 1971), pp. 143–152. Originally published in *New Worlds.*
        Consumer dystopia.

1955   **Anderson, Poul.** "Inside Straight," in his *Seven Conquests* (New York: Collier, 1969), pp. 92–116. Originally published in *Fantasy and Science Fiction.*
        Economic system based on gambling.

1955   **Anderson, Poul.** *No World of Their Own.* New York: Ace. **CSt, DLC**
        Computer Dystopia.

1955   **Asimov, Isaac.** "Franchise," in his *Earth Is Room Enough.* (Greenwich, Connecticut: Fawcett, 1957), pp. 57–73. Originally-published in *If.*
        One individual chosen by computer to vote in any given election.

1955   **Barr, Densil N.** *The Man With Only One Head.* London: Cowan. **L**
        Catastrophe — only one man fertile.

1955   **Blish, James.** *Earthman, Come Home.* London: Putnams. **DLC**
Social science fiction. Part of series *Cities in Flight.* See also
Blish 1956 (2), 1958, and 1962.

1955   **Brackett, Leigh.** *The Long Tomorrow.* Garden City: Doubleday.
DLC
Conflict between those accepting and those rejecting
technology.

1955   **Brown, Alec.** *Angelo's Moon.* London: The Bodley Head. **L**
Dystopia — degeneration of the human race.

1955   **Budrys, Algis.** "The Executioner," in *Spectrum,* edited by Kingsley
Amis and Robert Conquest (New York: Harcourt, Brace and
World, 1961), pp. 84–120. Originally published in *Astounding
Science Fiction.*
Dystopia — standard authoritarian except for judicial system
which is a trial by ordeal — if you survive you were innocent.

[1955]   **[Burke, John Frederick.]** *Deep Freeze,* by Jonathan Burke
(pseud.). London: Hamilton. **O**
Only women and children left on the planet; establish a
feminist eutopia. Conflict develops as men grow up.

1955   **Creedy, F[rederick].** *The Next Step in Civilization; A Star to Steer
By.* Vol. 3 of his *Truth is Enough.* Toronto: The Ryerson Press.
NcD
Become more like Christ.

1955   **Dick, Philip K.** *Solar Lottery.* New York: Ace. Also entitled *World
of Chance.* **L**
Power distributed and changed randomly. Corruption.

1955   **Elliott, H[arry] Chandler.** *Reprieve from Paradise.* New York:
Gnome. **DLC**
Dystopia — post-atomic war.

1955   **Gunn, James E.** *This Fortress World.* New York: Gnome Press.
DLC
Religious authoritarian dystopia.

1955   **[Harris, John Beynon.]** *Re-Birth,* by John Wyndham (pseud.).
New York: Ballantine. Also entitled *The Chrysalids.* **L, OU**
Post-nuclear war future. Religious dystopia. Emphasis on the
traditional physical form of human beings. All plants and
animals that mutate are killed. Mutant humans sterilized.
Telepathic mutants develop — discovered by a telepathic civilization that has developed elsewhere on earth.

1955   **[Hough, Stanley Bennett.]** *Utopia 239,* by Rex Gordon (pseud.).
London: Heinemann. **L, DLC**
Complete freedom produces dystopia.

1955   **Kee, Robert.** *A Sign of the Times.* London: Eyre & Spottiswoode.

L, DLC
Authoritarian dystopia.

1955 **[Klass, Philip.]** "The Servant Problem," by William Tenn (pseud.), in his *The Human Angle* (New York: Ballantine, 1956), pp. 44–75.
Authoritarian dystopia. Satire.

1955 **Knight, Damon.** *Hell's Pavement.* New York: Lion Books. Also entitled *Analogue Men.* **GU**
Attempts to control violence to produce eutopia produces dystopia.

1955 **Kornbluth, C.M.** *Not This August.* Garden City: Doubleday. Also entitled *Christmas Eve.* **DLC**
U.S. under Communism — dystopia.

1955 **Kreisheimer, H.C.** *The Whooping Crane.* New York: Pageant Press. **DLC, ViU**
Communist dystopia.

1955 **Lin Yutang.** *Looking Beyond.* New York: Prentice-Hall. Also entitled *The Unexpected Island.* **L, DLC**
Detailed conservative eutopia.

1955 **Mead, Harold.** *The Bright Phoenix.* London: Michael Joseph. **L**
Authoritarian dystopia.

1955 **Melling, Leonard.** *The Great Beyond. A.D. 2500. A Trilogy on Progress.* np.: Torch Pub. Co. **DLC**
Borderline — spiritualism. Unity.

1955 **Oliver, Chad.** "The Mother of Necessity," in his *Another Kind* (New York: Ballantine, 1955), pp. 1–14. **MiU**
Short story describing a future city called Fullcircle which incorporates the best of all previous city designs. It gradually replaces all previous social organizations.

1955 **Pawle, Hanbury.** *Before Dawn.* London: Hutchinson. **L**
Conflict between Christianity and Communism.

1955 **Pohl, Frederik and C.M. Kornbluth.** *Gladiator-at-Law.* New York: Ballantine. **DLC**
Dystopia — capitalist, machine.

1955 **[Pohl, Frederik and Lester Del Rey.]** *Preferred Risk,* by Edson McCann (pseud.). New York: Simon & Schuster. **DLC**
Insurance companies control the world.

1955 **Pohl, Frederik.** "Rafferty's Reasons," in his *Alternating Currents* (New York: Ballantine, 1956), pp. 83–96. Originally published in *Fantastic Universe.*
Dystopia — machine teaching.

1955 **Pohl, Frederik.** "Tunnel Under the World," in his *Alternating Currents* (New York: Ballantine, 1956), pp. 112–143. Originally

published in *Galaxy*.
Advertising dystopia.

1955   **Pohl, Frederik.** "What To Do Till the Analyst Comes," in his *Alternating Currents* (New York: Ballantine, 1956), pp. 143–154.
Drug dystopia.

1955   **St. Clair, Margaret.** *The Green Queen.* New York: Ace, 1957. Originally published as "The Mistriss of Virialis."
Class based authoritarian dystopia — primarily as background.

1955   **Sheckley, Robert.** "A Ticket to Trainai" in his *Citizen in Space* (New York: Ballantine, 1955), pp. 108–147.
Eutopia (no laws) except — all women kept in stasis, taxation by robbery, divorce by murder, governmental change by assassination.

1955   **Sieveking, Lance[lot de Giberne].** *A Private Volcano. A Modern Novel of Science and Imagination.* London: Ward, Lock. **DLC**
Abundance of gold brings misery, then prosperity.

1955   **Smith, H[arry] Allen.** *The Age of the Tail.* Boston: Little, Brown. **L**
Humor — people grow tails; changes in society as a result.

1955   **Wilson, Richard.** *The Girls from Planet 5.* New York: Ballantine. **DLC**
Women rule U.S. Texas is a man's state. Men take over again; the women had done a bad job.

1955   **[Youd, C.S.]** *The Year of the Comet,* by John Christopher (pseud.). London: Michael Joseph. **L**
Managerial dystopia.

1955   **Zuber, Stanley.** *The Golden Promise; A Novel of the Coming Era.* New York: Pageant Press. **DLC**
Detailed eutopia — the Global Union, a unification of all races and nations.

1956   **Blish, James.** *They Shall Have Stars.* London: Faber & Faber. Also entitled *Year 2018.* **OrU**
Social science fiction. Part of series *Cities in Flight.* See also Blish 1955, 1956, 1958, and 1962.

1956   **Blish, James.** *The Triumph of Time.* New York: Avon. Also entitled *A Clash of Cymbals.* **OrU**
Social science fiction. Part of series *Cities in Flight.* See also 1955, 1956, and 1962.

1956   **Boland, John.** *No Refuge.* London: Michael Joseph. **L**
Eutopia with flaws that make it a dystopia. Good life but authoritarian under the control of doctors and scientists.

1956   **Brebner, Winston.** *Doubting Thomas.* London: Rupert Hart-Davis. **L, DLC**
Authoritarian dystopia overcome by a clown.

1956   **Capon, Paul.** *Into the Tenth Millenium.* London: William Heinemann. **L**
Simple, agrarian eutopia. Everyone wealthy, self-assured. No Government. Free love.

1956   **Dick, Philip K.** *The Man Who Japed.* New York: Ace.
Moral Reclamation (Morec) — religion and advertising combined to produce dystopia.

1956   **Dick, Philip K.** *The World Jones Made.* New York: Ace. **DLC**
Authoritarian dystopia.

1956   **Fagan, Henry A[llan].** *Ninya; A Fantasy of a strange little world.* London: Jonathan Cape. **L**
Erewhonian, some eutopia — voluntary labor, freedom. Racial strife.

1956   **Hingley, Ronald.** *Up Jenkins!* London: Longmans Green. **L, MoU-St**
Satire — England split by a civil war into two warring states. Dystopia in the South — loyalty based on stupidity; education system based on stimulus response. Equality of women.

1956   **[Klass, Philip].** "A Man of Family," by William Tenn (pseud.), in his *The Human Angle* (New York: Ballantine, 1956), pp. 137–152.
Overpopulation dystopia.

1956   **[Lombino, S.A.]** *Tomorrow and Tomorrow,* by Hunt Collins (pseud.). New York: Pyramid. Also entitled *Tomorrow's World.* **GU, WaF**
Vicarious movement (drugs, sex, etc.) versus realism. Latter wins.

1956   **[Marshall, James Scott.]** *The Planet Mars and Its Inhabitants, by Eros Urides (A Martian)* (pseud.). np:np. **MoU-St**
Detailed communal eutopia on Mars.

1956   **Mason, Gregory.** *The Golden Archer; A Satirical Novel of 1975.* New York: Twayne. **CtY**
Combined church and state.

1956   **[Morley, Felix.** *Gumption Island; A Fantasy of Coexistence.* Caldwell, Idaho: Caxton. **NcD**
Capitalist eutopia.

1956   **Pohl, Frederik.** "My Lady Green Sleeves," in his *The Case Against Tomorrow* (New York: Ballantine, 1957), pp. 111–150. Originally published in *Galaxy.*
Dystopia — class society based on occupation. Civil Service, which includes Congress, at top.

1956   **Schneider, John.** *The Golden Kazoo.* New York: Rinehart. **TxU**
Future election campaign dominated by a computer.

1956   **Sheckley, Robert.** "Pilgrimage to Earth," in *Spectrum,* edited by
Kingsley Amis and Robert Conquest (New York: Harcourt,
Brace and World, 1961), pp. 209–220. Originally published in
Playboy.
Earth, exhausted of its natural resources, is a vacation planet
selling true love (by hypnotizing the women), vicarious vio-
lence, and sexual perversion.

1956   **Silverberg, Robert.** *Invaders from Earth.* New York: Ace. **CSt**
Dystopia — capitalism, public relations.

1956   **Stark, Raymond.** *Crossroads to Nowhere.* London: Ward, Lock.
DLC, L
Barbarianism.

1956   **Vance, Jack.** *To Live Forever.* New York: Ballantine. **TxU**
Dystopia — overpopulation, class system.

1956   **Waller, Robert.** *Shadow of Authority.* London: Jonathan Cape. **L**
Bureaucratic dystopia.

1956   **Walter, W[illiam] Grey.** *Further Outlook.* London: Gerald Duckworth. Also entitled *The Curve of the Snowflake.*
Egalitarian eutopia.

1956   **Wouk, Herman.** *The "Lomokome" Papers.* New York: Simon and
Schuster. First published in *Colliers* (February 17), pp. 70–84.
Satire on the arms race.

1957   **Aldiss, Brian W.** "The Shubshub Race," in his *Space, Time and
Nathaniel* (London: New English Library, 1971), pp. 63–79.
Satire — includes a planet called Utopia, the health planet —
constant pleasant climate.

1957   **Anderson, Poul.** "License," in his *Seven Conquests* (New York:
Collier Books, 1969), pp. 140–166. Originally published in *Fan-
tasy and Science Fiction.*
Overpopulation dystopia.

1957   **Asimov, Isaac.** "Profession" in his *Nine Tomorrows* (Greenwich,
Connecticut: Fawcett, 1959), pp. 11–68. Originally published in
Astounding.
Imprinting knowledge directly into the brain leads to an un-
creative society.

1957   **Asimov, Isaac.** "Strikebreaker," in his *Nightfall and Other Stories*
(Garden City: Doubleday, 1969), pp. 268–281. Originally pub-
lished as "Male Strikebreaker" in *The Original Science Fiction
Stories.*
Rigid class structure based on occupation, which is inherited.

1957   **Barlow, James.** *One Half of the World.* London: Cassell. **L**
Authoritarian dystopia.

1957 **Biggle, Lloyd, Jr.** "The Tunesmith," in his *The Metallic Muse* (Garden City: Doubleday & Co., 1972), pp. 4–48. Originally published in *Worlds of If.*
  All art in the form of commercials.

1957 **Clifton, Mark and Frank Riley.** *They'd Rather Be Right.* New York: Gnome Press. Alternate title *The Forever Machine.* **GU**
  Computer perfects humans and the reaction of society.

1957 **Enright, D[ennis] J[oseph].** *Heaven Knows Where.* London: Secker & Warburg. **L**
  Satire — South Sea Island Utopia.

1957 **Gaskell, Jane.** *Strange Evil.* New York: E.P. Dutton. **NIC**
  Detailed eutopia — struggle between good and evil. Author was fourteen when she wrote it.

1957 **Heinlein, Robert A.** *Citizen of the Galaxy.* New York: Scribner's. **NcD**
  Each space ship a sovereign state. Slave trade.

1957 **[Lehrburger, Egon.]** *You'll See; Report from the Future,* by Egon Larsen (pseud.). London: Rider. **L**
  Technological eutopia.

1957 **Loutrel, Anna Gregson.** *A Constitution for the Brotherhood of Man. The United Communities Bill, and How It Came to Be Written.* New York: Greenwich Book Publishers. **DLC**
  Constitution for an eutopia.

1957 **McGrath, Thomas.** *The Gates of Ivory, The Gates of Horn.* New York: Mainstream Publishers. **DLC**
  Authoritarian dystopia.

1957 **Maddux, Rachel.** *The Green Kingdom.* New York: Simon & Schuster. **NcD**
  Primitive, arcadian eutopia.

1957 **Maxwell, Edward** (pseud.). *Quest for Pajaro.* London: Heinemann. **L**
  Future world destroyed in war — replaced by world government, a universal language, technology.

1957 **Mead, Harold.** *Mary's Country.* London: Michael Joseph. **L, DLC, GU, MoU-St**
  Authoritarian dystopia.

1957 **Moore, C.E.** *Doomsday Morning.* Garden City: Doubleday. **L**
  Authoritarian dystopia and revolt.

1957 **Morgan, Arthur E.** *The Community of the Future and The Future of Community.* Yellow Springs, Ohio: Community Service, Inc. **NcD**
  Borderline — description of a face-to-face community as an eutopia — essay form.

1957   **Rand, Ayn.** *Atlas Shrugged.* New York: Random House. **MH**
Authoritarian dystopia replaced by individualistic eutopia.

1957   **Sizemore, Julius C. and Wilkie G.** *The Sea People.* New York: Exposition Press. **MoU-St**
Eutopia under the sea.

1957   **Vance, Jack.** *The Languages of Pao.* New York: Ace.
Social science fiction — characterization of society dependent on language.

1958   **Blish, James.** *A Case of Conscience.* London: Faber & Faber. **L, NjR**
Two societies, Lithia, an eutopia, and earth, a dystopia. Earth — Shelter Society — stratified, hedonistic, but considerable alienation. Lithia — eutopia of reason.

1958   **Bloch, Robert.** *This Crowded Earth.* New York: Belmont Books.
Overpopulation dystopia.

1958   **Charbonneau, Louis.** *No Place on Earth.* Garden City: Doubleday. **L**
Authoritarian dystopia.

1958   **Coblentz, Stanton A[rthur].** *The Blue Barbarians.* New York: Avalon. **DLC**
Satire — capitalist culture on Venus — either at war or in extreme competition.

1958   **Cooper, Edmund.** *The Uncertain Midnight.* London: Hutchinson. Also entitled *Deadly Image.* **L**
Machine eutopia which is really a dystopia.

1958   **Hadley, Arthur T.** *The Joy Wagon.* New York: Viking. **TxU**
Humor — computer runs for President.

1958   **Heyne, William P.** *Tale of Two Futures; A Novel of Life on Earth and the Planet Paliades in 1975.* New York: Exposition.
Earth as dystopia — class, gangs, inflation. Paliades as eutopia — religion, monogamy.

1958   **Huxley, Aldous.** *Brave New World Revisited.* New York: Harper.
Essay arguing that extrapolation of 1932 Huxley was coming true.

1958   **Jones, Ewart C[harles].** *Head in the Sand.* London: Arthur Barker. **L**
Dystopia — England controlled by the U.S.S.R.

1958   **[Klass, Philip.]** "Eastward Ho," by William Tenn (pseud.), in his *The Wooden Star* (New York: Ballantine, 1968), pp. 73–93.
Originally published in *Fantasy and Science Fiction.* Satire — Indians retake the American continent.

1958   **Sheckley, Robert.** *Immortality Delivered.* New York: Avalon.
Expanded version entitled *Immortality Inc.* **L, KyU**

Suicide Act of 2102 — join a game as the Hunted and elude professional killers.

1958 **Updike, John.** *The Poorhouse Fair.* New York: Alfred A. Knopf. **MoU-St**
Borderline — background of the novel is a future United States that is slowly degenerating, becoming stagnant.

1958 **Young, Michael.** *The Rise of the Meritocracy 1870–2033; An Essay on Education and Equality.* London: Thames and Hudson.
Development of a class system based on I.Q.

1959 **Anderson, Poul.** *Virgin Planet.* New York: Avalon. **TxU**
Planet occupied only by women. Religion had developed around the expected return of men.

1959 **Appel, Benjamin.** *The Funhouse; An Eyewitness Report of the historic search for the world's most dangerous weapon, the A-I-D....* New York: Ballantine. Also entitled *The Death Master.* **N**
Two worlds, the Pleasure State and the Reservation. Reservation — no machinery invented after 1879, seen as ideal. Pleasure State — computer controlled eutopia solely based on pleasure.

1959 **Coury, Phil.** *Anno Domini 2000.* New York: Vantage. **NN, MoU-St**
Anti-socialist dystopia.

1959 **Dick, Philip K.** *Time Out of Joint.* Philadelphia: J.B. Lippincott. **IU**
Militaristic dystopia.

1959 **Ellison, Harlan.** "Eyes of Dust," in *Alone Against Tomorrow* (New York: Macmillan, 1971), pp. 171–179. Originally published in *Rogue Magazine.*
Eutopia based on the suffering of a few.

1959 **Heinlein, Robert A.** *Starship Troopers.* New York: Putnam. **L**
Pro-military.

1959 **Knight, Damon.** *Masters of Evolution.* New York: Ace.
City-country split. Latter is anti-machine.

1959 **Kornbluth, C.M. and Frederik Pohl.** *Wolfbane.* New York: Ballantine. **DLC**
Authoritarian dystopia.

1959 **Leiber, Fritz.** "The Haunted Future," in *A Day in the Life,* edited by Gardner Dozois (New York: Harper and Row, 1973), pp. 154–199.
Conditioning for freedom.

1959   **Mackenzie, Compton.** *The Lunatic Republic.* London: Chatto and Windus. **MoU-St**
        Authoritarian dystopia — everyone does the same thing at the same time.

1959   **Roshwald, Mordecai.** *Level 7.* New York: McGraw-Hill.
        Bomb shelter society.

1959   **Swados, Harvey.** *False Coin.* Boston: Little, Brown. **L**
        Authoritarian dystopia.

1959   **Van Petten, Albert Archer.** *The Great Man's Life 1925–2000 A.D.* New York: Utopian Publishers, Inc. **MoU, NN**
        Detailed eutopia — improved democracy.

1960   **Ballard, J.G.** "Build-Up," in his *Chronopolis and Other Stories* (New York: G.P. Putnam's Sons, 1971), pp. 175–193.
        Overpopulation dystopia.

1960   **Booth, Philip.** "The Tower," in *New Poets of England and America. Second Selection,* edited by Donald Hall and Robert Pack (Cleveland: Meridian Books, 1962), pp. 190–196. Originally published in *Poetry.*
        Poem using utopian imagery.

1960   **Casewit, Curtis W.** *The Peacemakers.* New York: Bouregy.
        Militaristic dystopia.

1960   **Dick, Philip K.** *Vulcan's Hammer.* New York: Ace.
        Computer gives power over government.

1960   **Ferguson, Merrill.** *Village of Love.* London: Macgibbon and Kee. **L**
        Commune and its problems.

1960   **Fitz Gibbon, Constantine.** *When the Kissing Had to Stop.* London: Cassell. **DLC**
        Communist takeover.

1960   **Hartley, L.P.** *Facial Justice.* London: Hamish Hamilton. **L**
        Egalitarian, authoritarian dystopia.

1960   **Hersey, John.** *The Child Buyer; A Novel in the Form of Hearings Before the Standing Committee on Education, Welfare, and Public Morality of a certain State Senate, Investigating the conspiracy of Mr. Wissey Jones, with others to Purchase a Male Child.* New York: Alfred A. Knopf.
        Satire — attempt to establish a pool of pliant brain power.

1960   **Hunt, H.L.** *Alpaca.* Dallas: H.L. Hunt Pub. Co. **MoU-St**
        Capitalist eutopia — power to money.

1960   **Keene, Day and Leonard Pruyn.** *World Without Women.* Greenwich, Connecticut: Fawcett.
        Most women die; gang wars.

1960   **Miller, Walter M., Jr.** *A Canticle for Leibowitz.* Philadelphia: J.B. Lippincott (c. 1959). **NcD**

Three stages of re-birth after war — religion, science, new war.

1960   **Sheckley, Robert.** *The Status Civilization.* New York: Dell. Originally published in *Amazing* as "Omega."
Dystopia — prison planet, success by murder. Violence. Religion of evil.

1960   **Sturgeon, Theodore.** *Venus Plus X.* New York: Pyramid.
Eutopia — hermaphrodite. Emphasis on change, forward movement.

1960   **Szilard, Leo,** "The Voice of the Dolphins," in his *The Voice of the Dolphins and Other Stories* (New York: Simon and Schuster, 1961), pp. 19–72. **MoU-St**
Institute supposedly run by dolphins controls world affairs and avoids war.

1960   **[White, William A. P.]** "Barrier," by Anthony Boucher (pseud.), in Kingsley Amis and Robert Conquest, eds., *Spectrum IV* (London: Victor Gollancz, 1965), pp. 134–188. Originally published in *Astounding Science Fiction.*
Authoritarian dystopia.

1961   **Aldiss, Brian.** *The Interpreter.* London: Brown, Watson (c. 1960). Also entitled *Bow Down to Nul.* **L**
Earth a colony.

1961   **Aldiss, Brian.** *Primal Urge.* New York: Ballantine. **ICarbS**
Effects of a device that allows everyone to know the sexual desires of people vis-a-vis each other.

1961   **Allighan, Garry.** *Verwoerd — The End; A look-back from the Future.* London: T. V. Broadman. **L**
Apartheid as eutopia.

1961   **Ball, F.N.** *Metatopia.* Ipswich: Thames Bank Pub. Co. Ltd. **MoU-St**
Detailed eutopia by 2023. Equality, but recognizes merit. Press controlled by the universities. Planning to decrease population, provide better housing and more green space.

1961   **Ballard, J.G.** "Billenium," in his *Chronopolis and Other Stories* (New York: G. P. Putnam's Sons, 1971), pp. 137–151. Originally published in *New Worlds Science Fiction.*
Overpopulation dystopia.

1961   **Ballard, J. G.** "Chronopolis," in his *Chronopolis and Other Stories* (New York: G. P. Putnam's Sons, 1971), pp. 152–174. Originally published in *New Worlds Science Fiction.*
Illegal to have a watch or a clock. People had been too concerned with time and timed people could be made to work faster.

1961   **Biggle, Lloyd, Jr.** *Monument.* Garden City: Doubleday, 1974. First published in *Analog.*
        Social science fiction stressing conflict between a capitalist and a paradise world. Ecology.

1961   **Biggle, Lloyd, Jr.** "Well of the Deep Wish," in his *The Metallic Muse* (Garden City: Doubleday, 1972), pp. 138–157. Originally published in *Worlds of If.*
        Twenty-three hours a day watching TV.

1961   **Dreifuss, Kurt.** *The Other Side of the Universe.* New York: Twayne. **DLC**
        Little government, free association, equal income.

1961   **Fox, William McKinely.** *Our Castle.* New York: Carlton Press. **ViU**
        Marriage tie evil. Free love.

1961   **Gillon, Diana and Meir Gillon.** *The Unsleep.* London: Barrie & Rockliff. **L**
        Dystopia caused by no longer needing to sleep — desperate need to fill time.

1961   **Gunn, James.** *The Joy Makers.* New York: Bantam. **L**
        Whole society focused on pleasure. Perversion of hedonism.

1961   **Heinlein, Robert A.** *Stranger in a Strange Land.* New York: G.P. Putnam's Sons. **DLC**
        Communal eutopia set in a dystopia.

1961   **Leiber, Fritz.** *The Silver Eggheads.* New York: Ballantine. **L**
        Automation of the publishing industry. Computers write books. Female robot (colored pink) is the censor. People lose the ability to write.

1961   **Martineau, Louis.** *The Ecumen of Nations.* New York: Carlton Press.
        Detailed eutopia of world order presented as a religious book.

1961   **Pease, Tom.** *Pudoria.* New York: Lyle Stuart.
        Open, free love eutopia. Money indecent.

1961   **Pohl, Frederik and C.M. Kornbluth.** "Critical Mass," in their *The Wonder Effect* (New York: Ballantine, 1962), pp. 11–46. Originally published in *Galaxy.*
        Shelter dystopia.

1961   **Pohl, Frederik, and C.M. Kornbluth,** "A Gentle Dying," in their *The Wonder Effect* (New York: Ballantine, 1962), pp. 47–54. Originally published in *Galaxy.*
        Child-dominated dystopia.

1961   **Vonnegut, Kurt, Jr.** "Harrison Bergeron," in his *Welcome to the Monkey House* (New York: Dell, 1970), pp. 7–13. Originally published in *Fantasy and Science Fiction Magazine.*
        Future tale in which equality is achieved by handicapping the superior.

1961   **Winterburn, Katherine.** *Mystery-Wisdom From Mars.* New York: Printed by Photolith Printing Co. **MoU-St**
Detailed eutopia — Mars advanced both technically and spiritually.

1962   **Anvil, Christopher.** "Gadget Vs. Trend," in *Spectrum IV,* edited by Kingsley Amis and Robert Conquest (London: Victor Gollancz, 1965), pp. 55–69. Originally published in *Analog.*
Effect of technological development allowing complete privacy and inviolability.

1962   **Blish, James.** *A Life for the Stars.* New York: Putnams. **DLC**
Social science fiction. Part of series *Cities in Flight.* See also Blish 1955, 1956 (2), and 1958.

1962   **Bone, J.F.** *The Lani People.* London: Transworld. **L**
Development of women bred to perfectly please men.

1962   **Del Rey, Lester.** *The Eleventh Commandment.* New York: Ballantine. Revised edition 1970.
Overpopulation dystopia due to Roman Catholic dominance.

1962   **Dick, Philip K.** *The Man in the High Castle.* New York: G.P. Putnam's Sons. **DLC**
Dystopia using alternate history. Germans and Japanese had won World War II and divided up the world.

1962   **Gunn, James.** *The Immortals.* New York: Bantam.
Transplant dystopia — society controlled by doctors.

1962   **Harrison, Harry.** *Planet of the Damned.* New York: Bantam. Also entitled *Sense of Obligation.*
Authoritarian, overpopulation dystopia.

1962   **Harrison, Helga.** *The Catacombs.* London: Chatto & Windus. **L**
Authoritarian dystopia — underground Christian group.

1962   **Hugli, Edwin E. H.** *The A-M-O F-O-R-M-U-L-A.* Toronto: Edwin E. H. Hugli. **CaOTU**
Democratic socialist eutopia.

1962   **Huxley, Aldous.** *Island.* New York: Harper & Row.
Free love, psychedelic drugs, science and religion brings eutopia.

1962   **Jones, Raymond F.** *The Cybernetic Brains.* New York: Avalon.
Computer dystopia.

1962   **King, [Frank] Harvey.** *The Inaugurator.* Southport, England: Holsum Pub. Co. **L**
New system of international trade.

[1962]   **Leach, Decima.** *The Garthians.* Ilfracombe, England: Arthur H. Stockwell. **L**
Technologically advanced. Basis for the good society the correct early training of children.

1962   **Roshwald, Mordecai.** *The Small Armageddon.* London: Heinemann.
Dystopia — militarism.

1962   **Russell, Eric Frank.** *The Great Explosion.* New York: Distributed by Dodd, Mead. **DLC**
Three societies of the far future described. The first is the result of a planet peopled by transported criminals. They develop into a series of isolated strongholds adept at war and opposed to labor. The second comes from nudists and is a success. The third is founded on Gandhian principles and is clearly an eutopia.

1962   **Sheckley, Robert.** *Journey Beyond Tomorrow.* New York: Signet, 1960.
Abridged as "Journey of Joenes" in *Fantasy and Science Fiction.* Machine dominated dystopia and a simple life eutopia.

1962   **Smith, Evelyn E.** *The Perfect Planet.* New York: Avalon.
Satire — eutopia of health food and exercise. Ruled by beautiful women.

1962   **[Wilson, John Anthony.]** *Clockwork Orange,* by Anthony Burgess (pseud.). London: Heinemann.
Dystopia — violence, drugs, youth gangs.

1962   **[Wilson, John Anthony.]** *The Wanting Seed,* by Anthony Burgess (pseud.). London: Heinemann.
Overpopulation dystopia — homosexuality encouraged to keep down population growth.

1963   **Anderson, Poul.** "No Truce With Kings," in his *Time and Stars* (London: Panther, 1966), pp. 9–66. Originally published in *The Magazine of Fantasy and Science Fiction.*
Argument for feudal eutopia against centralized state.

1963   **Bateman, Robert.** *When the Whites Went.* New York: Walker & Co. **IEN**
Almost all whites disappear; blacks discover cooperation after many problems.

1963   **Bernard, Edward.** *A World To Be.* New York: Vantage Press. **MoU**
Detailed eutopia.

1963   **Borgese, Elizabeth Mann.** "My Own Utopia," in her *Ascent of Woman* (New York: George Braziller, 1963), pp. 209–227. **MoU-St**
All people feminine until forty-four then become masculine.

1963   **Charbonneau, Louis.** *The Sentinel Stars.* New York: Bantam. **DLC, L**
Authoritarian dystopia.

1963   **Charkin, Paul.** *The Living Gem.* London: Brown, Watson. **L**
Authoritarian dystopia. Small free love sect.

1963   **Dagmar, Peter.** *Sands of Time.* London: Brown, Watson. **L**
        Revolt against rule by computer.

1963   **Disch, Thomas.** "Utopia? Never!!," in his *White Fang Goes Dingo and other funny s.f. stories* (London: Arrow Books, 1971), pp. 67–69. Book first published in 1966 as *102 H-Bombs*. Story first published in *Amazing Stories.*
        Perfect society except for one flaw.

[1963] **Finlay, J[ames] C[olin].** *Time Shall be Neutral (A Study of the Road to Utopia).* Auckland, New Zealand: Author. **NcD**
        Capitalist eutopia but develops a State Investment program.

1963   **[Goodrich, Charles H.]** *The Wheel Comes a Turn; A Novel Based on Scientific Study of War of the Sexes,* by Charles H. Good (pseud.). New York: Vantage Press.
        Communist dystopia. Sex-role reversal.

1963   **Halle, Louis J.** *Sedge.* New York: Frederick A. Praeger.
        Small town eutopia. Emphasis on keeping things small.

1963   **Jakes, John.** "The Sellers of the Dream," in *Spectrum,* edited by Kingsley Amis and Robert Conquest (London: Victor Gollancz, 1965), pp. 86–123. Originally published in *Galaxy.*
        Planned obsolescence.

1963   **Pohl, Frederik and Jack Williamson.** *The Reefs of Space.* New York: Ballantine, 1964. Originally published in *Worlds of If.*
        Authoritarian dystopia.

1963   **Streichl, Karl.** *The Better World.* New York: Vantage Press.
        Detailed eutopia — stress on quality, physical fitness, education.

1963   **Thinkwell, Senator** (pseud.). *No Laughing Matter.* Vol. 1. np: National Purpose Associates. No evidence of further volumes. **DLC**
        Newtopia — a series of essays describing a better world.

1963   **Vonnegut, Kurt, Jr.** *Cat's Cradle.* New York: Holt, Rinehart & Winston. **DLC**
        Authoritarian dystopia but includes a religion providing the basis for a better existence — catastrophe.

1963   **Wallace, Irving.** *The Three Sirens.* New York: Simon and Schuster. **DLC, L, O**
        Borderline — community in which all must be sexually happy.

1963   **Woodman, George [David].** *The Heretic.* Whitestable: Shipyard Press. **L**
        Written in 1938. Scientific dystopia; loss of emotion.

1963   **Yasugi, Issho.** *A View of New World for World State.* Tokyo: Author. **LLL**
        Moral rearmament. Common property.

1964   **Brook-Rose, Christine.** *Out.* London: Michael Joseph. **InU**
        Light skinned people suppressed.

1964   **Burroughs, William S.** *Nova Express.* New York: Grove Press.
        Dystopian imagery — addicts world.

1964   **Cooper, Susan.** *Mandrake.* London: Hodder & Stoughton. **L**
        Authoritarian dystopia.

1964   **[Dakers, Elaine.]** *A State of Mind,* by Jane Lane (pseud.). London:
        Frederick Muller. **L**
        Authoritarian dystopia.

1964   **Dick, Philip K.** *The Penultimate Truth.* New York: Leisure Books.
        Authoritarian dystopia.

1964   **Dick, Philip K.** *The Simulacra.* New York: Ace.
        Authoritarian dystopia.

1964   **Disch, Thomas M.** "Thesis on Social Forms and Social Control in
        the U.S.A.," in his *Fun With Your New Head* (Garden City:
        Doubleday & Co., 1968), pp. 177–192. Originally published in
        Fantastic.
        Schizophrenia as a form of social organization.

1964   **Harrison, Harry.** *Deathworld 2.* New York: Bantam. **CSt**
        Dystopia of violence. See also Harrison 1960 and 1968.

1964   **Heinlein, Robert A.** *Farnham's Freehold.* New York: G.P.
        Putnam's.
        Authoritarian dystopia — blacks rule whites.

1964   **Hugli, Edwin E.H.** *Proposed Canadian Amo Party; Based on the*
        Amo Formula. Toronto: Author. **CaOTU**
        See 1962 Hugli.

1964   **Lawrence, Josephine.** *Not a Cloud in the Sky.* New York: Har-
        court, Brace and World. **WMU**
        Society rejects elderly — forces them all into rest homes.

1964   **Long, Frank Belknap.** *It Was the Day of the Robot.* London:
        Dennis Dobson. **L**
        Robot controlled dystopia.

1964   **Wallis, Dave.** *Only Lovers Left Alive.* New York: Dutton. **DLC**
        Teenage gangs, high suicide rate. Finally a new clan system
        develops — good society.

1965   **Aldiss, Brian W.** "Man on Bridge," in his *Who Can Replace a Man*
        (New York: New American Library), pp. 82–98. English edition
        entitled *Best Science Fiction Stories of Brian W. Aldiss.*
        Anti-intellectual dystopia.

1965   **Bailey, Hilary.** "The Fall of Frenchy Steiner," in *SF12,* edited by
        Judith Merrill (New York: Dell, 1968), pp. 94–126. Originally
        published in *New Worlds,* No. 143 (November 1965).
        Authoritarian dystopia.

1965   **Brunner, John.** *The Squares of the City.* New York: Ballantine.
        Authoritarian dystopia.

1965   **Charbonneau, Louis.** *Psychedelic-40.* New York: Bantam. Also
        entitled *The Specials.* **L**
        Drug dystopia — authoritarian.

1965   **Daventry, Leonard [John].** *A Man of Double Deed.* London: Vic-
        tor Gollancz. **L**
        ESP. Pleasure oriented world.

1965   **Dick, Philip K.** *The Three Stigmata of Palmer Eldritch.* Garden
        City: Doubleday (c. 1964). **MoR**
        Dystopia — drug can induce eutopia to hide the horrors of
        contemporary life.

1965   **Harrison, Harry.** *Bill, The Galactic Hero.* Garden City: Double-
        day.
        Militaristic dystopia.

1965   **Harrison, Harry,** "I Always Do What Teddy Says," in *The New
        Improved Sun,* edited by Thomas M. Disch (New York: Harper
        & Row, 1975), pp. 157–166. Originally published in *Ellery
        Queen's Mystery Magazine.*
        Socialization by robots.

1965   **Herbert, Frank.** *Dune.* Philadelphia: Chilton Books.
        Borderline — Detailed picture of an unusual country. See also
        1969 Herbert.

1965   **Hersey, John.** *White Lotus.* New York: Alfred A. Knopf.
        Authoritarian dystopia — Chinese suppress whites.

1965   **[Klass, Philip.]** "The Masculinist Revolt," by William Tenn
        (pseud.), in his *The Wooden Star* (New York: Ballantine, 1968),
        pp. 213–251. Originally published in *Fantasy and Science
        Fiction.*
        Abortive pro-male revolt.

1965   **Ludlow, Edmund.** *The Coming of the Unselves.* New York:
        Exposition Press.
        Horrors of honesty and equality.

1965   **Pohl, Frederik.** *A Plague of Pythons.* New York: Ballantine. **IaU**
        Dystopia — corruption by power.

1965   **Pohl, Frederik and Jack Williamson.** *Starchild.* New York: Ballan-
        tine.
        Authoritarian dystopia.

1965   **Shriver, Gary G.** "Cynia: An Original Utopia," Unpublished M.A.
        thesis, University of Wyoming.
        Individualist anarchist eutopia.

1966   **Barth, John.** *Giles Goat-Boy or, The Revised New Syllabus.*
        Garden City: Doubleday.

Borderline — dystopia set in a university. Rule by a computer. Comic novel.

1966 **Coblentz, Stanton A[rthur].** *Lord of Tranerica.* New York: Avalon. Satire — dictatorship in computer-perfect, business-based, pleasure-oriented society of the future.

1966 **Compton, D[avid] G[uy].** *Farewell, Earth's Bliss.* London: Hodder & Stoughton.
Authoritarian dystopia.

1966 **Coover, Robert.** *The Origin of the Brunists.* New York: Putnam.
Origin, development, and collapse of a religious sect.

1966 **Disch, Thomas M.** "Invaded by Love," in his *White Fang Goes Dingo and other funny s.f. stories* (London: Arrow, 1971), pp. 82–102. Book first published as *102 H-Bombs.* Story first published in *New Worlds Science Fiction.*
Pills that make everyone love one another. Civilization collapses.

1966 **Disch, Thomas M.** "102 H-Bombs," in his *White Fang Goes Dingo and other funny s.f. stories* (London: Arrow Books, 1971), pp. 7–33. First published as *102 H-Bombs.*
Dystopia — militarism and apathy.

1966 **Harrison, Harry.** *Make Room! Make Room!* Garden City: Doubleday. **IU**
Overpopulation dystopia.

1966 **High, Philip E.** *The Mad Metropolis.* New York: Ace. Also entitled *Double Illusion.* **L**
Computer eutopia that is actually a dystopia.

1966 **[Hough, Stanley Bennett.]** *The Paw of God,* by Rex Gordon (pseud.). London: Tandem, 1967. Also entitled *Utopia Minus X.*
Perfect world dystopia — machine controlled.

1966 **Hunter, Jim.** *The Flame.* London: Faber & Faber. **DLC**
New Vigour Movement — Christian.

1966 **Jones, D[ennis] F[eltham].** *Colossus.* London: Rupert Hart-Davis. **L**
Computer dystopia. See also 1974 Jones.

1966 **Lafferty, R.A.** "The Primary Education of the Camiroi," in *SF 12,* edited by Judith Merrill (New York: Dell, 1968), pp. 161–174. Originally published in *Galaxy.*
Educational eutopia.

1966 **Petty, John.** *The Last Refuge.* London: Ronald Whiting & Wheaton. **L**
Authoritarian dystopia — countryside paved over. Private homes replaced by huge apartment blocks.

1966 **[Rankine, John.]** *From Carthage Then I Came,* by Douglas R.

Mason (pseud.). Garden City: Doubleday. Also entitled *Eight Against Utopia*. **DLC**
Authoritarian dystopia.

1966   **Reynolds, Mack.** *Of Godlike Power*. New York: Belmont. **CSt**
Prophet, preaching perfect society, disrupts the current one.

1966   **Rimmer, Robert.** *The Harrad Experiment*. Los Angeles: Sherburne Press.
One of Rimmer's novels of the good life through sex. See also 1975 Rimmer.

1966   **Sheckley, Robert.** *The Tenth Victim*. London: Mayflower.
Legalized hunt — killing of humans by each other.

1966   **Shodall, Reuben Sam.** *The Enlightened Ones Beyond The Icebergs*. New York: Exposition Press. **PSt**
Atlantis relocated in Far North. History of Atlantis. Fairly standard enlightened eutopia.

1967   **Anderson, Poul.** "Eutopia," in *Dangerous Visions,* edited by Harlan Ellison (Garden City: Doubleday, 1967), pp. 274–291.
An eutopia so planned and ordered as to become a dystopia.

1967   **Biggle, Lloyd, Jr.** "And Madly Teach," in *The Best From Fantasy and Science Fiction. Sixteenth Series,* edited by Edward L. Ferman (Garden City: Doubleday, 1967), pp. 25–58.
Extrapolation of effect of technology on teaching and response of one excellent teacher.

1967   **Blish, James and Norman L. Knight.** *A Torrent of Faces*. Garden City: Doubleday. **DLC**
High population but earth can support it if well organized.

1967   **Bourne, John.** *Computer Takes All*. London: Cassell. **DLC**
Computer dystopia.

1967   **Brunner, John.** *Quicksand*. Garden City: Doubleday.
Flawed eutopia. Dictatorship of immortals. Sex as a drug.

1967   **Dick, Philip K.** *Counter Clock World*. New York: Berkeley. **CSt**
Black power.

1967   **Duke, Madelaine.** *This Business of Bomfog, A Cartoon*. London: Heinemann. **L, DLC**
Bomfog means Brotherhood-of-Man-Fatherhood-of-God. Coalition to end war, get rid of politicians.

1967   **Geston, Mark S.** *Lords of the Starship*. New York: Ace.
Militarism.

1967   **Hunt, H. L.** *Alpaca Revisited*. Dallas: H. L. H. Products.
Capitalist eutopia.

1967   **Jones, D[ennis] F[eltham].** *Implosion*. London: Hart Davis.
Fall in birthrate produces dystopia.

1967   **Laumer, Keith.** "The Day before Forever," in his *The Day Before*

Forever and Thunderhead (Garden City: Doubleday, 1968), pp. 7–112. **IU**
Authoritarian dystopia focusing on transplants.

1967   **[Lewin, Leonard D.]** *Report from Iron Mountain on the Possibility and Desirability of Peace.* New York: Dell.
Problems if permanent peace should occur.

1967   **McMichael, R. Daniel.** *The Journal of David O. Little.* New Rochelle, New York: Arlington House. **DLC, CoU**
Communist takeover of the United States.

1967   **Mason, Lowell B.** *The Bull on the Bench.* Oak Park, Illinois: Arcturus Pub. **MoU-St**
Satire — cattle rule world and produce a eutopia.

1967   **[Murray, John Middleton, Jr.]** *Phoenix,* by Richard Cowper (pseud.). New York: Ballantine.
Authoritarian dystopia and barbarianism.

1967   **Nolan, William F. and George Clayton Johnson.** *Logan's Run.* New York: Dial. **DLC**
Dystopia — violence, drugs, sex. Youth — all killed at 21.

1967   **Peters, Ludovic.** *Riot '71.* New York: Walker and Co. **DLC**
Fascist, racist dystopia.

1967   **Saberhagen, Fred.** *Berserker.* New York: Ballantine.
Militaristic dystopia. See also, 1969 Saberhagen.

1967   **Shirley, George E.** *A World Beyond.* New York: Vantage Press. **MoU-St**
Simple life eutopia taken over by Communists from U.S.S.R. — brings dystopia.

1967   **Silverberg, Robert.** *The Time-Hoppers.* Garden City: Doubleday. **NjP**
Overpopulation dystopia.

1967   **Silverberg, Robert.** *To Open the Sky.* New York: Ballantine.
Overpopulation dystopia.

1967   **Simak, Clifford D.** *Why Call Them Back from Heaven?* New York: Ace.
Society based on longevity. Highly puritanical, safety oriented.

1967   **Sladek, John T.** "The Happy Breed," in *Dangerous Visions,* edited by Harlan Ellison (Garden City: Doubleday, 1967), pp. 414–431.
Man degenerates due to takeover by machines.

1967   **Spinrad, Norman.** *Agent of Chaos.* New York: Belmont.
Authoritarian dystopia.

1967   **Spinrad, Norman.** *The Men in the Jungle.* Garden City: Doubleday.
Militarism.

1967   **[Westlake, Donald.]** *Anarchaos,* by Curt Clark (pseud.). New York: Ace.
Lawless world.

1967   **Zelazny, Roger.** *Lord of Light.* Garden City: Doubleday.
Authoritarian dystopia — based on control of technology by a group ruling as the Hindu pantheon.

1968   **Aldiss, Brian W.** "Total Environment," in *World's Best Science Fiction 1969,* edited by Donald A. Wollheim and Terry Carr (New York: Ace, 1969), pp. 287–331. Originally published in *Galaxy.*
Overpopulation dystopia.

1968   **Bloch, Robert.** *Ladie's Day.* New York: Belmont Books.
Sex-role reversal. Lesbian dystopia.

1968   **Brautigan, Richard.** "All Watched Over by Machines of Loving Grace," in his *The Pill versus The Springhill Mine Disaster* (New York: Delta, 1968), p. 1. Originally published: San Francisco: Four Seasons Foundation, 1968. *Writing 20.*
Borderline — poem. A computer Cockaigne but with an element of irony.

1968   **Brautigan, Richard.** *In Watermelon Sugar.* San Francisco: Four Seasons Foundation. *Writing 21.*
Eutopia rather on the Cockaigne model.

1968   **Brunner, John.** *Stand on Zanzibar.* Garden City: Doubleday.
Overpopulation dystopia.

1968   **Bulmer, Kenneth.** *The Doomsday Men.* Garden Ctiy: Doubleday. **L, DLC**
Dystopian background. Violence.

1968   **Caidin, Martin.** *The God Machine.* New York: E. P. Dutton.
Computer dystopia.

1968   **Chandler, A[rthur] Bertram.** *Spartan Planet.* New York: Dell, 1969. Also entitled *False Fatherland.*
Militaristic dystopia. Homosexuality.

1968   **Clark, Laurence Walter.** *A Father of the Nation.* Ricksmansworth, England: Veracity Ventures. **L**
England failing due to party influence and socialist policy — saved.

1968   **Cooper, Edmund.** *Five to Twelve.* New York: G. P. Putnam's Sons.
Dystopia — rule by women.

1968   **Disch, Thomas M.** *Camp Conçentration.* London: Rupert Hart-Davis. **DLC**
Authoritarian dystopia.

1968   **Durrell, Lawrence.** *Tunc.* New York: E.P. Dutton.

> Dystopian background — growth of control of world by one company.

1968   **Fairman, Paul W.** *I, The Machine.* New York: Lancer.
> Machine dystopia.

1968   **Frayn, Michael.** *A Very Private Life.* London: Collins.
> Dystopia — technology brings isolation of people from each other.

1968   **Green, Robert.** *The Great Leap Backward.* London: Hale. **DLC**
> Machine dystopia.

1968   **Groves, John William.** *Shellbreak.* London: Robert Hale. **L**
> Authoritarian dystopia.

1968   **[Jacob, Piers A.D.] and Robert E. Margroff.** *The Ring,* by Piers Anthony (pseud.) and Robert E. Margroff. New York: Ace. **GU**
> Authoritarian dystopia — technologically enforced conformity to too rigid moral standards.

1968   **Jones, Gonnar.** *The Dome.* London: Faber & Faber. **DLC**
> Machine that can project feelings into the brain — feelies.

1968   **Lafferty, R[aphael] A[loysius].** *Past Master.* London: Rapp & Whiting. **DLC**
> Future utopia, sick — boredom, lack of religion. Bring More to cure it.

1968   **Laski, Audrey.** *The Keeper.* London: Eyre & Spottiswoode. **IEdS**
> Religious commune.

1968   **Levene, Malcolm.** *Carder's Paradise.* London: Rupert Hart-Davis. **DLC**
> Dystopia — authoritarian, too much leisure. Man degenerates.

1968   **McCutchan, Philip.** *The Day of the Coastwatch.* London: Harrap. **DLC**
> Authoritarian dystopia.

1968   **[MacGregor, James Murdoch.]** *Six Gates from Limbo,* by J. T. McIntosh (pseud.). London: Michael Joseph. **L**
> Various dystopias.

1968   **Mannes, Marya.** *They.* Garden City: Doubleday.
> Computer, authoritarian, youth dystopia.

1968   **Niven, Larry.** *A Gift from Earth.* New York: Ballantine.
> Transplant dystopia — power of doctors.

1968   **Oliver, M.** *A New Constitution for a New Community.* Revised edition [Reno: Published by arrangement with Fine Arts Press] 1st edition, 1968. **MiU**
> Detailed capitalist eutopia — contains a complete constitution.

1968   **Orr, Paul and Violet.** *1993; The World of Tomorrow.* Altadena,

California: Pacific Progress Publishers. **MiU**
Detailed socialist eutopia stressing decentralization.

1968   **Palmer, William J.** *The Curious Culture of the Planet Loretta.*
New York: Vantage. **MoU-St**
Capitalist eutopia.

1968   **Patterson, James Ernest William.** *The Call of the Planets.* Bala,
North Wales: A. J. Chapple. **O**
Serenity, equality.

1968   **[Rankine, John.]** *Ring of Violence,* by Douglas R. Mason (pseud.).
London: Robert Hale. **L**
Dystopia of violence.

1968   **Roberts, Keith.** *Pavane.* Garden City: Doubleday.
Parallel history. Papal domination of Europe has slowed
progress and a dystopian medievalism has lasted into the 20th
century.

1968   **Sheckley, Robert.** "The People Trap," in his *The People Trap and
other Pitfalls, Snares, Devices and Delusions, as well as Two
Sniggles and a Contrivance* (London: Pan, 1972), pp. 7–27.
Originally published in the *Magazine of Fantasy and Science
Fiction.*
Overpopulation dystopia.

1968   **Sheckley, Robert.** "Street of Dreams, Feet of Clay," in *The Liberated Future,* edited by Robert Hoskins (Greenwich, Connecti-
cut: Fawcett, 1974), pp. 139–158. Originally published in
Galaxy.
Overpopulation dystopia — automated city with a mother
complex.

1968   **Taylor, Geoff.** *Day of the Republic.* London: Peter Davies. **CLU**
Fascist dictatorship in Australia.

1968   **Theobald, Robert.** *An Alternative Future for America II. Essays
and Speeches.* Chicago: Swallow. 2nd edition, 1970.
Borderline — essay, but detailed eutopia.

1968   **Thom, Robert.** *Wild in the Streets.* New York: Pyramid. **IEN**
Dystopia — teenage takeover.

1968   **[Thompson, Anthony A.]** *Catharsis Central,* by Antony Alban
(pseud.). London: Dennis Dobson. **L**
Computer dystopia.

1968   **[Tucker, Allan James.]** *The Alias Man,* by David Craig (pseud.).
London: Jonathan Cape. **DLC**
Britain is a satellite of Moscow. U.S. is isolationist. Soviet-
Bonn bloc. See also Tucker 1969 and 1970.

1968   **[Upchurch, Boyd.]** *The Last Starship from Earth,* by John Boyd
(pseud.). New York: Weybright and Talley.
Eugenic dystopia. Science rules.

1968   **Vonnegut, Kurt, Jr.** "Welcome to the Monkey House," in his *Welcome to the Monkey House* (New York: Dell, 1970), pp. 28–47. Originally published in *Playboy.*
Birth Control through deadening sensation below the waist and reducing the population by voluntary euthanasia. A few people fight back.

1968   **Young, Frank Herman.** *Neocracy; A Plan for Social Order and Co-operative Capitalism.* New York: Exposition Press. **LSE**
"Neocracy is co-operative capitalism utilizing representative rule of the people, by the people, for the people, in both business and government," p. 119.

1969   **Blish, James.** "We All Die Naked," in *Three for Tomorrow* (New York: Meredith Press, 1969), pp. 139–180.
Pollution dystopia.

1969   **Brien, Alan.** "Give-and-Take Utopia," *New Statesman,* 78 (August 22), 243–244.
Short eutopian sketch.

1969   **Brunner, John.** *The Jagged Orbit.* New York: Ace. **CSt**
Dystopia of violence.

1969   **Bulmer, Kenneth.** *The Patient Dark.* London: Robert Hale. **L, DLC**
Authoritarian dystopia.

1969   **Bulmer, Kenneth.** *The Ulcer Culture.* London: Macdonald. **L**
Dystopia of drugs.

1969   **Carroll, Gladys Hasty.** *Man on the Mountain.* Boston: Little Brown. **DLC**
Status dependent on age.

1969   **Cooper, Hughes.** *Sexmax.* New York: Paperback Library. **L, CSt**
Computer dystopia.

1969   **Donson, Cyril.** *The Perspective Process.* London: Robert Hale. **L**
Women in power. Eutopia.

1969   **Elgin, Suzette Haden.** "For the Sake of Grace," in *World's Best Science Fiction 1970,* edited by Donald A. Wollheim and Terry Carr (New York: Ace, 1970), pp. 105–127. Originally published in *Fantasy and Science Fiction.*
Women inferior. Occupation by competitive exam. See also 1972 Elgin.

1969   **Hale, John.** *The Paradise Man; A Black and White Farce.* London: Rapp and Whiting. **InU**
Racial turmoil. Constant conventional war by international agreement to keep economies going.

1969   **Herbert, Frank.** *Dune Messiah.* New York: G. P. Putnam.
Sequel to 1965 Herbert.

1969   **Hodgart, Matthew,** ed. [written by]. *A New Voyage to the Country of the Houyhnhnms. Being the Fifth Part of the Travels into Several Remote Parts of the World by Lemuel Gulliver* (pseud.) *First a Surgeon and then a Captain of Several Ships. Wherein the Author returns and finds a New State of Liberal Horses and Revolting Yahoos.* New York: G. P. Putnam's Sons, 1970. **MoU-St**
        Satire on the 1960's using 1726 Swift.

1969   **Kettle, Pamela.** *The Day of the Women.* London: Leslie Frewin. **L**
        Sex role reversal. Authoritarian dystopia.

1969   **Keyes, Kenneth S., Jr. and Jacque Fresco.** *Looking Forward.* South Brunswick, New Jersey: A. S. Barnes.
        Computer-based eutopia set in the future. Extensive genetic engineering. Production and distribution computer controlled; no industrial work for people. Work is administrative and creative.

1969   **Kneale, Nigel.** "The Year of the Sex Olympics," in his *The Year of the Sex Olympics and Other TV Plays.* (London: Ferret Fantasy, 1976), pp. 93-143. Produced July 29, 1969.
        Shows sexual athletics on TV to suggest to people that since they can't perform as well, they shouldn't try.

1969   **Koontz, Dean R.** *The Fall of the Dream Machine.* New York: Ace. **GU**
        Extrapolation of the ideas of Marshall McLuhan into a dystopia.

1969   **Le Guin, Ursula K.** *The Left Hand of Darkness.* London: Walker and Co.
        Hermaphrodite society.

1969   **Leiber, Fritz.** *A Spector Is Haunting Texas.* New York: Walker & Co. (c. 1968). **MB**
        Dystopia — Texas has taken over most of North America. Racial, ethnic, financial and political discrimination. Black republics in California and Florida. Circumluna — satellite of scientists, hippies, etc.

1969   **Lightner, A[lice] M.** *The Day of the Drones.* New York: W. W. Norton.
        Post-catastrophe. Blacks rule, whites are drones.

1969   **Pohl, Frederik.** *The Age of the Pussy Foot.* New York: Ballantine. **CSt**
        Everyone has a personal computer, widespread drug use, much leisure, sexual freedom, immortality through freezing.

1969   **Rankine, John.** *The Weisman Experiment.* London: Dennis Dodson. **L**
        Authoritarian dystopia.

1969 **Reed, Kit.** *Armed Camps.* London: Faber & Faber. **DLC**
  Military dominated dystopia.

1969 **Reynolds, Mack.** *The Cosmic Eye.* New York: Belmont.
  Standard dystopia.

1969 **Ryder, James.** *Kark.* London: Robert Hale. **L**
  Authoritarian dystopia.

1969 **Saberhagen, Fred.** *Brother Berserker.* London: Macdonald.
  Science Fiction. Also entitled *Brother Assassin.*
  Sequel to 1967 Saberhagen.

1969 **Saxton, Mark.** *The Islar; A Narrative of Lang III.* Boston: Houghton Mifflin.
  Sequel to 1942 Wright.

1969 **Seymour, Alan.** *The Coming Self-Destruction of the United States
  of America.* New York: Grove Press. **DLC**
  Violence. Race war.

1969 **Spinrad, Norman.** *Bug Jack Barron.* New York: Walker.
  Race relations of the future. Dystopia.

1969 **Theobald, Robert and J. M. Scott.** *Teg's 1994; An Anticipation of
  the Near Future,* np:np. New edition — Chicago: Chicago Swallow Press, 1972.
  Detailed eutopia.

1969 **[Tucker, Allan James.]** *Message Ends,* by David Craig (pseud.).
  London: Jonathan Cape. **DLC**
  See 1968 [Tucker] and also 1970 Tucker.

1969 **[Upchurch, Boyd.]** *The Rakehells of Heaven,* by John Boyd
  (pseud.). New York: Weybright & Talley.
  Satire — promiscuity, anarchy, nudity, return to nature.

1969 **[Vance, John Holbrook.]** *Emphyrio,* by Jack Vance (pseud.). Garden City: Doubleday. **GU**
  Authoritarian dystopia based on control of utilities, religion
  and monopoly of trade.

1969 **Weatherhead, John.** *Transplant.* London: George G. Harrap. **L**
  Transplant dystopia. Power of doctors.

1970 **[Aiken, John.]** *World Well Lost,* by John Paget (pseud.). London:
  Robert Hale. 1971 U.S. edition under author's name. **GU**
  Religious dystopia.

1970 **Anderson, Colin.** *Magellan.* New York: Walker. **DLC**
  Welfare dystopia.

1970 **Asimov, Isaac.** "2430 A.D.," in his *Buy Jupiter and Other Stories*
  (Garden City: Doubleday, 1975), pp. 159–166.
  Conformist dystopia.

1970 **Bennett, Diana.** *Adam and Eve and Newbury.* London: Hodder &
  Stoughton. **L**
  Welfare dystopia.

1970   **Bova, Ben.** "Blood of Tyrants," in his *Forward in Time* (New York: Walker & Co., 1973), pp. 17–34. Originally published in *Amazing*.
Authoritarian dystopia.

1970   **Brown, James Cooke.** *The Troika Incident. A Tetralogue in Two Parts.* Garden City: Doubleday & Co. **MoU-St**
Detailed eutopia — decentralized, craft-based economy, free love.

1970   **Compton, D[avid] G[uy].** *The Steel Crocodile.* New York: Ace. Also entitled *The Electric Crocodile.*
Authoritarian dystopia.

1970   **Cook, Robin.** *A State of Denmark or a Warning to the Incurious.* London: Hutchinson. **DLC**
Welfare dystopia.

1970   **Cooper, Edmund.** *Son of Kronk.* London: Hodder & Stoughton. Also entitled *Kronk.* **L**
Dystopia — pollution, violence.

1970   **DeGrazia, Alfred.** *Kalos; What Is To Be Done With Our World.* New York: Kalos Press. **MoU-St**
Detailed eutopia — decentralization. Tutors similar to the Samurai in 1905 Wells.

1970   **Dirac, Hugh.** *The Profit of Doom.* London: Sidgwick & Jackson. **L**
Transplant dystopia.

1970   **Durrell, Lawrence,** *Nunquam.* New York: E. P. Dutton. **MoU-St**
Continuation of 1968 Durrell.

1970   **Elder, Michael.** *Paradise Is Not Enough.* London: Robert Hale. **L**
Dystopia of mechanical perfection.

1970   **Glass, L. A.** *Journey to Utopia.* New York: Vantage Press.
Search for utopia.

1970   **Goulart, Ron.** *After Things Fell Apart.* New York: Ace. **CNoS**
Satire — future U.S. broken into small enclaves. Women's group killing men.

1970   **Hartridge, Jon.** *Earthjacket.* London: Macdonald. **DLC**
Authoritarian dystopia — catastrophe.

1970   **Heinlein, Robert A.** *I Will Fear No Evil.* New York: Putnam's. **DLC**
Dystopia — violence.

1970   **Hoyle, Fred and Geoffrey Hoyle.** *Seven Steps to the Sun.* London: Heinemann.
Dystopia — authoritarian decentralized political system.

1970   **Jonas, Gerald.** "The Shaker Revival," in *World's Best Science Fiction 1971,* edited by Donald A. Wollheim and Terry Carr

(New York: Ace, 1971), pp. 263–292.
>Apartheid. New Shaker sect — "No hate, No War, No money, No sex."

1970   **Levin, Ira.** *This Perfect Day. New York: Random House.*
>Computer dystopia.

1970   **Mitchell, Adrian.** *The Bodyguard.* London: Jonathan Cape. **DLC**
>Dystopia — violence.

1970   **Priest, Christopher.** *Indoctrinaire.* London: Faber.
>Anarchist eutopia.

1970   **Reynolds, Mack.** "Utopian," in *The Year 2000,* edited by Harry Harrison (Garden City: Doubleday, 1970), pp. 91–110.
>Eutopia brings degeneration.

1970   **Russ, Joana.** *And Chaos Died.* New York: Ace.
>ESP on eutopian planet. Earth an authoritarian dystopia.

1970   **Silverburg, Robert,** "Black Is Beautiful," in *The Year 2000,* edited by Harry Harrison (Garden City: Doubleday, 1970), pp. 175–193.
>Apartheid.

1970   **[Tucker, Allan James.]** *Contact Lost,* by David Craig (pseud.). London: Jonathan Cape. **DLC, CaOTP**
>See 1968 [Tucker] and also 1969 Tucker.

1970   **[Upchurch, Boyd.]** *Sex and the High Command,* by John Boyd (pseud.). New York: Weybright and Talley. **IU**
>Satire on male chauvinism and women's liberation.

1970   **[Youd, C. S.]** *The Guardians,* by John Christopher (pseud.). London: Hamish Hamilton. **L, DLC**
>Dystopia — overcrowded cities for the proletariat. Rural life for the aristocracy. Maintained by psychological conditioning and brain surgery.

1971   **Adlard, Mark.** *Interface.* London: Sidgwick & Jackson. **IU**
>First of a series about Stahlnex (only building material) Corp. — controls world. Few live in splendour and isolation. Others live in a overpopulation dystopia.

1971   **Bass, T.J.** *Half Past Human.* New York: Ballantine.
>Overpopulation dystopia.

1971   **Brunner, John.** *The Wrong End of Time.* Garden City: Doubleday.
>Dystopia — U.S. controlled by the Department of Defense.

1971   **Bunch, David R.** *Moderan; Extraordinary Chronicles of the World of the Future.* New York: Avon.
>Militaristic dystopia.

1971   **Dickson, Gordon R.** *Sleepwalker's World.* Philadelphia: Lippincott.
>Overpopulation dystopia.

1971   **Ehrlich, Max.** *The Edict.* Garden City: Nelson Doubleday.
        Overpopulation dystopia — ruling that there be no children
        for thirty years.

1971   **Ellison, Harlan.** "Silent in Gehenna," in *The Many Worlds of
        Science Fiction,* edited by Ben Bova (New York: E.P. Dutton,
        1971), pp. 196–217.
        Dystopia — patriotism. Universities run by the military.

1971   **Keilty, James.** "The People of Prashad," in *The New Improved
        Sun,* edited by Thomas M. Disch (New York: Harper & Row,
        1975), pp. 49–80. Originally published in *Quark.*
        Anarchist, nature-oriented eutopia.

1971   **Lange, Oliver.** *Vandenberg.* New York: Stein & Day. **MoU-St**
        Communist takeover of U.S.

1971   **McAllister, Bruce.** "Benji's Pencil," in *The Best from Fantasy and
        Science Fiction. Nineteenth Series,* edited by Edward L. Ferman
        (Garden City: Doubleday, 1971), pp. 273–283.
        Dystopia — art dead, no grass, mandatory death at seventy.

1971   **MacLean, Katherine.** *The Missing Man.* New York: Berkeley, 1975.
        Originally published in *Analog.*
        Dystopia — overpopulation leads to break up into small, hos-
        tile communities.

1971   **Percy, Walker.** *Love in the Ruins.* London: Eyre & Spottiswoode.
        Racial conflict. General collapse of civilization.

1971   **Sillitoe, Alan.** *Travels in Nihilon.* London: W. H. Allen.
        Satire on anarchism (nihilism).

1971   **Silverberg, Robert.** *A Time of Changes.* Garden City: Nelson
        Doubleday. **DLC**
        Dystopia — emphasis on group cohesion.

1971   **Wager, W. Warren.** *Building the City of Man; Outlines of a World
        Civilization.* New York: Grossman Publishers.
        Borderline — mostly on current crisis of civilization. Detailed
        eutopia — new world culture must develop if people are to
        survive.

1971   **Wylie, Philip.** *Los Angeles A.D. 2017.* New York: Popular Library.
        Overpopulation dystopia.

1972   **Adlard, Mark.** *Volteface.* London: Sidgwick & Jackson.
        Authoritarian dystopia.

1972   **Biggle, Lloyd, Jr.** *The Light That Never Was.* Garden City:
        Doubleday.
        Planet devoted to art. Much adventure. Anti-alien pogroms.

1972   **Brunner, John.** *The Sheep Look Up.* New York: Harper & Row.
        Pollution dystopia.

1972   **Disch, Thomas M.** *334.* London: MacGibbon & Kee.

Near future U.S. as dystopia — violence, overpopulation, poverty.

1972 **Dozois, Gardner R.** "Machines of Loving Grace," in Damon Knight, ed., *Orbit 11* (New York: G. P. Putnam's Sons, 1972), pp. 147–152.
Overpopulation and machine dystopia.

1972 **Du Maurier, Daphne.** *Rule Britannia.* London: Victor Gollancz.
Dystopia — U.S. becomes all Disneyland.

1972 **Elgin, Suzette Haden.** *At the Seventh Level.* New York: DAW Books.
Development of 1969 Elgin, "For the Sake of Grace."

1972 **Herbert, Frank.** *Hellstrom's Hive.* New York: Bantam. Originally published in *Galaxy* as "Project 40."
Future man becomes hive creature.

1972 **Hill, Richard.** "Moth Race," in *Again, Dangerous Visions,* edited by Harlan Ellison (Garden City: Doubleday, 1972), pp. 538–548.
Overpopulation dystopia.

1972 **Hoffman, Lee.** "Soundless Evening," in *Again, Dangerous Visions,* edited by Harlan Ellison (Garden City: Doubleday, 1972), pp. 422–426.
Overpopulation dystopia.

1972 **Lewin, Leonard C.** *Triage.* New York: Dial Press. **MoU-St**
Presents a picture of a near future where the "unfit," and many others, are being eliminated by a planned campaign of murder, accident and genocide.

1972 **Lupoff, Richard A.** "With the Bentfin Boomer Boys on Little Old New Alabama," in *Again, Dangerous Visions,* edited by Harlan Ellison (Garden City: Doubleday, 1972), pp. 676–765.
Racial conflict.

1972 **[McIlwain, David.]** *Alph,* by Charles Eric Maine (pseud.). Garden City: Nelson Doubleday.
Society without men and the effect of the creation of one.

1972 **Malzberg, Barry N.** *Revelations.* New York: Warner.
Technological dystopia — emphasis on a TV talk show.

1972 **Moorcock, Michael.** *An Alien Heat,* Vol. 1 of *The Dancers at the End of Time.* London: MacGibbon & Kee.
World where each individual has control over matter. A balanced, loving society. Continued in *The Hollow Lands* which is not a utopia.

1972 **Norman, Alfred Lorn.** *Informational Society.* Paper Number Five. Office for Applied Social Science and the Future, Center for Urban and Regional Affairs, University of Minnesota, Minneapolis, June 1972.
Detailed eutopia — automation, stress on information flow.

1972   **Peck, Richard E.** "Gantlet," in *Orbit 10,* edited by Damon Knight (New York: G. P. Putnam's Sons, 1972), pp. 157–168.
Dystopia — overpopulation, pollution.

1972   **Phillifent, John T.** *Genius Unlimited.* New York: DAW Books.
Eutopia of geniuses has problems.

1972   **Priest, Christopher.** *Fugue for a Darkening Island.* London: Faber & Faber. U.S. edition entitled *Darkening Island.* **DLC**
Race war.

1972   **Rocklynne, Ross.** "Ching Witch!," in *Again, Dangerous Visions,* edited by Harlan Ellison (Garden City: Doubleday, 1972), pp. 10–26.
Dystopia — rule by teenagers.

1972   **Russ, Joanna.** "Nobody's Home," in *Women of Wonder,* edited by Pamela Sargent (New York: Vintage, 1974), pp. 231–256. Originally published in Robert Silverberg, ed., *New Dimensions 2.*
Eutopia — extended family.

1972   **Russ, Joanna.** "When It Changed," in *Again, Dangerous Visions,* edited by Harlan Ellison (Garden City: Doubleday, 1972), pp. 253–260.
Eutopia without men.

1972   **Sargent, Pamela.** "A Sense of Difference," in *and walk gently through the fire and other science fiction stories,* edited by Roger Elwood (Philadelhia: Chilton Book Co., 1972), pp. 137152.
Clones.

1972   **Silverberg, Robert.** *The Second Trip.* Garden City: Nelson Doubleday.
Dystopian background — criminals have personality wiped out, new personality implanted.

1972   **Skal, Dave.** "They Cope," in *Orbit 11,* edited by Damon Knight (New York: G. P. Putnam's Sons, 1972), pp. 153–157.
Dystopia of sensory overload.

1972   **Tubb, E.C.** *Century of the Manikin.* New York: DAW Books.
Future society — non-violent, heavy drug use, free sexuality. Underground sadism.

1972   **Vale, Eugene.** *Some State of Affairs.* London: W. H. Allen. **L**
A group of capitalists buy an island and hire an idealistic college professor to write a constitution. They want a sovereign state free from taxes, hippies, etc. Conflict develops between the capitalists' desires and the ideals of the professor. Arcadia.

1972   **Vonnegut, Kurt, Jr.** "The Big Space Fuck," in *Again, Dangerous Visions,* edited by Harlan Ellison (Garden City: Doubleday,

1972), pp. 267–272.
Pollution dystopia.

1972   **Watkins, William Jon and E.V. Snyder.** *Ecodeath.* Garden City: Doubleday. **IaSU**
Pollution dystopia.

1972   **Wilhelm, Kate.** "The Funeral," in *Again, Dangerous Visions,* edited by Harlan Ellison (Garden City: Doubleday, 1972), pp. 218–241.
Borderline — post catastrophe dystopia. Society divided into castes. Teachers hold great authority. Children are under complete control. Old resent the young and had most killed in the past.

1972   **Yarbro, Chelsea Quinn.** "False Dawn," in *Strange Bedfellows, Sex and Science Fiction,* edited by Thomas N. Scortia (New York: Random House, 1972), pp. 117–134.
Borderline — post catastrophe dystopia. Barbarianism. Violence — rape is common. Gang warfare. Mutants.

1973   **Anderson, Poul.** *The People of the Wind.* New York: New American Library.
Eutopia — limited government.

1973   **Anderson, Poul.** "The Pugilist," in *20/20 Vision,* edited by Jerry Pournelle (New York: Avon, 1974), pp. 85–117.
Authoritarian dystopia.

1973   **Benello, C. George.** "A Serviceable Past," in 1973 American Anthropological Association Experimental Symposium on Cultural Futuristics: Pre-Conference Volume.
Detailed eutopia — two societies set in 2010. In one depletion of resources has produced a poor society. In the other an eutopia is presented that rejects growth and emphasizes ecology and religion. Decentralizatiaon, crafts, education through apprenticeship.

1973   **Berger, Thomas.** *Regiment of Women.* London: Eyre Methuen.
Sex-role reversal.

1973   **Brunner, John.** *The Stone That Never Came Down.* Garden City: Doubleday.
Dystopia — religion and morals too strict.

1973   **Bryant, Edward.** "The Legend of Cougar Lou Landis," in *Universe 3,* edited by Terry Carr (New York: Random House, 1973), pp. 135–150.
Plutocracy.

1973   **Carr, Terry.** "Saving the World," in *Saving Worlds,* edited by Roger Elwood and Virginia Kidd (Garden City: Doubleday & Co. 1973), pp. 2–16.
Ecology dystopia with hopeful ending.

1973   **Cooper, Edmund.** *The Cloud Walker.* New York: Ballantine. **GU**
Luddite reaction in the future after a catastrophe. Religious dystopia.

1973   **Cooper, Edmund.** *The Tenth Plant.* New York: G. P. Putnam.
Stapledonian future.

1973   **Dickinson, Peter.** *The Green Gene.* New York: Pantheon.
Apartheid — Irish.

1973   **Dickson, Gordon R.** *The R-Master.* Philadelphia: J.B. Lippincott.
Flawed eutopia.

1973   **Disch, Thomas M.** "Pyramids for Minnesota — A Serious Proposal," in *The New Improved Sun,* edited by Thomas M. Disch (New York: Harper & Row, 1975), pp. 167–170. Originally published *Harper's Magazine*
Modern version of 1905 Wells' samurai.

1973   **Dobbert, Marion L.** "London Times, 2075 July 15. Reporter Visits Lincoln. First Reporter in 100 Years," in 1973 American Anthropological Association Experimental Symposium on Cultural Futuristics: Pre-Conference Volume.
Detailed eutopia — ecologically sound society that stresses the human scale

1973   **Effinger, George Alec.** "The Ghost Writer," in *Universe 3,* edited by Terry Carr (New York: Random House, 1973), pp. 61–73.
Society of high technical ability that is strongly opposed to change or difference.

1973   **Frayn, Michael.** *Sweet Dreams.* London: Collins.
Satire — fantasy of ordinary individuals in the process of creating the world. Humor.

1973   **Heinlein, Robert A.** *Time Enough for Love: The Lives of Lazarus Long.* New York: Putnam. **DLC**
Wide ranging detailed eutopia — dystopia.

1973   **Judson, [Lyman Spicer] Vincent.** *Solution PNC and PNCland.* [Oshkosh, Wisconsin:] Apex University Press. **DLC**
Anarcho-capitalist eutopia. Developed in *The AQUA Declaration* (1976).

1973   **Kenwood, Robin.** *The U.F.O. Story.* [Richmond, Virginia:] International Friends. **DLC**
Detailed eutopia — low population, one race, one universal language, world government.

1973   **Kuer, Dorothy and Russell La Due.** "Univaria; A Cultural Alternative," in 1973 American Anthropological Association Experimental Symposium on Cultural Futuristics: Pre-Conference Volume.
Detailed eutopia — leadership by people like 1905 Wells' samurai. Ceiling on income, no inheritance — no taxes.

Decentralization. Limit on family size.

1973   **Le Guin, Ursula K.** "The Ones Who Walk Away from Omelas (Variations on a Theme by William James)," in *New Dimensions 3,* edited by Robert Silverberg (Garden City: Doubleday & Co., 1973), pp. 1–8.
Flawed eutopia.

1973   **MacLean, Katherine.** "Small War," in *Saving Worlds,* edited by Roger Elwood and Virginia Kidd (Garden City: Doubleday & Co., 1973), pp. 61–67.
Ecology dystopia.

1973   **Malzberg, Barry N.,** "Conversation's at Lothar's," in *The Liberated Future,* edited by Robert Hoskins (Greenwich, Connecticut: Fawcett, 1974), pp. 229–234. Originally published in *Children of Infinity,* edited by Roger Elwood.
Overpopulation dystopia.

1973   **Mano, D. Keith.** *The Bridge.* Garden City: Doubleday & Co.
MoUK
Authoritarian dystopia — disaster tale.

1973   **Muir, John.** *The Velvet Monkey Wrench.* Santa Fe: John Muir Publications.
Detailed eutopia with plans of how to attain it.

1973   **Neville, Lil and Kris.** "The Quality of the Product," in *Saving Worlds,* edited by Roger Elwood and Virginia Kidd (Garden City: Doubleday & Co., 1973), pp. 31–54.
Ecology dystopia.

1973   **Niven, Larry.** "Cloak of Anarchy," in *20/20 Vision,* edited by Jerry Pournelle (New York: Avon, 1974), pp. 41–61.
Anti-anarchy. Freedom possible only through control.

1973   **Norton, André.** "Desirable Lakeside Residence," in *Saving Worlds,* edited by Roger Elwood and Virginia Kidd (Garden City: Doubleday & Co., 1973), pp. 69–88.
Ecology dystopia.

1973   **O'Neil, Dennis.** "Noonday Devil," in *Saving Worlds,* edited by Roger Elwood and Virginia Kidd (Garden City: Doubleday & Co., 1973), pp. 105–115.
Ecology dystopia.

1973   **Reynolds, Mack.** *Looking Backward, From the Year 2000.* New York: Ace.
Modernized 1888 Bellamy.

1973   **Rocklynne, Ross.** "Randy-Tandy Man," in *Universe 3,* edited by Terry Carr (New York: Random House, 1973), pp. 101–112.
Society in which hate is controlled by forcing everyone to hate until they purge themselves.

1973   **Rositzke, Harry.** *Left On! The Glorious Bourgeois Cultural*

Revolution. New York: Quadrangle/*The New York Times* Book Co.
Satire — U.S. Along Maoist lines.

1973   **[Sheldon, Alice.]** "The Girl Who Was Plugged In," by James Tiptree, Jr. (pseud.), in *New Dimensions 3,* edited by Robert Silverberg (Garden City: Doubleday & Co., 1973), pp. 60-97.
Authoritarian dystopia.

1973   **Thomas, Cogswell.** "Paradise Regained," in *Saving Worlds,* edited by Roger Elwood and Virginia Kidd (Garden City: Doubleday & Co., 1973), pp. 173-191.
Ecology dystopia.

1973   **Van Vogt, A. E.** "Don't Hold Your Breath," in *Saving Worlds,* edited by Roger Elwood and Virginia Kidd (Garden City: Doubleday & Co., 1973), pp. 205-226.
Ecology dystopia.

1973   **Van Vogt, A.E.** *Future Glitter.* New York: Ace.
Authoritarian dystopia.

1973   **Van Vogt, A.E.** "Future Perfect," in *20/20 Vision,* edited by Jerry Pournelle (New York: Avon, 1974), pp. 151-174.
Flawed eutopia.

1973   **Zebrowski, George.** "Parks of Rest and Culture," in *Saving Worlds,* edited by Roger Elwood and Virginia Kidd (Garden City: Doubleday & Co., 1973), pp. 17-29.
Ecology dystopia.

1974   **Arnason, Eleanor.** "A Clear Day in Motor City," in *The New Improved Sun,* edited by Thomas M. Disch (New York: Harper & Row, 1975), pp. 108-116. Originally published in *New Worlds 6.*
Drug induced eutopia.

[1974]   **Brameld, Theodore.** *The Teacher As World Citizen.* [The 1974 Kappa Delta Pi Lecture] np: [Kappa Delta Pi Press]. **MoU-St**
Eutopia stressing world government, socialist humanism and ecology.

1974   **Compton, D[avid] G[uy].** *The Unsleeping Eye.* New York: DAW Books. Also entitled *The Continuous Katherine Mortenhoe.*
Media dystopia.

1974   **Darrow, Frank M.** *Wife Styles and Life Styles.* Trona, California: Author. Cover has subtitle *Science Fiction Sociology and Instant V.D.* **MoU-St**
Presents two societies, each a mixture of good and bad. One is a matriarchy and polygamous. The other is monogamous and very conservative. Attack on the pill.

1974   **Dick, Philip K.** *Flow my tears, the policeman said.* Garden City: Doubleday & Co. **DLC**
Authoritarian dystopia.

1974   **Eklund, Gordon.** *All Times Possible.* New York: DAW
        Authoritarian dystopia.

1974   **Girad, Dian.** "Eat, Drink, and Be Merry," in *20/20 Vision,*
        edited by Jerry Pournelle (New York: Avon, 1974), pp. 121–126.
        Computer dystopia.

1974   **Hersey, John.** *My Petition for More Space.* New York: Alfred
        A. Knopf.
        Overpopulation dystopia.

1974   **Janifer, Laurence M.** *Power.* New York: Dell.
        Guild system as eutopia.

1974   **Jones, D[ennis] F[eltham].** *The Fall of Colossus.* New York:
        Putnams.
        Sequel to 1966 Jones.

1974   **Jones, Robert F.** *Blood Sport; A Journey Up the Hassayampa.*
        New York: Simon & Schuster. 1975 edition entitled *Ratnose.*
        Dystopia of overpopulated, polluted future compared to
        dystopia/eutopia of violent but integrated outlaw com-
        munity.

1974   **Karlins, Marvin and Lewis M. Andrews.** *Gomorrah.* Garden
        City: Doubleday & Co.
        Dystopia — violence.

1974   **Le Guin, Ursula K.** *The Dispossessed: An Ambiguous Utopia.*
        New York: Harper & Row. **MoU-St**
        Detailed anarchist eutopia with problems.

1974   **McDaniel, Dave.** "Prognosis: Terminal," in *20/20 Vision,* edited
        by Jerry Pournelle (New York: Avon, 1974), pp. 129–148.
        Authoritarian, but generally a good society.

1974   **Morland, Dick.** *Albion! Albion.* London: Faber & Faber.
        Dystopia — violence.

1974   **Nozick, Robert.** *Anarchy, State, and Utopia.* New York: Basic
        Books.
        Expository but Part III "Utopia" describes in detail an
        anarcho-capitalist eutopia.

1974   **Reynolds, Mack.** *Commune 2000 A.D.* New York: Bantam.
        Commune system.

1974   **Saberhagen, Fred.** *Berserker's Planet.* New York: DAW Books,
        1975. First published in *If.*
        Sequel to Saberhagen 1967 and 1969.

1974   **Stableford, Brian.** *The Paradise Game.* New York: DAW Books.
        Real paradise of no conflict, but based on viruses that kill
        human beings.

1974   **Tralins, Robert.** *Android Armageddon.* New York: Pinnacle.
        Authoritarian dystopia.

1974   **[Upchurch, Boyd.]** *The Doomsday Gene,* by John Boyd (pseud.).

New York: Weybright & Talley.
Gene for short, intense life.

1975   **Adlard, Mark.** *Multiface.* London: Sidgwick & Jackson.
Picture of a controlled society of the future that is presented as an eutopia, albeit with problems.

1975   **Aldiss, Brian W.** "What You Get For Your Dollar," in *The New Improved Sun,* edited by Thomas M. Disch (New York: Harper & Row, 1975), pp. 38–48.
Future development of the Middle East. Cooperation of Arabs and Israelis. Development of science and art.

1975   **Asimov, Isaac.** "The Life and Times of Multivac," *The New York Times Magazine* (January 5), pp. 12, 51, 56, 58, 70.
Computer eutopia — flawed.

1975   **Ballard, J. G.** *High-Rise.* London: Jonathan Cape.
Dystopia of violence within an apartment block.

1975   **Bass, T. J.** *The Godwhale.* London: Eyre Methuen.
Authoritarian dystopia — degeneration.

1975   **Brunner, John.** *The Shockwave Rider.* New York: Harper & Row.
Computer dystopia — authoritarian.

1975   **Callenbach, Ernest.** *Ecotopia. The Notebooks and Reports of William Weston.* Berkeley: Banyan Tree Books. **DLC**
Ecological eutopia.

1975   **Davidson, Michael.** *The Karma Machine.* New York: Popular Library.
Computer dystopia.

1975   **Drennan, Paul.** *Wooden Centauri.* Morley: Elmfield. **L**
Authoritarian dystopia.

1975   **Elliott, Sumner Locke.** *Going.* New York: Harper & Row.
Future dystopia of love and patriotism.

1975   **Gibbs, Barbara and Francis Golffing.** "A Prologue to Utopia: The Six Days of its Creation (out of the conditions of the now-existing world)," *Northern New England Review,* 1:68–73.
Short description of the beginnings of a eutopia based on "a psychological revolution" which allows human beings to see themselves as one world-wide society.

1975   **Gotschalk, Felix C.** *Growing Up in Tier 3000.* New York: Ace.
Grotesque — children kill parents as part of the rites of passage. Constraint on energy resources necessitates limit on population.

1975   **Hyams, Edward [S.].** *Morrow's Ants.* London: Allen Lane. **DLC**
Industrialist applies knowledge of ant colonies to human workers, and develops a new community on the same principles.

1975   **Le Guin, Ursula K.** "The New Atlantis," in *The New Atlantis and Other Novellas of Science Fiction,* edited by Robert Silverberg (New York: Hawthorne Books, 1975), pp. 59–85.
Bureaucratic, authoritarian dystopia.

1975   **Malzberg, Barry N.** "Going Down," in *Dystopian Visions,* edited by Roger Elwood (Englewood Cliffs, New Jersey: Prentice-Hall, 1975), pp. 146–67.
Dystopia of sexual gratification — all fantasies and fetishes fulfilled.

1975   **Malzberg, Barry N.** "Uncoupling," in *Dystopian Visions,* edited by Roger Elwood (Englewood Cliffs, New Jersey: Prentice-Hall, 1975), pp. 26–37.
Overpopulation dystopia.

1975   **Mitchison, Naomi.** *Solution Three.* New York: Warner Books.
Overpopulation — eutopia turns into dystopia. Cloning.

1975   **Monteleone, Thomas F.** "Breath's a Ware That Will Not Keep," in *Dystopian Visions,* edited by Roger Elwood (Englewood Cliffs, New Jersey: Prentice-Hall, 1975), pp. 2–19.
Breeder tanks. Hosts mothers.

1975   **Nye, Cassandra.** "Drumble," in *The New Improved Sun,* edited by Thomas M. Disch (New York: Harper & Row, 1975), pp. 98–107.
Authoritarian eutopia; completely controlled environment.

1975   **Payes, Rachel Cosgrove.** "Come Take a Dip With Me in the Genetic Pool," in *Dystopian Visions,* edited by Roger Elwood (Englewood Cliffs, New Jersey: Prentice-Hall, 1975), pp. 20–24.
Authoritarian genetic council.

1975   **Powe, Bruce.** *The Last Days of the American Empire.* New York: St. Martins (c. 1974).
Class based dystopia.

1975   **Reynolds, Mack.** *Amazon Planet.* New York: Ace.
Sex-role reversal.

1975   **Reynolds, Mack.** *Tomorrow Might Be Different.* New York: Ace.
Future in which a successful, hedonistic, consumer-oriented Soviet Union dominates the world. New religion developed to encourage moderation.

1975   **Rimmer, Robert H.** *The Premar Experiments.* New York: Crown.
Another version of Rimmer's good life through sex.

1975   **Russ, Joanna.** *The Female Man.* New York: Bantam Books.
Feminist eutopia.

1975   **Sargent, Pamela and George Zebrowski.** "Weapons," in *Dystopian Visions,* edited by Roger Elwood (Englewood Cliffs, New Jersey: Prentice-Hall, 1975), pp. 55–73.

1975   **Sladek, John.** "Heavens Below: Fifteen Utopias," in *The New*

Improved Sun, edited by Thomas M. Disch (New York: Harper & Row, 1975), pp. 5–16.
Series of short utopias.

1975 **Spencer, John.** *The Electronic Lullaby Meat Market.* London: Quartet.
Authoritarian dystopia.

1975 **Weekley, Richard.** *The Adventures of Chet Blake — Plastic Man.* Los Angeles: Crescent Publications.
Satire set in the future — impact of a rock group.

1975 **Wyatt, Patrick.** *Irish Rose.* London: Michael Joseph.
Depopulated future. Women kept solely for breeding. All affection is homosexual.

1975 **[Zachary, Hugh.]** *The Stork Factor,* by Zack Hughes (pseud.). New York: Berkeley.
Authoritarian dystopia.

WORKS NOT LOCATED

1799 *Travels in Andamothia.* London.
Cited in *Notes and Queries* (July 12, 1873).

1887 **[Waterhouse, Elizabeth.]** *The Brotherhood of Rest,* by E.W. London: Simpkin. 2nd edition — London: E. Langley, 1889.
Cited in *English Catalogue.*

1888 **Batchelor, John.** *A Strange People.* New York: Ogilvie.
Cited in *National Union Catalog.* Stuart Teitler provided the annotation found in the Chronological List.

1890 *The Angel and the Idiot. A Story of the Next Century.* London: Stott Library.
Cited in *English Catalogue.*

1897 **Flower, Benjamin Orange.** *Equality and Brotherhood.* Boston: Arena.
Cited in *National Union Catalog.*

1900 **Ramsey, Milton Worth.** *Future Dark Ages.* Minneapolis: Nation.
Cited in *National Union Catalog.*

1900 **Ramsey, Milton Worth.** *Two Billion of Miles; or, The Story of a Trip Through the Solar System.* [Minneapolis:] np.
Cited in *National Union Catalog.* In a letter to me the Library of Congress verified that they "discarded" this book some years ago.

1903 **Van Laun, Henri.** *The Gates of Afree A.D. 1928.* London: W. H. White.
Author's name is often listed as Laun, Henri Van. Cited in I.F. Clarke, *Tale of the Future,* who also provided the annotation that appears in the Chronological List.

1912   **L'Hermite de Prague.** *What Will Posterity Say of Us?*
Cited in Creel de la Barra, *Esquema de una teoria del estado utopica.*

1957   **Bowers, R. L.** *Second Earth.* London: Cobra Books.
Cited in I. F. Clarke, *Tale of the Future.*

1958   **Carlton, Mary Shaffer.** *The Golden Phoenix.* New York: Vantage.
Cited in Tuck, *The Encyclopaedia of Science Fiction and Fantasy,* Vol. 1.

ADDENDUM

1840   **Shelley, Percy Bysshe.** "The Assassins. A Fragment of a Romance" in his *Essays, Letters from Abroad, Translations and Fragments.* 2 Vols. ed. Mrs. Shelley (London: E. Moxon. 1840). 1. pp. 182–211. Written in 1814.
Isolated Christian sect as eutopia of innocence and purity.

1926   **Walsh, William.** "Utopia Lost." *Catholic World.* 122 (January, February 1926). p. 433–42. 600–607.
Satire attacking modern science.

1929   **West, Wallace G.** "The Last Man." in Sam Moskowitz (ed.) *When Women Rule.* (New York: Walker. 1972). pp. 104–30. Originally published February 1929 in *Amazing Stories.* **NcRS**
NcRS
Sexless women rule a dull dying world. Last man and an atavistic woman meet and fall in love.

1930   **Sutherland, James.** *The Narrative of Jasper Weeple; Being an Account of His Strange Journey to the Land of Midanglia.* London: Eric Partridge.**L,LL**
Eutopia with a benevolent monarchy. All people are paid equally. Education by Apprenticeship. No marriage, religion or technology.

1932   **Gardner, Thomas S.** "The Last Woman" in Sam Moskowitz (ed.) *When Women Rule* (New York: Walker. 1972). pp. 131–48. Originally published April 1932 in *Wonder Stories.* **NcRs**
Last woman and the man who came to love her killed in a world of macho men.

1955   **Cogswell, Theodore R.** "Consumer's Report" in Rob Sauer (ed.) *Voyagers: Scenarios for a Ship Called Earth* (New York: Zero Population Growth and Ballantine. 1971). pp. 250–62. **GU**
Dystopia — conditioning. Violence.

1955   **Gunn, James.** "Little Orphan Android" in his *Future Imperfect* (New York: Bantam, 1964). pp. 17–45. Originally published in *Galaxy Science Fiction.* **KU**
Consumer androids developed to keep industrial society con-

suming goods at the highest possible level. Compare to 1954 Pohl. "The Midas Plague."

1956 **Dickson, Gordon R.** *Mankind on the Run.* New York: Ace. **CSt**
Authoritarian dystopia.

1957 **Gunn, James.** "Every Day is Christmas" in his *Future Imperfect* (New York: Bantam. 1964). pp. 61–80. Originally published in *Super Science Fiction.* **KU**
Dystopian world in which subliminal advertising is aired 24 hours a day.

1967 **Tubb, E. (dwin) C.(harles).** *Death Is a Dream* London: Rupert Hart-Davis. **L,O,DCC**
Dystopia — a future world with the knowledge of previous reincarnations. Extreme capitalism. Selfishness.

1970 **Pendleton, Don.** *1989: Population Doomsday.* New York. **NcD**
Overpopulation and pollution dystopia

1970 **Spinrad, Norman.** "The Lost Continent" in Anthony Cheetham (ed.) *Science Against Man* (New York: Avon, 1970). pp. 9–56. **CNSt**
Future with Africa dominant. American degenerated due to extensive pollution.

1970 **Stapp, Robert.** *A More Perfect Union.* N.Y.: Harper's Magazine Press in Association with Harper and Row. **IaStU**
Borderline — South receded and in 1981 the Confederacy is a totalitarian dystopia in conflict with the United States.

1971 **Bova, Ben.** THX 1138. New York: Warner Books. Based on the screenplay by George Lucas and Walter Murch.
Authoritarian dystopia.

1971 **Donis, Miles.** *The Fall of New York.* New York: David McKay. **MoSW**
Borderline New Left revolution leaves New York deserted except for children. Violence. Sadism. Army finally wins.

1972 **Farmer, Philip Jose.** "Seventy Years of Decpop." *Galaxy.* (July 1972). pp. 96–104.
Effects of a radical drop in population. Causes serious problems at first, but results in a better life for most people.

1972 **Offutt, Andrew J.** *The Castle Keeps.* New York, Berkeley. **AzU**
Overpopulation and pollution dystopia. Isolated, fortified homes provide the only hope for the future.

1974 **Charnas, Suzy McKee.** *Walk to the End of the World.* New York: Ballantine. **MoU-St**
Post-catastrophe future. Supression of women and their revolt.

1974 **Leguin, Ursula K.** "The Day Before the Revolution" in James Gunn (ed.) *Nebula Award Stories Ten.* New York: Harper &

Row. 1975.) pp. 129–45.

First published August 1974 in *Galaxy*. See 1974 Leguin. *The Dispossessed*. The Story of Odo, theorist of the revolution, as an old woman just before the revolution.

1975   **Peter, Laurence J.** *The Peter Plan; A Proposal for Survival*. New York: William Morrow.

Borderline, but presents a future eutopia based on ecology and participation.

Secondary Works on Utopian Literature

BOOKS

Aalders, W. J. *Toekomstbeelden uit vijf, eeuwen. More — Bunyan — Mandeville — Fichte — Wells.* Groningen, The Netherlands: J. B. Wolters, 1939.

Aaron, Daniel. *Men of Good Hope.* New York: Oxford University Press, 1951.

Abellán, José Luis. *Mito y cultura.* Madrid: Seminarios y Ediciones, 1971.

Adams, Frederick B., Jr. *Radical Literature in America.* Stanford, Connecticut: Overbrook Press, 1939.

Adams, Percy G. *Travellers and Travel Liars 1660–1800.* Berkeley: University of California Press, 1962.

Adams, Robert P. *The Better Part of Valor; More, Erasmus, Colet, and Vives, on Humanism, War, and Peace, 1496–1535.* Seattle: University of Washington Press, 1962.

Adams, Robert P. *Utopias and Social Ideals.* Seattle: University of Washington, Division of Independent Studies, 1976.

Adamson, Jack H. *The Golden Savage Land* (31st Annual Frederick William Reynolds Lecture, University of Utah) Salt Lake City: Division of Continuing Education, University of Utah, 1967.

Adler, Georg. *Geschichte des Sozialismus und Kommunismus von Plato bis zur Gegenwart.* Leipzig: C. L. Hirschfeld, 1899.

Adriani, Maurilio. *L'Utopia.* Rome: Editrice Studium, 1961.

Akin, William. E. *Technocracy and the American Dream; The Technocrat Movement, 1900–1941.* Berkeley: University of California Press, 1977.

Aldiss, Brian W. *Billion Year Spree.* London: Weidenfeld & Nicolson, 1973.

Allinson, A. A. and F. E. Hotchkin. *SF.* Melbourne: Chesire, 1968.

Althaus, Friedrich. *Samuel Hartlib; Ein deutsch-englische Characterbild.* Leipzig: np, [1884]. Reprinted from *Historischen Taschenbuch.*

Altheim, Franz. *Utopie und Wirtschaft; eine geschichtliche Betrachtung.* Frankfurt am Main: V. Klostermann, 1957.

Amersin, Ferdinand. *Das Land der Freihiet. Ein Zukunftsbild in schilichter Erzälungsform.* Graz: Commissions-Verlag "Leykam-Josefstahl," 1874. (*Weisheit und Tugend des reinen Menschenthums,* Vol. 2).

Ames, Russell Abbot. *Citizen Thomas More and His Utopia.* Princeton: Princeton University Press, 1949.

Amis, Kingsley. *New Maps of Hell.* New York: Ballantine, 1960.

Andrade, Oswald De. *A marcha das utopias.* [Rio de Janeiro:] Serviço de Documentação, Ministerio da Educação Cultura, 1966.

Armytage, W. H. G. *Yesterday's Tomorrows; A Historical Survey of Future Societies.* London: Routledge & Kegan Paul, 1968.

Ash, Brian. *Faces of the Future.* New York: Taplinger, 1975.

Atkinson, Geoffroy. *The Extraordinary Voyage in French Literature Before 1700.* New York: Columbia University Press, 1920.

Atkinson, Geoffroy. *The Extraordinary Voyage in French Literature from 1700 to 1720.* Paris: Edouard Champion, 1922.

Atkinson, Geoffroy. *Les Relations de voyages du XVIIe siècle et l'évolution des idées. Contribution à l'étude de la formation de l'esprit du XVIIIe siècle.* Paris: Edouard Champion, [1924].

Autran, Ch[arles]. *"Utopie;" ou, du rationnel à l'humain.* Paris: L'Éditions d'art et d'histoire, [1941].

Axhausen, Gunther. *Utopie und realismus im betriebsrätegedanken; eine Studie nach Freese und Godin.* Berlin: E. Ebering, 1920. (Betriebs-und fianz-wirtschaftliche Forshungen --- No. 4).

Babcock, William H. *Legendary Islands of the Atlantic. A Study in Medieval Geography.* New York: American Geographical Society, 1922.

Bailey, J. O. *Pilgrims Through Space and Time; Trends and Patterns in Scientific and Utopian Fiction.* New York: Argus, 1947.

Baldini, Massimo. *Il lenguaggio delle Utopie: Utopia e ideologia, una rilettura epistemologia.* Rome: Studium, 1974.

Baldini, Massimo. *Il Pensiero Utopico.* Rome: Città Nuova Editriu, 1974.

Baldry, H. C. *Ancient Utopias.* Southampton: University of Southampton, 1956.

Baring-Gould, S[abine]. *Curious Myths of the Middle Ages.* London: Rivingtons, 1866.

Barkun, Michael. *Disaster and the Millenium.* New Haven: Yale University Press, 1974.

Barmeyer, Eike, ed. *Science Fiction: Theorie und Geschichte.* Munich: Wilhelm Fink Verlag, 1972.

Barron, Neil. *Anatomy of Wonder: Science Fiction.* New York: R. R. Bowker, 1976.

Baudet, Henri. *Paradise on Earth. Some Thoughts on European Images of Non-European Man.* Translated by Elizabeth Wentholt. New Haven: Yale University Press, 1965.

Baudin, Henri. *La Science-Fiction; Un univers en espansion.* Paris: Bordas, 1971.

Bauer, Hermann. *Kunst und Utopie. Studien über das Kunst- und Staatsdenken in der Renaissance.* Berlin: de Gruyter, 1965.

Bauer, Wolfgang. *China and the Search for Happiness; Recurring Themes in Four Thousand Years of Chinese Cultural History.* Translated by Michael Shaw. New York: Seabury Press, 1976.

Baumann, Zygmunt. *Socialism; The Active Utopia.* New York: Holmes and Meier, 1976.

Baumer, Franz. *Paradiese der Zukunft; Die Menschheitsträume vom besseren Leben.* Munich: Langen-Muller, 1967.

Becker, Carl. *The Heavenly City of the Eighteenth Century Philosophers.* New Haven: Yale University Press, 1932.

Berger, Harold L. *Science Fiction and the New Dark Age.* Bowling Green, Ohio: Bowling Green University Popular Press, 1976.

Bentley, Wilder. *The Communication of Utopian Thought; Its History, Forms, & Use. I. The Bibliography.* San Francisco: San Francisco State College Bookstore, 1959.

Beres, Louis René and Harry R. Targ. *Reordering the Planet; Constructing Alternative World Futures.* Boston: Allyn and Bacon, 1974.

Beresford, J[ohn] D[avys]. *H. G. Wells.* London: Nisbet & Co., 1915.

Bergonzi, Bernard. *The Early H. G. Wells: A Study of the Scientific Romances.* Manchester: Manchester University Press, 1961.

Bernal, J[ohn] D[esmond]. *The World, the Flesh and the Devil; An Inquiry into the Future of the Three Enemies of the Rational Soul.* 2nd edition. Bloomington: Indiana University Press, 1969.

Bernardi, Walter. *Utopia e socialismo nel '700 francese.* Florence: Sansoni, 1974.

Berneri, Marie Louise. *Journey Through Utopia.* London: Routledge & Kegan Paul, 1950.

Bernstein, Eduard. *Cromwell and Communism.* London: George Allen & Unwin, 1930.

Bidez, J[oseph]. *La cité du monde et la cité du soleil chez les Stoïciens.* Paris: Les Belles Lettres, 1932. Originally published in *Bulletin de l'Academie royale de Belgique,* 5th series 18, Nos. 7-9, pp. 244-94.

Biese, Y. M. *Notes on the Vocabulary in Compton Mackenzie's Novel "The Lunatic Republic."* Series B, Vol. 78 of *Turun Yliopiston Julkaisuja. Annales Universitatis Turkuensis.* Turku, Finland: Yurun Yliopisto, 1963.

Biesterfeld, Wolfgang. *Die literarische Utopie.* Stuttgart: Metzler, 1974.

Bingenheimer, Heinz. *Transgalaxis. Katalog der deutschsprachigen utopisch-phantastischen Literatur, 1460–1960.* [Friedrichsdorf:] Trans-galaxis, 1959/1960.

Bisinger, Josef. *Der Agrarstaat in Platons Gesetzen.* Leipzig: Deiterich'sche Verlagsbuchhandlung, 1925. *Klio. Beiträge zur Alten Geschichte,* Supplement 17, New Series, No. 4.

Blanchet, Léon. *Campanella.* Paris: Felix Alcan, 1920.

Bleiler, Everett F., ed. *The Checklist of Fantastic Literature; A bibliography of fantasy, weird and science fiction books published in the English language.* New edition. Naperville, Illinois: FAX Collector's Editions, 1972.

Bleymehl, Jakob. *Beiträge zur Geschichte und Bibliographie der Utopischen und phantastischen Literatur.* Privately Printed, 1965.

[Blish, James.] *The Issue at Hand,* by William Atheling, Jr. (pseud.). Chicago: Advent, 1964.

[Blish, James.] *More Issues at Hand,* by William Atheling, Jr. (pseud.). Chicago: Advent, 1970.

Blitzer, Charles. *An Immortal Commonwealth; The Political Thought of James Harrington.* New Haven: Yale University Press, 1960.

Bloch, Ernst. *Freiheit und Ordnung; Abriss der Sozial-Utopien.* New York: Aurora Verlag, 1946.

Bloch, Ernst. *Geist der Utopie.* Munich: Duncker & Humblot, 1918.

Bloch, Ernst. *Das Prinzip Hoffnung.* 3 Vols. Berlin: Aufbau-Verlag, 1955–1959.

Bloch, Ernst. *Thomas Munzer als Theologe der Revolution.* Frankfurt am Main: Suhrkamp Verlag, 1960.

Bloch, Ernst. *Tübinger Einleitung in die Philosophie.* 2 Vols. Frankfurt am Main: Suhrkamp Verlag, 1963.

Bloomfield, Paul. *Imaginary Worlds or The Evolution of Utopia.* London: Hamish Hamilton, 1932.

Blüher, Rudolf. *Moderne Utopien: ein Beitrag zur Geschichte des Sozialismus.* Bonn: Kurt Schroeder, 1920.

Bodin, Felix. *Le Roman de l'avenir.* Paris: Lecointe et Pougin, 1834.

Boguslaw, Robert. *The New Utopians; A Study of System Design and Social Change.* Englewood Cliffs, New Jersey: Prentice-Hall, 1965.

Bohrer, Karl Heinz. *Der Lauf des Freitag: die ladiërte Utopie und die Dichter. Eine Analyse* (Reihe Hanser, 123). Munich: Carl Hanser, 1973.

Borries, Achim Von and Ingeborg Brandies, comps. *Anarchismus. Theorie, Kritik, Utopie. Texte und Kommentare.* Frankfurt am Main: Melzer, 1970.

Bortone, Leone, [ed.]. *L'Utopia; una antologia dagli scritti di Moro, Campanella, Bacone.* Torino: Loescher, 1957.

Bossle, Lother. *Utopie und Wirklichkeit im politischen Denken von Reinhold Schneider.* Mainz: Hase and Koehler, [1965].

Bourgin, Hubert. *Étude sur les sources de Fourier.* Paris: Société Nouvelle de Librairie et d'edition, 1905.

Bowman, Sylvia E., et al. *Edward Bellamy Abroad; An American Prophet's Influence.* New York: Twayne Publishers, 1962.

Bowman, Sylvia E., *The Year 2000, A Critical Biography of Edward Bellamy.* New York: Bookman Associates, 1958.

Bozza, Tommaso. *Scrittori Politici Italiani dal 1550 al 1650; Saggio di Bibliografia.* Rome: Edizioni di 'Storia e letteratura', 1949.

Bramwell, James. *Lost Atlantis.* London: Cobden-Sanderson, [1937].

Braunert, Horst. *Utopia. Antworten griechischen Denkens auf die Herausforderung durch soziale Verhältnisse.* New series No. 51 of *Veröffentlichungen der Schleswig-Holsteinischen Universitätsgesellschaft.* Kiel: Ferdinand Hirt, 1969.

Bretnor, Reginald, ed. *Modern Science Fiction, Its Meaning and Its Future.* New York: Coward-McCann, 1953.

Bretnor, Reginald, ed. *Science Fiction; Today and Tomorrow.* New York: Harper & Row, 1974.

Briney, Robert E. and Edward Wood. *SF Bibliographies; An Annotated Bibliography of Bibliographical Works on Science Fiction and Fantasy Fiction.* Chicago: Advent, 1972.

Brockhaus, Heinrich. *Die Utopia-Schrift des Thomas Morus.* Leipzig: B. G. Teubner, 1929. Beiträge zur Kulturgeschichte des Mittelalters und der Renaissance. Vol. 37.

Brooks, Robert E. *Utopian Universe.* New York: R. J. R. Press, [1973].

Brüggemann, Fritz. *Utopie und Robinsonade: Untersuchungen zu Schnabels Insel Felsenburg (1731–1743).* Vol. 46 of *Forschungen zur neueren Literaturgeschichte,* edited by Franz Muncker. Weimar: Alexander Muncker, 1914.

Brüggemann, Fritz, ed. *Verboten der bürgerlichen Kultur; Johann Gottfried Schnabel und Albrecht von Haller.* Leipzig: Phillip Reclam, 1931.

Brussels. Université libre. Institut pour l'étude de la Renaissance et de l'humanisme. *Les Utopies à la Renaissance.* Brussels: Presses Universitaires, 1963.

Buber, Martin. *Paths in Utopia,* translated by R. F. C. Hull. Boston: Beacon, 1949.

Buchner, Hermann. *Programmiertes Glück. Soziakritik in der utopischen Sowjetliteratur.* Vienna: Europa Verlag, [1970].

Bühler, Theodor. *Von der Utopie zum Sozialstaat; [Randbemerkungen zu einem zeitgemässen Problem].* Stuttgart: W. Kohlhammer Verlag, 1942.

Cabodevilla, Jose Maria. *Feria de utopias; estudio sobre la felicidad humana.* Madrid: Biblioteca de Autores Cristianos, 1974.

Campbell, W[illiam] E[dward]. *More's Utopia and His Social Teaching.* London: Eyre and Spottiswoode, 1930.

Cantimori, Delio. *Utopisti e Riformatori Italiani 1794–1847. Ricerche Storiche.* Florence: G. C. Sansoni, [1943].

[Carandell, José Maria.] *Las Utopias.* Barcelona: Salvat Editores, [1974].

Case, Arthur E. *Four Essays on Gulliver's Travels.* Princeton: Princeton University Press, 1945.

Castro, Giovanni De. *Vecchie Utopie.* Milan: Max Kantorowicz, Editore, 1895.

Cepeda, Alfredo. *Los Utopistas: Owen — Saint Simon — Fourier — Leroux — Considerant.* Buenos Aires: Editorial Futuro, 1944.

Chambers, R. W. *Thomas More.* Ann Arbor: University of Michigan Press, 1958.

Chambon, Guy. *Les Utopistes et l'urbanisation.* [Paris:] Editions Cujas, 1975.

Chaudoir Roberti, Maurice. *L'Autorité, essai de sociologie et d'economie politique. Critériologie des bases du principe d'autorité. Le socialisme dans le passé. Le socialisme et ses promesses. Histoire analytique de 256 utopies. La crise. La panne. Le carnet independant.* Paris: "Les Clématites," 1923.

Cheng, J[ames] C[hester]. *Chinese Sources for the Taiping Rebellion 1850–1864.* Hong Kong: Hong Kong University Press, 1963.

Chianese, Robert L., ed. *Peaceable Kingdoms; An Anthology of Utopian Writings.* New York: Harcourt Brace Jovanovich, 1971.

Choay, François. *L'Urbanisme; Utopies et réalités. Une anthologie.* Paris: Éditions du Seuil, 1965.

Cioran, E. M. *Histoire et utopie.* Paris: Gallimard, 1960.

Cioranescu, Alexandre. *L'Avenir du passé; Utopie et littérature.* Paris: Gallimard, 1972.

Clareson, Thomas D., ed. *Many Futures Many Worlds; Theme and Form in Science Fiction.* [Kent, Ohio:] Kent State University Press, 1977.

Clareson, Thomas D. *SF: A Dream of Other Worlds.* College Station, Texas: Texas A&M University Library, 1973. Texas A&M University Library Miscellaneous Publication 6.

Clareson, Thomas D. *Science Fiction Criticism; An Annotated Checklist.* [Kent, Ohio:] Kent State University Press, 1972.

Clarke, I. F. *The Tale of the Future from the Beginning to the Present Day. An Annotated Bibliography of those satires, ideal states, imaginary wars and invasions, potential warnings and forecasts, interplanetary voyages and scientific romances — all located in an imaginary future period — that have been published in the United Kingdom between 1644 and 1976.* 3rd edition. London: The Library Association, 1978.

Clarke, I. F. *Voices Prophesying War 1763–1984.* London: Oxford University Press, 1966.

Coates, J. B. *Ten Modern Prophets.* London: Frederick Muller, 1944.

Cobo Suero, J. B. *Un ensayo de pensamiento social postcomunista.* Madrid: Editorial Razón y Fe, [1965].

Cocchiara, Giuseppe. *Il Mito del Buon Selvaggio; Introduzione alla Storia della Teorie Etnologische.* Messina: G. D'Anna, 1948.

Cohn, Norman. *The Pursuit of the Millenium; Revolutionary messianism in medieval and Reformation Europe and its bearing on modern totalitarian movements.* 2nd edition. New York: Harper & Row, 1961.

Coletta, Mario. *Lo spazio sociologico nell'urbanistica dell'utopia.* Bologna: Istituto Aldini-Valeriani, [1969].

Connes, Georges. *Étude sur la pensée de Wells.* [Paris:] Librarie Hachette, 1926.

Conrads, Ulrich and Hans G. Sperlich. *The Architecture of Fantasy; Utopian Building and Planning in Modern Times.* Translated, edited and expanded by Christiane Crasemann Collins and George R. Collins. New York: Frederick A. Praeger, 1962.

Corbin, Mrs. Carol Elizabeth (Fairfield). *The Position of Women in the Socialistic Utopia.* [Chicago: American Association Opposed to Socialism, 1901].

Cornelius, Paul. *Languages in seventeenth- and early eighteenth-century imaginary voyages.* Geneva: Librairie Droz, 1965.

Cox, Carlos Manuel. *Utopía y realidad en el Inca Garcilaso: pensamiento económica, interpretación histórica.* Lima: Universidad, [1965].

Crawford, Joseph H., Jr., James J. Donahue, and Donald M. Grant. *"333" A Bibliography of the Science-Fantasy Novel.* Providence: The Grandon Co., 1953.

Creel de la Barra, Enrique. *Esquema de una teoria del estado Utopico.* Mexico City: Universidad Nacional Autonoma Facutad De Derecho, 1950.

Crowe, Charles. *George Ripley, Transcendentalist and Utopian Socialist.* Athens, Georgia: University of Georgia Press, 1967.

Csiszár, Jolán, ed. *Utópisztikus, Tudományos-Fantasztikus Müvek Bibliográfiája.* Miskolc, Hungary: np, 1970.

Curcio, Carlo. *Utopisti e riformatori sociali del cinquecento.* Bologna: Nicola Zanichelli, [1941]. Enlarged edition *Utopisti Italiani del cinquecento.* np: Colombo, [1944].

Dameron, Louise. *Utopias: Bibliography.* Revised edition. Baltimore: Enoch Pratt Free Library, 1938.

Dareste de la Chavanne, Antoine Elisabeth Cléophas. *Thomas Morus et Campanella; ou, Essai sur les utopies contemporaines de la renaissance et de la réforme.* Paris: P. Dupont, 1843.

Dark, Sidney. *An Outline of Wells; The Superman in the Street.* New York: G. P. Putnam's Sons, 1922.

Davenport, Basil. *Inquiry into Science Fiction.* London: Longmans, Green & Co., 1955.

Davenport, Basil. *Introduction to 'Islandia.'* New York: Farrar, 1942.

Davenport, Basil, et al. *The Science Fiction Novel; Imagination and Social Criticism.* Chicago: Advent, 1959.

Davidson, Morrison. *The Wisdom of Winstanley the "Digger"; Being Outlines of the Kingdom of God on Earth.* London: Francis Riddell Henderson, 1904. *Fiat Lux* No. 2.

De Camp, L. Sprague and Willy Ley. *Lands Beyond.* New York: Rinehart and Co., 1952.

De Camp, L. Sprague and Willy Ley. *Lost Continents: The Atlantis Theme in History, Science, and Literature.* New York: Gnome Press, 1954.

De la Mare, W. John. *Desert Islands and Robinson Crusoe.* London: Faber & Faber, 1930.

Delvaille, Jules. *Essai sur l'histoire de l'idée de progrès jusqu'a la fin du XVIIIe siècle.* Paris: Félix Alcan, 1910.

Dermenghem, Emile. *Thomas Morus et les utopistes de la Renaissance.* Paris: Plon, 1927.

Desanti, Dominique. *Les socialistes de l'utopie.* Paris: Payot, 1970.

Desroche, Henri. *Les Dieux rêvés. Théisme et athéisme en Utopie.* Paris: Desclée, 1972.

Desroche, Henri. *La société festive: du fourierisme écrit aux fourierismes pratiques.* Paris: Éditions du Seuil, 1975.

Doig, Ivan, ed. *Utopian America: Dreams and Realities.* Rochelle Park, New Jersey: Hayden, 1976.

Döll, Emil. *Das Schicksal aller Utopien oder socialen Charlatanerien und das verstandesgemäss Reformatorische.* Leipzig, C. G. Naumann, [1897].

Donner, H. W. *Introduction to Utopia.* London: Sidgwick and Jackson, 1945.

Dottin, Paul. *Daniel Defoe et ses Romans.* 3 Vols. Paris: Presses Universitaires de France, 1924.

Doughty, F. H. *H. G. Wells Educationist.* London: Jonathan Cape, 1926.

Doxiadis, Constantinos. *Between Dystopia and Utopia.* Hartford: Trinity College Press, 1966.

Dubois, Claude Gilbert. *Problemes de l'utopie.* No. 85 of *Archives des lettres modernes,* Paris: [1968?].

Dubos, René. *The Dreams of Reason; Science and Utopias.* New York: Columbia University Press, 1961.

Dudok, Gerard. *Sir Thomas More and His Utopia.* Paris: Kruyt, 1923.

Dumont, Rene. *L'Utopie ou la Mort.* Paris: Editions du Seuil, 1973. Translated by Vivienne Menkes as *Utopia or Else.* New York: Universe Books, 1974.

Dupont, V[ictor]. *L'Utopie et le Roman Utopique dans la Littérature Anglaise.* Paris: Librarie M. Didier, 1941.

Durning, Russell E. *Margaret Fuller, Citizen of the World: An Intermediary Between European and American Literature.* Heidelberg: Carl Winter, 1969.

Duveau, Georges. *Sociologie de l'utopie et autre 'essais.'* Paris: Presses Universitaires de France, 1961.

Eddy, William A. *Gulliver's Travels; A Critical Study.* Princeton: Princeton University Press, 1923.

Egbert, Donald Drew and Stow Persons, eds. *Socialism and American Life.* 2 Vols. Princeton: Princeton University Press, 1952.

Eichner, Henry M. *Atlantean Chronicles.* Alhambra, California: Fantasy Pub. Co., 1971.

Elliott, Robert C. *The Shape of Utopia; Studies in a Literary Genre.* Chicago: University of Chicago Press, 1970.

Ely, Richard T. *French and German Socialism in Modern Times.* New York: Harper and Brothers, 1883.

Engels, Friedrich. *Die Entwicklung des Sozialismus von der Utopie zur Wissenschaft.* Zurich: Schweizerische Genossenschaftsdruckerei, 1882.

Engländer, Sigmund. *Geschichte der französischen Arbeiten-Assoziation.* 4 Vols. Hamburg: Hofmann and Campe, 1864.

Erdmannsdörffer, Hans Gustav. *Ein Phantasiestaat. Darstellung und Kritik von Bellamys "Im Jahre 2000, Rückblick auf 1887," Vortrag.* Leipzig: Werther, 1891.

Escalante, Manuel F. *Libertad natural y poder politico en el estado perfecto de Tomas Campanella.* [Seville]: Publicacions de la universidad Hispalense, 1969.

Eurich, Nell. *Science in Utopia; A Mighty Design.* Cambridge: Harvard University Press, 1967.

Evans, Bergan. *Utopias; Five talks by Dr. Bergan Evans . . . on Of Men and Books; Presented by Northwestern University and the Department of Education of the Columbia Broadcasting System. . . .* [Evanston?: np., 1940].

Fakkar, Rouchdi [Rushdi]. *L'influence internationale de Saint-Simon et de ses disciples Bilan en Europe et portée extraeuropéene.* Geneva: Victor Chevalier, 1967. Dissertation, Geneva, 1966.

Fakkar, Rouchdi [Rushdi]. *Sociologie Socialisme et Internationalisme prémarxistes. Contribution à l'étude de l'influence internationale de Saint-Simon et de des disciples (Bilan en Europe et portée extraeuropéene).* Neuchâtel: Delachaux & Niestlé, 1968.

Falkiner, C[aesar] Litton. *The New Voyage to Utopia. Address delivered in the dining hall of Trinity College . . . on Thursday evening, November 5th, 1885.* University of Dublin Philosophical Society Proceedings, pp. 4–19.

Falter, G[ustav]. *Staastideale unserer Klassiker.* Leipzig: C. L. Hirschfeld, 1911.

Fedeli, Ugo. *Un Viaggio alle 'Isole Utopia'; Conversazioni tenue in Ivrea al 'Centro Culturale Olivetti' (gennaio-febbraio 1953).* Quaderni del "Centro Culturale Olivetti," np: [1958?].

Ferguson, John. *Utopias of the Classical World.* London: Thames and Hudson, 1975.

[Fernandez de la Mora, Gonzalo.] *Del Estado ideal al Estado de razón. Discurso de ingreso en la Real Academia de Ciencias Morales y Políticas del Excmo.* Madrid: np, 1972.

Ferry, W. H., Michael Harrington, and Frank L. Kugan. *Conversation: Cacotopias and Utopias.* Santa Barbara: Fund for the Republic, 1965.

Filley, Alan C. *Organization Invention: A Study of Utopian Organizations.* Madison: University of Wisconsin, Bureau of Business Research and Service, 1973. Wisconsin Business Papers No. 3.

Firestone, Clark B. *The Coasts of Illusion; A Study of Travel Tales.* New York: Harper & Brothers, 1924.

Firpo, Luigi. *Lo Stato ideale della Controriforma Ludovico Agostini.* Bari. Editori Laterze, 1957.

Fisher, Robert T. *Classical Utopian Theories of Education.* New Haven: College and University Press, 1963.

Fishman, Robert. *Urban Utopias in the 20th Century. Ebenezer Howard, Frank Lloyd Wright, and Le Corbusier.* New York: Basic Books, 1977.

Flammarion, Camille. *Les Mondes imaginaires et les mondes réels; voyage astronomique pittoresque dans le ciel et revue critique des théories humaines scientifiques et romanesques, anciennes et modernes sur les habitants des astres.* Paris: Didier, 1865.

Flashar, Hellmut. *Formen utopischen Denkens bei den Griechen: Vortag, gehalten am 19. Juni 1973.* Innsbruck: Institut für Sprachwissenschaft der Universität Innsbruck, 1974.

Fleisher, Martin. *Radical Reform and Political Persuasion in the Life and Writings of Thomas More.* Geneva: Librarie Droz, 1973.

Flory, Claude R. *Economic Criticism in American Fiction, 1792–1900.* Philadelphia: University of Pennsylvania Press, 1936.

Flower, B[enjamin] O[range]. *The Century of Sir Thomas More.* Boston: Arena Pub. Co., 1896.

Fogg, Walter L. and Peyton E. Richter. *Philosophy Looks to the Future; Confrontation, Commitment, and Utopia.* Boston: Holbrook Press, 1974.

Fraenkel, Heinrich. *Gegen Bellamy!: eine Widerlegung des Sozialistischen Romans Ein Rückblick aus dem Jahre 2000, und des sozialistichen Zunkunftsstaat überhaupt.* 10th edition Würzburg: Stuber, 1891.

Francastel, Pierre, ed. *Utopie et institutions au XVIIIe siècle. Le Pragmatisme du lumières.* Paris: Mouton, 1963.

Francoeur, Robert T. *Utopian Motherhood. New Trends in Human Reproduction.* Garden City: Doubleday, 1970.

Franklin, H. Bruce. *Future Perfect; American Science Fiction of the Nineteenth Century.* New York: Oxford University Press, 1966.

Frei, Bruno. *Die anarchistische Utopie; Freiheit und Ordnung.* Frankfurt am Main: Marxistische Blätter, 1971.

Frei, Bruno. *Zur Kritik der Sozialutopie.* Frankfurt am Main: S. Fischer, [c. 1973].

Freyer, Hans. *Die Politische Insel. Eine Geschichte der Utopien von Platon bis zur Gegenwart.* Leipzig: Bibliographischer Institut ag., 1936.

Friedberg, Morris. *L'influence de Charles Fourier sur le Mouvement Social Contemporain.* Paris: Marcel Giard, 1926.

Friedrich, Gerhard. *Utopie und Reich Gottes; zur Motivation politischen Verhaltens.* Göttingen: Vandenhouk & Ruprecht, [1974].

Fuller, R. Buckminster. *Utopia or Oblivion. The Prospects for Humanity.* New York: Bantam, 1969.

Furter, Pierre. *A dialética da esperança: uma interpretação do pensamento utópico de Ernest Bloch.* Rio de Janeiro: Paz e Terra, 1974.

Fuz, Jerzy Konstanty. *Welfare Economics in Some English Utopias From Francis Bacon to Adam Smith.* Rotterdam: Nederlandsche Economische Hogeschool, 1951.

Gallagher, Buell G. *A Preface to the Study of Utopias* (Antioch College Founders Day Lecture). Yellow Springs, Ohio: Antioch Press, 1960.

Gallagher, Ligeia, ed. *More's Utopia and Its Critics.* Chicago: Scott, Foresman, 1964.

Garcia Cantú, Gastón. *Utopías mexicanas.* México City: Era, 1963.

Garcia San Miguel, L[uis]. *La sociedad autogestionada: Una utopia demogrática.* Madrid: Seminarios y Ediciones, 1972.

Garnier, Charles Georges Thomas, ed. *Voyages Imaginaires, Songes, Visions, et Romans Cabalistiques.* 39 Vols. Amsterdam: np, 1787–1795.

Garrett, John Charles. *Utopias in Literature.* Christchurch: University of Canterbury, 1968.

Gehrke, Dr. A[lbert]. *Communistische Idealstaaten.* Breman: Verlag von C. Schünemann, 1878.

Gerber, Richard. *Utopian Fantasy; A Study of English Utopian Fiction since the End of the Nineteenth Century.* London: Routledge & Kegan Paul, 1955.

Gerhards, Hans-Joachim. *Utopie als innergeschichtlicher Aspeckie der Eschatologie: die konkrete Utopie Ernst Blochs unter dem eschatologischen Gutersloh: Vorbehalt der Theologie Paul Tillichs.* Gutersloh, Germany: Gutersloher Verlagehaus Mohen, 1973.

Gerlich, Fritz. *Der Kommunismus als Lehre vom Tausendjährigen Reich.* Munich: Hugo Bruckmann, 1920.

Gernsback, Hugo. *Evolution of Modern Science Fiction.* [New York: Privately Printed, 1952].

Giamatti, A. Bartlett. *The Earthly Paradise and the Renaissance Epic.* Princeton: Princeton University Press, 1966.

Gilison, Jerome M. *The Soviet Image of Utopia.* Baltimore: The Johns Hopkins University Press, 1975.

Gillet, Mathurin. *L'Utopie de Condorcet.* Paris: Guillaumin et Cie, 1883.

Giordani, Pier Luigi. *il futuro dell'utopia.* Bologna: Calderini, 1969.

Girsberger, Hans. *Der utopische Sozialismus des 18. Jahrhunderts in Frankreich und seine philosophischen und materiellen Grundlagen.* Zürich: Rascher & Cie. A.-G. Verlag, 1924.

Gonnard, René. *Le légende du bon sauvage; Contribution à l'étude des origines du socialisme.* Paris: Librarie de Médicis, 1946.

González, Regino. *Utopiás y realidades socialistes.* Madrid: Imprenta Torrent, 1932.

González Casanova, Pablo. *Una utopía de América.* Mexico City: El Colegio de México, 1953.

Goodheart, Eugene. *The Utopian Vision of D. H. Lawrence.* Chicago: University of Chicago Press, 1963.

Goodman, Paul. *Utopian Essays and Practical Proposals.* New York: Random House, 1962.

Götz, Ina. *Tradition und Utopie in den Dramen Fritz von Unruhs.* Bonn: Bouvier Verlag Herbert Grundmann, 1975.

Gouhier, Henri. *La Jeunesse d'Auguste Comte et la formation du positivisme.* 3 Vols. Paris: Librairie J. Vrin, 1933, 1936, 1941.

Goulding, Sybil. *Swift en France; Essai sur la fortune et l'influence de Swift en France au XVIIIe siècle, suivi d'un aperçu sur la fortune de Swift en France au cours du XIXe siècle.* Paris: Edouard Champion, 1924.

Gove, Philip Babcock. *The Imaginary Voyage in Prose Fiction — A History of Its Criticism and A Guide for Its Study, with an Annotated Check List of 215 Imaginary Voyages from 1700 to 1800.* London: Holland Press, 1961.

Graaf, Vera. *Homo Futurus; Eine Analyse der modernen Science-fiction.* Hamburg: Claassen, 1971.

Gray, Alexander. *The Socialist Tradition: Moses to Lenin.* London: Longmans, Green, & Co., 1946.

Gray, Donald J. and Allan H. Orrick. *Designs of Famous Utopias: Materials for Research Papers.* New York: Holt, Rinehart & Winston, 1959.

Green, Roger Lancelyn. *Into Other Worlds; Space-Flight in Fiction from Lucian to Lewis.* London: Abelard-Schuman, 1957.

Gremmels, Christian and Wolfgang Herrmann. *Vorurteil und Utopie; Zur Aufklärung der Theologie.* Stuttgart: Kohlhammar, [1971].

Grillo, Francesco. *Tommaso Campanella in America; A Critical Bibliography and a Profile.* New York: S. F. Vanni, 1954.

Grimm, Reinhold and Jost Hermand, eds. *Deutsches utopisches Denken im 20. Jahrhundert.* Stuttgart: W. Kohlhammer, 1974.

Gronau, Karl. *Der Staat der Zukunft von Plato bis Dante.* Braunschweig: Georg Westermann, 1933.

Grube, Frank and Gerhard Richter, eds. *Die Utopie der Konservativen: Antworten auf Helmut Schelskys konservatives Manifest.* Munich: Piper, 1974.

Guarnieri, Silvio. *Utopia e realtà.* [Torino:] Guilio Einaudi, 1955.

Guiomar, Michel. *Imaginaire et Utopie.* Geneva: Librarie José Corti, 1976.

Gunn, James E. *Alternate Worlds: The Illustrated History of Science Fiction.* Englewood Cliffs, New Jersey: Prentice-Hall, 1975.

Gunnarson, Gunner. *Socialdemokratiskt idéarv. Utopism, Marxism, Socialism.* Stockholm: Tidens förlag, 1971.

Gunnarson, Gunner, ed. *De stora utopisterna.* 2 Vols. Stockholm: Tidensförlag, 1973.

Gusfield, Joseph R. *Utopian Myths and Movements in Modern Societies.* Morristown, New Jersey: General Learning Press, 1973.

Gustafsson, Lars. *Utopier, och andra essäer om 'dikt' och 'liv'.* Stockholm: Pan/Norstedts, 1969.

Guter, Josef. *Pädagogik in Utopia; Erziehung und Arbeitswelt in sozialpolitischen Utopien der Neuzeit.* Neuwied am Rhein: Hermann Luchterhand, 1968.

Guthrie, W. B. *Socialism Before the French Revolution; A History.* New York: Macmillan, 1907.

Guzmán, Mauricio. *Cautiverio del hombre; proyecciones del utopismo.* Mexico City: B. Costa-Amic, [1968].

H.G. Wells Society. *H. G. Wells: A Comprehensive Bibliography.* London: H. G. Wells Society, 1966.

Hahn, Arnold. *Grenzenloser Optimismus. Die Biologischen und Technischen Möglichkeiten der Menschheit. Utopiologie.* Prague: Arnold Hahn, [1939].

Hamburg. Museum für Kunst und Gewerbe. *Die wilden Leute des Mittelalters.* Hamburg: Museum für Kunst und Gewerbe, 1963.

Hansot, Elisabeth. *Perfection and Progress: Two Modes of Utopian Thought.* Cambridge: MIT Press, 1974.

Harris, John F[rederick]. *Samuel Butler, Author of Erewhon; The Man and His Work.* London: Richards, 1916.

Hausenstein, Wilhelm. *Die grossen Utopisten. Fourier, Saint-Simon, Owen.* Berlin: Paul Singer, 1920.

Heiss, Robert. *Utopie und Revolution; ein Beitrag zur Geschichte des fort-schrittlichen Denkens.* Munich: R. Piper, [1973].

Helm, Rudolf. *Utopia.* Rostock, Germany: Verlag von H. Warkentiens Universitätsbuchhandlung, 1921.

Hennig, Richard. *Wo lag das Paradise? Rätselfragen der Kulturgeschichte und Geographie.* Berlin: Verlag des Druckhauses Tempelhof, 1950.

Herp, Jacques Van. *Panorama de la science fiction: Les thèmes les genres, les écoles, les problèmes.* Marabout: André Gérard, 1973.

Hertzler, Joyce Oramel. *The History of Utopian Thought.* New York: Macmillan, 1923.

Hettner, Hermann. *Robinson und die Robinsonaden.* Berlin: Wilhelm Hertz, 1854.

Hevesi, Ludwig. *Katalog einer Merkwürdigen Sammlung von Werken utopichen Inhalts 16.-20. Jahrh[underts] aus dem Nachlasse des Schrift-stellers.* Vienna: Gilhofer and Ranschberg, [1914?].

Hienger, Jörg. *Literarische Zukunftsphantastik; eine Studie über Science Fiction.* Göttingen, Germany: Vandenhoeck & Ruprecht, 1972.

Higginson, Thomas Wentworth. *Tales of the Enchanted Islands of the Atlantic.* New York: Macmillan Co., 1898.

Hillegas, Mark R. *The Future As Nightmare; H. G. Wells and the Anti-Utopians.* New York: Oxford University Press, 1967.

Hillegas, Mark R. *Shadows of Imagination; The Fantasies of C. S. Lewis, J. R. R. Tolkien, and Charles Williams.* Carbondale, Illinois: SIU Press, 1969.

Hillquit, Morris. *History of Socialism in the United States.* 4th edition. New York: Funk & Wagnalls, 1963.

Hinterhäuser, Hans Heinrich. *Utopie und Werklichkeit bei Diderot; Studien zum 'Supplément au Voyage de Bougainville'.* Heidelberg: C. Winter, 1957.

Hippel, Olga von. *Die pädagogische Dorf-Utopie der Aufklärung.* Langensalza, Germany: Verlag von Julius Beltz, 1939.

Holbrook, Stewart H. *Dreamers of the American Dream.* Garden City: Doubleday & Co., 1957.

Hollins, Dorothea, ed. *Utopian Papers. Being Addresses to 'The Utopians.'* London: Masters, 1908.

Holz, Hans Heinz. *Utopie und Anarchismus; zur Kritik der kritischen Theorie Herbert Marcuse.* Cologne: Pahl-Rugenstein, 1968.

Hough, Robert L. *The Quiet Rebel: William Dean Howells as Social Commentator.* Lincoln: University of Nebraska Press, 1959.

Howe, Irving, ed. *Orwell's Nineteen Eighty-Four; Text, Sources, Criticism.* New York: Harcourt, Brace & Co., 1963.

Hurbon, Laënnes. *Ernst Bloch; Utopie et esperance.* Paris: Editions du Cerf, 1974.

Hutchins, Robert M. *The University of Utopia.* 2nd edition. Chicago: University of Chicago Press, 1964.

Hutchinson, Tom. *British Science Fiction and Fantasy.* [London:] National Book League in association with The British Council, 1975.

Hyndman, H. M. *An Introduction to the "Life to Come."* London: Hyndman Literary Committee, 1926.

Iggers, Georg. *The Cult of Authority. The Political Philosophy of Saint-Simonism; A Chapter in the Intellectual History of Totalitarianism.* The Hague: Martinus Nijhoff, 1958.

Imaz, Eugenio. *Topia y Utopia.* Mexico City: Tezontle, 1946.

Isaacs, Leonard. *Darwin to Double Helix; The Biological Theme in Science Fiction.* London: Butterworths, 1977.

Jackson, Holbrook. *Dreamers of Dreams; The Rise and Fall of the 19th Century Idealism.* London: Faber, 1948.

Jaher, Frederic Cople. *Doubters and Dissenters; Cataclysmic Thought in America, 1885–1918.* New York: Free Press of Glencoe, 1964.

Japy, Gaston. *Réalités et utopies. Les idées jaunes.* Paris: Plon, 1906.

Jaritz, Kurt. *Utopischer Mond. Mondreisen aus drei Jahrtausenden.* Graz: Stiasny, 1965.

Jaurès, Jean, ed. *Histoire socialiste (1789–1900).* 13 Vols. Paris: Rouff, nd.

Jeanmarie, Henri. *La Sibylle et le retour de l'age d'or.* Paris: Librairie Ernest Leroux, 1939.

Johnson, J. W., ed. *Utopian Literature.* New York: Modern Library, 1968.

Johnson, Robbin S. *More's Utopia: Ideal and Illusion.* New Haven: Yale University Press, 1969.

Just, Klaus Günther. *Aspekte der Zukunft. Zwei Essays.* Bern: Francke Verlag, [1971].

Kalin, Martin G. *The Utopian Flight from Unhappiness: Freud Against Marx on Social Progress.* Chicago: Nelson-Hall, 1974.

Kamlah, Wilhelm. *Utopie, Eschatologie, Geschichtsteleologie; Kritische Untersuchungen zum Ursprung und zum futuristischen Denken der Neuzeit.* Mannheim: Bibliographisches Institut, 1969.

Kateb, George, ed. *Utopia.* New York: Atherton Press, 1971.

Kateb, George. *Utopia and Its Enemies.* New York: Free Press of Glencoe, 1963.

Kaufmann, M[oritz]. *Utopias; or, Schemes of Social Improvement. From Sir Thomas More to Karl Marx.* London: C. Kegan Paul & Co., 1879. Also: *The Leisure Hour,* 27 (March 2, April 20, May 11, June 1, July 13, August 17, August 31, September 21, October 12, October 26, November 9, November 23, December 14, December 28, 1878), pp. 134–136, 245–248, 293–295, 349–352, 436–440, 524–528, 558–560, 602–605, 652–655, 681–684, 715–719, 746–750, 788–792, 821–825.

Kautsky, Karl. *Thomas More and His Utopia,* translated by H. J. Stenning. London: A. & C. Black, Ltd., 1927.

Kautsky, Karl. *Vorläuffer des neueren Sozialismus.* 2 Vols. Berlin: Dietz, 1947.

Kelly, Leo P., ed. *Themes in Science Fiction; A Journey into Wonder.* New York: McGraw-Hill, 1972.

Ketterer, David. *New Worlds for Old: The Apocalyptic Imagination, Science Fiction and American Literature.* Garden City: Anchor Books, 1974.

Kippenberg, August. *Robinson in Deutschland bis zur Insel Felsenburg (1731–43); Ein Beitrag zur Litteraturgeschichte des 18 Jahrhunderts.* Hannover: Norddeutsche Verlagsanftalt, O. Goedel, 1892.

[Kirchenheim, Arthur Von.] *Schlaraffia politica; Geschichte der Dichtungen vom besten Staate.* Leipzig: Fr. Milh. Grunow, 1892.

Kirk, Clara Marburg. *W. D. Howells, Traveller from Altruria, 1889–1894.* New Brunswick, New Jersey: Rutgers University Press, 1962.

Kleinwächter, Friedrich. *Die Staatsromane; Ein Beitrag zur lehre vom Communismus und Sozialismus.* Vienna: M. Breitenstein's Verlagsbuchhandlung, 1891.

Knight, Damon. *In Search of Wonder.* 2nd edition revised & enlarged Chicago: Advent, 1967.

Krämer-Badoni, Rudolf. *Anarchismus: Geschichte und Gegenwart einer Utopie.* Vienna: Moden, 1970.

Kränzle, Karl. *Utopie und Ideologie. Gesellschaftskritik und politisches Engagement im Werk Ernst Blochs.* Bern: Herbert Lang, 1970.

Krarup, Søren, Per Stig Møller and Ebbe Kløvedal Reich. *Utopi og Virkelighed.* [Copenhagen:] Stig Vendelkaer, 1973.

Kremser, Rudolf. *Staat und Überstaat. Ein Streifzug durch Utopie und Wirklichkeit.* Vienna: E. Wancura-Verlag, [1949].

Krysmanski, Hans-Jürgen. *Die Utopische Methode; Eine literatur- und wissenssoziologische Untensuchung deutscher utopischer Romane des 20. Jahrhunderts.* Cologne: Westdeutscher Verlag, 1963. *Dortmunder Schriften zur Sozialforschung* Vol. 21.

Kunz, Hans. *Die anthropologische Bedeutung der Phantasie.* 2 Vols. Supplements 3 and 4 to *Studia Philosophica, Jahrbuch der Schweizerischen Philosophischen Gesellschaft.* Basel: Verlag für Recht und Gesselschaft, 1946.

Kyle, David. *A Pictorial History of Science Fiction.* London: Hamlyn, 1976.

Labougle, Eduardo. *Los Utopicos de todos los tiempos.* Caracas: Vargas, 1920.

Lachèvre, Frédéric. *Les Successeurs de Cyrano de Bergerac.* Paris: E. Champion, 1922.

Laidler, Harry W. *History of Socialism, A Comparative Survey of Socialism, Communism, Trade Unionism, Cooperation, Utopianism, and Other*

Systems of Reform and Reconstruction. London: Routledge & Kegan Paul, 1969. Updated and expanded version of *Social-Economic Movements,* 1944.

Lampa, Anton. *Das naturwissenschaftliche Märchen.* Reichenberg: Verlag Deutsche Arbeit, 1919.

Lampo, Hubert. *Toen Herakles spitte en Kirke spon zijnde het verhaal van Charles-Joseph de Grave en zijn "République des Champs Elysées," waarin bewezen wordt, dat Plato's Atlantis in de Nederlanden gelegen was.* Brussels: Manteau, [1967].

Lang, Leoni. *Urbane Utopien der Gegenwart: Analyse ihrer formalen und sozialen Zielsetzungen.* Stuttgart: Kramer, 1972.

Lansac, Maurice. *Les Conceptions méthodologiques et sociales de Charles Fourier. Leur influence.* Paris: J. Vrin, 1926.

Lapouge, Gilles. *Utopie et civilisations.* [Paris:] Weber, 1973.

Lasky, Melvin J. *Utopia and Revolution.* Chicago: University of Chicago Press, 1976.

Law, Richard Kidson. *Return from Utopia.* London: Faber & Faber, 1950.

Leblond, Marius-Ary. *L'ideal du XIXᵉ siècle.* Paris: Félix Alcan, 1909.

Leclair, Sister St. Ida. *Utopias and the Philosophy of Saint Thomas* (Catholic University of America Philosophical Studies, Vol. 60). Washington: Catholic University of America Press, 1941.

Leflamanc, Auguste. *Les Utopies prérévolutionnaires et la philosophie des 18ᵉ siècle.* Paris: J. Vrin, 1934. [Tipped over Brest: L. LeGrand, 1933, Cover says Paris, etc.].

Le Guin, Ursula K. *From Elfland to Poughkeepsie.* Portland, Oregon: Pendragon Press, 1973.

Lehouck, Emile. *Fourier, aujourd'hui.* Paris: Editions Denoel, 1966.

Leroy, Maxime. *Le Socialisme des Producteurs; Henri de Saint-Simon.* Paris: Librairie des Sciences politiques et sociales, 1924.

Le Sueur, Theodore. *A French Draft Constitution of 1792 Modelled on James Harrington's Oceana.* Paris: Droz, 1932.

Levin, Harry. *The Myth of the Golden Age in the Renaissance.* Bloomington: Indiana University Press, 1969.

Lewis, Arthur O., Jr. *Utopian Literature.* New York: Arno Press, 1971.

Lewis, Joan. "Utopias As Alternative Futures." Menlo Park: Stanford Research Institute, Educational Policy Research Center, Research Memorandum, EPRC-6747-7, March, 1970.

Leyburn, Ellen Douglass. *Satiric Allegory: Mirror of Man.* New Haven: Yale University Press, 1956. Vol. 130 of Yale Studies in English.

Lichtenberger, André. *Le Socialisme utopique; Études sur quelques précurseurs inconnus du socialisme.* Paris: Félix Alcan, 1898.

Lief, Ruth Ann. *Homage to Oceania; The Prophetic Vision of George Orwell.* [Columbus:] Ohio State University Press, 1969.

Liljegren, S[ten] B[odvar.] *Studies on the Origin and Early Tradition of English Utopian Fiction.* Vol. 23 of Uppsala University English Institute *Essays and Studies on English Language and Literature.* Uppsala: A. B. Lundequistake, 1961.

Locke, George. *Voyages in Space; A Bibliography of Interplanetary Fiction 1801–1914.* London: Ferret Fantasy, 1975.

Loewenthal, Eduard. *Der Staat Bellamy's und seine Nachfolge.* Berlin: H. Muskalla, 1905.

Löffler, Henner. *Macht und Konsens in den klassischen Staatsutopien. Eine studie zur Ideengeschichte des Totalitarismus.* Cologne: Carl Heymans, [1972].

Loubere, Leo. *Utopian Socialism: Its History Since 1800.* Cambridge, Massachusetts: Schenkman, 1974.

Louis, Gustave. *Thomas Morus und seine Utopia.* Berlin: R. Gaertners, 1895.

Lovejoy, Arthur O. and George Boas. *Primitivism and Related Ideas in Antiquity.* New York: Octagon Books, 1965.

Lundwall, Sam J. *Science Fiction: What it's All About.* New York: Ace, 1971.

Lyon, Jean. *Les Utopies et le royaume.* Paris: Editions du Centurion, 1973.

McHale, John. *The Future of the Future.* New York: George Braziller, 1969.

Machovcová, Markéta, *Utopie blouznivců a sektářů.* Prague: Nakladatelství Československé Akademie Ved, 1960.

Macnair, Everett W. *Edward Bellamy and the Nationalist Movement, 1889–1894.* Milwaukee: Fitzgerald Co., 1957.

Mähl, Hans-Joachim. *Die Idee des goldenen Zeitalters im Werk des Novalis. Studien zur Wesensbestimmung der frühromantischen Utopie und zu ihren ideengeschichtlichen Voraussetzungen.* Heidelberg: Carl Winter, 1965.

Mannheim, Karl. *Ideology and Utopia: An Introduction to the Sociology of Knowledge,* translated Louis Wirth and Edward Shils. New York: Harcourt, Brace & Co., [1936].

Mannin, Ethel Edith. *Bread and Roses; An Utopian Survey and Blueprint.* London: Macdonald & Co., [1945].

Manuel, Frank E. *The Prophets of Paris.* New York: Harper & Row, 1962.

Manuel Frank E., ed. *Utopias and Utopian Thought.* Boston: Beacon Press, 1967.

Manuel, Frank E. and Fritzie P. Manuel, eds. & trans. *French Utopias.* New York: Free Press, 1966.

Maravall, José Antonio. *Utopía y Contrautopia en el 'Quijote.* Santiago de Compostela, Spain: Pico Sacco, 1976.

Marcuse, Herbert. *Das Ende der Utopie.* Berlin: Verlag Peter von Maikowski, 1967.

Marin, Louis. *Utopiques; jeux d'espaces.* Paris: Minuit, 1973.

Massingham, Harold John. *The Golden Age; The Story of Human Nature.* London: Gerald Howe, 1927.

Massó, Gildo. *Education in Utopias.* No. 257 of Teachers College, Columbia University, *Contributions to Education.* New York: Bureau of Publications, Teachers College, Columbia University, 1927.

Mathews, R. D. *An Introductory Guide to the Utopian and Fantasy Writing of William Morris.* [London:] William Morris Centre, 1976.

Meier, Paul. *La Pensée utopique de William Morris.* Paris: Editions sociales, 1972.

Melchiorre, Virgilio. *La coscienza utopica.* Milan: Vita e pensiero, 1970.

Mellen, Philip A. *Gerhart Hauptmann und Utopia.* No. 17 of Stuttgarter Arbeiten zur Germanistik. Stuttgart: Akademischer Verlag Hans-Dieter Heinz, 1976.

Meozzi, Antero. *L'Utopia politica di Dante.* Milan: Edizioni Athena, 1929.

Merian, P[aul]. *Die Utopie der 'Welt als Werk.'* Basel: Verlag Mathaus Merian, [1950?].

Messac, Régis. *Esquisse d'une chrono-bibliographie des utopies.* Lausanne: Club Futopia, Collection Denebienne, No. 1, 2962 [1962].

Meyers, Jeffrey. *A Reader's Guide to George Orwell.* London: Thames and Hudson, 1975.

Meyers, Jeffrey and Valerie Meyers. *George Orwell; An Annotated Bibliography of Criticism.* New York: Garland Pub. Co., 1977.

Miller, Marjorie M. *Isaac Asimov: A Checklist of Works Published in the United States, March 1939–May 1972.* [Kent, Ohio:] Kent State University, 1972.

Möbus, Gerhard. *Macht und Menschlichkeit in der Utopia des Thomas Morus.* Berlin: Weiss, 1953.

Möbus, Gerhard. *Die Politik des Heiligen. Geist und Gesetz der Utopia des Thomas Morus.* Berlin: Morus-Verlag, 1953.

Modelmog, Ilse. *Die andere Zukunft; zur Publizistik und Soziologie der utopischen Kommunikation.* Dusseldorf: Bertelsmann, 1970.

Molina Quirós, Jorge. *La Novela utopica inglesa (Tomás Moro, Swift, Huxley, Orwell).* Madrid: Editorial Prensa Española, 1967.

Molnar, Thomas. *Utopia: The Perennial Heresy.* New York: Sheed & Ward, 1967.

Moniz, Milton. *Meditando sobre o homen. . .* Lisbon: Editorial Polis, 1970.

Moos, Rudolf and Robert Brownstein. *Environment and Utopia; A Synthesis.* New York: Plenum Press, 1977.

Morgan, Arthur E. *Edward Bellamy.* New York: Columbia University Press, 1944.

Morgan, Arthur E. *Nowhere Was Somewhere; How History Makes Utopias* *and How Utopias Make History.* Chapel Hill: University of North Carolina Press, 1946.

Morgan, Arthur E. *The Philosophy of Edward Bellamy.* New York: King's Crown Press, 1945.

Morgan, Arthur E. *Plagiarism in Utopia; A Study of the Continuity of the Utopian Tradition With Special Reference to Edward Bellamy's "Looking Backward."* Yellow Springs, Ohio: Author, 1944.

Morrow, Glenn R. *Plato's Cretan City; A Historical Interpretation of the Laws.* Princeton: Princeton University Press, 1960.

Morton, A[rthur] L[eslie]. *The English Utopia.* London: Lawrence & Wishart, 1952.

Moskowitz, Sam[uel]. *Explorers of the Infinite; Shapers of Science Fiction.* Cleveland: World Pub. Co., 1963.

Moskowitz, Sam[uel], ed. *Science Fiction by Gaslight; A History and Anthology of Science Fiction in the Popular Magazines, 1891–1911.* Westport, Connecticut: Hyperion Press, 1974.

Moskowitz, Sam[uel]. *Seekers of Tomorrow. Masters of Modern Science Fiction.* Cleveland: World Pub. Co., 1966.

Moskowitz, Sam[uel], ed. *Under the Moon of Mars: A History and Anthology of "The Scientific Romance" in the Munsey Magazine, 1912–1930.* New York: Holt, Rinehart and Winston, 1970.

Mucchielli, Roger. *Le Mythe de la cité idéale.* Paris: Presses Universitaires de France, 1960.

Mumford, Lewis. *The City in History.* New York: Harcourt, Brace & World, 1961.

Mumford, Lewis. *The Story of Utopias.* New York: Boni and Liveright, 1922.

Mundt, Theodor. *Die Geschichte der Gesellschaft in ihren neueren Entwicklungen und Probleme.* Berlin: M. Simion, 1844.

Nagl, Manfred. *Science Fiction in Deutschland; Untersuchungen zur Genese, Soziographie und Ideologie der Phantastischen Massenliteratur.* Tübingen: Tübingen Vereinigung für Volkskunde, 1972. Vol. 30 of Untersuchungen des Ludwig-Uhland-Instituts der Universität Tübingen.

Naudé, Gabriel. *La Bibliographie du Sr. Naudé.* Paris: G. Pelé, 1642.

Negley, Glenn, ed. *Utopia Collection of the Duke University Library.* Durham: Friends of Duke University Library, 1965. Supplement dated February, 1967.

Negley, Glenn and J. Max Patrick, eds. *The Quest for Utopia.* New York: Henry Schuman, 1952.

Nelson, William, ed. *Twentieth Century Interpretations of Utopia.* Englewood Cliffs, New Jersey: Prentice-Hall, 1968.

Nettlau, Max. *Esbozo de Historia de las Utopias,* translated by D. Abod de Santillan. Buenos Aires: Iman, 1934.

Neusüss, Arnhelm, ed. *Utopie; Begriff und Phanomen des Utopischen.* Neuwied, Germany, Luchterhand, 1968.

Neusüss, Arnhelm. *Utopisches Bewusstsein und freischwebende Intelligenz Zur Wissenssoziologie Karl Mannheim* (Marburger Abhandlungen zur politischen Wissenschaft, Vol. 10). Meisenheim am Glan, Germany: Verlag Anton Hain, 1968.

Nicholson, Normen. *H. G. Wells.* London: Arthur Barker Ltd., 1950.

Nicolson, Marjorie Hope. *Voyages to the Moon.* New York: Macmillan, 1948.

Nipperdey, Thomas. *Reformation, Revolution, Utopie. Studien zum 16. Jahrhundert.* Gottingen, Germany: Vandenhoeck & Ruprecht, 1975.

Noyelle, Henri. *Utopie libérale. Chimère socialiste economie dirigée.* Paris: Sirey, 1934.

Obloy, Elaine, comp. *Beyond Tomorrow; Utopian Fantasies.* Cleveland: Cleveland Public Library, 1975.

Odegard, Holtan P. *The Politics of Truth: Toward Reconstruction in Democracy.* University, Alabama: University of Alabama Press, 1971.

Oncken, Hermann. *Die Utopia des Thomas Morus and das machtproblem in der staatslehre.* Heidelberg: Winter, 1922.

Orlans, Harold. *Utopia Ltd. The Story of the English New Town Stevenage.* New Haven: Yale University Press, 1953.

Ortega, Félix. *Sociología, utopía y revolución.* Valencia: Torres, [c. 1976].

Ozman, Howard. *Utopias and Education.* Minneapolis: Burgess Pub. Co., 1969.

Palmgren, Raoul. *Toivon ja pelon utopiat.* Helsinki: Kansankultturi ϕy, 1963.

Panshin, Alexei. *Heinlein in Dimension; a Critical Analysis.* Chicago: Advent, 1968.

Papademetriou, Costas B[asileiou]. *La part du réel dans l'utopie de Platon.* Paris: Arthur Rousseau, 1937.

Paraf, Pierre. *Les cités du bonheur.* Paris: Editions du Myrte, 1945.

Pariset, Georges. *L'Utopie de deux Lorrains sous Napoléon Ier* in *Études d'histoire revolutionnaire et contemporaine.* Paris: Publications de la Faculté des Lettres de l'Université de Strasbourg, fasc, 46, 1929.

Parrington, Vernon Louis, Jr. *American Dreams: A Study of American Utopias.* 2nd edition New York: Russell and Russell, 1964.

Patch, Howard Rollin. *The Other World According to Descriptions in Medieval Literature.* Cambridge: Harvard University Press, 1950.

Patrick, J. Max. *Inside Utopia. For an Exhibition of the Paul Klapper Library, Queens College, 1957.* [New York: Paul Klapper Library, Queens College, 1957].

Pehlke, Michael and Norbert Lingfeld. *Roboter und Gartenlaube: Ideologie und Unterhaltung in der Science-Fiction-Literatur.* Munich: Hanser, 1970.

Penta, Clement Della. *Hope and Society. A Thomistic Study of Social Optimism and Pessimism.* Washington, D.C.: Catholic University of America, 1942.

[Perry-Coste, Frank Hill.]. *Towards Utopia, (Being Speculations in Social Evolution),* by A Free Lance (pseud.). New York: D. Appleton, 1894.

Philmus, Robert M. *Into the Unknown; The Evolution of Science Fiction from Francis Godwin to H. G. Wells.* Berkeley: University of California Press, 1970.

Picht, Georg. *Mut zur Utopie; die grossen Zukunftsaufgaben; zwölf Vorträge.* Munich: Piper, 1969.

Picht, Georg. *Prognose. Utopie. Planung. Die Situation des Menschen in der Zukunft der technischen Welt.* Stuttgart: Ernst Klett, 1967.

Pierret, M. *Utopies et perversions.* Paris: Debresse, 1973.

Pirker, Theo, ed. *Utopie und Mythos der Weltrevolution. Zur Geschichte der Komintern, 1926–1940.* Munich: Deutscher Taschenbuch Verlag, 1964.

Piroschow, Vera. *Alexander Herzen. Der Zusammenbruch einer Utopie.* Munich: Anton Pustet, 1961.

Pitocca, Francesco. *Utopia e riforma religiosa nel Risorgimento; Il sansimonismo nella cultura toscana.* Bari: Laterza, 1972.

Planhol, René de. *Les utopistes de l'amour.* Paris: Garnier, 1921.

Plank, Robert. *The Emotional Significance of Imaginary Beings; A Study of the Interaction Between Psychopathology, Literature, and Reality in the Modern World.* Springfield, Illinois: Charles C. Thomas, 1968.

Plank, Robert. *Josef Popper-Lynkeus, der Gesellschaftsingenieur.* Vienna: Saturn-Verlag, 1938.

Plath, David. W., ed. *Aware of Utopia.* Urbana: University of Illinois Press, 1971.

Plattel, Martin G. *Utopian and Critical Thinking.* Pittsburgh: Duquesne University Press, 1972.

Plum, Werner. *English Utopian Schemes; Models of Social and Technological Cooperation.* Bonn Bad Godesberg: Friedrich-Evert-Stiftung, 1974.

Poggioli, Renato. *Definizione dell'utopia; e, Morte del senso della tragedia; due saggi di critica delle idee.* [Pisa:] Nistri-Lischi, [1964].

Poisson, Ernest. *The Co-operative Republic,* translated W. P. Watkins. London: T. Fisher Unwin, 1925.

Polak, Fred[erick] L. *The Image of the Future; Enlightening the Past, Orientating the Present, Forecasting the Future.* 2 Vols. New York: Oceana Pub., 1961.

Pompery, E[douard] de. *Les thélémites de Rabelais et les harmoniens de Fourier.* Paris: C. Reinwald, 1892. At head of title: *Appel aux vrais socialistes.*

Popper, Karl R. *The Open Society and Its Enemies.* 3rd edition 2 Volumes. London: Routledge & Kegan Paul, 1957.

Poster, Mark. *The Utopian Thought of Restif de la Bretonne.* New York: New York University Press, 1971.

Prager, R. L., Booksellers. *Marx, Engels, Lasselle: Eine Bibliographie des Sozialismus.* 3 Vols. in 1. Berlin: R. L. Prager Booksellers, 1924.

La Première Utopie Francaise. Le Royaume d'Antangil (inconnu jusqu'à présent). Paris: La Connaissance, 1933.

Privat, Edmond. *Le Chancelier Décapité; Saint Thomas More, Henri VIII et la République des Utopiens.* Neuchatel: Viator, [1935].

Prudhommeaux, Jules. *Etienne Cabet et les Origines du Communisme Icarien.* Nimes: Imprimerie "La Laborieuse," 1907.

Prÿs, Joseph. *Der Staatsroman des 16. und 17. Jahrhunderts und sein Erziehungsideal.* Würzburg: Franz Staudenraus, 1913.

Pulvermann, M. *Die gleichheit des Zukunftsstaates.* Berlin: Reichsverbands Verlag, 1906.

Quabbe, Georg. *Das letzte Reich: Wandel und Wesen der Utopie.* Leipzig: Meiner, 1933.

Quarta, Cosima. *Per una definzione dell'utopia.* [Naples]: Glauz, 1971.

Quel avenir attend l'homme? Rencontre internationale de Royaumont (17–20 Mai 1961). Paris: Presses Universitaires de France, 1961.

Rabkin, Eric S. *The Fantastic in Literature.* Princeton: Princeton University Press, 1976.

Raghavacharyulu, D[hupaty] V. K. *Utopia: The Quest and the Crisis; A Study of the English Utopians.* Waltair: Andhra University Press, 1965.

Raknem, Ingvald. *H. G. Wells and His Critics.* Oslo: Universitetsforlaget, 1962.

Ransom, Arthur. *Dr. Hertzka's Freeland.* Bedford: Times Office, 1892.

Reiner, Julius. *Berühmte Utopisten und ihr Staatsideal.* Jena, Germany: Hermann Costenoble, 1906.

Reiner, Thomas A. *The Place of the Ideal Community in Urban Planning.* Philadelphia: University of Pennsylvania Press, 1963.

Reybaud, Louis. *Etudes sur les réformateurs ou socialistes modernes.* 7th edition. 2 Vols. Paris: Guillaurmin et Cie, 1864.

Reynolds, Thomas. *Preface & Notes, Illustrative, Explanatory, Demonstrative, Argumentative, and Expostulatory to Mr. Edward Bellamy's Famous Book, "Looking Backward."* London: Thomas Reynolds, 1890.

Rhodes, Harold V. *Utopia in American Political Thought.* Tucson: University of Arizona Press, 1967.

Richter, Peyton E., ed. *Utopia/Dystopia?* Cambridge, Massachusetts; Schenkman Pub. Co., 1975.

Richter, Peyton E., ed. *Utopias.* Boston: Holbrook Press, 1971.

Rideout, Walter B. *The Radical Novel in the United States 1900–1954.* Cambridge: Harvard University Press, 1956.

Rihs, Charles. *Les Philosophes utopistes; le mythe de la cité Communautaire en France au XVIIIe siècle.* Paris: Marcel Rivière et cie, 1970.

Ritter, Gerhard. *Machstaat und Utopie; vom Streit um die Damonie der Macht seit Machiavelli und Morus.* Munich: R. Oldenbourg, 1940.

Rodenstein, Heinrich. *Die Utopisten.* No. 14 of *Beitrage zum Geschichtsunterricht.* Braunschweig: Verlag Albert Limbach, 1949.

Roemer, Kenneth M. *Build Your Own Utopia; Instructions and Feedbacks.* Arlington, Texas: University of Texas at Arlington, 1978.

Roemer, Kenneth M. *Build Your Own Utopia; Study Guide.* Arlington, Texas: University of Texas at Arlington, 1978.

Roemer, Kenneth M. *The Obsolete Necessity: America in Utopian Writings, 1888–1900.* Kent, Ohio: Kent State University Press, 1976.

Roper, William. *The Life of Syr Thomas More.* London: Scolar Press, 1970. [1626] edition entitled *The Mirrour of Vertue in Worldly Greatnes.*

Rose, Lois and Stephen Rose. *The Shattered Ring; Science Fiction and The Quest for Meaning.* Richmond, Virginia: John Knox Press, 1970.

Ross, Harry. *Utopias Old and New.* London: Nicholson and Watson, 1938.

Rosteutscher, Joachim. *Der Gedanke des kulturellen Fortschritts in der englischen Dichtung.* Vol. 13 of *Sprache und Kultur der Germanischen und Romanischen Völkes.* Breslau: Priebatsch, 1933.

Røstvig, Maren-Sofie. *The Happy Man; Studies in the Metamorphoses of a Classical Ideal 1600–1760.* 2 Vols. Oslo: Oslo University Press, 1954, 1958. Nos. 2 and 7 of Oslo Studies in English.

Rowley, H. H. *The Relevance of Apocalyptic: A Study of Jewish and Christian Apocalypses From Daniel to the Revelation.* 2nd edition revised. New York: Association Press, 1963.

Rubert de Ventós, Xavier. *Utopias de la sensualidad y metodos del sentido.* [Barcelona:] Editorial Anagrama, [1973].

Rudhart, Georg Thomas von. *Thomas Morus: Aus den Quellen bearbeitet.* Nürnberg: Fredrich Campe, 1829.

Rushdoony, Rousas John. *The Messianic Character of American Education; Studies in the History of the Philosophy of Education.* Philadelphia: Presbyterian and Reformed Publishing Co., 1963.

Russ, Jacqueline. *La pensée de precurseurs de Marx.* Paris: Bordas, 1973.

Russell, Frances Theresa. *Touring Utopia; The Realm of Constructive Humanism.* New York: Dial, 1932.

Russell-Smith, Hugh F. *Harrington and His Oceana; A Study of a 17th-Century Utopia and Its Influence in America.* Cambridge: Harvard University Press, 1914.

Ruyer, Raymond. *L'Humanité de l'avenir d'après Cournot.* Paris: F. Alcan, 1930.

Ruyer, Raymond. *L'Utopie et les utopies.* Paris: Presses Universitaires de France, 1950.

Sadoul, Jacques. *Histoire de la science-fiction moderne, 1911–1971.* Paris: A. Michel, 1973.

Säkularisation und Utopie. Ebracher Studien. Ernst Forsthoff zum 65. Geburtstag. Stuttgart: Kohlhammer, 1967.

Salin, Edgar. *Platon und die griechische Utopie.* Munich: Duncker and Humblot, 1921.

Sanford, Charles L. *The Quest for Paradise.* Urbana: University of Illinois Press, 1961.

Sargant, William Lucas. *Social Innovators and Their Schemes.* London: Smith, Elder & Co., 1858.

Sarti, Sergio. *Utopismo e mondo moderno.* [Palermo:] Palumbo, [1960].

Sauer, Gerda-Karla. *Kindliche Utopien.* Berlin: Beltz, 1954.

Schempp, Hermann. *Gemeinschaftssiedlungen auf religiöser und weltanschaulicher Grundlage.* Tübingen: Mohr, 1969.

Schimmelbusch, Heinz. *Kritik an Commutopia; zu einer wirtschaftspolitischen Konzeption der Neuen Linken.* Tubingen: Mohr, 1971.

[Schmidt, Willy.] *Das letzte Gesetz, der Durchbruch zum Weltbild der Kommenden Epoche,* by German Gerhold (pseud.). Stuttgart: Kulturaufbau-Verlag, 1946.

Schmitt, Eugen Heinrich. *Der Idealstaat.* Vol. 8 of *Kulturprobleme der Gegenwart.* Berlin: Johannes Räde, 1904.

Scholes, Robert. *Structural Fabulation; An Essay on Fiction of the Future.* Notre Dame: University of Notre Dame Press, 1975.

Scholes, Robert and Eric S. Rabkin. *Science Fiction: History. Science. Vision.* New York: Oxford University Press, 1977.

Scholtz, Harald. *Evangelischer Utopismus bei Johann Valentin Andreä. Ein Geistiges Vorspiel zum Pietismus.* Darstellungen aus der Wurttembergischen Geschichte Vol. 42. Stuttgart: W. Kohlhammer, 1957.

Schomann, Emilie. *Französische Utopisten und ihr Frauenideal.* Berlin: Verlag von Emil Felber, 1911.

Schulte Herbrüggen, Hubertus. *Utopie und Anti-Utopie: Strukturanalyse zur Strukturtypologie.* Bochum-Langendreer, Germany: H. Pöppinghaus, 1960.

Schwonke, Martin. *Vom Staatsroman zur Science Fiction; Eine Untersuchung über Geschichte und Funktion der naturwissenschaftlich-technischen Utopie.* Stuttgart: Ferdinand Enke, 1957.

Scudder, Vida D[utton]. *Social Ideals in English Letters.* Boston: Houghton, Mifflin & Co., 1898.

Seeber, Hans Ulrich. *Wandlungen der Form in der literarischen Utopie. Studien zur Entfaltung des utopischen Romans in England.* Goppingen, Germany: Alfred Kümmerle, 1970.

Seibt, Ferdinand. *Utopica; Modelle Totaler Sozialplanung.* Düsseldorf: L. Schwann, [1972].

Sera, Manfred. *Utopie und Parodie.* Bonn: H. Bouvier, 1969.

Servier, Jean. *Histoire de l'utopie.* Paris: Gallimard, 1967.

Shipley, Marie A. B. *The True Author of Looking Backward.* New York: John B. Alden, 1890.

Shklar, Judith. *After Utopia; The Decline of Political Faith.* Princeton: Princeton University Press, 1957.

Sibley, Mulford Q. *Technology and Utopian Thought.* Minneapolis: Burgess Pub. Co., 1971.

Silberling, E[douard]. *Dictionnaire de sociologie phalanstérienne. Guide des oeuvres complètes de Charles Fourier.* Paris: M. Riviere, 1911.

Simon, Wolfgang. *Die englische Utopie im Lichte der Entwicklungslehre.* Sprache und Kultur der Germanisch und Romanischen Völker. A. Anglistische Reihe, Band 25. Breslau: Priebatsch, 1937.

Small, Christopher. *The Road to Miniluv; George Orwell, the State, and God.* London: Victor Gollancz, 1975.

Soeffner, Hans-Georg. *Der geplante Mythos. Untersuchungen zur Struktur und Wirkungsbedingung der Utopie.* Hamburg: Helmut Buske, 1974.

Sofsky, Wolfgang. *Revolution und Utopie. Bemerkung zur Emanzipationstheorie im fortgeschrittenen Kapitalismus.* Frankfurt am Main: Makol-Verlag, 1971.

Spence, Lewis. *The History of Atlantis.* Philadelphia: David McKay, 1927.

Spina, Giorgio. *Utopia e satira nella fantascienza inglese.* Genova: Tilgher, [1974].

Stammhammer, Josef. *Bibliographie des Sozialismus und Communismus.* 3 Vols. Jena, Germany: Gustav Fischer, 1893, 1900, 1909.

Starr, Kevin. *Americans and the California Dream 1850–1915.* New York: Oxford University Press, 1973.

Stasio, Enzo. *The Romance of Communism.* Boston: Bruce Humphries, 1955.

Stegmann, Carl and C. Hugo (pseud.). *Handbuch der Sozialismus.* Zürich: Verlags-Magazin, 1897.

Steiner, Gerhard. *Franz Heinrich Ziegenhagen und seine Verhaltsnislehre: ein Beitrag zur Geschichte des utopischen Sozialismus in Deutschland.* Berlin: Akademie-Verlag, 1962.

Steinhoff, William R. *George Orwell and the Origins of "1984."* Ann Arbor: University of Michigan Press, 1975.

Steinhoff, William R. *The Road to "1984."* London: Weidenfeld and Nicolson, 1975.

Stent, Gunther S[iegmund], *The Coming of the Golden Age; A View of the End of Progress.* Garden City: American Museum of Natural History by Natural History Press, 1969.

Stiffoni, Giovanni. *Utopia e ragione in Gabriel Bonnot de Mably.* Lecce: Milella, 1975.

Sullivan, Frank and Majie Padberg. *Moreana; Material for the Study of Saint Thomas More.* 5 Vols. Los Angeles: Loyola University of Los Angeles, 1964–1971.

Surtz, Edward L., S.J. *The Praise of Pleasure; Philosophy, Education, and Communism in More's 'Utopia.'* Cambridge: Harvard University Press, 1957.

Surtz, Edward L., S.J. *The Praise of Wisdom; A Commentary on the Religious and Moral Problems and Backgrounds of St. Thomas More's "Utopia."* Chicago: Loyola University Press, 1957.

Süssmuth, Hans. *Studien zur Utopia des Thomas Morus. Ein Beitrag zur Geistesgeschichte des 16. Jahrhundert.* Münster: Aschendorffsche, 1967.

Suvin, Darko. *Russian Science Fiction 1956–1974: A Bibliography. Original Books, Translated Books, and an Annotated Checklist of Criticism; with an Appendix on Criticism of Russian SF before 1956.* Elizabethtown, New York: Dragon Press, 1976.

Suvin, Darko and Robert M. Philmus, eds. *H.G. Wells and Modern Science Fiction.* Lewisburg: Bucknell University Press, 1977.

Sviatlovskii, Vladimir Vladimirovich. *Katalog Utopii.* Moscow: np, 1923.

Świętochowski, Aleksander. *Utopie w Rozwoju Historycznym.* Warsaw: Nakład Gebethner i Wolffa, 1910.

Swoboda, Helmut, comp. *Der Traum vom besten Staat: Texte aus Utopien von Platon bis Morris.* Munich: Deutscher Taschenbuch-Verlag, 1972.

Swoboda, Helmut. *Utopia; Geschichte der Sehnsucht nach einer besseren Welt.* Vienna: Europaverlag, 1972.

Szacki, Jerzy. *Utopie.* Warsaw: Iskry, 1968.

Tafuri, Manfredo. *Architecture and Utopia: Design and Capitalist Development,* translated by Barbara Luigia La Penta. Cambridge: MIT Press, 1976.

Talmon, J[acob] L. *The Origins of Totalitarian Democracy.* New York: Frederick A. Praeger, 1960.

Talmon, J[acob] L. *Political Messianism; The Romantic Phase.* New York: Frederick A. Praeger, 1960.

Talmon, J[acob] L. *Utopianism and Politics.* London: Conservative Political Centre, 1957.

Tamisier, M. *L'Idée révolutionnaire et les Utopies modernes.* Paris: Lethielleux, 1914.

Tarbouriech, Ernest, *La Cité future; Essai d'une utopie scientifique.* Paris: P. V. Steck, 1902.

Taylor, Walter Fuller. *The Economic Novel in America.* Chapel Hill: University of North Carolina Press, 1942.

Teerink, Herman. *A Bibliography of the Writings of Jonathan Swift,* edited by Arthur H. Scouten. 2nd edition. Philadelphia: University of Pennsylvania Press, 1963.

[Teitler, Stuart.] *Eureka!* ...*A Survey of Archaeological Fantasies & Terrestrial Utopias.* Berkeley, California: Kaleidoscope Books, [1975].

Thoenes, Piet. *Utopie en ratio.* Meppel, The Netherlands: J. A. Boom, 1969.

Tillich, Paul. *Die politische Bedeutung der Utopie im Leben der Volker.* Berlin: Weiss, 1951.

Tinker, Chauncey Brewster. *Nature's Simple Plan; A Phase of Radical Thought in the Mid-Eighteenth Century.* Princeton: Princeton University Press, 1922.

Trautmann, Wolfgang. *Utopie und Technick; zum Erscheinungs- und Bedeutungswandel des utopischen Phänomens in der modernen Industriegessellschaft.* Berlin: Duncker & Humbolt, 1974.

Trousson, Raymond. *Voyage aux pays du nulle part: histoire littéraire de la pensée utopique.* [Brussels:] Université Libre de Bruxelles, Faculté de Philosophie et Lettres, 60, 1975.

Tuck, Donald H., comp. *The Encyclopedia of Science Fiction and Fantasy Through 1968,* 3 Vols. Chicago: Advent Publishers, 1974-.

Tuck, Donald H., comp. *A Handbook of Science Fiction and Fantasy.* 2 Vols. 2nd edition revised & enlarged. Hobart, Tasmania: Privately Printed, 1954.

Tuveson, Ernest Lee. *Millenium and Utopia: A Study in the Background of the Idea of Progress.* Berkeley: University of California Press, 1949.

Tuzinski, Konrad. *Das Individuum in der englischen devolutionistischen utopie.* Tübingen: Niemeyer, 1965.

Ullrich, Hermann. *Robinson und Robinsonaden. Bibliographie, Geschichte, Kritik. Ein Beitrag zur vergleichenden Litteraturgeschichte, im besonderen zur geschichte des Romans und zur Geschichte der Jugendlitterature.* Part I. Bibliographie. No. 7 of Litterarhistorische Forschungen. Weimar: Emil Felber, 1898.

U.S. Library of Congress. Division of Bibliography. *List of References on Utopias.* September 19, 1922.

U.S. Library of Congress. Division of Bibliography. *A List of References on Utopias (Supplementary to typewritten list of 1922)* by Florence S. Hellman, Chief Bibliographer, November 22, 1926.

U.S. Library of Congress. Division of Bibliography. *Memorandum on List of References on Utopias to be added to the list of 1922* submitted by Anne L. Baden, July 15, 1931.

[U.S. Library of Congress. Division of Bibliography.] [*List of References on Utopias.*] *Additional References.* August 15, 1935.

U.S. Library of Congress. Division of Bibliography. *Utopias. Additional References.* April 27, 1938.

U.S. Library of Congress. Division of Bibliography. *A List of References on Utopias (Supplementary to the typewritten lists of 1922 and 1926)* by Florence S. Hellman, Chief Bibliographer, January 31, 1940.

Urang, Gunnar. *Shadows of Heaven: Religion and Fantasy in the Writings of C. S. Lewis, Charles Williams, and J. R. R. Tolkien.* Philadelphia: Pilgrim Press, 1971.

Uscatescu, George. *Technica si Utopie.* Madrid: Destin, 1962.

Uscatescu, George. *Tempo Di Utopia.* Pisa: Giardini, 1967.

Uscatescu, George. *Utopia y Plenitud Historica.* Madrid: Ediciones Guaderrama, 1963.

Utopia e Fantascienza. Pubblicazioni dell'Istituto di Anglistica, Facoltà di Magistero dell'Università di Torino. Torino: Giappichelli, 1975.

L'Utopia nel mondo moderno. Florence: Vallecchi, 1969.

Utopiás del Renacimiento. Mexico City: Fondo de Cultura Económica, [1941].

Utopies de Justice. Neuchatel: Paul Attinger, 1898.

Vallentin, Antonina. *H. G. Wells: Prophet of Our Day,* translated by Daphne Woodward. New York: John Day Co., 1950.

Veldhuis, Ruurd. *Realism Versus Utopianism? Reinhold Neibuhr's Christian Realism and the Relevance of Utopian Thought for Social Ethics.* Assen, The Netherlands: Van Gorcum, 1975.

Vennerström, Ivar Teodor. *Svenska Utopister.* Stockholm: Tidens, [1913].

Versins, Pierre. *Encyclopédie de l'utopie et de la science fiction.* Lausanne: L'Age de Homme, 1972.

Versins, Pierre. comp. *Outrepart; anthologie d'Utopies, de Voyages extraordinaires, et de Science fiction, autrement dit, de Conjectures romanesques rationnelles. Ces textes de IIIᵉ millenaire avant J. C. à 1787.* Paris: Editions de la Tête de Feuilles, 1971.

Vida Najera, Fernando. *Estudios sobre el concepto y la organizacion del estado en las "utopias."* Madrid: Tesis, 1928.

Villgradter, Rudolf and Friedrich Krey. *Der Utopische Roman.* Darmstadt: Wissenschaftliche Buchgesellschaft, 1973.

Visionary Architects. Boullee, Ledoux, Lequece. [New York: S. W. Swan Services,] 1968.

Voigt, Andreas. *Die sozialen Utopien.* Leipzig: G. J. Goschen'sche Verlagshandlung, 1906.

Vom Sinn der Utopie; Eranos-Jahrbuch 1963. Zürich: Rhein-Verlag, 1964.

Von der Muhll, Emmanuel. *Denis Veiras et son Histoire des Sévarambes 1677-1679.* Paris: E. Droz, 1938.

Von Helmholtz-Phelan, Anna A. *The Social Philosophy of William Morris.* Durham: Duke University Press, 1927.

Vrankrijker, A[drianus] C[lemens] J[ohannes de]. *Onze anarchisten en uto-pisten rond 1900.* Bussum, The Netherlands: Fibula-Van Dishoeck, 1972.

Wagar, W. Warren. *The City of Man; Prophecies of a World Civilization in Twentieth-Century Thought.* Baltimore: Penguin Books, 1967.

Wagenknecht, Edward. *Utopia Americana.* Seattle: University of Washington Bookstore, 1929.

Walch, Jean. *Bibliographie du Saint-Simonisme avec trois textes inédits.* Paris: J. Vrin, 1967.

Walker, Roy. *The Golden Feast; A Perennial Theme in Poetry.* London: Rockliff, 1952.

Walkover, Andrew. *The Dialectics of Eden.* Stanford Honors Essay in Humanities No. 16, 1974.

Walsh, Chad. *From Utopia to Nightmare.* London: Geoffrey Bles, 1962.

Walter, L.-G. *Thomas Munzer (1489–1525) et les luttes sociales a l'époque de la reforme. Contributions a l'étude de la formation de l'ésprit révolutionnaire en Europe.* Paris: Auguste Picard, 1927.

Walther, Klaus, ed. *Marsmenschen; Kosmische und Kybernetische Abenteuer; Eine Anthologie internationaler utopischer Erzählungen.* Berlin: Verlag das Neue Berlin, 1966.

Wandlungen des Paradiesischen und Utopischen. Studien zum Bild eines Ideals. Vol. 2 of *Probleme der Kunstwissenschaft.* Berlin: Walter de Gruyter, 1966.

Ward, Colin. *Utopia.* Harmondsworth: Penguin Education, 1974.

Webb, Charles T. *The Kingdom Within; The Relation of Personal Character to the Problems of the World Without.* New York: Macmillan, 1934.

Webster, Charles, ed. *Samuel Hartlib and the Advancement of Learning.* Cambridge: Cambridge University Press, 1970.

Weinberg, Arthur and Lila Weinberg, eds. *Passport to Utopia; Great Panaceas in American History.* Chicago: Quadrangle, 1968.

Weinberg, Margarete. *Das Frauenproblem im Idealstaat der Vergangenheit und der Zukunft. Ein Streifzug durch das Wuderland der Utopien.* Leipzig: Kabitzsch, 1925.

Weiss, Miriam Strauss. *A Lively Corpse.* South Brunswick: A. S. Barnes & Co., 1969.

Weisskopf, Walter A., Raghavan N. Iyer, et al. *Looking Forward: The Abundant Society.* Santa Barbara: Center for the Study of Democratic Institutions, 1966.

Wershofen, Christian. *James Harrington und sein Wunschbild von germanischen Staat.* Bonn: Bonner Studien zur englischen Philologie. Vol. 26, 1935.

Whitman, John Pratt. *Utopia Dawns.* Boston: Utopia Publ. Co., 1934.

Williamson, Jack. *H. G. Wells: Critic of Progress.* Baltimore: Mirage Press, 1973.

Willink, M[argaret] D[orothea] R[ose]. *Utopia, According to Moses. A Study in the Social Teaching of the Old Testament.* London: Society for Promoting Christian Knowledge, 1919.

Willms, Bernard. *Planungsideologie and revolutionäre Utopie; Die zweifache Flucht und die Zukunft.* Stuttgart: W. Kohlhammer, 1969.

Wilson, Colin. *The Strength to Dream; Literature and the Imagination.* London: Victor Gollancz, 1962.

Wittels, Franz. *An End to Poverty,* translated by Eden and Cedar Paul. London: George Allen & Unwin, 1925.

Wittke, Carl. *The Utopian Communist, A Biography of Wilhelm Weitling.* Baton Rouge: Louisiana State University Press, 1956.

Wollheim, Donald A. *The Universe Makers: Science Fiction Today.* New York: Harper & Row, 1971.

Wootton, Mrs. Barbara. *Some Modern Utopias.* London: British Broadcasting Corp. (Aids to Study No. 42), [1929].

Yates, Frances A. *Giordano Bruno and the Hermetic Tradition.* New York: Vintage Books, 1969.

Yershov, Peter. *Science Fiction and Utopian Fantasy in Soviet Literature.* New York: Research Program on the U.S.S.R. (East European Fund, Inc.), 1954.

Yorburg, Betty. *Utopia and Reality. A Collective Portrait of American Socialists.* New York: Columbia University Press, 1969.

Young, Arthur Nichols. *The Single Tax Movement in the United States.* Princeton: Princeton University Press, 1916.

Zacharaslewicz, Waldemar. *Die "Cosmic voyage" und die "Excursion" in der englischen Dichtung, des. 17. und 18. Jahrhunderts.* Vienna: Verlag Notring, 1969.

Zavala, Silvio. *Ideario de Vasco de Quiroga.* Mexico City: Fondo de Cultura Economica, 1941.

Zavala, Silvio. *Recuerdo de Vasco de Quiroga.* Mexico City: Editorial Porrua, S.A., 1965.

Zavala, Silvio. *Sir Thomas More in New Spain; A Utopian Adventure of the Renaissance.* London: The Hispanic and Luso-Brazilian Councils, 1955.

Zecchi, Stefano. *Utopia e speranza nel comunismo: Un'interpretazione della prospettiva di Ernst Bloch.* Milan: Feltrinelli, 1974.

ARTICLES

Abrash, Merritt. "Missing the Point in More's *Utopia.*" *Extrapolation,* 19 (December 1977), 27–38.

"An Absence of Utopias," *Canadian Literature,* No. 42 (Autumn 1969), pp. 3–5.

Adams, Ephraim Douglass. "Democracy — A Vision," in his *The Power of*

Ideals in American History (New Haven: Yale University Press, 1913), pp. 127–151.

Adams, Robert P. "Designs by More and Erasmus for a New Social Order." *Studies in Philology,* 42 (April 1945), 131–145.

Adams, Robert P. "The Philosophic Unity of More's *Utopia.*" *Studies in Philology,* 38 (January 1941), 45–65.

Adams, Robert P. "The Social Responsibilities of Science in *Utopia, New Atlantis,* and After." *Journal of the History of Ideas,* 10 (June 1949), 374–398.

Adkins, Nelson F. "An Early American Story of Utopia." *Colophon,* NS 1 (July 1935), 123–132.

Adler, Georg. "Idealstaaten der Renaissance (More — Rabelais — Campanella)." *Annalen des Deutschen Reichs* (1899), pp. 409–455.

Adler, Max. "Der Utopismus bei Marx und Engels," in his *Die Staatsauffassung des Marxismus; Ein Beitrag zur Unterscheidung von Soziologischer und Juristischer Methode,* Vol. 4, Part 2 of *Marx-Studien. Blätter zur Theorie und Politik des Wissenschaftlichen Sozialismus.* Vienna: Verlag der Wiener Volksbuchhandlung, 1972.

Adorno, Theodor W. "Aldous Huxley und die Utopie," in his *Prismen; Kulturkritik und Gesselschaft* (Berlin: Suhrkamp, 1955), pp. 112–143.

Adriani, Maurilio. "La lezione dell'utopia." *Studium,* 66, No. 2 (February 1970), 101–112.

Adriani, Maurilio. "La mentalità utopica," in *L'Utopia nel mondo moderno* (Florence: Vallecchi, 1969), pp. 29–37.

Aggeler, Geoffrey, "Pelagius and Augustine in the Novels of Anthony Burgess." *English Studies,* 55 (February 1974), 43–55.

Aguilar Villanueva, Luis F. "Ernest Bloch, Filosofo de la Utopia," *Christus* (Mexico City), 41 (January 1976), 10–13.

Ainger, Canon Alfred. "Sir Thomas More's *Utopia.*" *Moreana,* No. 23 (August 1969), pp. 71–76.

Aldridge, Alexandra. "Myths of Origin and Destiny in Literature: Zamiatin's *We,*" *Extrapolation,* 19 (December 1977), 68–75.

Allen, Herbert F. "The Cynic Utopias," in his *The Play's the Thing* (Cedar Rapids: Torch Press, 1927), pp. 87–104.

Allen, Judson. "Utopian Literature: The Problem of Literary Reference." *Cithara,* 11 (May 1972), 40–55.

Allen, P. R. "*Utopia* and European Humanism: The Function of the Prefatory Letters and Verses." *Studies in the Renaissance,* 10 (1963), 91–107.

Allen, Ward. "Hooker and the Utopians." *English Studies,* 51, No. 1 (1970), 37–39.

Allen, Ward. "Hythloday and the Root of All Evil." *Moreana,* Nos. 31–32 (November 1971), pp. 51–59.

Allen, Ward. "Some Remarks on Gold in Utopia." *Moreana,* No. 18 (March 1968), pp. 5–6.

Améry, Jean. "Gewalt und Gefahr der Utopie." *Merkur,* 23, No. 5 (May 1969), 405–419.

Amón, Santiago. "Unità sociale d'emergenza." *Architettura,* 18 (December 1972), 536–541.

Anderegg, Michael A. "*Utopia* and early More Biography: Another Review." *Moreana,* No. 33 (February 1972), pp. 23–29.

Anderson, Poul. "The Creation of Imaginary Worlds: The World Builder's Handbook and Pocket Companion," in *Science Fiction; Today and Tomorrow,* edited by Reginald Bretnor (New York: Harper & Row, 1974), pp. 235–257.

Armand, E[mile] (pseud.) and Hugo Treni. "Les utopistes et la question sexuelle," in E[mile] Armand (pseud.), Hugo Treni, and Robin Hood, *Les Utopistes et la question sexuelle; la symbolisme sexuel de Sade, non conformiste et libre penseur.* (Orléans: Editions de l'En-dehors, [1935]), pp. 5–25.

Arms, George. "The Literary Background of Howell's Social Criticism." *American Literature,* 14 (November 1942), 260–276.

Armytage, W. H. G. "The Disenchanted Mechanophobes in Twentieth Century England." *Extrapolation,* 9 (May 1968), 33–60.

Armytage, W. H. G. "Extrapolators and Exegetes of Evolution." *Extrapolation,* 7 (December 1965), 2–17.

Armytage, W. H. G. "J. A. Etzler, an American Utopist." *American Journal of Economics and Sociology,* 16 (October 1956), 83–88.

Armytage, W. H. G. "Superman and the System." *Riverside Quarterly,* 2 (March 1967), 232–241; 3 (August 1967), 44–51.

Arndt, Hans-Joachim. "Die Figur des Plans als Utopie des Bewahrens," in *Säkularisation und Utopie. Ebracher Studien. Ernst Forsthoff zum 65. Geburtstag* (Stuttgart: W. Kohlhammer Verlag, 1967), pp. 119–154.

Ascoli, Georges. "Quelques notes biographiques sur Denis Veiras, d'Alais," in *Mélanges offerts par ses amis et ses élèves à M. Gustave Lanson* (Paris: Hachette, 1922), pp. 165–177.

Ashe, Geoffrey. "L. S. Mercier's L'An 2440: A Neglected Utopia published in 1772." *Wind and the Rain* (London), 7, Nos. 2-3 (1951), 136–141.

Ashe, Geoffrey. "Second Thoughts on *Nineteen Eighty-Four.*" *Month,* 4 (November 1950), 285–300.

Ashe, Geoffrey. "The Servile State in Fact and Fiction." *Month,* 4 (July 1950), 48–59.

Asimov, Isaac. "The Sword of Achilles." *Bulletin of the Atomic Scientists,* 19 (November 1963), 17–18.

Aucuy, M. "Peinture recente d'une société mecanisée, a propos du livre *Brave New World* d'A. Huxley." *Journal du Economistes,* 103 (January 1933), 7–17.

Audoin, Ch. "Tireur d'epine." *Topique,* Nos. 4-5 (October 1970), pp. 127-138.

Austin, H. "Edward Bellamy." *National Magazine,* 9 (October 1898), 69-72.

Ausubel, Herman. "General Booth's Scheme of Social Salvation." *American Historical Review,* 56 (April 1951), 519-525.

Avineri, Shlomo. "War and Slavery in More's Utopia." *International Review of Social History,* 7, No. 2 (1962), 260-290.

Ayer, A. J. "Viewpoint." *Times Literary Supplement,* No. 3757 (March 8, 1974), p. 236.

Babelon, Jean. "L'utopie," in *Humanisme actif. Mélanges d'art et de littérature offerts à Julien Cain.* 2 Vols. (Paris: Hermann, 1968). Vol. 1, pp. 63-72.

Bach, Marcus. "In Search of Utopia." *North Central Association Quarterly,* 32 (April 1958), 333-334.

Backvis, Claude. "Le courant utopique dans la Pologne de la Renaissance," in Université libre de Bruxelles. Institut pour l'etude de la Renaissance et de l'humanisme. *Les Utopies à la Renaissance* (Brussels: Presses Universitaire de Bruxelles, 1963), pp. 163-208.

Baczko, Bronislaw. "Lumière et utopie. Problèmes de recherche." *Annales,* 26 (March-April 1971), 355-386.

Baczko, Bronislaw. "L'utopie et l'idée de l'histoire-progrès." *Revue des sciences humaines,* 39, No. 155 (July-September 1974), 473-491.

Baget Bozzo, Gianni. "Utopia ed escatologia." *Giornale di metafisica* (Torino), 24, Nos. 4-6, 25; No. 1 (1969-1970), pp. 433-444; 13-29.

Bahr, Hans-Dieter. "Die Zukunft des Fortschritts." *Praxis,* 8, Nos. 3-4 (1972), 215-228.

Bailey, J. O. "An Early American Utopian Fiction." *American Literature,* 14 (November 1942), 285-293.

Bailey, J. O. "Shaw's Life Force and Science Fiction." *Shaw Review,* 16 (May 1973), 48-58.

Baker, Ernest A. "Utopian Fiction," in his *The History of the English Novel,* 10 Vols. (New York: Barnes and Noble, 1960). Vol. 2, pp. 264-271.

Baker, J. Wayne. "Populist Themes in the Fiction of Ignatius Donnelly." *American Studies,* 14 (Fall 1973), 65-83.

Baker, James H. "The Real Utopia," in *American Problems: Essays and Addresses* (London: Longmans, Green & Co., 1907), pp. 18-34.

Baldassarri, Mariano. "Intorno all'utopia di Giambulo." *Rivista di Filosofia Neo-Scholastica,* 65 (April-June 1973), 303-333.

Baldini, Massimo. "Epistemologia e Utopia." *La Critica Sociologica,* No. 27 (1973), pp. 161-183.

Baldissera, Alberta. "Il concetto di utopia: problemi e contraddizioni," *Concezione e previsione del futuro; Alcuni problemi di definizione e di* *metodo,* edited by Gianni Giannotti (Bologna: Mulino, 1971), pp. 95-158.

Baldry, H. C. "Zeno's Ideal State." *Journal of Hellenic Studies,* 79 (1959), 3-15.

Baldwin, Edward C. "Ezekiel's Holy State and Plato's *Republic.*" *Biblical World,* 41 (June 1913), 365-373.

Banning, Margaret Culkin. "Shopping for Utopia." *Saturday Evening Post,* 207 (January 19, 1935), 16-17.

Barberis, Pierre. "Les réalites d'un ailleurs: Chateaubriand et le 'voyage en Amerique.' " *Littérature,* No. 21 (February 1976), pp. 91-107.

Barfield, Rodney. "Lenin's Utopianism: *State and Revolution.*" *Slavic Review,* 30 (March 1971), 45-56.

Barion, Hans. "Das konziliare Utopia; Eine Studie zur Soziallehre des II. Vatikanischen Konzils," in *Säkularisation und Utopie. Ebracher Studien. Ernst Forsthoff zum 65. Geburtstag* (Stuttgart: W. Kohlhammer Verlag, 1967), pp. 187-233.

Barlow, George. "L'anti-utopie moderne." *Esprit,* 29 (March 1961), 381-396.

Barnes, S. B. "Edward Gibbon's Utopia." *Classical Journal,* 49 (October 1953), 13-17.

Baron, Lawrence, Gad Ben-Ami, Katherine Goodman, Asta Heller, Otto Koester and Anthony Niesz. "Der 'anarchische' Utopismus der westdeutschen Studentenbewegung," in *Deutsches utopisches Denken im 20. Jahrhundert,* edited by Reinhold Grimm and Jost Hermand (Stuttgart: W. Kohlhammer, 1974), pp. 120-135.

Barr, Alan. "The Paradise Behind '1984.' " *English Miscellany,* 19 (1968), 197-203.

Barron, Neil. "Anatomy of Wonder: A Bibliographic Guide to Science Fiction." *Choice,* 6 (January 1970), 1536-1545.

Barron, Neil. "Science Fiction Revisited." *Choice,* 10 (September 1973), pp. 920-928.

Barroso, Magdaleno Girao. "Ideologie, Ciencia e Utopia." *Revista Brasileira de Estudios Politicas,* 10 (January 1961), 34-43.

Barry, William. "Forecasts of To-morrow." *Quarterly Review,* 209 (July 1908), 1-27. Also, *Living Age,* 258 (August 29, September 5, 1908), 515-523, 614-623.

Barthes, Roland. "Fourier," in his *Sade Fourier Loyola,* translated by Richard Miller (New York: Hill and Wang, 1976), pp. 77-120. Originally published in Paris: Editions du Seuil, 1971.

Barthes, Roland. "L'Utopie du langage," in his *Le Degré zéro de l'écriture suivi de Nouveaux Essais critiques* ([Paris:] Éditions du Seuil, 1972), pp. 62-65.

Bartsch, Günter. "Demokratische oder totalitäre Utopie?" *Geist und Tat,* 19, No. 12 (December 1964), 373-377.

Bastide, Roger. "Mythes et utopie." *Cahiers internationaux de Sociologie,* 28, N.S. 7 (January-June 1960), 3–12.

Bathrick, David. "Die ästhetisch-utopistische Dimension der 'Weigerung' im Denken Herbert Marcuses," in *Deutsches utopisches Denken im 20. Jahrhundert,* edited by Reinhold Grimm and Jost Hermand (Stuttgart: W. Kohlhammer, 1974), pp. 104–119.

Bathrick, Serafina. "The Past as Future: Family and the American Home in *Meet Me in St. Louis.*" *Minnesota Review,* N.S. 6 (Spring 1976), pp. 132–139.

Batkin, Leonid M. "The Paradox of Campanella," translated by N. Slater. *Diogenes,* No. 83 (Fall 1973), pp. 77–102.

Battegazzore, Antonio M. "La Dimensione deontologica nella *Repubblica* Platonica." *Il Pensiero Politico,* 8, No. 3 (1975), 281–298.

Baxter, Sylvester. "The Author of *Looking Backward.*" *New England Magazine,* N.S. 1 (September 1889), pp. 92–98.

Beauchamp, Gorman. "Cultural Primitivism as Norm in the Dystopian Novel." *Extrapolation,* 19 (December 1977), 88–96.

Beauchamp, Gorman. "Future Words: Language and the Dystopian Novel." *Style,* 8 (Fall 1974), 462–476.

Beauchamp, Gorman. "Gulliver's Return to the Cave: Plato's *Republic* and Book IV of *Gulliver's Travels.*" *The Michigan Academician,* 7 (Fall 1974), 201–209.

Beauchamp, Gorman. "*The Iron Heel* and *Looking Backward:* Two Paths to Utopia," *American Literary Realism,* 9 (Autumn 1976), pp. 307–314.

Beauchamp, Gorman. "Of Man's Last Disobedience: Zamiatin's *We* and Orwell's *1984.*" *Comparative Literature Studies,* 10 (December 1973), 285–301.

Beauchamp, Gorman. "Themes and Uses of Fictional Utopias: A Bibliography of Secondary Works in English." *Science-Fiction Studies,* 4 (March 1977), 55–63.

Beauchamp, Gorman. "Utopia and Its Discontents." *Midwest Quarterly,* 16 (Winter 1975), 161–174.

Beck, Evelyn Torton. "Frauen, Neger und Proleten. Die Stiefkinder der Utopie," *Deutsches utopisches Denken im 20. Jahrhundert,* edited by Reinhold Grimm and Jost Hermand (Stuttgart: W. Kohlhammer, 1974), pp. 30–49.

Beck, J. H. "Dream or Vision?" *Month,* 158 (Augusut 1931), 110–116.

Becker, George J. "Edward Bellamy: Utopia, American Plan." *Antioch Review,* 14 (June 1954), 181–194.

Beckmann, Johannes. "Utopien als Missionarische Stosskraft." *Neue Zeitschrift für Missionswissenschaft. Nouvelle revue de science missionnaire,* 17 (1971), 361–407.

Beecher, Jonathan. "L'Archibras de Fourier; Un manuscrit censuré." *La Brèche,* No. 7 (December 1964), pp. 66–71.

Beger, Lina. "Thomas Morus und Plato. Ein Beitrag zur Geschichte des Humanismus." *Zeitschrift für die gesamte Staatswissenschaft,* 35, No. 2 (1879), 187–216.

Begley, Walter. "Bibliography of Romance from the Renaissance to the End of the Seventeenth Century," in *Nova Solyma the Ideal City; or Jerusalem Regained. An Anonymous Romance Written in the Time of Charles I. Now First Drawn From Obscurity, and Attributed to the Illustrious John Milton* [by Samuel Gott]. 2 Vols. (London: John Murray, 1902), Vol. 2, pp. 355–400.

Behl, C.F.W. "Überwindung der Utopie." *Völker-Friede,* 19 (March 1918), 31–32.

Bell, Daniel. "The Exhaustion of Utopia," in his *The End of Ideology* (New York: Free Press, 1960), pp. 265–375.

Bell, S. G. "Johan Eberlin von Gunzberg's Wolfaria: The First Protestant Utopia." *Church History,* 36 (June 1967), 122–139.

Bellamy, Edward. "How I Came to Write *Looking Backward." The Nationalist,* 1 (May 1889), 1–4.

Bellamy, Edward. "Progress of Nationalism in the United States." *North American Review,* 154 (May 1892), 742–752.

Bennett, Charles A. "What Price Utopia." *Harper's,* 156 (May 1928), 782–784.

Bennett, Donald C., Brian Walsh, and Brian Torode. "Anarchy as Utopia. The Poverty of Utopianism," *Studies,* 63 (Winter 1974), 323–341.

Benrekassa, Georges. "Le savior de la fable et l'utopie du savoir: Textes utopiques et recueils politiques 1764–1788." *Littérature,* No. 21 (February 1976), pp. 59–78.

Benrekassa, Georges. "Le statut du narrateur dans quelques textes dits utopiques," *Revue des sciences humaines,* 39, No. 155 (July-September 1974), 379–395.

Berenberg, David P. " 'Pie in the Sky,' A Study of Current Utopian Notions." *American Socialist Quarterly,* 4 (March 1935), 52–64.

Berger, Albert I. "The Magic That Works: John W. Campbell and the American Response to Technology." *Journal of Popular Culture,* 5 (Spring 1972), 867–943.

Berger, Harry, Jr. "The Renaissance Imagination: Second World and Green World." *Centennial Review,* 9 (Winter 1965), 36–78.

Bergues, Hélène. "La population vue par les utopistes." *Population,* 6, No. 2 (April-June 1951), 261–286.

Berlinger, Rudolph. "Humanität und Utopie, Eine Ontologische Skisse," *Praxis,* 8, Nos. 1-2 (1972), 63–69.

Bernard, L. L. "Early Utopian Social Theory in the United States." *Northwest Missouri State Teachers College Studies,* 2 (1938), 71–94.

Bernstein, Samuel. "From Social Utopia to Social Science," in his *Essays in Political and Intellectual History,* (New York: Paine-Whitman, 1955), pp. 113–120.

Bernstein, Samuel. "From Utopianism to Marxism." *Science and Society,* 14 (Winter 1949–1950), 58–67.

Berrigan, J. R. "An Explosion of Utopias." *Moreana,* No. 38 (June 1973), pp. 21–26.

Bertagnoni, Marialisa. "Discordia Concors: Utopie e il Dialogo del Conforta." *Moreana,* Nos. 31–32 (November 1971), pp. 183–188.

Bertanlaff, Ludwig von. "Die Klassische Utopie." *Preussische Jahrbücher,* 210 (December 1927), 341–357.

Bester, Alfred. "Science Fiction and the Renaissance Man," in *The Science Fiction Novel; Imagination and Social Criticism,* 3rd edition (Chicago: Advent Publishers, 1969), pp. 77–96.

Bevington, David M. "The Dialogue in Utopia: Two Sides to the Question." *Studies in Philosophy,* 58 (July 1961), 496–509.

Bianchi, Ruggero. "I Parametri della controutopia," in *Utopia e Fantascienza* (Torino: Giappichelli, 1975), pp. 159–172.

Bierman, Judah. "Ambiguity in Utopia: The Dispossessed." *Science-Fiction Studies,* 2 (November 1975), 249–255.

Bierman, Judah. "Science and Society in the *New Atlantis* and other Renaissance Utopias." *PMLA,* 78 (December 1963), 492–500.

Bikle, George B., Jr. "Utopia and the Planning Element in Modern Japan," in *Aware of Utopia,* edited by David Plath (Urbana: University of Illinois Press, 1971), pp. 33–54.

"Bi-Millenial Literature." *Literary World* (July 19, 1890), p. 240.

Bishop, Donald H. "Human Dignity and Ideal Society." *The Philosophy Forum,* 10 (December 1971), 305–316.

Bishop, Morchard. "The Natural History of Arcadia." *Cornhill,* No. 992 (1952), pp. 81–90.

Black, F. J. "Utopia as Reality." *College English,* 33 (December 1971), 304–316.

Bleich, David. "Eros and Bellamy." *American Quarterly,* 16 (Fall 1964), 445–459.

Bleich, David. "More's *Utopia:* Confessional Modes." *American Imago* 28 (Spring 1971), 24–59.

Blish, James. "Future Recall," in *The Disappearing Future,* edited by George Hay (London: Panther, 1970), pp. 97–105.

[Blish, James.] "S.F.: The Critical Literature," by William Atheling (pseud.). *S.F. Horizons,* No. 2 (1965), pp. 38–50.

Bloch, Ernst. "Antizipierte Realität-Wie geschieht und was leistet utopisches Denken?" *Universitätstage. Veröffenlichung der Freien Universität Berlin* (1965), pp. 5-15.

Bloch, Robert. "Imagination and Modern Social Criticism," in *The Science Fiction Novel; Imagination and Social Criticism,* 3rd edition (Chicago: Advent Publishers, 1969), pp. 97-121.

Bloch-Laine, Françoise. "The Utility of Utopias for Reformers," in *Utopias and Utopian Thought,* edited by Frank E. Manuel (Boston: Beacon Press, 1967), pp. 201-218.

Bloch-Laine, Françoise. "L'Utopie Constructive." *Esprit,* 35 (February 1966), 211-221.

Blodgett, Eleanor Dickinson. "Bacon's *New Atlantis* and Campanella's *Civitas Solis:* A Study in Relationships." *PMLA,* 46 (September 1931), 763-780.

Bloomfield, Paul. "The Eugenics of the Utopians: The Utopia of the Egenists." *Eugenics Review,* 40 (January 1949), 191-198.

Blotner, J. L. "The Novel of the Future," in his *The Modern American Political Novel* (Austin: University of Texas Press, 1966), pp. 139-163.

Bluck, R. S. "Plato's Ideal State." *Classical Quarterly,* 9 (1958), 166-168.

Bluhm, William T. "Place of the Polity in Aristotle's Theory of the Ideal State." *Journal of Politics,* 24 (November 1962), 743-753.

Blum, Irving D. "English Utopias from 1551 to 1699; A Bibliography." *Bulletin of Bibliography,* 21 (January-April 1955), 143-144.

Boas, George. "Earthly Paradises," in his *Essays on Primitivism and Related Ideas in the Middle Ages* (Baltimore: Johns Hopkins University Press, 1948), pp. 154-174.

Böckenförde, Ernst-Wolfgang. "Die Entstehung des Staates als Vorgang der Säkularisation," in *Säkularisation und Utopie. Ebracher Studien. Ernst Forsthoff zum 65. Geburtstag* (Stuttgart: W. Kohlhammer Verlag, 1967), pp. 75-94.

Bode, Helmut. "Die Wandlung Aldous Huxleys." *Literarisches Revue,* 4, No. 3 (1949), 181-184.

Bogardus, Emory, S[tephen]. "More and Utopian Social Thought," in his *The Development of Social Thought,* 4th edition (London: Longmans, Green, 1960), pp. 179-195.

Boggs, W. Arthur. "Looking Backward at the Utopian Novel, 1888-1900." *Bulletin of the New York Public Library,* 64 (June 1960), 329-336.

Bolitho, T. G. G. "Some Utopias." *Notes and Queries,* 193 (January 10, 1948), 522.

Bondy, M. von. "Der Untergang der Utopie." *Die Gegenwart,* 5, No. 15 (August 1950), 113-115.

Bonner, William Hallam. "Islandia," *Nature Magazine,* 37 (January 1944), 43.

Bonnet, Georges. "Intentions éthiques de l'utopie." *Le Supplement,* 119 (November 1976), 517–548.

Booth, Arthur J. "Fourier." *Fortnightly Review,* N.S. 12 (1872), pp. 530–553, 673–691.

Borecký, Bořivoj. "Platons Idealstaat in den 'nomoi' und die politische Theorie der Griechen." *Wissenschaftliche Zeitschrift der Humbolt-Universität zu Berlin. Gesellschafts und Sprachwissenschaftsliche Reihe,* 12, No. 3 (1963), 221–228.

Borges, Jorge Luis. "Utopia of a Tired Man," translated by Norman Thomas di Giovanni. *New Yorker,* 51 (April 14, 1975), 32–33.

Borgese, Elisabeth Mann. "The Feminine Revolution," in her *Ascent of Woman* (New York: George Braziller, 1963), pp. 111–132.

Borgese, Elisabeth Mann. "Women in Neverland," in her *Ascent of Woman* (New York: George Braziller, 1963), pp. 133–156.

Borinski, Ludwig. "Die Kritik der Utopie in der modernen englishchen Literatur." *Die Neueren Sprachen,* Supplement 2 [1957], 5–24.

Borinski, Ludwig. "Wells, Huxley und die Utopie," in *Literature — Kultur — Gesellschaft in England und Amerika. Aspekte und Forschungsbeiträge Friedrich Schubert zum 60. Gebrutstag,* edited by Gerhard Müller-Schwefe and Konrad Tuzinski (Frankfurt am Main; Verlag Mortiz Diesterweg, 1966), pp. 257–277.

Bosc, Robert. "Chronique de littérature allemande: les romans d'anticipation." *Etudes,* 269 (April 1951), 69–84.

Boschine, L.M. "Utopia come ipotesi di lavoro." *Casabella,* No. 305 (1966), pp. 16–25.

Bottero, Maria. "Astrazione scientifica e ricerca del concreto nell' utopia di B. Fuller." *Zodiac,* No. 19, pp. 50–57.

Bottiglia, William F. "The Eldorado Episode in *Candide.*" *PMLA,* 73 (September 1958), 339–347.

Boulding, Elise. "Religion, Futurism, and Models of Social Change." *The Humanist* (November/December 1973), pp. 35–39.

Bova, Ben. "The Role of Science Fiction," in *Science Fiction: Today and Tomorrow,* edited by Reginald Bretnor (New York: Harper & Row, 1974), pp. 3–14.

Bowes, G. K. "The Doom of Social Utopias — A Study of Population," *Hibbert Journal,* 35 (January 1937), pp. 161–175.

Bowman, Frank Paul. "Utopie, Imagination, Espérance: Northrop Frye, Ernst Bloch, Judith Schlanger." *Littérature,* No. 21 (February 1976), pp. 10–19.

Bowman, Sylvia E. "Bellamy's Missing Chapter," *New England Quarterly,* 31 (March 1958), pp. 47–65.

Bowman, Sylvia E. "Utopian Views of Man and the Machine," *Studies in the Literary Imagination,* 6 (Fall 1973), 105–120.

Bradbury, Ray. "Day After Tomorrow; Why Science Fiction?" *Nation,* 176 (May 2, 1953), 364–367.

Brady, Charles A. "Utopias Between the Wars." *America,* 66 (January 3, 1942), 353–354.

Brandis, Evgeni and Vladimir Dmitravsky. "In the Land of Science Fiction." *Soviet Literature,* No. 5 (1968), pp. 145–150.

Brandt, Dr. "Utopie und Kulturgeschichte." *Beilage zur allegemeinen Zeitung,* No. 108 (May 14, 1898), pp. 1–4.

Brann, Eva. " 'An Exquisite Platform': Utopia." *Interpretation,* 3 (Autumn 1972), 1–26.

Brasch, Moritz. "Socialistische Phantasiestaaten," in his *Gesammelte Essays [und charakterkopf] zur neuren philosophie und literatur* (Leipzig: Theodor Huth, [1887], pp. 57–125.

Brauer, Theodor. "Utopischer Sozialismus," in *Staatslexikon.* 5 Vols. (Freiburg im Breisgau: Herder, 1926–1932), Vol. 5, pp. 587–590.

Braunert, Horst. "Die Heilige Insel des Euhemeros in der Dioder-Überlieferung." *Reinisches Museum für Philologie,* N.S. 108 (1965), pp. 255–268.

Bredvold, Louis. "Prospects of Utopia," in his *The Brave New World of the Enlightenment* (Ann Arbor: University of Michigan Press, 1962), pp. 99–124.

Breines, Paul. "Utopie und Partei. Anmerkungen zum jungen Lukács," in *Detusches utopisches Denken im 20. Jahrhundert,* edited by Reinhold Grimm and Jost Hermand (Stuttgart: W. Kohlhammer, 1974), pp. 96–103.

Bretnor, Reginald. "Science Fiction in the Age of Space," in *Science Fiction; Today and Tomorrow,* edited by Bretnor (New York: Harper & Row, 1974), pp. 150–178.

Brie, Friedrich. "Machtpolitik und Kreig in der Utopia des Thomas More." *Historisches Jahrbuch,* 61 (1941), 116–137.

Briefs, Goetz A. "The Rise and Fall of the Proletarian Utopias." *Review of Politics,* 1 (January 1939), 31–50.

Brinton, Crane. "Utopia and Democracy," in *Utopias and Utopian Thought,* edited by Frank E. Manuel (Boston: Beacon Press, 1967), pp. 50–68.

Bristol, Michael. "Acting Out Utopia; The Politics of Carnival," *Performance,* 1 (May-June 1973), 13–15, 22–28.

Bronner, Stephen Eric. "Revolutionary Anticipation and Tradition; In Honor of Ernst Bloch's 90th Birthday." *Minnesota Review,* N.S. 6 (Spring 1976), pp. 88–95.

Brooks, Collin. "What are We to do With Our Wells?" *The Bookman,* 81 (February 1932), 272–273.

Brophy, Liam, "Century of Utopian Dreams and Catholic Realism." *Social Justice Review,* 48 (August 1955), 116–119.

Brophy, Liam. "Grave New Worlds." *Catholic World,* 179 (April 1954), 40–43.

Brown, Truesdell S. "Euhumerus and the Historians." *Harvard Theological Review,* 39 (October 1946), 259–274.

Browning, Gordon. "Toward a Set of Standards for Evaluating Anti-Utopian Fiction." *Cithara,* 10 (1970), 18–32.

Brubacher, J. S. "Utopian Perspectives on the University." *Educational Record,* 50 (Spring 1969), 213–219.

Bruck, Max von. "Der Untergang der Utopie," in *Der Gesichtskreis. Joseph Drexel zum 60. Geburtstag* (Munich: Beck, 1956), pp. 71–81.

Brüggemann, F[ritz]. "Einführung," *Vorboten der bürgerlichen Kultur. Johann Gottfried Schnabel und Albrecht von Haller,* edited by Brüggemann (Leipzig: Phillip Reclam, 1931), pp. 5–18.

Brugmans, Henri. "Morus' 'Utopia' . . . en Verder." *Moreana,* Nos. 15–16 (November 1967), pp. 165–180.

Bryson, Lyman. "Humanism and Utopia," in his *Next America; Prophecy and Faith* (New York: Harper, 1952), pp. 197–204.

Buddecke, Eckhart. "Utopisches Denken in der Biochemie," in *Säkularisation und Utopie. Ebracher Studien, Ernst Forsthoff zum 65 Geburtstag* (Stuttgart: W. Kohlhammer Verlag, 1967), pp. 279–298.

Buhle, Paul. "Dystopia as Utopia: Howard Phillips Lovecraft and the Unknown Content of American Horror Literature." *Minnesota Review,* N.S. 6 (Spring 1976), pp. 118–131.

Bullough, Geoffrey. "The Later History of Cockaigne," in *Festschrift Prof. Dr. Herbert Koziol zum Siebzigsten Geburtstag (Wiener Beiträge zur englischen Philologie, 75),* edited by Gero Bauer, Franz K. Stanzel, and Franz Zaic (Stuttgart: Wilhelm Baraunmüller, 1973), pp. 22–35.

Bunge, Mario. "On William Morris' Socialism." *Science and Society,* 20 (Spring 1956), 142–144.

Burckhardt, Lucius. "Lernen von den Utopien." *Werk,* 60 (September 1973), 1075–1080.

Burgess, Anthony. "Utopias and Dystopias," in *The Novel Now: A Guide to Contemporary Fiction.* (New York: W. W. Norton, 1967), pp. 38–47.

Burkhardt, Francois and Burghart Schmidt. "Blick auf Möglichen Vorschein in jungen Stadtentwürfen." *Werk,* 60 (September 1973), 1093–1103.

Burkhardt, Francois, Matthias Eberle, and Burghart Schmidt. "Erläufterung des Begriffs 'Konkrete Utopie' Darstellung des Sinnes." *Werk,* 60 (September 1973), 1056–1057.

Burkhardt, Francois, and Burghart Schmidt, eds. "Stadutopie/Stadplanung." *Werk,* 60 (September 1973), pp. 1055–1103.

Burschell, Friedrich. "Der Geist Der Utopie," in *Ernst Bloch zu ehren: Beitrage zu seinem Werk,* edited by Siegfried Unseld ([Frankfurt am Main:] Suhrkamp, [1965]), pp. 375–381. Reprinted from *Die neue Rundschau.*

Busch, Günther. "Utopie als Vermögen und Gehäuse." *Begegnung,* 13 (1958), 99–100.

Bush, Robert D. "Technology and Elitism: The Legacy of Saint-Simon." *McNeese Review,* 22 (1975–1976), 51–61.

Butor, Michel. "La politique des Charmeuses." *Topique,* Nos. 4–5 (October 1970), pp. 99–101.

Butor, Michel. "Science Fiction: The Crisis of Its Growth." *Partisan Review,* 34 (1967), 595–602.

Buve, Sergius. "Utopie als Kritik," in *Säkularisation und Utopie. Ebracher Studien. Ernst Forsthoff zum 65. Geburtstag* (Stuttgart: W. Kohlhammer Verlag, 1967), pp. 11–35.

Cadman, Harry. "The Future of Industrialism." *Overland Monthly,* 2nd series, 15 (June 1890), 577–591.

Caillois, Roger. "De la féerie à la science fiction; l'image fantastique," in his *Images, images...* (Paris: Jose Corti, 1966), pp. 11–59.

Caillois, R[oger]. "Negative Utopia and Religion." *Diogenes,* No. 87 (Fall 1974), pp. 34–49.

Campbell, W. E. "More's *Utopia,*" *Dublin Review,* 185 (October 1929), 194–216.

Campbell, W. E. "The Utopia of Sir Thomas More," in *The King's Good Servant; Papers read to The Thomas More Society of London* (Oxford: Basil Blackwell, 1948), pp. 26–39.

Canaday, Nicholas, Jr. "Community and Identity at Blithedale." *South Atlantic Quarterly,* 71 (Winter 1972), 30–39.

Canary, Robert H. "Utopian and Fantastic Dualities in Robert Graves' *Watch the North Wind Rise,*" *Science-Fiction Studies,* 1 (Fall 1974), 248–255.

Cansler, Ronald Lee. "*Stranger in a Strange Land:* Science Fiction as Literature of Creative Imagination, Social Criticism, and Entertainment." *Journal of Popular Culture,* 5 (Spring 1972), 944–954.

Carlisle, Robert B. "The Birth of Technocracy: Science, Society, and Saint-Simonians." *Journal of the History of Ideas,* 35 (July/September 1974), 445–464.

Carlisle, Robert B. "Saint-Simonian Radicalism: A Definition and a Direction." *French Historical Studies,* 5 (Fall 1968), 430–445.

Carlson, William A. "Professor Macnie as a Novelist." *The Alumni Review* (University of North Dakota) (December 1934), pp. 4, 16.

Carlton, Frank T. "An American Utopia." *Quarterly Journal of Economics,* 24 (February 1910), 428–433.

Carmichael, Montgomery. "Blessed Thomas More, Utopist." *Tablet* (July 27, 1929), pp. 102–104.

Carmichael, Montgomery. "Sir Thomas More's Utopia; Its Doctrine of the Common Life." *Dublin Review,* 191 (October 1932), 173–187.

Carr, Edward Hallett. "Utopia and Reality," in his *The Twenty Years' Crisis 1919–1939*. 2nd edition (London: Macmillan, 1946), pp. 11–21.

Carson, Clarence B. "Their Young Men Dream No Dreams." *Spiritual Life,* 9 (Spring 1963), 27–35.

Carter, John. "Modern Utopias As Seen in Recent Books." *Outlook,* 157 (February 11, 1931), 232.

Cary, Francine C. *"The World A Department Store:* Bradford Peck and the Utopian Endeavor." *American Quarterly,* 29 (Fall 1977), 370–384.

Caso, Alfonso. "Presencia de don Vasco." *Cuadernos Americanos,* 141, No. 4 (July-August 1965), 139–147.

Cataldi, Margherita. "Mito Edenico, Utopia e fantascienza nella narrativa di Flann O'Brien," in *Utopia e Fantascienza* (Torino: Giappichelli, 1975), pp. 143–158.

Caterinussi, Bernardo. "Le dimensioni dell'utopia." *Rivista di Sociologia* (Rome) 12, No. 3 (September-December 1974), 89–110.

Cavanaugh, John R. "Utopia: Sound from Nowhere." *Moreana,* No. 35 (September 1972), pp. 27–38.

Cepeda, Alfredo. "El pensamiento utopista," in his *Los Utopistas: Owen — Saint Simon — Fourier — Leroux — Considerant* (Buenos Aires: Editorial Futuro, 1944), pp. 9–41.

Cepeda, Alfredo. "El socialismo utopico y el pensamiento argentino," in his *Los Utopistas: Owen — Saint Simon — Fourier — Leroux — Considerent* (Buenos Aires: Editorial Futuro, 1944), pp. 42–51.

Chafer, Rollin Thomas. "Christian Socialism: Its Historical Background and Successor." *Bibliotheca Sacra,* 94-95 (October 1937-January 1938), 430–442, 69–75.

Chalpin, Lila. "Anthony Burgess's Gallows Humor in Dystopia." *Texas Quarterly,* 16 (Autumn 1973), 73–84.

Chambers, R. W. "The Saga and Myth of Sir Thomas More." *Proceedings of the British Academy* (1926), pp. 179–225.

Chase, Stuart. "A Modest Utopia." *The Futurist,* 9 (October 1975), 249–253.

Cheney, Brainard. "Christianity and the Tragic Vision — Utopianism USA." *Sewanee Review,* 69 (Autumn 1961), 515–533.

Chenu, Marie-Dominique. "La paura delle utopie." *Civitas,* 5, No. 24 (1969), 386–388.

Chesneaux, Jean. "Egalitarian and Utopian Traditions in the East." *Diogenes,* 62 (1968), 76–102.

Chevallier, Jean-Jacques. "Platon, médicin de la Cité ou la tentation idéocratique." *Revue francaise de Science politique,* 1 (October-December 1951), 417–432.

Chiaromonte, Nicola. "Nota sulla civiltà e le utopie." *Solaria* (Florence), 8, No. 4/5:5–18.

Child, Harold. "Some English Utopias." *Essays by Divers Hands being the Transactions of the Royal Society of Literature of the United Kingdom,* New [3rd] Series 12 (1933), pp. 31-60.

Chipraz, Francois. "Plaidoyer pour l'utopie." *Esprit,* 42 (April 1974), 567-584.

Choay, Françoise. "L'urbanisme en question," in his *L'Urbanisme. Utopies et realités. Une anthologie.* (Paris:Éditions du Seuil, 1965), pp. 7-83.

Christopher, J. R. "Methuselah, Out of Heinlein by Shaw." *Shaw Review,* 16 (May 1973), 79-88.

Chroust, Anton-Hermann. "The Ideal Polity of the Early Stoics: Zeno's Republic." *Review of Politics,* 27 (April 1965), 173-183.

Churchman, C. West. "Ethics, Ideals, and Dissatisfaction." *Ethics,* 63 (October 1952), 64-65.

Cioran, E.-M. "Essai sur l'utopie." *La Nouvelle Nouvelle Revue française* 6, No. 67 (July 1, 1958), 59-75.

Cioranescu, Alexandre, "*Epigone,* le premier roman de l'avenir." *Review des sciences humaines,* 39 (July-September 1974), 441-448.

"Les Cites ideales." "IV. — Lettres Modernes." "Bibliographie sommaire pour les Agregations de Lettres et de Grammaire." *L'Information Litteraire,* 19, No. 4 (September-October 1967), 185-186.

Clareson, Thomas D. "An Annotated Checklist of American Science Fiction: 1880-1915," *Extrapolation,* 1 (December 1959), 5-20.

Clareson, Thomas D. and Edward S. Lauterbach. "A Checklist of Articles Dealing with Science Fiction." *Extrapolation,* 1 (May 1960), 29-34.

Clareson, Thomas D. "The Classic: Aldous Huxley's *Brave New World.*" *Extrapolation,* 2 (May 1961), 33-40.

Clareson, Thomas D. "Major Trends in American Science Fiction: 1880-1915." *Extrapolation,* 1 (December 1959), 2-4.

Clark, Dennis J. "Utopia in the Sixties: Current Expressions of Utopian Idealism." *Catholic World,* 196 (March 1963), 357-363.

Clark, E. Roger. "L'Utopie: Tentative de réintegration universelle." *Studies in the Eighteenth Century,* 6 (1977), 417-426.

Clark, Roger. Voyages curieux d'un Philadelphe (1755): An Anonymous Utopia of the Mid-18th Century," in *The Varied Pattern; Studies in the 18th Century,* edited by Peter Hughes & David Williams (Toronto: A.M. Hakkert, Ltd., 1971), pp. 39-49.

Clark, Walter H. "Drugs and Utopia/Dystopia," in *Utopia/Dystopia,* edited by Peyton E. Richter (Cambridge, Massachusetts: Schenkman Pub. Co., 1973), pp. 111-123.

Clarke, I.F. The First Forecast of the Future." *Futures,* 1 (June 1969), 325-330.

Clarke, I.F. "Harrington's Oceana: or, the long arm of Utopia." *Futures,* 5 (June 1973), 317-322.

Clarke, I.F. "The Nineteenth Century Utopia." *Quarterly Review* (London), 296 (January 1958), 80–91.

Clayton, Alan. "The Twentieth Century and the Utopian Perspective." *Melbourne Journal of Politics,* No. 5 (1972), pp. 61–71.

Clayton, Bertram. "Utopias Unlimited." *Quarterly Review,* 231, No. 459 (April 1919), 510–524.

Cleghorn, S. N. "Prospects of Futurity." *Harvard Graduates Magazine,* 32 (December 1923), pp. 219–229.

Cleghorn, S. N. "Utopia Interpreted." *Atlantic Monthly,* 134 (July 1924, August 1924), 55–67, 216–224.

Clément, Catherine. "A-topie: Description d'un rituel." *Littérature,* No. 21 (February 1976), pp. 105–110.

Coe, Richard N. "*Nineteen Eighty-Four* and the Anti-Utopian Tradition." *Geste* (University of Leeds), 6, No. 7 (October 27, 1960): unpaged.

Colberg, Eckard. "Ideologie, Utopie und politische Theorie." *Gesellschaft, Staat, Erziehung,* 16, No. 1 (1971), 7–22.

Cole, G. D. H. "The New *New Atlantis.*" *The Fortnightly,* 158 (November 1942), 293–300.

Cole, Susan Ablon. "The Evolutionary Fantasy: Shaw and Utopian Fiction." *Shaw Review,* 16 (May 1973), 89–97.

Coleman, D.C. "Bernard Shaw and *Brave New World,*" *Shaw Review,* 10 (January 1967), 6–8.

Collins, Christopher. "Zamyatin, Wells and the Utopian Literary Tradition." *Slavonic and East European Review,* 44 (July 1966), 351–360.

Colquitt, Betsey Feagan. "Orwell: Traditionalist in Wonderland." *Discourse,* 8 (1965), pp. 370–383.

"The Coming Age." *The Saturday Review of Politics, Literature, Science and Art,* 37 (May 23, 1874), 645–646.

Connelly, Wayne. "H. G. Wells's 'The Time Machine': Its Neglected Mythos," *Riverside Quarterly,* 5, No. 3 (August 1972), 178–191. Correcting errors as indicated by errata sheet.

Connes, George. "Leçon finale d'un cours public sur 'Quelques utopistes Anglo-saxons.' " Publications de l'Université de Dijon, Vol. 1 (1928). Part I, Mélanges, pp. 37–57.

Connors, James. " 'Do It to Julia': Thoughts on Orwell's *1984.*" *Modern Fiction Studies,* 16 (Winter 1970–1971), 463–473.

Connors, James. "Zamyatin's *We* and the Genesis of *1984.*" *Modern Fiction Studies,* 21 (Spring 1975), 107–124.

Conquest, Robert. "Science Fiction and Literature." *Critical Quarterly,* 5 (Winter 1963), 355–367.

Coogan, Robert, C. F. C. "Nŭnc VIVOVT Volo." *Moreana,* Nos. 31–32 (November 1971), pp. 29–45.

Cooperman, Stanley. "Utopian Realism: The Futuristic Novels of Bellamy and Howells." *College English,* 24 (March 1963), pp. 464–467.

Corbin, Henry. "Au pays de l'Imân Caché," in *Vom Sinn der Utopie. Eranos-Jahrbuch 1963* (Zürich: Rhein-Verlag, 1964), pp. 31–87.

Cornu, Auguste. "German Utopianism: 'True Socialism,' " translated by Henry F. Mins. *Science and Society,* 12 (Winter 1948), 97–112.

Cornu, A[uguste]. "Utopisme et marxisme," in *A la lumière du marxisme (essais).* 2 Vols. (Paris: Editions sociales internationales, 1935, 1937), Vol. 2, pp. 127–150.

Corsano, Antonio. "Jérôme Cardan et l'utopie," in Université libre de Bruxelles. Institut pour l'étude de la Renaissance et de l'humanisme. *Les Utopie à la Renaissance* (Brussels: Presses Universitaires de Bruxelles, 1963), pp. 89–98.

Coser, Lewis A. "The Sexual Requisites of Utopia," in his *Greedy Institutions; Patterns of Individual Commitment* (New York: The Free Press, 1973), pp. 136–149.

Cotgrove, Stephen. "Environmentalism and Utopia." *Sociological Review,* 24 (February 1976), pp. 23–42.

Courcelle, Pierre. "Les exégèses chrétiennes de la quatrième éclogue." *Revue des études anciennes,* 59 (1957), 294–319.

Cox, J. Sullivan. "Imaginary Commonwealths." *United States Magazine and Democratic Review,* 19 (September 1846), 175–185.

Crane, R. S. "The Houyhnhnms, the Yahoos, and the History of Ideas," in *Reason and Imagination; Studies in the History of Ideas 1600–1800,* edited by J.A. Mazee (New York: Columbia University Press, 1962), pp. 231–253.

Creel, George. "Utopia Unlimited." *Saturday Evening Post,* 207 (November 24, 1934), 5–7.

Cro, Stelio. "Introduction," in *Descripcion de la Sinapia; Peninsula en la Tierra Austral. A Classical Utopia of Spain,* edited by Stelio Cro (np: McMaster University, 1975), pp. i–lvii.

Croce, Benedetto. "Problemi di metodologia storica: L'Utopia della forma sociale perfetta." *Quaderni della "Critica,"* 6, No. 16 (March 1950), 21–26.

Crozier, John Beattie. "Mr. Wells as a Sociologist." *Fortnightly Review,* 84 (September 1905), 417–426.

Cunis, Reinmar. "Wunschbild und Alptraum. Eine soziologische Betrachtung moderner literarischer Utopien." *Die neue Gesellschaft,* 8 (May 1961), 219–225.

Curcio, Carlo. "Introduzione. Formazione e carattesi dell'utopia italiana nel Rinascimento," in *Utopisti Italiani del Cinquecento,* edited by Carlo Curcio (np: Colombo Editore, 1944), pp. 5–34.

Dagron, Gilbert. "Histoire et Utopie; Discours utopiques et récit des origines.

Une lecture de Cassiodore-Jordanès: les Goths de Scanza à Ravenne."
Annales, 26 (March-April 1971), 290–305.

Dahrendorf, Ralf. "In Praise of Thrasymachus," in his *Essays in the Theory of Society* (Stanford: Stanford University Press, 1968), pp. 129–150.

Dahrendorf, Ralf. "Out of Utopia: Toward a Reorientation of Sociological Analysis." *America Journal of Sociology,* 64 (September 1958), 115–127.

Daniel-Rops. "Thomas More, Planiste de l'*Utopie.*" *Moreana,* No. 6 (May 1965), pp. 5–8.

D'Astorg, Bernard. "Du roman d'anticipation." *Esprit,* N.S. 21 (May 1953), 657–673.

Dator, James Allen. "Political Futuristics: Toward the Study of Alternative Political Futures," in *Aware of Utopia,* edited by David Plath (Urbana: University of Illinois Press, 1971), pp. 55–63.

Dautry, Jean. "Fourier et les questions d'éducation." *Revue Internationale de philosophie,* No. 60 (1962), pp. 234–260.

Davidson, Donald. "The Shape of Things and Men." *The American Review,* 7 (June 1936), 225–248.

Davies, H. Neville. " 'Symzonia' and 'The Man in the Moone.' " *Notes and Queries,* 15 (Summer 1968), 342–345.

Davies, James C. "Political Fiction." *International Encyclopedia of the Social Sciences,* Vol. 9: 430–440.

Davies, Wallace Evan. "A Collectivist Experiment Down East: Bradford Peck and the Cooperative Association of America." *New England Quarterly,* 120 (December 1947), 471–491.

Davis, J. C. "Utopia and History." *Historical Studies* (Melbourne), 13 (April 1968), 165–176.

Davis, Jerome. "Utopias," in his *Contemporary Social Movements* (New York: Century, 1930), pp. 15–68.

Davis, Natalie Zemon. "René Choppin on More's Utopia." *Moreana,* Nos. 19–20 (November 1958), pp. 91–96.

Dawes, Anna L. "Mr. Bellamy and Christianity." *Andover Review,* 15 (April 1891), 413–418.

Debout, Simone. "L'illusion réele." *Topique,* Nos. 4–5 (October 1970), pp. 11–78.

Debout-Oleszkiewicz, Simone. "L'analogie ou 'Le poème mathématique' de Charles Fourier." *Revue internationale de philosophie,* No. 60 (1962), pp. 176–199.

Debus, Karl. "Raumschiffahrtsdichtung und Bewohnbarkeitsphantasien seit der Renaissance bis Heute," in *Der Möglichkeit der Weltraumfahrt; allgemeinverständliche beiträge zum raumschiffahrtsproblem,* edited by Willy Ley (Leipzig: Hachmeister & Thal, 1928), pp. 67–105.

Decobert, Jacques. "Au procès de l'utopie, un 'roman des illusions pardues':

Prévost et la 'Colonie Rochelloises.' " *Revue des sciences humaines,* 39, No. 155 (July-September 1974), 493–504.

De Corte, Marcel. "Gli intellettuali e l'utopia," in *L'Utopia nel mondo moderno* (Florence: Vallecchi, 1969), pp. 41–64.

De Jouvenal, Bertrand. "Utopia for Practical Purposes," in *Utopias and Utopian Thought,* edited by Frank E. Manuel (Boston: Beacon Press, 1967), pp. 219–235.

Delany, Selden Peabody. "Golden Age or Millenium." *Commonweal,* 21 (April 19, 1935), 702–703.

Delcourt, Marie. "Utopiana." *Latomus,* 25, No. 2 (1966), pp. 305–309.

Demaison, Michel. "Les sentiers de l'utopie chrétienne." *Lumière et vie,* 18, No. 95 (1969), 87–110.

Demoris, René. "L'utopie, *Autre* du roman: *La Terre Australe Connue. . .* de G. de Foigny (1676)." *Revue des sciences humaines,* 39, No. 155 (July-September 1974), 397–409.

Demos, Raphael. "A Note on Plato's *Republic.*" *Review of Metaphysics,* 12 (December 1958), 300–307.

Demos, Raphael. "Paradoxes in Plato's Doctrine of The Ideal State." *Classical Quarterly,* 51 (July-October 1957), 164–174.

Derleth, August. "Contemporary Science Fiction." *English Journal,* 41 (January 1952), 1–8.

Derrett, J. Duncan M. "More's Utopia and Indians in Europe." *Moreana,* No. 5 (February 1965), 17–18.

Derrett, J. Duncan M. "The Utopian Alphabet." *Moreana,* No. 12 (November 1966), pp. 61–64.

Desanti, Dominique. "San Francisco: Des hippies pour Fourier." *Topique,* Nos. 4–5 (October 1970), pp. 205–212.

Desroche, Henri. "De Thomas More à Etienne Cabet." *Moreana,* Nos. 31–32 (November 1971), pp. 215–219.

Desroche, Henri. "Dissidence religieuses et socialismes utopiques." *Année Sociologique,* 3rd series (1952), pp. 393–429.

Desroche, Henri, "Fouriérisme ambigu. Socialisme ou religion?." *Revue internationale de philosophie,* No. 60 (1962), pp. 200–220.

Desroche, Henri. "L'origine utopique." *Esprit,* 42 (October 1974), 337–366.

Desroche, Henri. "Owenisme et utopies françaises: Symposium commémoratif du deuxième Centenaire de Robert Owen (1771–1971)." *Communautes Archives Internationales de Sociologie de la Coopération et du Développement,* No. 30 (July-December, 1971), pp. 5–192.

Desroche, Henri. "Petite bibliothèque de l'utopie." *Esprit,* 42 (April 1974), 663–670.

Desroche, Henri. "La Phalanstère." *Esprit,* 42 (April 1974), 585–602.

Desroche, Henri. "Saint Simon ou l'utopie d'une science sociale en action."

Communautes Archives Internationales de Sociologie de la Coopération et du Développement, No. 27 (January-June, 1970), pp. 21-34.

Desroche, Henri. "Voyages en ucoopies...." *Esprit,* 35 (February 1966), 224-245.

Deutscher, Isaac. "*1984* — The Mysticism of Cruelty," in his *Russia in Transition and Other Essays* (New York: Coward-McCann, 1957), pp. 230-245.

Devoto, Bernard. "What the Next Hour Holds." *Harpers,* 173 (June 1936), 109-112.

Dewey, John. "A Great American Prophet." *Common Sense,* 3 (April 1934), 6-7.

Diamant, Alfred. "Anti-Bureaucratic Utopias in Highly Industrialized Societies: A Preliminary Assessment." *Journal of Comparative Administration,* 4, No. 1 (May 1972), 3-34.

Dickinson, J.A. "Antecedents of the Community-School Concept in the Utopian Theories." *National Society for the Study of Education Yearbook,* 52, part 2 (1952), 238-250.

Dietzel, H. "Beiträge zur Geschichte des Sozialismus und des Kommunismus. III. Morus Utopien und Campanellas Sonnenstaat." *Vierteljahrsschrift für Staats- und Volkswirtschaft, für Litteratur und Geschichte der Staatswissenschaften aller Länden,* 5, No. 2, 4 (1896, 1897), 217-238, 372-412.

Ditz, Gerhard W. "Utopian Symbols in the History of the British Labour Party." *British Journal of Sociology,* 17 (June 1966), 145-150.

"Dokumentation Concilium. Utopia." *Concilium,* 5, No. 1 (1969), 74-81.

Domenach, Jean-Marie. "L'Homme parti à la conquête de l'avenir ne doit pas renoncer à ses vieux rêves." *Le Magazine Maclean,* 3 (January 1963), 50.

Domenach, Jean-Marie. "L'Utopie ou la raison dans l'imaginaire." *Esprit,* 42 (April 1974), 546-556.

Domhoff, G. William. "Blueprints for a New Society." *Ramparts,* (February 1974), pp. 13-16.

Donoso Núñez, Guido. "En Torno a una utopia de Fenelon." *Atenea,* No. 399 (1963), pp. 18-35.

Doren, Alfred. "Campanella-als Chiliast und Utopist,"in *Kultur und Universalgeschichte. Walter Goetz zu seinem 60. Geburtstage* (Leipzig: B. G. Teubner, 1927), pp. 242-259.

Doren, Alfred. "Wunschräume und Wunschzeiten." Bibliothek Warburg *Vorträge,* 1924-1925, edited by Fritz Saxl (Leipzig: Teubner, 1927), pp. 158-205.

Dorsch, T. S. "Sir Thomas More and Lucian. An Interpretation of Utopia." *Archiv für das Studium der neueren Sprachen und Literaturen,* 203, No. 5 (1967), 345-463.

Doty, Madelaine Z. "The Socialist in Recent Fiction." *Charities and the Commons,* 17 (December 15, 1906), 485-488.

Doxiadis, C. A. "Entopia." *Ekistics,* 38 (November 1974), 302–304.

Doyle, Charles Clay. "*Utopia* and the Proper Place of Gold: Classical Sources and Renaissance Analogues." *Moreana,* Nos. 31–32 (November 1971), pp. 47–49.

Doyon, René-Louis. "Variations de l'utopie," in *La Première utopie française* (Paris: La Connaissance, 1933), pp. vii–xxi.

Dubois, Claude-Gilbert. "De la première 'utopie' à 'la première utopie française.' Bibliographie et refléxion sur la création utopique au XVIe siècle." *Répertoire analytique de littérature française,* 1 2 (1970), 7–25, 11–31.

Dubois, Claude-Gilbert. "Une architecture fixionnelle." *Revue des sciences humaines,* 39, No. 155 (July-September 1974), 449–471.

Dubos, René Jules. "Medical Utopias." *Daedalus,* 88 (Summer 1959), 410–424.

Dubos, René Jules. "Utopias and Human Goals," in his *Mirage of Health* (New York: Harper & Brothers, 1959), pp. 216–236.

Duchet, Michèle. "Clarens, 'Le Lac-d'amour où l'on se noie.' " *Littérature,* No. 21 (February 1976), pp. 79–90.

Dudden, Arthur P. "Looking Backward: 2000-1887," in *Landmarks of American Writing,* edited by Hennig Cohen (New York: Basic Books, 1969), pp. 207–218.

Duhamel, P. Albert. "Medievalism of More's *Utopia.*" *Studies in Philology,* 52 (April 1955), 99–126.

Duncan, Graeme. "In Defense of Political Utopianism." *Dissent* (Australia), No. 20 (Winter 1967), pp. 23–33.

Duparc, Jean. "Utopie ou theorie?" *La Pensée,* No. 168 (March-April 1973), pp. 116–122.

Dupré, Louis. "Religion, Ideology, and Utopia in Marx." *New Scholasticism,* 50 (Fall 1976), 415–434.

Dupuy, Jean R. "Un utopiste du passé, Péguy, penseur politique." *Annales de la Faculté de Droit d'Aix-en-Provence,* N.S. 49 (1957), pp. 43–66.

Durant, William J. "How we made Utopia," in his *Pleasures of Philosophy* (New York: Simon & Schuster, 1958), pp. 319–332.

Durić, Mihailo. "Die Doppelsinnigkeit der Utopie." *Praxis,* 8, Nos. 1–2 (1972), 27–38.

Dust, Philip. "Alberico Gentili's Commentaries on Utopian Wars." *Moreana,* No. 37 (February 1973), pp. 31–40.

Duveau, Georges. "Approches de l'utopie." *Bulletin de la faculté des lettres de Strasbourg,* 33, No. 6 (1955), 259–263.

Duveau, Georges. "Introduction à une Sociologie de l'Utopie." *Cahiers internationaux de Sociologie,* 9 (1951), 17–41.

Duveau, Georges. "Le resurrection de l'utopie." *Cahiers internationaux de sociologie,* 23 (1957), 3–22.

Duveau, Georges. "Utopie et planification." *Cahiers internationaux de sociologie,* 16 (July-December 1954), 75–92.

Ebner, Dean. "*Tempest:* Rebellion and the Ideal State." *Shakespeare Quarterly,* 16 (Spring 1965), 161–173.

Edrich, Emanuel. "George Orwell and the Satire in Horror." *Texas Studies in Literature and Language,* 4 (1962/63), 96–108.

Edwards, Scott. "Reich, Roszak and the New Jerusalem." *Midwest Quarterly,* 13 (Winter 1972), 185–198.

Ehrenpreis, Irvin. "Orwell, Huxley, Pope." *Revue des langues vivantes,* 23 (1957), 215–230.

Ehrmann, Jacques. "Live in Utopia? Habiter l'utopie?" *Perspecta,* No. 14, pp. 209–219.

Ehrmann, Jacques. "Tribune libre; habiter l'utopie?." *L'Architecture d'aujourd'hui,* 41, No. 150 (June-July 1970), ix–xi.

Eisermann, Gottfried. "Ideologia e utopia." *Revue internationale de sociologie,* 3, Nos. 1–3 (1967), 28–73.

Eliade, Mircea. "Paradise and Utopia: Mythical Geography and Eschatology." in *Utopias and Utopian Thought,* edited by Frank E. Manuel (Boston: Beacon Press, 1967), pp. 260–280.

Elliott, Robert C. "Literature and the Good Life: A Dilemma," *Yale Review,* 65 (Autumn 1975), 24–37.

Ellison, Lee Monroe. "*Guadentio Di Lucca:* A Forgotten Utopia." *PMLA,* 50 (June 1935), 494–509.

Ellul, Jacques. "Search for an Image." *The Humanist,* (November/December 1973), pp. 22–25.

Elsbree, Langdon. "The Structured Nightmare of 1984." *Twentieth Century Literature,* 5 (October 1959), 135–141.

End, Heinrich. "Utopische Elemente in der Friedensforschung. Selbstverständnis und Kritik neuerer politikwissenschaftlicher Forschungsansätze." *Zeitschrift für Politik,* 20 (June 1973), 109–119.

Engelhardt, Werner Wilhelm. "Utopien als Problem der Social- und Wirtschaftswissenschaften." *Zeitschrift für die gesamte Staatswissenschaft,* 125, No. 4 (October 1969), 661–676.

Epps, P. H. "The Golden Age." *The Classical Journal,* 29 (January 1934), 292–296.

Epstein, J. H. "Ueber Utopien." *Berichte des Freien Deutschen Hochstiftes zu Frankfurt am Main,* N.S. 3 (1886/87), pp. 294–299.

Epting, K. "Vom Geist der Utopie; Sehnsucht nach dem Glück — Zerrbild eines Traumes." *Christ und Welt,* 17, No. 50 (1964), 21.

Erisman, Fred. " 'Where We Plan to Go': The Southwest in Utopian Fiction." *Southwestern American Literature,* 1 (September 1971), pp. 137–143.

Ermecke, Gustav. "Ideologie und Utopie." *Jahrbuch für Christliche Sozial-wissenschaften,* 10 (1969), 259–271.

Erzgräber, Willi. "Zur *Utopia* des Thomas Morus," in *Literature — Kultur — Gesellschaft in England und Amerika. Aspekte und Forschungsbeiträge Friedrich Schubel zum 60 Geburtstag,* edited by Gerhard Müller-Schwefe and Konrad Tuzinski (Frankfurt am Main: Verlag Moritz Diesterweg, 1966), pp. 229–56.

Eschmann, Wilhelm Ernst. "Die grossen Gehirne. Vom Computer in Utopien und Wirklichkeit." *Merkur,* 19, No. 209 (August 1965), 720–735.

Eschmann, Wilhelm Ernst. "Die Raumsucher; zur amerikanischen Literatur der Space-Fiction." *Merkur,* 12 (1958), 368–378.

Evans, John X. "The Kingdom within More's Utopia." *Moreana,* 14, Nos. 55–56 (December 1977), pp. 5–21.

Evans, K. W. "*Sejanus* and the Ideal Prince Tradition." *Studies in English Literature,* 11 (Spring 1971), 249–264.

Evans, Robert O. "The *Nouveau Roman,* Russian Dystopias, and Anthony Burgess." *Studies in the Literary Imagination,* 6 (Fall 1973), pp. 27–38.

Fabre, Jean. "Realite et utopie dans la pensée politique de Rousseau." *Annales da la Sociéte, J.-J. Rousseau* (Geneva), 35 (1962), 181–221.

Faguet, Emile. "Charles Fourier." *Revue des deux mondes,* 136 (August 1, 1896), pp. 570–594.

Falke, Rita. "Utopie-logische Konstruktion und chimère." *Germanischroma-nische Monatsschrift,* 6 (1956), pp. 76–81.

Falke, Rita. "Utopies d'heir et d'aujourd'hui." *Diogène,* No. 23 (July-September 1958), pp. 18–28.

Falke, Rita. "Versuch einer Bibliographie der Utopien," *Romanistisches Jahr-buch,* 6 (1953–1954), 92–109.

Farrar, Clarence B. "The Quest for Utopia." *American Journal of Psychiatry,* 109, No. 2 (1952–1953), 153–154.

"Fatherlands and Utopias." *Tablet,* 177 (April 12, 1941), 284–285.

Fensch, Ludwig. "Das Land Nirgendwo une seine Geschichte." *Protestan-tische Monatshefte* (1913), pp. 307–317, 357–368.

Ferguson, Arthur B. "The Complete Works of St. Thomas More, Volume 4, *Utopia.*" *Journal of the History of Ideas,* 29 (April-June 1968), 303–310.

Ferry, W. H. "The White Nation and the Black." *Liberation,* 10 (April 1965), 12–15.

Fiedler, Leslie. "Introduction," in *In Dream_ Awake; A Historical-Critical Anthology of Science Fiction,* edited by Fiedler (New York: Laurēl, 1975), pp. 11–23.

Fiedler, Leslie. "The New Mutants." *Partisan Review,* 32 (Fall 1965), 505–525. Reprinted in *Innovations,* edited by Bernard Bergonzi (London: Macmillan, 1968), pp. 23–45.

Finer, S. E. "A Profile of Science Fiction." *Sociological Review,* Series 2, 2 (December 1954), 239–255.

Fingarette, Herman. "Eros and Utopia." *Review of Metaphysics,* 10 (June 1957), pp. 660–665.

Fink, Conrad. "Die Utopie des Thomas Morus und die Klosterrepublik auf dem Berge Athos." *Historisches Jahrbuch* (1930), pp. 237–242.

Fink, Howard. "*Coming Up For Air:* Orwell's Ambiguous Satire on the Wellsian Utopia." *Studies in the Literary Imagination,* 6 (Fall 1972), 51–60.

Finley, M. I. "Utopianism Ancient and Modern," in *The Critical Spirit; Essays in Honor of Herbert Marcuse,* edited by Kurt Wolff and Barrington Moore, Jr. (Boston: Beacon, 1967), pp. 3–20.

Firpo, Luigi. "La Città ideale del Filarete," in *Studi in memoria di Gioele Solari* (Torino: Edizioni Ramella, 1954), pp. 11–59.

Firpo, Luigi. "Kaspar Stiblin, utopiste," in Université libre de Bruxelles. Institut pour l'étude de la Renaissance et de l'humanisme. *Les Utopies à la Renaissance* (Brussels: Presses Universitaire de Bruxelles, 1963), pp. 107–133.

Firth, Sir Charles. "The Political Significance of Gulliver's Travels," in his *Essays Historical and Literary* (Oxford: Oxford University Press, 1938), pp. 210–241.

Fischer, Andreas. "Utopisches Denken als Kategorie von Bildung und Erziehung." *Pädagogische Rundschau,* 5, No. 26 (1972), 357–378.

Fisher, James A. and Peyton Richter. "Education for Citizenship: A Utopian Approach to General Education." *Journal of Higher Education,* 28 (April 1957), 220–224.

Fisher, Marvin. "The Pattern of Conservatism in Johnson's *Rasselas* and Hawthorne's *Tales.' Journal of the History of Ideas,* 19 (April 1958), 173–196.

Fisher, Peter F. "Plato's *Republic* and Modern Utopianism." *Queen's Quarterly,* 67 (Spring 1960), 18–27.

Fissori, Valerio. "Modi narrativi comparati dei racconti di utopia e di SF," in *Utopia e Fantascienza* (Torino: Giappichelli, 1975), pp. 45–62.

Fiz, S. Marchán. "Arquitectura visionario-utópics en Berlin. 1918–1922." *Goya,* 115 (July 1973), 16–23.

Flach, Jacques. "Thomas Morus et l'ile d'utopie." *Revue bleue* (November 23, 30, 1912), pp. 645–652, 678–686.

Flechtheim, Ossip K. "Utopie, gegenutopie und Futurologie," in his *Eine Welt oder keine? Beiträge zur Politik, Politologie und Philosophie* ([Frankfurt am Main:] Europäische Verlagsanstalt, 1964), pp. 31–47.

Flechtner, Hans-Joachim. "Die phantastische Literatur; eine literarästhetische Untersuchung." *Zeitschrift für Ästhetik und allgemeine Kunstwissenschaft,* 24 (1943), 37–46.

Florescano, Enrique. "Tomas Moro, la 'Utopia' y el experimente de Vasco de Quiroga." *La Palabra y el Hombre,* No. 25 (1963), 21–49.

Flower, B. O. "The Divine Quest; or, The Age-Long Dream of the Fraternal State." *Arena,* 28 (August, October 1902), 152–159, 386–397.

Flower, B. O. "The Latest Social Vision." *Arena,* 18 (October 1897), 517–534.

Flower, B. O. "The Utopia of Sir Thomas More." *Arena,* 15 (January, February 1896), 296–303, 391–398.

Flürscheim, Michael. "Modell-Gemeinwesen." *Schweizerische Blätter fur Wirtschafts- und Sozialpolitik,* 2, No. 1 (1894), 145–154, 229–241.

Flynn, John T. "Why Utopias Always Fail." *American Mercury,* 82 (January 1956), 149–155.

Flynn, Thomas R. "The Use and Abuse of Utopias." *Modern Schoolman,* 53 (March 1976), 235–264.

Fogg, Walter E. "Technology and Dystopia," in *Utopia/Dystopia?,* edited by Peyton E. Richter (Cambridge, Massachusetts: Schenkman Pub. Co., 1975), pp. 59–73.

Foley, Joseph and James Ayer. "Orwell in English and Newspeak: A Computer Translation." *College Composition and Communication,* 17 (February 1966), 15–18.

Fontaine, Paul. "De la justice en Utopie." *Canada Française,* 28 (February 1941), 633–646.

Forbes, Allyn B. "The Literary Quest for Utopia, 1880–1900." *Social Forces,* 6 (December 1927), 179–189.

Foriers, Paul. "Les Utopies et le Droit," in Université libre de Bruxelles. Institut pour l'étude de la Renaissance et de l'humanisme. *Les Utopies à la Renaissance* (Brussels: Presses Universitaires de Bruxelles, 1963), pp. 231–261.

Foxwell, H. S. "Bibliography of the English Socialist School," appended to Anton Menger, *The Right to the Whole Produce of Labour; The Origin and Development of the Theory of Labour's Claim to the Whole Product of Industry,* translated by M. E. Tanner (London: Macmillan, 1899), pp. 189–267.

Francis, K. "Political Myths, Utopias and Political Theories." *Political Science Review* (Jaipur, Rajasthan), 15, No. 1 (January-March 1976), 1–9.

Francke, Kuno. "A German Utopia of the Seventeenth Century." *Nation,* 109 (October 4, 1919), 458–459.

Francoeur, Robert T. "Human Nature and Human Relations." *The Humanist* (November/December 1973), pp. 32–35.

Francon, Marcel. "Two Nineteenth Century Utopias: The Influence of Renan's *L'Avenir de la Science* on Wilde's *The Soul of Man Under Socialism.*" *Modern Language Review,* 59 (July 1964), 361–370.

Frank, S. L. "The Utopian Heresy." *Hibbert Journal,* 52 (April 1954), 213–223.

Franklin, Fabian. "The Bellamy Utopia," in his *People and Problems* (New York: Henry Holt, 1908), pp. 149–153.

Franklin, H. Bruce. "Fictions of the Future." *Stanford Today,* Ser. 1, No. 17 (Summer 1966), pp. 6–11.

Franklin, John Hope. "Edward Bellamy and the Nationalist Movement." *New England Quarterly,* 11 (December 1939), 739–772.

Frenzel, Ivo. "Utopia and Apocalypse in German Literature." *Social Research,* 39 (Summer 1972), 306–321.

Freund, Julien. "Das Utopische in den gegenwärtigen politischen Ideologien," in *Säkularisation und Utopie. Ebracher Studien. Ernst Forsthoff zum 65. Geburtstag* (Stuttgart: W. Kohlhammer, 1967), pp. 95–118.

Freund, Michael. "Zur Deutung der Utopia des Thomas Morus; Ein Beitrag zur Geschichte der Staatsräson in English." *Historische Zeitschrift,* 142, No. 2 (1930), 254–268.

Freyer, Hans. "Das Problem der Utopia." *Deutsche Rundschau,* 183 (June 1920), 321–345.

Friedrich, Bruno. "Die Utopie als Krankheit des Politischen." *Geist und Tat,* 19, No. 10 (October 1964), 308–312.

Friedrich, Otto. "George Orwell." *Points* (Paris), 19 (1954), 25–36.

Friend, Beverly. "Virgin Territory: The Bonds and Boundaries of Women in Science Fiction," in *Many Futures Many Worlds; Theme and Form in Science Fiction,* edited by Thomas D. Clareson ([Kent, Ohio:] Kent State University Press, 1977), pp. 140–163.

Froelich, J. C. "Utopies et millénarismes modernes." *L'Afrique et l'Asie,* No. 80 (1967), pp. 34–38.

Fromm, Erich. "Afterword," in *1984,* by George Orwell (New York: Signet, 1971), pp. 257–267.

Frye, Northrop. "Variety of Literary Utopias," in *Utopias and Utopian Thought,* edited by Frank E. Manuel (Boston: Beacon Press, 1967), pp. 25–49.

Fueyo, Jesús. "Tomas Moro y el utopismo politico." *Revista de Estudios politicos,* 86–87 (March-June 1956), pp. 61–107.

Fuller, Mary Breese. "Is Sir Thomas More Utopian?" *Survey,* 37 (December 2, 1916), 223–225.

Furter, Pierre. "Utopie et marxisme selon Ernst Bloch." *Archives de Sociologie des Religions,* 21 (January-July 1966), pp. 3–21.

Fuson, Ben W. "A Poetic Precursor of Bellamy's 'Looking Backward' " *Extrapolation,* 5 (May 1964), 31–36.

Fyfe, W. H. "Tacitus's *Germania* and More's *Utopia.*" *Transactions of the Royal Society of Canada,* 3rd Series 30, Section 2 (May 1936), pp. 57–59.

G., J. *"Utopie et schizophrénie."* *Encyclopaedia Universalis* (Paris: Encyclopaedia Universalis, 1975), 16, pp. 559–561.

Gandillac, Maurice De. "Les 'semi-utopies' scientifiques, politiques et religieuses du Cardinal Nicolas de Cues," in Université libre de Bruxelles. L'Institut pour l'étude de la Renaissance et de l'humanisme. *Les Utopies à la Renaissance* (Brussels: Presses Universitaires de Bruxelles, 1963), pp. 39–71.

Garagnon, Jean. "L'Abbé Prévost et l'Utopie." *Studies in the Eighteenth Century,* 6 (1977), 439–457.

Garavaglia, Gian-Paolo. "I Livallatori e L'*Utopia*." *Moreana,* No. 31–32 (November 1971), pp. 191–196.

García Cantú, Gastón. "De la República de lot Trabajadores (Una utopia mexicana del sigle XIX)." *Revista Mexicana de Sociologiá,* 29 (April-June 1967), 347–360.

Garin, Eugenio. "La Cité idéale de la Renaissance italienne," in Université libre de Bruxelles. L'Institut pour l'étude de la Renaissance et de l'humanisme. *Les Utopies à le Renaissance* Brussels: Presses Universitaires de Bruxelles, 1963), pp. 11–37.

Gasparetto, Pier Francesco. "Un archetipo di fantautopia lunare nel '600 Inglese," in *Utopia e Fantascienza* (Torino: Giappichelli, 1975), pp. 81–97.

Gaudibert, Pierre. "Fourier et l'organisations des libertés amoureuses." *Arguments,* (1st trimester 1961), pp. 29–33.

Gaumann, Gladys Valcourt. "Year of Utopias." *English Journal,* 61 (February 1972), 234–238, 251.

Gay, William T. "Edward Bellamy Nineteenth Century Futurist." *Futurist,* 1 (June 1967), 40–41.

Geering, R.G. " 'Darkness at Noon' and '1984': A Comparative Study." *Australian Quarterly,* 30 (September 1958), pp. 90–96.

Gehlen, Arnold. "Die Säkularisierung des Fortschritts," in *Säkularisation und Utopie. Ebracher Studien. Ernst Forsthoff zum 65. Geburtstag* (Stuttgart: W. Kohlhammer, 1967), pp. 63–72.

Geipel, Robert. "Über die Behandlung von Utopien im Unterricht." *Gesselschaft Staat Erziehung,* 3 (1958), 373–380.

Gemorah, Solomon. "Laurence Gronlund — Utopian or Reformer?" *Science and Society,* 33 (Fall-Winter 1969), 446–458.

Gérard, Albert. "George Orwell et l'utopie de notre temps." *Revue Générale Belge,* 5 (May 1958), 13–24.

Gerber, Richard. "The English Island Myth: Remarks on the Englishness of Utopian Fiction." *Critical Quarterly,* 1 (Spring 1959), 36–43.

Gerlo, Alois. "Der Friedensgedanke im griechisch-römanisch Altertum." *Wissenschaftliche Zeitschrift der Humboldt-Universität zu Berlin.*

Gesellschafts- und Sprachwissenschaftsliche Reihe, 12, No. 3 (1963), 203–214.

Ghent, W. J. "Utopias and Other Forecasts," in his *Our Benevolent Feudalism* (New York: Macmillan, 1902), pp. 1–10.

Giachino, Enzo. "Per Recuperare il miracolo," in *Utopia e Fantascienza* (Turin: Giappichelli, 1975), pp. 63–79.

Giannini, Alessandro. "Mito e utopia nella letteratura greca prima di Platone," *Rendiconti,* 101, No. 1 (1967), 101–132.

Giard, Luce. "Voyageuse raison." *Esprit,* 42 (April 1974), 557–566.

Gibaud, Henri. "Thomas Morus en Icarie." *Moreana,* Nos. 43–44 (November 1974), pp. 71–80.

Gibson, R. W. and J. Max Patrick, compilers. "Utopias and Dystopias 1500–1750," in *St. Thomas More: A Preliminary Bibliography of His Works and of Moreana to the Year 1750,* compiled by R.W. Gibson (New Haven: Yale University Press, 1961), pp. 291–412.

Gilbert, George Holley. "Religion in an Ideal Commonwealth." *Atlantic,* 101 (April 1908), 566–568.

Gilman, Nicholas P. "Bellamy's *Equality.*" *Quarterly Journal of Economics,* 12 (October 1897), 76–82.

Gilman, Nicholas P. "Nationalism in the United States." *Quarterly Journal of Economics,* 4 (October 1889), 50–76.

Gilman, Nicholas P. "The Way to Utopia," *Unitarian Review,* 34 (July 1890), 48–66.

Glass, James M. "The Yogin and the Utopian: Nirvana and the Discovery of Being." *Polity,* 5 (Summer 1973), 427–450.

Gleckner, Robert F. "1984 or 1948?" *College English,* 18 (November 1956), 95–99.

Glicksberg, Charles I. "Anti-Utopianism in Modern Literature." *Southwest Review,* 37 (Summer 1952), 221–228.

Gobetz, G. E. and R. M. Frumkin. "Teaching About Utopian Ideas and Practices." *Improving College and University Teaching,* 19 (Winter 1971), 26–32.

Golffing, Francis. "Notes Toward a Utopia." *Partisan Review,* 27 (Summer 1960), 514–525.

Golffing, Francis and Barbara Golffing. "An Essay on Utopian Possibility." *Centennial Review,* 7 (Fall 1963), 470–480.

Golffing, Francis and Barbara Gibbs. "Notes Towards a Utopia." *Stand,* 6 (Winter 1962), 51–58.

Golub, Leon. "Utopia/Anti-Utopia; Surplus Freedom in the Corporate State." *Artforum,* 10 (May 1972), 33–34.

Gombin, Richard. "Actualité de Fourier." *Esprit,* 42 (April 1974), 603–613.

Gondor, Lily H. "The Fantasy of Utopia." *American Journal of Psychotherapy,* 17 (October 1963), pp. 606-618.

Goodey, Brian. "Mapping 'Utopia': A Comment on the Geography of Sir Thomas More." *Geographical Review,* 60 (January 1970), 15-30.

Goodheart, Eugene. "Utopia and the Irony of History," in his *Culture and the Radical Conscience* (Cambridge: Harvard University Press, 1973), pp. 97-124.

Goodman, Paul. "Le réalisme utopique." *Esprit,* 42 (April 1974), 625-642.

Goodman, Paul. "Utopian Means They Don't Want to Do It!" *Anarchy 85,* 8 (March 1968), 87-89.

Goret, J. "L'essai d'une 'phalangette' d'enfants." *Topique,* Nos. 4-5 (October 1970), pp. 191-204.

Gothein, Eberhard. "Platos Staatslehre in der Renaissance." *Sitzungsberichte der Heidelberger Akademie der Wissenschaften. Philosophisch-historische Klasse,* No. 5 (1912), pp. 3-25.

Gottfried, Alex and Sue Davidson. "Utopia's Children: An Interpretation of Three Political Novels." *Western Political Quarterly,* 15 (March 1962), 17-32.

Gottschling, Ernst, Horst Kunlaschke, and Horst Schröder. "Marxistisch-leninistischer Geschichtsbegriff und staats und rechtswissenschaftliches Erbe." *Wissenschaftsliche Zeitschrift der Humbolt-Universtät zu Berlin. Gesellschafts- und Sprachwissenschaftsliche Reihe,* 13, No. 3 (1963), 285-291.

Gould, Harold. "The Utopian Side of the Indian Uprising," in *Aware of Utopia,* edited by David Plath (Urbana: University of Illinois Press, 1971), pp. 86-116.

Goulemot, Jean-Marie. "Écriture et lecture de l'ailleurs, l'*Eldorado* ou le fusil à deux coups des ingenus qui feignent de l'être." *Revue des sciences humaines,* 39, No. 155 (July-September 1974), 425-40.

Gourcuff, O[livier], de. "Deux voyages imaginaires écrits par des Bretons." *Revue de Bretagne, de Vendée et d'Anjou,* 6 (September, October 1891), 215-223, 306-315.

Gove, Phillip Babcock. "Gildon's 'Fortunate Shipwreck' as Background for *Gulliver's Travels.*" *Review of English Studies,* 18 (October 1942), 470-478.

Grabowsky, Adolf. "Die politischen Utopien und ihre Probleme." *Schweizer Rundschau,* N.S. 48 (May 1948), pp. 89-100.

Grace, William J. "The Conception of Society in More's 'Utopia.'" *Thought,* 22 (June 1947), 283-296.

Graham, Bessie. "Utopias." *Unpopular Review,* 10 (October 1918), 355-367.

Graham, Daniel F. "A Cheerful Word for Timid Teachers." *Education,* 55 (June 1935), 622-625.

Grahame, Kenneth. "Ideals and Day-Dreams." *Yale Review,* 12 (January 1923), 238–252.

Grant, H. Roger. "Henry Olerich and Utopia: The Iowa Years." *Annals of Iowa,* 43 (Summer 1976), 349–361.

Grant, H. Roger. "Henry Olerich and the Utopian Ideal." *Nebraska History,* 56 (Summer 1975), 248–258.

Grant, H. Roger. " 'One who dares to plan': Charles W. Caryl and the New Era Union." *Colorado Magazine,* 51 (Winter 1974), 13–27.

Grant, H. Roger. "Viola Olerich, 'The Famous Baby Scholar': An Experiment in Education." *The Palimpsest,* 56, No. 3 (May/June 1975), 82–88.

Graus, F. "Social Utopias in the Middle Ages." *Past and Present,* No. 38 (December 1967), pp. 3–19.

Gray, J. H. "To Hell with Utopias." *Canadian Forum,* 15 (April 1935), 249–250.

Green, Eleanor. "Blueprints for Utopia: The Political Ideas of Nietzsche and D. H. Lawrence." *Renaissance and Modern Studies,* 18 (1974), 141–161.

Green, J. F. "Looking Forward," *Positivist Review,* 26 (September 1918), 196–200.

Green, John. "The Tyranny of an Idea: George Orwell's 'Nineteen-Eighty-Four.' " *Sixty one* (University of Leeds), 5 (October 1964), 11–16.

Greenbaum, Leonard. "Herzl's Utopia." *Commentary,* 34 (July 1962), 82–88.

Greene, James J. "Utopia and Early More Biography," *Moreana,* Nos. 31–32 (November 1971), pp. 199–207.

Gregg, Richard A. "Two Adams and Eve in the Crystal Palace: Dostoevsky, The Bible and *We.* " *Slavonic Review,* 24 (December 1965), 680–687.

Greive, Bernhard. "Wandel der Utopie." *Die lebenden Fremdsprachen,* 3 (November 1951), 327–334.

Grendler, Paul F. "Utopia in Renaissance Italy: Doni's 'New World.' " *Journal of the History of Ideas,* 26 (October 1965), 479–494.

Grlić, Danko. "Die Ewige Wiederkehr des Gleichen als die Wiederkehr des Künsterischen in der Kunst." *Praxis,* 8, Nos. 1–2 (1972), 129–139.

Gronlund, Laurence. "Nationalism." *Arena,* 1 (January 1890), 153–165.

Grube, G. M. A. "Marriage Laws in Plato's *Republic.*" *Classical Quarterly,* 21 (April 1927), 95–99.

Grunwald, Henry Anatole. "From Eden to the Nightmare," *Horizon,* 5 (March 1963), 72–79.

Guérard, Albert. "Literature in Utopia." *Nineteenth Century,* 111 (February 1932), 239–246.

Guhrauer, G[ottschalk] E[duard]. "Der erste deutsche Staatsroman." *Deutsche Museum* (Leipzig), (July, September, 1852), pp. 734–54.

Gulbin, Suzanne. "Parallels and Contrasts in *Lord of the Flies* and *Animal Farm.*" *English Journal,* 55 (January 1966), 86–90, 92.

Gümpel, C. Godfrey. "A Possible Solution of the Social Question." *Westminster Review,* 138 (July-December 1892), 270–285.

Gurney, Peter. "Utopia Ltd." *National Review,* 118 (January 1942), 48–51.

Gury, Jacques. "The Abolition of the Rural World in Utopia." *Moreana,* Nos. 43–44 (November 1974), pp. 67–69.

Gury, Jacques. "L'Utopie tous azimuts." *Moreana,* Nos. 43–44 (November 1974), pp. 65–66.

Gusfield, Joseph. "Economic Development as a Modern Utopia," in *Aware of Utopia,* edited by David Plath (Urbana: University of Illinois Press, 1971), pp. 75–85.

Gussmann, Wilh[elm]. "Reipublicae Christianopolitanae Descriptio. Eine Erinnerung an Johann Valentin Andreae zu seinem dreihundersten Geburtstag." *Zeitschrift für Kirchlich-Wissenschaft und Kirchliches Leben* (1886), pp. 326–333.

Gutek, Gerald. "An Analysis of Formal Education in Edward Bellamy's 'Looking Backward.' " *History of Education Quarterly,* 4 (December 1964), 251–263.

Guy, Alain. "Vives Socialiste et L'*Utopie* du More." *Moreana,* Nos. 31–32 (November 1971), pp. 263–279.

H., D. "Utopie." *Encyclopaedia Universalis* (Paris: Encyclopaedia Universalis, 1975), 16, pp. 557–559.

H., J. F. "Utopias in Literature." *The Eagle* (St. Johns College, Cambridge), 37–38 (June, December 1916, March 1917), 340–347, 34–42, 157–164.

Haac, Oscar A. "Toward a Definition of Utopia." *Studies in the Eighteenth Century,* 6 (1977), 407–416.

Hacker, Andrew. "In Defense of Utopia." *Ethics,* 65 (January 1955), pp. 135–138.

Hacker, Andrew. "Original Sin vs. Utopia in British Socialism." *Review of Politics,* 18 (April 1956), 184–206.

Hadas, Moses. "Utopian Sources in Herodotus." *Classical Philology,* 30 (April 1935), 113–121.

Hahn, István. "Die Eigentumsverhaltnisse der Qumrán-Sekte." *Wissenschaftliche Zeitschrift der Humbolt-Universität zu Berlin, Gesellschafts- und Sprachwissenschaftsliche Reihe,* 12, No. 3 (1963), 236–272.

Hahn, István. "Die Soziale Utopie der Spätantike." *Wissenschaftliche Zeitschrift der Martin-Luther-Universität Halle-Wittenberg. Gesellschafts- und Sprachwissenschaftsliche Reihe,* 11, No. 10 (October 1962), 1357–61.

Halewood, William H. "Gulliver's Travels I, vi." *ELH,* 33 (December 1966), 422–433.

Halkin, Léon E. "Mithra dans l'*Utopie*." *Moreana,* Nos. 31–32 (November 1971), pp. 157–159.

Hall, A. R. "Science, Technology and Utopia in the Seventeenth Century," in *Science and Society 1600–1900,* edited by Peter Mathias (Cambridge: Cambridge University Press, 1972), pp. 33–53.

Hamburger, Bernard. "Industrie eutopie." *L'Architecture d'aujourd'hui,* 41, No. 148 (February-March 1970), 13.

Hamilton, Kenneth M. "G. K. Chesterton and George Orwell: A Contrast in Prophecy." *Dalhousie Review,* 31 (Autumn 1951), 198–205.

Hamilton, Robert. "More's *Utopia:* Its Bearing on Present Conditions." *Hibbert Journal,* 44 (April 1946), 242–247.

Harary, F. and J. Rockey. "A City is not a semilattice either." *Environment and Planning A,* 8 (1976), 375–384.

Hare, William Loftus. "Utopia Rediscovered." *Open Court,* 39 (July 1925), 405–423.

Harlow, Benjamin C. "Houyhnhnmland: A Utopian Satire." *McNeese Review,* 13 (1963), 44–58.

Harris, W. T. "Edward Bellamy's Vision." *The Forum,* 8 (October 1889), 199–208.

Hauser, Richard. "Utopie und Hoffnung," in *Säkularisation und Utopie. Ebracher Studien. Ernst Forsthoff zum 65. Geburtstag* (Stuttgart: W. Kohlhammer Verlag, 1967), pp. 235–251.

Hauskeer, Herman. "Etienne Cabet's Utopia and Its French Medical Background." *Bulletin of the History of Medicine,* 9 (March, April, May 1941), 294–310, 401–435, 517–529.

Hawthorne, Julian. "A Popular Topic." *Lippincott's Magazine,* 45 (June 1890), 883–888.

Haynes, Renee. "Castles in Spain or Nineteen Ninety-nine." *Blackfriars,* 28 (June 1947), 270–275.

Hébraud, Raymonde. "Mythe et utopie approche de Rousseau." *Homo,* N.S. 6, No. 4 (1970), pp. 37–52.

Heilbroner, Robert L. "The Beautiful World of the Utopian Socialists," in his *The Worldly Philosophers,* revised edition (New York: Simon & Schuster, 1961), pp. 85–111.

Heinisch, Klaus J. "Zum Verständnis der Werke," in *Der utopische Staat* ([Hamburg:] Rowohlt, 1960), pp. 216–265.

Heinlein, Robert A. "Science Fiction: Its Nature, Faults and Virtues," in *The Science Fiction Novel; Imagination and Social Criticism,* 3rd edition (Chicago: Advent Publishers, 1969), pp. 14–48.

Heiserman, A. R. "Satire in the *Utopia,*" *PMLA,* 78 (June 1963). 163–174.

Held, Felix Emil. "Andreae's 'Christianopolis,' Its Origin and Influence," in *Christianopolis; An Ideal State of the Seventeeth Century,* by Johan Valentin Andreae and translated by Felix Emil Held (New York: Oxford University Press, 1916), pp. 3–128.

Helleiner, Karl F. "Prester John's Letter: A Medieval Utopia." *The Phoenix,* 13 (Summer 1959), 47–57.

Hellin, F.P. and Robert Plank. "Der Plan des Josef Popper-Lynkeus." *Quarber Merkur,* 13/1–13/2, Nos. 39–40 (January-March 1975), 14–39, 3–26.

Hendrix, Pjotr. " 'Garten' und 'Morgan' als Ort und Zeit für das *Mysterium Paschale* in der Orthodoxen Kirche," in *Vom Sinn der Utopie. Eranos-Jahrbuch 1963* (Zürich: Rhein-Verlag, 1964), pp. 147–171.

Henningsen, Jürgen. "Utopie und Erfahrung." *Bildung und Erziehung,* 2, No. 23 (1970), 82–86.

Henríquez Ureña, Pedro. "La utopía de América," in *Universidad y Educación* (Mexico City: Dirección General de Difusion Cultural, 1969), pp. 49–56.

Herbert, Beda. "Woman's Place in Utopia." *Irish Monthly,* 76 (February 1948), 73–76.

Herbert, Frank. "Science Fiction and a World in Crises," in *Science Fiction; Today and Tomorrow,* edited by Reginald Bretnor (New York: Harper & Row, 1974), pp. 69–95.

Hermand, Jost. "Brecht on Utopia." *Minnesota Review,* N.S. 6 (Spring 1976), pp. 96–113.

Hermand, Jost. "Von der Notwendigkeit utopischen Denkens," in *Deutsches utopisches Denken im 20. Jahrhundert,* edited by Reinhold Grimm and Jost Hermand (Stuttgart: W. Kohlhammer, 1974), pp. 10–29.

Hernlund, Patricia. "Author's intent: *In Watermelon Sugar.*" *Critique,* 16, No. 1 (1974), 5–17.

Hertzler, J. O. "On Golden Ages: Then and Now." *South Atlantic Quarterly,* 39 (July 1940), 318–329.

Herzog, Bert. "Utopische Romane." *Schweizer Rundschau,* 50 (March 1951), 764–768.

Hessen, Sergius. "Der Zusammenbruch des Utopismus," in *Festschrift für Th. G. Masaryk zum 80. Geburtstag,* 2 Vols. (Bonn: Verlag von Friedrick Cohen, 1930), Vol. 1, pp. 107–120.

Hewlett, Maurice. "Eutopia." *Nation and the Athenaeum,* 29 (September 24, 1921), 883–884.

Hewlett, Maurice. "A Materialist's Paradise." *National Review,* 17 (August 1891), 818–827.

Hexter, J. H. "The Composition of *Utopia.*" "Introduction," in *Utopia,* edited by Edward Surtz, S. J. and J. H. Hexter. Vol. 4 of *The Complete Works of St. Thomas More* (New Haven: Yale University Press, 1965), pp. xv–xxiii.

Hexter, J. H. "Thomas More: On the Margins of Modernity." *Journal of British Studies,* 1 (November 1961), 20–37.

Hexter, J. H. "*Utopia* and its Historical Milieu," Introduction" in *Utopia,* edited by Edward Surtz, S.J. and J.H. Hexter. Vol. 4 of *The Complete Works of St. Thomas More* (New Haven: Yale University Press, 1965), pp. xxiii–cxiv.

Hicks, George L. "Utopian Communities and Social Networks," in *Aware of Utopia,* edited by David Plath (Urbana: University of Illinois Press, 1971), pp. 135–150.

Hieronimus, Ekkehard. "Utopie und Science Fiction." *Leserzeitschrift,* No. 5 (1965), pp. 4–11.

Hillegas, Mark. "The Clarkson Collection of Science-Fiction at Harvard." *Extrapolation,* 5 (December 1963), 2–14.

Hillegas, Mark. "Dystopian Science Fiction: New Index to the Human Situation." *New Mexico Quarterly,* 31 (Autumn 1961), 238–249.

Hillegas, Mark. "Science Fiction and the Idea of Progress." *Extrapolation,* 2 (May 1960), 25–28.

Hillegas, Mark. "Science Fiction as a Cultural Phenomenon: A Reevaluation." *Extrapolation,* 4 (May 1963), 26–33.

Hillkowitz, Max. "Das Agrargesetz in James Harringtons 'Oceana' (Ein Beitrag zur Geschichte des agrarutopismus)." *Jahrbuch der Philosophischen Fakultät der Rheinischen Friedrich-Wilhelms-Universität zu Bonn,* 1 (1923), 82–85.

Himmelfarb, Gertrude. "Bentham's Utopia: The National Charity Company." *Journal of British Studies,* 10 (November 1970), 80–125.

Hirsch, Walter. "The Image of the Scientist in Science Fiction; A Content Analysis." *American Journal of Sociology,* 63 (March 1958), 506–512.

"Historical Fictions." *The Times* (London) *Literary Supplement,* No. 969 (August 12, 1920), pp. 509–510.

Hobson, J. A. "The New Aristocracy of Mr. Wells." *Contemporary Review,* 89 (April 1906), 487–497.

Hochart, Patrick. "La science de Charles Fourier." *Topique,* Nos. 4–5 (October 1970), pp. 143–174.

Hodgart, Matthew. "From *Animal Farm* to *1984,*" in *The World of George Orwell,* edited by Miriam Gross (London: Weidenfeld and Nicolson, 1971), pp. 136–142.

Hofe, Harold Von. "Heinse, America, and Utopianism." *PMLA,* 72 (June 1957), 390–402.

Hoffman, Frederick J. "Aldous Huxley and the Novel of Ideas." *College English,* 8 (December 1946), pp. 129–137.

Hoffmann, Gerhard. "Utopien und christliche Hoffnung." *Evangelisch lutherische Kirchenzeitung,* 9 (1955), 231–234.

Höffner, Joseph. "Existenzangst und Fürsorgestaat; die sozialutopien und die Wirklichkeit." *Rheinischer Merkur* (December 2, 1950), p. 6.

Höffner, Joseph. "Wandel der Sozialutopien." *Trierer Theologische Zeitschrift,* 59 (1950), 377.

Hogan, Patrick G., Jr. "The Philosophical Limitations of Science Fiction." *Journal of General Education,* 28 (Spring 1976), 1–15.

Hogan, Patrick G., Jr. "Philosophical Limitations of Utopian Science Fiction." *Journal of the American Studies Association of Texas,* 6 (1975), 55–62.

Hohoff, Curt. "Gefährliche Utopien." *Neue Schweizer Rundschau,* 19, No. 8 (December 1951), 514–517.

Hohoff, Curt. "Utopische Schreckbilder. Der Sog zum Ameisenstaat im modernen Roman." *Rheinischer Merkur* (December 2, 1950), p. 9.

Hollander, John, Marshall Cohen, and George Kateb. "Utopias." *Yale Reports,* No. 366 (June 6, 1965).

Hollander, Paul. "The Ideological Pilgrim: Looking for Utopia, Then and Now." *Encounter,* 41 (November 1973), 3–15.

Höllerer, Walter and Richard Figge. "The Prospects for Literature in Future Society." *Comparative Literature Studies,* 10 (December 1973), 353–363.

Holquist, Michael. "How to play Utopia: Some brief notes on the distinctiveness of utopian fiction." *Yale French Studies,* No. 41 (1968), pp. 106–123.

Holt, Lee Elbert. "Samuel Butler's Revisions of *Erewhon.*" *Papers of the Bibiliographical Society of America,* 38, No. 1 (1944), 22–38.

Holynski, A. "Cabet et les icariens." *Revue socialiste,* 14–16 (November 1891, January-April, September 1892), 539–550, 40–49, 201–205, 315–321, 449–456, 296–307.

Hönncher, E. "Bemerkungen zu Godwin's 'Voyage of Domingo Gonsales to the Moon.' " *Anglia,* 10 (1888), 452–456.

Hönncher, E. "Quellen zu Dean Jonathan Swift's 'Gulliver's Travels' (1727)." *Anglia,* 10 (1888), 397–427.

Horkheimer, Max. "Die Utopie," in *Utopie; Begriff und Phänomen des Utopischen,* edited by Arnhelm Neüsuss (Neuwied: Luchterhand, 1968), pp. 178–192.

Hornsby, Samuel. "Utopia and Auburn." *Moreana,* Nos. 31–32 (November 1971), pp. 197–198.

Horowitz, Irving Louis. "American Futurology and the Pursuit of the Millennium," in his *Ideology and Utopia in the United States 1956–1976* (New York: Oxford University Press, 1977), pp. 113–130.

Horowitz, Irving Louis. "Fortalizacíon de la theoría General de la Ideologiá y la Utopiá." *Revista mexicana de Sociologiá,* 24 (January–April 1962), 87–99.

Horsburgh, H. J. N. "The Relevance of the Utopian." *Ethics,* 67 (January 1957), 127–138.

Horváth, Barna. "Der Sinn der Utopie." *Zeitschrift für öffentliches Recht,* 20, No. 2 (1940), 198–230.

Hough, Rev. T. W. "Ideal Commonwealth's." *Transactions of the Leicester*

Literary and Philosophical Society, 13, Part I (January 1909), 1–14.

Howe, Irving. "The Fiction of Anti-Utopia," in his *A World More Attractive; A View of Modern Literature and Politics* (New York: Horizon Press, 1963), pp. 216–226.

Howe, Irving, with Lewis Coser. "Images of Socialism," in his *A World More Attractive; A View of Modern Literature and Politics* (New York: Horizon Press, 1963), pp. 227–250.

Howe, Irving. "*1984* — Utopia Reversed." *New International,* 16 (November-December 1950), 360–368.

Howe, Irving. "Orwell: History as Nightmare." *American Scholar,* 25 (Spring 1956), 193–207.

Howells, William Dean. "Edward Bellamy." *Atlantic Monthly,* 82 (August 1898), 253–256.

Hubalek, Felix. "Die Utopie der Gegenwart, oder der trübe Blick in der Zukunft." *Zukunft,* No. 8 (August 1950), pp. 213–215.

Hughes, David Y. "H. G. Wells: Ironic Romancer," *Extrapolation,* 6 (May 1965), 32–38.

Hughes, David Y. "The Mood of *A Modern Utopia.*" *Extrapolation,* 19 (December 1977), 59–67.

Hughes, Merritt Y. "Spenser and Utopia." *Studies in Philology,* 17 (April 1920), 132–146.

Hummert, Paul A. "Bernard Shaw's Marxist Utopias." *Shaw Review,* 2 (September 1959), 7–26.

Huntemann, Georg H. "Der Gedanke der Selbstentfremdung bei Karl Marx und in den Utopien von E. Cabet bis G. Orwell." *Zeitscrift für Religions und Geistesgeschichte,* 6 (1954), 138–146.

Hunter, Doris. "Christian Atheism: A Divine Utopia." *Christian Advocate* (December 18, 1967), pp. 7–8.

Hunter, Doris and Howard Hunter. "*Siddhartha* and *A Clockwork Orange:* Two Images of Man in Contemporary Literature and Cinema," in *Utopia/Dystopia?* edited by Peyton E. Richter (Cambridge, Massachusetts: Schenkman Pub. Co., 1975), pp. 127–141.

Huntington, John. "Public and Private Imperatives in Le Guin's Novels." *Science-Fiction Studies,* 2 (November 1975), 237–242.

Hutchins, Robert M[aynard]. "University for Utopians." *Saturday Review,* 36 (October 17, 1953), 11–12.

Hutchins, Robert Maynard. "The University of Utopia." *Yale Review,* 20 (March 1931), 456–468. Condensed in *Proceedings of the Southern Conference on Education,* 1930, pp. 5–13.

Huxley, Aldous. "Boundaries of Utopia." *Virginia Quarterly Review,* 7 (January 1931), 47–54.

Huxley, Aldous. "Ozymandias, the Utopia that failed," in his *Tomorrow and* *tomorrow and tomorrow, and other essays* (New York: Harper, 1956), pp. 84–102.

Hyde, William J. "The Socialism of H. G. Wells in the Early Twentieth Century." *Journal of the History of Ideas,* 17 (April 1956), 217–234.

Idiotes (pseud.). "Mechanism and Modern Life." *Economic Review,* 18 (January 1908), 43–58.

Imaz, Eugenio. "Topia y Utopia," in *Utopías del Renacimiento* (Mexico City: Fondo de Cultura Económica, [1941]), pp. vii–xl.

Ince, Richard. "Nowhere Land: The Search for the Perfect Polity." *Blackfriar's,* 13 (November 1932), 672–80.

Ingerflom, Claudio. "A propos du socialisme utopique." *La Pensée,* No. 169 (May-June 1973), pp. 80–84.

Irby, James E. "Borges and the Idea of Utopia." *Books Abroad,* 45 (Summer 1971), 411–420.

Isaacs, Reginald R. "Das Bauhaus. Eine Utopie?," in *Deutsches utopisches Denken im 20. Jahrhundert,* edited by Reinhold Grimm and Jost Hermand (Stuttgart: W. Kohlhammer, 1974), pp. 70–81.

Israeli, Nathan. "Some Aspects of the Social Psychology of Futurism." *Journal of Abnormal and Social Psychology,* 25 (July 1930), 121–132.

Iyer, Raghavan N. "The Social Structure of the Future," in *Looking Forward: The Abundant Society* (Santa Barbara: Center for the Study of Democratic Institutions, 1966), pp. 16–29.

Jäckel, Eberhard. "Utopia und Utopie zum Ursprung eines Begriffs." *Geschichte in Wissenschaft und Unterricht,* 7 (1956), 655–667.

Jähnig, Dieter. "Kunst und Wirklichkeit." *Praxis,* 8, Nos. 1–2 (1972), 79–92.

Jakoby, Hans and Lewis A. Coser. "Rückblick auf Utopia." *Aufklärung,* 2 (1953), 215–228.

Jameson, Frederic. "Introduction/Prospectus: To Reconsider the Relationship of Marxism to Utopian Thought." *Minnesota Review,* N.S. 6 (Spring 1976), pp. 53–58.

Jameson, Frederic. "Of Islands and Trenches: Naturalization and the Production of Utopian Discourse." *Diacritics,* 7 (June 1977), 2–21.

Jameson, Frederic. "World Reduction in Le Guin: The Emergence of Utopian Narrative." *Science-Fiction Studies,* 2 (November 1975), 221–230.

Janet, Paul. "Le socialisme au XIXe siècle: La philosophie der Charles Fourier." *Revue des deux mondes,* 35 (October 1, 1879), 619–645.

Janssen, Jörn. "Die graue Stadt am Meer." *Werk,* 60 (September 1973), 1083–1090.

Jay, Martin. "Marcuse's Utopia." *Radical America,* 4 (April 1970), 21–28.

Jeannière, Abel. "Utopies du Modialisme politique." *Revue de l'action populaire,* 173 (December 1963), 1157–1169.

Jenkins, Alan. "Utopia Round the Corner." *World Review* (January 1941), pp. 55–60.

Jevons, H. Stanley. "Contemporary Models of Sir Thomas More; Utopia and the Socialist Inca Empire." *Times Literary Supplement,* No. 1761 (November 2, 1935), p. 692.

Jevons, H. Stanley. "Utopia and the Incas." *Tribune* (London), No. 579 (February 13, 1948), p. 14.

Joachimson, Paul. "Johann Valentin Andreae und die evangelische utopie." *Zeitwende,* 2 (1926), 485–503, 623–642.

Joad, C. E. M. "An Open Letter to H. G. Wells." *New Statesman and Nation* (August 17, 1940), pp. 154–155. Reply: (August 24, 1940), p. 180. Reply: (August 31, 1940), p. 208.

Joedicke, Jürgen. "Utopisten der zwanziger Jahre in Deutschland." *Bauen + Wohnen,* 22, No. 5 (May 1967), 193–197.

Joedicke, Jürgen. "Zu diesem Heft. Stadtplanung-Experimente und Utopien." *Bauen + Wohnen,* 22, No. 5 (May 1967), 163–164.

John, Augustus. "Fourier's Utopia — and Mine." *Anarchy 10,* 1 (December 1961), 298–304.

Johnson, Robbin S. "The Argument for Reform in More's *Utopia.*" *Moreana,* Nos. 31–32 (November 1971), pp. 123–134.

Jonas, Gerald. "S.F." *New Yorker,* 48 (July 29, 1972), 33–36, 38, 43–44, 46, 48–52.

Jones, Joseph. "Utopia as Dirge." *American Quarterly,* 2 (Fall 1950), 214–226.

Jones, Judith P. "The *Philebus* and the Philosophy of Pleasure in Thomas More's *Utopia.*" *Moreana,* Nos. 31–32 (November 1971), 61–69.

Jones, Stephen K. "The Authorship of 'Nova Solyma.' " *The Library,* 3rd series, 1 (July 1910), 225–238.

Juin, Hubert. "Présence de Charles Fourier dans la poésie moderne." *Topique,* Nos. 4–5 (October 1970), pp. 103–125.

Julie, Sister. "Thomas More and the Soviets." *Commonweal,* 22 (September 13, 1935), 462–464.

Jungk, Robert. "Toward an Experimental Society." *The Humanist,* (November/December 1973), pp. 39–41.

Justus, James H. "Hawthorne's Coverdale: Character and Art in the *Blithedale Romance.*" *American Literature,* 47 (March 1975), 21–36.

Kaempffert, Waldemar Bernhard. "Evangelist of Utopia," in his *Explorations in Science* (New York: Viking, 1953), pp. 263–269.

Kagarlitski, Julius. "Bernard Shaw and Science Fiction: Why Raise the Question?," translated by Roger Freling. *Shaw Review,* 16 (May 1973), 59–66.

Kagarlitski, Julius. "Wissenschaftlich-utopische Literatur aus dem Ausland in russischer Übertragung." *Sowjetliteratur,* 20 (May 1968), 174–179.

Kahler, Erich. "Die Wirklichkeit der Utopie (1945)," in his *Die Verantwortung des Geistes; Gesammelte Aufsätze* (Frankfurt am Main: S. Fischer Verlag, 1952), pp. 214–227.

Kandel, I. L. "Educational Utopias," *Annals of the American Academy of Political and Social Science,* No. 235 (September 1944), pp. 41–48.

Kangrga, Milan. "Wirklichkeit und Utopie." *Praxis,* 8, Nos. 1–2 (1972), pp. 9–25.

Kanters, Robert. "Fantomes et martiens; ou la littérature entre la magie et la science." *Revue de Paris,* 65 (May 1958), 122–131.

Kantorowicz, Alfred. "La Fin de l'utopie." *Etudes* (Brussels), 5, No. 4 (1963), 1–17.

Karpf, Fritz. "Ein englischer Utopist des XVII Jahrhunderts." *Neue Jahrbücher für Wissenschaft und Jugendbildung,* 1, No. 2 (1925), 235–244.

Kasper, Walter. "Politische Utopie und christliche Hoffnung," in *Erwartung, Verheissung, Erfüllung,* edited by Wilhelm Heinen and Joseph Schreiner (Wurzburg: Echter-Verlag, 1969), pp. 230–253.

Kasson, John F. "Technology and Utopia," in his *Civilizing the Machine; Technology and Republican Values in America 1776–1900* (New York: Grossman, 1976), pp. 183–234.

Kateb, George. "Utopia and the Good Life," in *Utopias and Utopian Thought,* edited by Frank E. Manuel (Boston: Beacon Press, 1967), pp. 239–259.

Kateb, George. "Utopias and Utopianism." *International Encyclopedia of the Social Sciences.* Vol. 16: 267–271.

Kaufholz, Elaine. "L'Utopie-asile: 'Die Insel Felsenburg.' " *Littérature,* No. 21 (February 1976), pp. 52–58.

Kaufmann, Rev. A. "Utopian Experiments and Social Pioneerings." *Leisure Hour,* 28 (1879), 10+. I. "Communism of the Early Christians and Essenes" (January 4, 1879), pp. 10–13; II. "Medieval Communism" (February 15, 1879), pp. 106–110; III. "Waldenses, Lollards, and Hussites" (March 22, 1879), pp. 186–190; IV. "During the Reformation" (April 12, 1879), pp. 234–238; V. "Moravian Settlements" (May 3, July 26, 1879), pp. 282–286, 479–480; VI. "The Jesuit Settlement in Paraguay" (June 7, 1879), pp. 362–367; VII. "Communistic Societies in North America" (August 16, 23, 1879), pp. 516–520, 541–544; VIII. "Utopian Experiments in the United States" (September 27, 1879), pp. 618–622; IX. "Co-operation Abroad" (October 18, 1879), pp. 667–670; X. "The History and Progress of Co-operation in England" (November 22, 1879), pp. 749–752.

Kaufmann, M. "The Society of The Future." *Contemporary Review,* 37 (April 1880), 626–638.

Kaufmann, V. Milo. "Brave New Improbable Worlds: Critical Notes on 'Extrapolation' as a Mimetic Technique in Science Fiction." *Extrapolation,* 5 (December 1963), 17–24.

Kaupp, Peter. "Ein Neuer Utopie — Verständnis?" *Archiv für Rechts und Sozialphilosophie,* 55, No. 2 (1969), 249–258.

Kegel, Charles H. " 'Nineteen Eighty-Four' A Century of Ingsoc," *Notes and Queries,* 10 (April 1963), 151–152.

Kelley, Maurice W. "Thomas Cooper and Pantisocracy." *Modern Language Notes,* 45 (April 1930), 218–220.

Kelly, R. Gordon. "Ideology in Some Modern Science Fiction Novels." *Journal of Popular Culture,* (Fall 1968), pp. 211–227.

Keniston, Kenneth. "Alienation and the Decline of Utopia." *American Scholar,* 29 (Spring 1960), 161–200.

Kenkel, William F. "Marriage and the Family in Modern Science Fiction." *Journal of Marriage and the Family,* 31 (February 1969), 6–14.

Kerényi, Karl. "Ursinn und Sinnwandel des Utopischen," in *Vom Sinn der Utopie. Eranos-Jahrbuch 1963* (Zürich: Rhein-Verlag, 1964), pp. 9–29.

Kessler, Martin. "Power and the Perfect State: A Study in Disillusionment as Reflected in Orwell's *Nineteen Eighty-Four* and Huxley's *Brave New World.*" *Political Science Quarterly,* 72 (December 1957), 565–577.

Kesting, Hanno. "Utopie und Eschatologie. Zukunftserwartungen in der Geschichtsphilosophie des 19. Jahrhunderts." *Archiv für Rechts- und Sozialphilosophie,* 41, No. 2 (1954), 202–230.

Ketterer, David. "Utopian Fantasy as Millenial Motive and Science-Fictional Motif." *Studies in the Literary Imagination,* 6 (Fall 1973), 79–104.

Khanna, Lee Cullen. "No Less Real Than Ideal: Images of Women in More's Work." *Moreana,* 14, Nos. 55–56 (December 1977), 35–51.

Khanna, Lee Cullen. "*Utopia:* The Case for Open-Mindedness in the Commonwealth." *Moreana,* Nos. 31–32 (November 1971), 91–105.

Khouri, Nadia. "Utopia and Epic: Ideological Confrontation in Jack London's *Iron Heel.*" *Science-Fiction Studies,* 3 (July 1976), 174–181.

Kimmerle, Heinz. "Eschatologie und Utopie im Denken von Ernst Bloch." *Neue Zeitschrift für systematische Theologie und Religionsphilosophie,* 7 (1965), 297–316.

Kinkade, Kathleen. "Power and the Utopian Assumption." *Journal of Applied Behavioral Science,* 10 (July 1974), 402–414.

Klages, Helmut. "Models for a Future Society: Literature and the Sociologist." Translated by Richard Figge, Vincent Dell'Orto, and Gerrit Den Hartog, *Comparative Literature Studies,* 10 (December 1973), 323–333.

Klaw, Spencer. "Harvard's Skinner: The Last of the Utopians." *Harper's Magazine,* 226 (April 1963), 45–51.

Klein, Robert. "L'Urbanisme utopique de Filarete à Valentin Andreae," in Université libre de Bruxelles. Institut pour l'etude de la Renaissance et de l'humanisme. *Les Utopies à la Renaissance* (Brussels: Presses Universitaires de Bruxelles, 1963), pp. 209–230.

Klossowski, Pierre. "Sade et Fourier." *Topique,* Nos. 4–5 (October 1970), pp. 79–98.

Kloten, Norbert. "Utopie und Leitbild im wirtschaftspolitischen Denken." *Kyklos,* 20, No. 1 (1967), 331–354.

Knapp, Friedrich. "Über den utopischen Roman." *Welt und Wort,* 3 (September 1948), 284–286.

Knepper, B[ill] G[arton]. "Shaw and the Unblessed Poor." *Iowa English Yearbook* (Fall 1968), pp. 12–17.

Knepper, Bill Garton. "Shaw's Debt to *The Coming Race*." *Journal of Modern Literature,* 1 (March 1971), 339–353.

Knight, Damon. "Science Fiction Basics." *Library Journal,* 91 (June 1, 1966), 2777–2779.

Knight, Isabel F. "Utopian Dream as Psychic Reality." *Studies in the Eighteenth Century,* 6 (1977), 427–438.

Knowlson, James R. "A Note on Bishop Godwin's *Man in the Moone:* The East Indies Trade Route and a 'Language' of Musical Notes." *Modern Philology,* 65 (May 1968), 357–361.

Knox, George. "Apocalypse and Sour Utopias." *Western Humanities Review,* 16 (Winter 1962), 11–22.

Knox, George. "The *Divine Comedy* in *1984*." *Western Humanities Review,* 9 (Autumn 1955), 371–372.

Knust, Herbert. "Utopian Thought and Modern Society: Interdisciplinary Perspectives (summary of a panel discussion)." *Comparative Literature Studies,* 10 (December 1973), 374–386.

Koebner, Richard. "Oceana." *Englische Studien,* 68, No. 3 (1934), 358–396.

Koestler, Arthur. "The Boredom of Fantasy," in his *The Trail of the Dinosaur and Other Essays* (London: Hutchinson, 1955), pp. 82–85.

Kofler, Leo. "Das Apollinische und das Dionysische in der utopischen und antagonistischen Gesellschaft," in *Festschrift zum achtzigsten Geburtstag von Georg Lukacs,* edited by Frank Benseloer (Neuweid: Luchterland, 1965), pp. 556–587.

Köhler, Bernhard. "Das Recht auf Arbeit — eine Utopie?" *Die Deutsche Volkswirtschaft,* 4, No. 1 (1935), 9–11.

Kolnai, Aurèle. "La Mentalité utopienne." *La Table ronde,* No. 153 (September 1960), pp. 62–84.

Kolnai, Aurèle. "Notes sur l'utopie réactionnaire." *Cité libre* (1955), pp. 9–20.

"Konkrete Utopie. Zweiundsiebenzig Gedanken für die Zukunft." *Kursbuch,* 14 (1968), 110–145.

Korinman, Michel. "Les sens de la pérégrination: Fernão Mendes Pinto." *Littérature,* No. 21 (February 1976), pp. 20–34.

Kornbluth, C. M. "The Failure of the Science Fiction Novel as Social Criticism," in *The Science Fiction Novel; Imagination and Social Criticism,* 3rd edition (Chicago: Advent Publishers, 1969), pp. 49–76.

Kovaly, Pavel. "Marxism and Utopia," in *Utopia/Dystopia?*, edited by Peyton E. Richter (Cambridge, Mass.: Schenkman Pub. Co., 1975), pp. 77–92.

Kragalott, Robert. "Mahatma Gandhi's Concept of Trusteeship Socialism: A Hindu Search for Utopia." *Praxis,* 8, Nos. 3–4 (1972), pp. 325–337.

Krappe, Alexander H. "Subterraneous Voyage." *Philological Quarterly,* 20 (April 1941), 119–130.

Kraus, Michael. "America and the Utopian Ideal in the Eighteenth Century." *Mississippi Valley Historical Review,* 22 (March 1936), 487–504.

Krause, Gerd. "George Orwell's Utopia 'Nineteen Eighty-Four.' Ein Beitrag zur Wurdigung des Dichters und politischen Kritikers." *Die neueren Sprachen,* N.S., No. 12 (1954), pp. 529–543.

Krause, Gerd. "Die Kulturkrise in der Utopie Aldous Huxleys." *Die Neuren Sprachen,* Beiheft 2 [1957], pp. 25–44.

Krauss, Werner. "Fontenelle und die 'Republik der Philosophen.' " *Romanische Forschungen,* 75, No. 1/2 (1964), pp. 11–21.

Krauss, Werner. "Geist und Widergeist der Utopien," in *Science Fiction; Theorie und Geschichte,* edited by Eike Barmeyer (Wilhelm Fink, 1972), pp. 23–47.

Kretzman, Edwin M. J. "German Technological Utopias of the Pre-War Period." *Annals of Science,* 3 (October 15, 1938), 417–430.

Kristol, Irving. "Foolish Americanism: utopianism." *New York Times Magazine* (November 14, 1971), p. 31 + ; "Reply," by A. F. Reel (December 5, 1971), p. 32 +.

Kristol, Irving. "Utopianism." *Vital Speeches,* 39 (July 1, 1973), 500–505.

Kritschewsky, S. B. "Saint-Justes Utopie; Ein Beitrag zur Beleuchtung der historischen Stellung der Bergpartie." *Die Neue Zeit,* 13, Nos. 39–40 (1894/95), 388–95, 420–431.

Krog, Fritz. "Butlers *Erewhon:* eine Utopie?" *Anglia,* 60 (May 1936), 423–433.

[Kropotkin, Peter.] "Le Vingtième Siècle." *La Révolte,* 3, Nos. 12–16 (November 30, 1889 — January 10, 1890), pp. 1–2, 1, 1–2, 1–2.

Krutch, Joseph Woos. "But I Wouldn't Like to Live There," in his *And Even If You Do* (New York: Morrow, 1967), pp. 266–277.

Krutch, Joseph Wood. "Danger: Utopia Ahead." *Saturday Review,* 49 (August 20, 1966), 17–18 +.

Krutch, Joseph Wood. "Ignoble Utopias," in his *The Measure of Man* (Indianapolis: Bobbs-Merrill, 1954), pp. 55–76.

Krutch, Joseph Wood. "Men, Apes, and Termites," in his *And Even If You Do* (New York: Morrow, 1967), pp. 35–46.

Krysmanski, Hans-Jürgen. "Die Eigenart des utopischen Romans," in *Science Fiction: Theorie und Geschichte,* edited by Eike Barmeyer (Munich: Wilhelm Fink, 1972), pp. 47–57.

Kühn, Johannes. "Geschichtsphilosophie und Utopie." *Welt als Geschichte,* 11 (1951), 1–11.

Kühn, Johannes. "Thomas Morus und Rousseau. Die Geburt Gesellschafts-lehre aus einem Menschenideal." *Historische Vierteljahrschrift,* 23, No. 2 (1926), 161–187.

Kulemann, W. "Der Socialistiche Zukunftsstaat." *Protestantische Kirchen-zeitung für das evangelische Deutschland,* No. 8 (February 22, 1893), pp. 169–176.

Küng, Emil. "Utopie von heute — Realität von morgen?" *Weltwoche* (Zurich), 24, No. 1207 (December 28, 1956), 15.

Kuypers, Julien. "Utopia in Flanderen." *Nieuwe Stem,* 8 (1953), 680–693.

Kvačala, J. "Thomas Campanella und die Pädagogik." *Die Deutsche Schule,* 9, Nos. 10–11 (1905), 621–639, 677–688.

L., M. "Une Utopie rare, L'Utopie du Ruvarebohni." *Bulletin of the Inter-national Institute for Social History,* No. 1 (1937), pp. 26–33.

La Bossiere, C[amille] R. and R. D. Mullen. "Sunken Atlantis and the Utopia Question: Parry's *The Scarlet Empire* and Coblentz's *The Sunken World.*" *Science-Fiction Studies,* 1 (Fall 1974), 290–297.

La Bossière, Camille R. "Zamiatin's 'We' A Caricature of Utopian Sym-metry." *Riverside Quarterly,* 6, No. 1 (August 1973), pp. 40–43.

Lacas, M. M. "Social Welfare Organizer in Sixteenth-Century New Spain: Don Vasco de Quiroga, First Bishop of Michoacán." *Americas,* 14 (July 1957), 57–86.

Lacombe, M.-M. "La Sagesse d'Epicure dans L'*Utopie.*" *Moreana,* Nos. 31–32 (November 1971), pp. 169–182.

Lalande, André. "Utopie," in his *Vocabulaire technique et critique de la philosophie,* 4th edition, 3 Vols. (Paris: Félix Alcan, 1932), Vol. 2, pp. 933–936.

Landshut, S. "Utopisten," in *Die Religion in Geschichte und Gegenwart,* 2nd edition, 5 Vols. (Tübingen: Mohr, 1927–1931), Vol. 5, pp. 1430–1431.

Lang, Hans-Joachim. "Orwells dialektischer Roman 'Nineteen Eight-Four,' " in *Rationalität-Phänomenalität Individualität, Festgabe für Hermann und Marie Glockner,* edited by Wolfgang Ritzel (Bonn: H. Bouvier, 1966), pp. 301–341.

Lasky, Melvin J. "The Birth of a Metaphor: On the Origins of Utopia and Revolution." *Encounter,* 34 (February, March 1970), 35–45, 30–42.

Lasky, Melvin J. "Der grüne Stab; zur Verteidigung der Utopien und der Uto-pisten." *Der Monat,* 3, No. 26 (November 1950), pp. 213–217.

Lasky, Melvin J. "Sweet Dream: Kant and the Revolutionary Hope for Utopia." *Encounter,* 33 (October 1969), 14–27.

Lassmann, Alfred. "Utopien und ihre Leser." *Neue Volksbildung,* N.S. 8 (1957), 327–335.

Laveleye, Émile [Louis Victor] de. "Deux Utopies nouvelles," in his *Essais et Études,* 3rd edition (Paris: Felix Alcan, 1897), pp. 269–291.

Laver, James. "Countries of the Imagination." *Essays by Divers Hands; being the transactions of the Royal Society of Literature of the United Kingdom,* New [i.e., 3d] series, 28 (1956), 138–154.

Lawton, H. W. "Bishop Godwin's *Man in the Moone." Review of English Studies,* 7 (January 1931), 23–55.

Leary, Daniel J. "The Ends of Childhood: Eschatology in Shaw and Clarke." *Shaw Review,* 16 (May 1973), 67–78.

Leavitt, Harvey. "Regained Paradise of Brautigan's *In Watermelon Sugar." Critique,* 16, No. 1 (1974), 18–24.

Lederer, Richard. "Shaping the Dystopian Nightmare." *English Journal,* 56, No. 8 (November 1967), 1132–1135.

Leeper, Geoffrey. "The Happy Utopias of Aldous Huxley." *Meanjin Quarterly,* 24 (1965), 120–124.

Lefebvre, Henri. "Engels et l'utopie." *Espaces et Societe,* 4 (December 1971), 3–9.

Leiber, Fritz. "Utopia for Poets and Witches." *Riverside Quarterly,* 4, No. 3 (June 1970), 194–205.

Leithauser, Joachim G. "Weltuntergänge broschiert und in Leinen; die schrecklichen Zukunftsbilder der schönen Literatur." *Der Monat,* 4, No. 41 (February 1952), 474–481.

Lemberg, Eugen. "Ideologie und Utopie im unserer politischen Bildung." *Gesellschaft-Staat-Erziehung,* 3, No. 2 (1958), 57–65.

Lerner, Laurence. "Arcadia and Utopia," in his *The Uses of Nostalgia* (New York: Schocken, 1972), pp. 63–80.

Lerner, Laurence. "Sex in Arcadia," in his *The Uses of Nostalgia* (New York: Schocken, 1972), pp. 81–104.

Leroux, Pierre. "Lettres sur le fouriérisme," *Revue sociale,* 1, Nos. 9–12 (June-November 1846), 129–135, 145–154, 161–175, 177–192; 2, Nos. 1-2, 4, 7 (January, April 1847), 1–7, 17–22, 57–60, 97–112.

Leroy, Gaylord C. "A.F. 632 to 1984." *College English,* 12 (December 1950), 135–138.

Levi, Albert William. "Edward Bellamy: Utopian." *Ethics,* 55 (January 1945), 131–44.

Levin, Harry. "Paradises, Heavenly and Earthly," in his *The Myth of the Golden Age in the Renaissance* (Bloomington: Indiana University Press, 1969), pp. 168–87.

Levin, Harry. "Some Paradoxes of Utopia," in his *The Myth of the Golden Age in the Renaissance* (Bloomington: Indiana University Press, 1969), pp. 187–93.

Levy, David. "Reality, Utopia, and Tradition." *Modern Age,* 20, No. 2 (Spring 1976), 153–163.

Lewis, Arthur O. "The Anti-Utopian Novel: Preliminary Notes and Checklist." *Extrapolation,* 2 (May 1961), 27–32.

Lewis, Arthur O. "Introduction," in *American Utopias: Selected Short Fiction* (New York: Arno Press and *The New York Times,* 1971), pp. vii–xxi.

Lewis, Arthur O. "Introduction," in *The Art of Real Pleasure,* by Calvin Blanchard (New York: Arno Press and *The New York Times,* 1971), pp. i–x.

Lewis, Arthur O. "Introduction," in *A.D. 2000,* by Alvarado M. Fuller (New York: Arno Press and *The New York Times,* 1971), pp. i–viii.

Lewis, Arthur O. "Introduction," in *Looking Backward and What I Saw,* by W. W. Satterlee (New York: Arno Press and *The New York Times,* 1971), pp. i–xii.

Lewis, Arthur O. "The Utopian Dream," in *Directions in Literary Criticism,* edited by Stanley Weintraub and Philip Young (University Park: The Pennsylvania State University Press, 1973), pp. 192–200.

Lewis, C. S. "On Science Fiction," in his *Of Other Worlds; Essays and Stories* (London: Geoffrey Bles, 1966), pp. 59–73.

Lewis, C. S., Brian W. Aldiss and Kingsley Amis. "Unreal Estates [A Conversation]," in *Spectrum IV; A Science Fiction Anthology,* edited by Kingsley Amis and Robert Conquest (London: Victor Gollancz, 1965), pp. 13–22.

Lewis, Sinclair. "Mr. Lorimer and Me." *Nation,* 127 (July 25, 1928), 81.

Lippmann, Walter. "White Passion." *New Republic,* 8 (October 21, 1916), 293–95.

Littlefield, Henry M. "The Wizard of Oz: Parable on Populism." *American Quarterly,* 16 (Spring 1964), 47–58.

Livingston, Dennis. "Science Fiction as an Educational Tool," in *Learning for Tomorrow; The Role of the Future in Education,* edited by Alvin Toffler (New York: Random House, 1974), pp. 234–256.

Lodge, David. "Post-Pill Paradise Lost: John Updike's *Couples,*" in his *The Novelist at the Crossroads and other Essays in Fiction and Criticism* (Ithaca: Cornell University Press, 1971), pp. 233–244.

Lodge, David. "Utopia and Criticism: The Radical Longing for Paradise." *Encounter,* 32 (April 1969), 65–75.

Lokke, Virgil L. "The American Utopian Anti-Novel," in *Frontiers of American Culture,* edited by Ray B. Browne et al. ([Lafayette:] Purdue University Studies, 1968), pp. 123–153.

Lopez Estrada, Francisco. "Mas Noticias sobre la Sinapia o utopia española." *Moreana,* 14, Nos. 55–56 (December 1977), pp. 23–33.

López-Morillas, Juan. "Sueños de la razón y la sinrazón: Utopiá y anti-utopiá." *Sistema: Revista de Ciencias sociales,* No. 5 (April 1974), pp. 5–19.

Lopez-Morillas, Juan. "Utopia and Anti-Utopia; From 'Dreams of Reason' to 'Dreams of Unreason.' " *Survey,* 18 (Winter 1972), 47–62.

Lorenz, Jakob. "Utopie und Werklichkeit." *Schweizerische Rundschau,* 31: 21–30.

Lougy, Robert E. "William Morris' *News from Nowhere:* The Novel as Psychology of Art." *English Literature in Transition,* 13 (1970), 1–8.

Love, Joseph L. "Utopianism in Latin American Cultures," in *Aware of Utopia,* edited by David Plath (Urbana: University of Illinois Press, 1971), pp. 117–134.

Lowry, C. B. "City on a Hill and Kibbutzim: Seventeenth Century Utopias as Ideal Types." *American Jewish History Quarterly,* 64 (Summer 1974), 24–41.

Lüdtke, Franz. "Rückblick aus dem Jahre 2000." *Westermanns Monatshefte,* 163 (November 1937), 217–218.

Ludwig, Albert. "Homunculi und Androiden." *Archiv für das Studium der neueren Sprachen und Literaturen,* 137–139 (1918-19), 137–53, 141–55, 1–25.

Ludz, Peter Christian. "Utopie und Utopisten," in *Religion in Geschichte und Gegenwart,* 3rd edition (Tübingen: J.C.B. Mohr, 1956-65), Vol. 6, pp. 1217–1220.

Lupton, J. H. "Introduction," in Sir Thomas More, *The Utopia of Sir Thomas More,* edited by J. H. Lupton (Oxford: Clarendon Press, 1895), pp. xvii–lxxvi.

Lyons, John O. "George Orwell's Opaque Glass in *1984.*" *Wisconsin Studies in Comparative Literature,* 2 (Fall 1961), 39–46.

McCutcheon, Elizabeth. "Denying the Contrary: More's Use of Litotes in the *Utopia.*" *Moreana,* Nos. 31–32 (November 1971), pp. 107–121.

McDonald, Christie V. "The Reading and Writing of Utopia in Denis Diderot's *Supplement au voyage du Bougainville.*" *Science-Fiction Studies,* 3 (November 1976), 248–254.

MacFadden, Gary. "The Press in Utopia." *Montana Journalism Review,* 19 (1976), 2–10.

McKenzie, Allan. "The History of Utopias." *Canadian Banker,* 46 (January 1939), 213–224.

Mackie, J. L. "Theism and Utopia." *Philosophy,* 37 (April 1962), 153–158.

MacLeish, Archibald. "Preface to an American Manifesto." *Forum,* 91 (April 1934), 195–198.

McNaught, Kenneth. "American Progressives and the Great Society." *Journal of American History,* 53 (December 1966), 504–520.

McNeely, J. A. "Historical Relativism in Wieland's Concept of the Ideal State." *Modern Language Quarterly,* 22 (Summer 1961), 269–282.

McNelis, James I., Jr. "Introduction," in Ludvig Holberg *The Journey of Niels Klim to the World Underground* (Lincoln, Neb.: University of Nebraska Press, 1960), pp. vii–xxxi.

Macy, John. "H. G. Wells and Utopia," in his *The Critical Game* (New York: Boni & Liveright, 1922), pp. 267–276.

Madarević, Vlado. "Literatur und revolutionärer Mythos als Kategorie der Utopie." *Praxis*, 8, Nos. 3–4 (1972), 313–19.

Maddison, Michael. "The Case Against Tomorrow." *Political Quarterly*, 36 (April-June 1965), 214–227.

Maddison, Michael. "1984: A Burnhamite Fantasy." *Political Quarterly*, 32 (January-March 1961), 71–79.

Madison, Charles A. "Edward Bellamy, Social Dreamer." *New England Quarterly*, 15 (September 1942), 444–466.

Madison, Charles A. "The Utopians," in his *Critics and Crusaders* (New York: Henry Holt, 1948), pp. 83–154.

Mahlmann, Theodor. "Eschatologie und Utopie im geschichtsphilosophischen Denken Paul Tillichs." *Neue Zeitschrift für systematische Theologie und Religionsphilosophie*, 7, No. 3 (1965), pp. 339–370.

Malkin, Lawrence. "Halfway to 1984." *Horizon*, 12 (Spring 1970), 33–39.

Mallock, W. H. "Trade-Unionism and Utopia." *The Forum*, 11 (April 1891), 204–214.

Manicardi, Luigi. "La 'Repubblica immaginaria' di L. Agostini." *La Rassegna* (Genoa), Ser. 4, 34 (February 1926), 1–10.

Mann, Fritz Karl. "Fontenelles Republik, eine Dichtung vom besten Staat." *Zeitschrift für Politik*, 4 (1911), 495–521.

Manndorf, Rudolf Freih. V. "Staatsromane und Gesellschaftsideale." *Monatsschrift für christliche Social-Reform*, 19 (1897), 350–356, 438–444, 526–529.

Mannheim, Karl. "Utopia," in *Encyclopedia of the Social Sciences*, Vol. 15 (New York: Macmillan, 1935), pp. 200–203.

Manuel, Frank E. "The Golden Age: A Mythic Prehistory for Western Utopia," in his *Freedom from History and Other Untimely Essays* (New York: New York University Press, 1971), pp. 69–88.

Manuel, Frank E. "Introduction," in his *Utopias and Utopian Thought* (Boston: Beacon Press, 1967), pp. vii–xxiv.

Manuel, Frank E., and Fritzie P. Manuel. "Sketch for a Natural History of Paradise," in *Myth, Symbol and Culture*, edited by Clifford Geertz (New York: W. W. Norton, 1971), pp. 83–128.

Manuel, Frank E. "Toward a Psychological History of Utopias," in his *Freedom from History and Other Untimely Essays* (New York: New York University Press, 1971), pp. 115–148.

Manzalauoi, Mahmoud. "Reflexions on Professor S. B. Liljegren's *Studies on the Origin and Early Tradition of Utopian Fiction*." *Moreana*, No. 2 (February 1964), pp. 37–50.

Maravall, José Antonio. "El pensamiento utopico y el dinamismo de la historia europea." *Sistema*, 14 (July 1976), 13–44.

Marcuse, Herbert. "The End of Utopia." *Ramparts,* 8 (April 1970), 27–32.

Marcuse, Herbert. "Friede als Utopie." *Neues Forum,* 15, Nos. 179–180 (November-December 1968), 705–707.

Marcuse, Herbert. "Phantasy and Utopia," in his *Eros and Civilization; A Philosophical Inquiry into Freud* (London: Sphere Books, 1969), pp. 119–131.

Marcuse, Ludwig. "Vom Wesen der Utopie; Die Sehnsucht nach einer besseren Gesellschaft." *Der Monat,* 3, No. 26 (November 1950), 120–125.

Marin, Louis. "Les Corps utopiques Rabelaisiens." *Litterature,* No. 21 (February 1976), pp. 35–51.

Marin, Louis. "Historie et Utopie; Discours utopiques et récit des origines. 2. De l' 'Utopia' de More à la Scandza de Cassiodore-Jordanes." *Annales,* 26 (March-April 1971), 306–327.

Marin, Louis. "Theses On Ideology and Utopia." *Minnesota Review,* N.S. 6 (Spring 1976), pp. 71–75.

Markov, Walter. "Die Utopie des Citoyen," in *Festschrift Ernst Bloch zum 70. Geburtstag,* edited by Rugard Otto Gropp (Berlin: VEB Deutscher Verlag der Wissenschaften, 1955), pp. 229–240.

Marriott, J. W. "Modern Utopians." *Hibbert Journal,* 13 (October 1914), 124–137.

Marsch, Wolf-Dieter. "Dein Reich komme! Über die Utopie als theologisches Problem." *Monatschrift für Pastoral Theologie,* 46 (1957), 16–30, 151–164.

Marsch, W[olf-] D[ieter]. "Utopie," in *Evangelisches Kirchenlexikon,* 3 Vols. (Gottingen: Vandenhoeck und Ruprecht, 1959), Vol. 3, pp. 1602–1604.

Martin, David A. "Some utopian aspects of the concept of secularization," in *Theoretische Aspekte der Religionssoziologie,* 2 Vols. (Köhn: West-deutscher Verlag, 1966), Vol. 1, pp. 87–97. *Internationale Jahrbuch für Religionssoziologie.*

Martin, Jay. "Paradises (To Be) Regained," in his *Harvests of Change; American Literature, 1865–1914* (Englewood Cliffs: Prentice-Hall, 1967), pp. 202–239.

Martinez Estrada, Ezequiel. "El nuevo mundo, la Isle de Utopia y la Isla de Cuba." *Cuadernos Americanos,* 22, No. 2 (March/April 1963),

Mattei, Rodolfo de'. "Contenuto ed Origini dell'Utopia Cittadina nel Seicento." *Revista Internazionale di Filosophia di Diritto,* 9 (1929), 414–425.

Mattes, William W. "The Utopian Tradition and Aldous Huxley." *Science-Fiction Studies,* 2 (July 1975), 146–151.

Maurin, Peter. "The Case for Utopia." *Catholic Worker,* 1 (April 1, 1934), 1, 3.

Mayer, Hans. "Ernst Bloch, Utopie, Literatur," in *Deutsches utopisches*

Denken im 20. Jahrhundert, edited by Reinhold Grimm and Jost Hermand (Stuttgart: W. Kohlhammer, 1974), pp. 82–95.

Mead, Margaret. "Towards More Vivid Utopias." *Science,* 126 (November 8, 1957), 957–961.

Meaney, J. W. "Mexico. Vasco de Quiroga's Adaptation of Thomas More's Utopian System." *American Catholic Historical Records,* 60 (December 1949), 197–212.

"Mechanism and Modern Life, With Reference to the Views of H. G. Wells." *Economic Review,* 18 (January 1908), 43–58.

Meckier, Jerome. "Cancer in Utopia: Positive and Negative Elements in Huxley's Island." *Dalhousie Review,* 54 (Winter 1974–75), 619–633.

Meckier, Jerome. "Dickens and a Dystopian Novel," in *The Novel and Its Changing Form,* edited by R. G. Collins (Winnipeg: University of Manitoba Press, 1972), pp. 51–58.

Meckier, Jerome. "Utopian Counterpoint and the Compensatory Dream," in his *Aldous Huxley; Satire and Structure* (London: Chatto and Windus, 1969), pp. 175–205.

Meisel, Sandra. "Challenge and Response: Poul Anderson's View of Man." *Riverside Quarterly,* 4, No. 2 (January 1970), pp. 80–95.

Meisner, Maurice. "Maoist Utopianism and the Future of Chinese Society." *International Journal,* 26 (Summer 1971), 535–555.

Melchiorre, Virgilio. "La coscienza utopica." *Studi di Sociologia,* 2, No. 4 (October-December 1964), 371–385.

Melchiorre, Virgilio. "L'utopismo politico," in *L'Utopia nel mondo moderno* (Firenze: Vallecchi, 1969), pp. 87–97.

Ménard, Guy. "Entre rêve et realité; approche de l'utopie — La Rehabilitation d'un concept." *Relations* (Montreal), 36 (June 1976), 178–183.

Mencken, H. L., "Utopian Flights," in his *Mencken Chrestomathy* (New York: Knopf, 1949), pp. 378–391.

Mencken, H. L., "What Is This Talk About Utopia?" *Nation,* 126 (June 13, 1928), 662–663.

Merlaud, André. "L'Utopie, une bouteille à la mer." *Moreana,* Nos. 15–16 (November 1967), pp. 181–192.

Merriam, Alexander R., "Some Literary Utopias," *Hartford Seminary Record,* 8 (May 1898), pp. 203–226.

Mesnard, Pierre. "L'Utopie de Robert Burton," in Université libre de Bruxelles. L'Institut pour l'etude de la Renaissance et de l'humanisme. *Les Utopies à la Renaissance* (Brussels: Presses Universitaires de Bruxelles, 1963), pp. 73–88.

Messac, Régis. "Voyages moderne au centre de la terre." *Revue de littérature comparée,* 9 (1929), 74–104.

Messineo, A. "Utopistie reformation sociali del Cinquecento, A. F. Doni, U. Foglietta ecc." *Civilta Cattolica* (Rome), 83. A. Vol. 2, pp. 41–45.

Metzger, Arnold. "Utopie und Transzendenz," in *Ernst Bloch zu ihren; Beitrage zu seinem Werk,* edited by Siegfried Unseld ([Frankfurt am Main:] Suhrkamp, [1965]), pp. 69–82.

Meyer, Karl Ernest. "Signposts to Futopia," in his *The New America: Politics and Society in the Age of the Smooth Deal* (New York: Basic Books, 1961), pp. 167–180.

Meyers, Jeffrey. "George Orwell: A Bibliography." *Bulletin of Bibliography,* 31 (July-September 1974), 117–121.

Meyers, Jeffrey. "George Orwell: A Selected Checklist." *Modern Fiction Studies,* 21 (Spring 1975), 133–136.

Meyerson, Martin. "Utopian Traditions and the Planning of Cities." *Daedalus,* 90 (Winter 1961), 180–193.

Meyrick, Geraldine. "The Ethics of Nationalism." *Overland Monthly,* 2nd series, 15 (June 1890), 566–568.

Miller, Clarence H. "The English Translation in the Yale *Utopia:* Some Corrections." *Moreana,* No. 9 (February 1966), pp. 57–64.

Miller, Jane. "Rasselas and Other Heavens." *Folio* (Winter 1975), pp. 27–32.

Minattus, Joseph. "More's *Utopia* and Kerala." *Moreana,* No. 22 (May 1969), pp. 39–43.

Minder, Robert. "Das Wesen der Gemeinschaft in der deutschen und in der französischen Literatur," in *Akademie der Wissenschaften und der Literatur. Abhandlungen der Klasse der Literatur* (1953), pp. 181–196.

Mish, Charles C. "A Voyage to the Moon." *Notes and Queries,* 200 (December 1955), 527–529.

Mitcham, Alison. "Northern Utopia." *Canadian Literature,* No. 63 (Winter 1975), pp. 35–39.

Mitchell, R. "Satire and Utopia." *Tribune* (January 18, 1946), p. 15.

"A Modern Prophet." *The Independent,* 58 (June 8, 1905), 1307–1308.

"A Modern Review." *Edinburgh Review,* (July 1905), pp. 805–817.

"A Modern Utopia." *Edinburgh Review,* (July 1905), pp. 56–78.

"Moderne Utopien." *"Protestantenblatt,* 24 (1891), 74–76.

Mohl, Robert Von. "Die Staatsromane," in his *Die Geschichte und Literatur der Staatswissenschaften,* 2 Vols. (Erlangen: Ferdinand Enke, 1855), Vol. 1, pp. 165–214.

Mohl, R[obert] von. "Die Staats-Romane. Ein Beitrag zur Literatur-Geschichte der Staats-Wissenschaften." *Tübingen Zeitschrift für die gesamte Staatswissenschaft,* 2 (1845), 24–74.

Molina Quiros, Jorge. " '1984': Fuentes Literarias." *Filologia Moderna,* 6 (1967), 145–153.

Mölk, Ulrich. "Philologische Bemerkungen zu Thomas Morus' *Utopia.*" *Anglia,* 82, No. 3 (1964), 309–320.

Molnar, Thomas. "A Critique of Utopian Catholics: Where Marx and the Jesuits Meet." *Modern Age,* 7 (Spring 1963), 163–175.

Molnar, Thomas. "Myth and Utopia." *Modern Age,* 17 (Winter 1973), 71–77.

Mongardini, Carlo. "L'Utopia dal punto di vista sociologica." *Cultura e scuola,* No. 11 (1964), pp. 196–203.

Monk, Samuel H. "The Pride of Lemuel Gulliver." *Sewanee Review,* 63 (Winter 1955), 48–71.

Montalenti, Giuseppe. "Utopie." *Rivista di psicologia,* 35 (1939), 197–199.

Monti, Alessandro. "Appunti preliminari per un saggio su Wells," in *Utopia e Fantascienza* (Torino: Giappichelli, 1975), pp. 99–128.

Moore, John W. "Freud, Marx, and Tomorrow." *Kinesis,* 4 (Fall 1971), 31–41.

Moore, Mary. "Utopia. Plato and Sir Thomas More." *Theology,* (August 1922), 89–95.

Moore, Stanley. "Utopian Themes in Marx and Mao: A Critique for Modern Revisionists." *Monthly Review,* 21 (June 1969), 33–44.

Moore, W. George. "The Futility of Utopianism." *Search,* 3 (July 1933), 432–445.

Moore, Wilbert E. "The Utility of Utopias." *American Sociological Review,* 31 (December 1966), 765–772.

Moreana: Organe de l'Association Amici Thomae Mori, No. 1, September 1963–

"More's *Utopia* and Four Hundred Years After." *Outlook,* 116 (July 4, 1917), 359–360.

Morf, Otto. "Ernst Bloch und die Utopie," in *Festschrift Ernst Bloch zum 70. Geburtstag,* edited by Rugard Otto Gropp (Berlin: VEB Deutscher Verlag der Wissenschaften, 1955), pp. 257–262.

Morgan, Alice B. "Philosophic Reality and Human Construction in the Utopia." *Moreana,* No. 39 (September 1973), pp. 15–23.

Morgan, Arthur E. "Beyond Utopia." *Saturday Review of Literature,* 28 (December 29, 1945), 5–6.

Morgan, H. Wayne. "The Utopia of Eugene V. Debs." *American Quarterly,* 11 (Summer 1959), 120–135.

Morra, Gianfranco. "L'utopia tecnocratica," in *L'Utopia nel mondo moderno* (Florence: Vallecchi, 1969), pp. 101–114.

Morton, A. L. "Utopias Yesterday and Today." *Science and Society,* 17 (Summer 1953), 258–263.

Mosca, Mariangela. "Fantascience, q.b., nelle prime opera di William Golding," in *Utopia e Fantascienza* (Turin: Giappichelli, 1975), pp. 129–141.

Moschkowskaja, J. "Zwei vergessene deutsche Utopien aus dem achtzehnten. Jahrhundert." *Neue Welt,* 9 (1954), 2128–2149.

Moser, Simon. "Mythos, Utopie, Ideologie." *Zeitschrift für philosophische Forschung,* 12, No. 3 (1958), 423–436.

Moses, Bernard. "Social Transformation." *Overland Monthly,* 2nd series, 15 (June 1890), 561–565.

Moskowitz, Sam. "A History of 'The Scientific Romance' in the Munsey Magazines, 1912–1930," in his *Under the Moons of Mars: A History and Anthology of 'The Scientific Romance' in the Munsey Magazines, 1912–1920* (New York: Holt, Rinehart and Winston, 1970), pp. 291–433.

Mosse, George L. "Tod, Zeit und Geschichte. Die völkische Utopie der Überwindung," in *Deutsches utopisches Denken im 20. Jahrhundert,* edited by Reinhold Grimm and Jost Hermand (Stuttgart: W. Kohlhammer, 1974), pp. 50–69.

Mucchielli, Roger. "L'Utopie de Thomas Morus," in Université libre de Bruxelles. Institut pour l'étude de la Renaissance et de l'humanisme. *Les Utopies à la Renaissance* (Brussels: Presses Universitaires de Bruxelles, 1963), pp. 99–106.

Mullen, Richard D. "Blish, van Vogt, and the uses of Spengler." *Riverside Quarterly,* 3, No. 3 (August 1968), 172–186.

Mullen, Richard D. "H. G. Wells and Victor Rousseau Emanuel: *When the Sleeper Wakes* and *The Messiah of the Cylinder.*" *Extrapolation,* 8 (May 1967), 31–63.

Müllenbrock, Heinz-Joachim. "Nationalismus und Internationalismus in Werk von H. G. Wells." *Die Neueren Sprachen,* 68, N.S. 18 (October 1969), 478–497.

Müllenbrock, Heinz-Joachim. "La position de Wells dans le développement de l'utopie anglaise moderne sous l'aspect sociologique." *Moreana,* No. 34 (May 1972), pp. 25–38.

Müller, Gert H. "Utopie in der Mathematik." in *Säkularisation und Utopie. Ebracher Studien. Ernst Forsthoff zum 65. Geburtstag* (Stuttgart: W. Kohlhammer Verlag, 1967), pp. 299–323.

Muller, Herbert J. "A Note on Utopia," in his *The Children of Frankenstein* (Bloomington: Indiana University Press, 1970), pp. 369–383.

Müller-Störmsdörfer, Ilse. "L'Art pour l'Espoir; Ernst Blochs Ästhetik des Utopischen," in *Wandlungen des Paradeisischen und Utopischen. Studien zum Bild eines Ideals.* Vol. 2 of *Probleme der Kunstwissenschaft* (Berlin: Walter de Gruyter, 1966), pp. 323–352.

Mumford, Lewis. "The Aftermath of Utopianism," in his *Values for Survival* (New York: Harcourt, Brace, 1946), pp. 61–77.

Mumford, Lewis. "Fashions Change in Utopia." *New Republic,* 47 (June 16, 1926), 114–115.

Mumford, Lewis. "Herzl's Utopia." *Menorah Journal,* 9 (August 1923), 155–169.

Mumford, Lewis. "Utopia, The City and The Machine," in *Utopias and Utopian Thought,* edited by Frank E. Manuel (Boston: Beacon Press, 1967), pp. 3–24.

Muminović, Rasim. "Utopicum als Indikation der Krise des Humanismus." *Praxis,* 8, Nos. 1–2 (1972), 47–61.

Munby, Lionel M. "William Morris' Romances and the Society of the Future." *Zeitschrift für Anglistik und Amerikanistik* 10, No. 1 (1962), 56–70.

Munson, Ronald. "The Clockwork Future: Dystopia, Social Planning, and Freedom," in *Ecology and the Quality of Life,* edited by Sylvan J. Kaplan and Elaine Kivy-Rosenbert (Springfield, Illinois: Charles C. Thomas, 1974), pp. 26–38.

Murdoch, Iris. "The Idea of Perfection." *Yale Review,* 53 (Spring 1954), 342–380.

Murphy, Walter F. "The Political Philosophy of Gerrard Winstanley." *Review of Politics,* 19 (April 1957), 214–238.

Murray, Matthew. "The English Utopians." *Twentieth Century,* 174 (Spring 1966), 12–15.

Murray, Robert H. "Utopian Toleration." *Edinburgh Review,* 219 (January 1914), 91–106.

Murry, John Middleton. "Art and Society." *Arts,* 14 (August 1928), 101–125.

Murry, John Middleton. "The Return to Fundamentals: Marx and Morris." *Adelphi,* 3 (October, November 1932), 19–29, 97–109.

"Musings Without Method." *Blackwood's Magazine,* 195 (June 1914), 859–864.

Negley, Glenn. "Utopia and Dystopia: A Look Backward," in *Utopia/Dystopia?,* edited by Peyton E. Richter (Cambridge, Massachusetts: Schenkman Publishing Co., 1975), pp. 21–27.

Neill, T. P. "Utopian Literature and the Historian." *Historical Bulletin,* 19 (May 1941), 75–76, 88–89.

Nelson, William. "Introduction," in his *Twentieth Century Interpretations of Utopia* (Englewood Cliffs, New Jersey: Prentice-Hall 1968), pp. 1–11.

Neri, Nicoletta. "Il viaggio nel tempo," in *Utopia e Fantascienza* (Turin: Giappichelli, 1975), pp. 7–43.

Neusüss, Arnhelm. "Schwierigkeiten einer Soziologie des utopischen Denkens," in his *Utopie; Begriff und Phänomen des Utopischen* (Neuwied: Luchterhand, 1968), pp. 13–119.

Neville, Pierre. "Economie et Utopie." *Praxis,* 8, Nos. 1–2 (1972), 71–77.

Newbolt, Henry. "A Modern Utopia," in his *Studies Green and Gray* (London: Thomas Nelson & Sons, 1926), pp. 102–134.

"A New Earth." *Spectator,* 113 (October 31, 1914), 585–586.

Newell, Peter E. "Communism — Primitive, Utopian, Authoritarian and Libertarian." *Freedom's Anarchist Review,* 38, No. 8 (April 30, 1977), 9–14.

Nicholas, Brian. "Two Nineteenth-Century Utopias: The Influence of

Renan's 'L'Avenir de la science' on Wilde's 'The Soul of Man Under Socialism.' " *Modern Language Review,* 59 (July 1964), 361-370.

Nicoletti, Manfredi G. "The End of Utopia." *Perspecta,* No. 14, pp. 268-279.

Nicoletti, Manfredi [G.]. "Flash Gordon and the Twentieth Century Utopia." *Architectural Review,* 140 (August 1966), 87-91.

Nicoletti, Manfredi G. "L'Utopia présent." *L'Architecture d'aujourd'hui,* 41, No. 148 (February-March 1970), xiv.

Niebuhr, Reinhold. "Modern Utopians." *Scribner's Magazine,* 100 (September 1936), 142-145.

Nipperdey, Thomas. "Die Funktion der Utopie im politischen Denken der Neuzeit." *Archiv für Kulturgeschichte* (Cologne), 44, No. 3 (1962), 357-378.

Nipperdey, Thomas. "Die Utopia des Thomas Morus und der Beginn der Neuzeit." in *Die moderne Demokratie und ihr Recht. Festschrift für Gerhard Leibholz zum 65. Geburtstag,* edited by Karl Dietrich Bracher, Christopher Dawson, Willi Geiger, and Rudolf Smend. 2 Vols. (Tübingen: J.C.B. Mohr, 1966), Vol. 1, pp. 343-368.

Noakes, Aubrey. "Lord Curzon on the Utopia: The Background Story of a Literary Find: Lord Curzon's Arnold Prize Essay of 1884 on Sir Thomas More." *Moreana,* Nos. 31-32 (November 1971), pp. 221-225. Text — pp. 227-249.

Nock, Albert Jay. "Thoughts on Utopia." *Atlantic,* 156 (July 1935), 14-25.

Normano, J. F. "A Neglected Utopian: Cyrano de Bergerac, 1619-55." *American Journal of Sociology,* 32 (November 1931), 454-457.

Normano, J. F. "Social Utopias in American Literature." *International Review for Social History,* 3 (1938), 287-300.

Norris, Darrell. "More's Utopia, A Geographical Approach." *Geographical Articles #10* (Cambridge: Cambridge University, Department of Geography, 1967), pp. 53-59.

Northbourne, Lord. "New Eschatology." *Studies in Comparative Religion,* 8 (Winter 1974), 33-39.

Nourse, Alan E. "Science Fiction and Man's Adaptation to Change." in *Science Fiction: Today and Tomorrow,* edited by Reginald Bretnor (New York: Harper & Row, 1974), pp. 116-132.

Novak, Maximillian E. "Robinson Crusoe and Economic Utopia." *Kenyon Review,* 25 (Summer 1963), 474-490.

Nuita, Seija. "Traditional Utopias in Japan and the West: A Study in Contrasts," in *Aware of Utopia,* edited by David Plath (Urbana: University of Illinois Press, 1971), pp. 12-32.

Nydahl, Joel. "Introduction," in Timothy Savage, *Amazonian Republic* (Delmar, New York: Scholars' Facimiles & Reprints, 1976), pp. v-xv.

Oates, Whitney J. "The Ideal States of Plato and Aristotle." in *The Greek Political Experience: Studies in Honor of William Kelly Prentice* (Princeton: Princeton University Press, 1941), pp. 187-213.

Oleszkiewicz, Antoine. "A Dieu et au génie." *Topique,* Nos. 4–5 (October 1970), pp. 139–142.

Oliver, Kenneth. *"Islandia* Revisited." *Pacific Spectator,* 9 (Spring 1955), 178–182.

Ollero, Andres. "La Utopia Rousseauiana: Democracia y Participación," in *IVR X: Equality and Freedom: International and Comparative Jurisprudence,* edited by Gray Dorsey. 3 Vols. (Dobbs Ferry, New York: Oceana & Leiden: A.W. Sijthoff, 1977), Vol. 1, pp. 367–377.

Oncken, Hermann. "Einleitung," in Thomas Morus, *Utopia,* edited by Gerhard Ritter. Vol. 1 of *Klassiker der Politik* (Berlin: Reimer Hobbing, 1922), pp. 5–45.

Oncken, Hermann. "Die Utopia des Thomas Morus und Machtproblem in der Staatslehre," in *Sitzungsberichte der Heidelberger Akademie der Wissenschaften. Philosophisch-historische Klasse.* Jahrgang 1922. 2 Abhandlung.

Oppel, Horst. "Die Gonzalo-Utopie in Shakespeares 'Sturm.' " *Deutsche Vierteljahrsschrift,* 28, No. 2 (1954), 194–220.

Ortlieb, Heinz-Dietrich. "Utopie als Gefahr?" *Das sozialistische Jahrhundert,* 1, Nos. 13–14 (1946), pp. 198–199.

Osgerby, J. R. *"Animal Farm* and *1984." Use of English,* 17 (1966), 237–243.

Osinovsky, Igor N. "Thomas More's *Utopia* in Russia," translated by I. V. Victorov, *Moreana,* No. 22 (May 1969), pp. 33–38.

Ozmon, Howard A. "Education and Utopia." *Liberal Education,* 51 (May 1965), 235–270.

P., G. "Zukunftsmusik." *Christliche Welt,* 7 (1893), 519–524, 540–545, 647–653.

[Paget, Victoria.] "On Modern Utopias: An Open Letter to Mr. H. G. Wells," by Vernon Lee (pseud.). *Fortnightly Review,* 86 (December 1906), 1123–1137.

[Paget, Victoria.] "A Postscript on Mr. Wells and Utopias," by Vernon Lee (pseud.) in her *Gospels of Anarchy and Other Contemporary Studies* (London: T. Fisher Unwin, 1908), pp. 353–372.

Panshin, Alexei. "Books in the Field: Science Fiction." *Wilson Library Bulletin,* 44 (February 1970), 616–620.

"Paradise Indeed." *Scribner's Magazine,* 44 (November 1908), 634–636.

Parekh, Bhiku. "Utopianism and Manicheism: A Critique of Marcuse's Theory of Revolution." *Social Research,* 39 (Winter 1972), 622–651.

Park, James W. "Utopian Economics of Sir Thomas More." *American Journal of Economics and Sociology,* 30 (July 1971), 275–288.

Parks, George B. "More's *Utopia* and Geography." *Journal of English and Germanic Philology,* 37 (April 1938), 224–236.

Parrinder, Patrick. "Imagining the Future: Wells and Zamyatin," in *H. G. Wells and Modern Science Fiction,* edited by Darko Suvin and Robert M.

Philmus (Lewisburg, Pennsylvania: Bucknell University Press, 1977), pp. 126–143.

Parssinen, T. M. "Bellamy, Morris and the Image of the Industrial City in Victorian Social Criticism." *Midwest Quarterly,* 14 (Spring 1973), 257–266.

Pass, Rudolf A. "Die Utopie im Urteil der Wirklichkeit." *Die Neue Gesellschaft,* 3 (1956), 273–282.

Patai, Daphne. "Utopia for Whom." *Aphra,* 5 (Summer 1974), 2–16.

"Patent Five-Cent Utopia." *Atlantic Monthly,* 154 (July 1934), 126–128.

Patrick, J. Max. "A Consideration of *La Terre Australe Connue,* by Gabriel de Foigny." *PMLA,* 61 (September 1946), 739–751.

Patrick, J. Max. "*The Free State of Noland,* A Neglected Utopia From the Age of Queen Anne." *Philological Quarterly,* 25 (January 1946), 79–88.

Patrick, J. Max. "Iconoclasm, the Complement of Utopianism." *Science-Fiction Studies,* 3 (July 1976), 157–161.

Patrick, J. Max. "Robert Burton's Utopianism." *Philological Quarterly,* 27 (October 1948), 345–358.

Patrick, J. Max. "*Scydromedia,* a Forgotten Utopia of the Seventeenth Century." *Philological Quarterly,* 25 (January 1946), 79–88.

Patterson, R[obert] H[ogarth]. "Utopias," in his *Essays in History and Art* (Edinburgh: William Blackwood & Sons, 1862), pp. 151–161.

Peardon, Thomas P. "Bentham's Ideal Republic." *Canadian Journal of Economics and Political Science,* 17 (May 1951), 184–283.

Pechel, Rudolf. "Bei Dr. Leete." *Deutsche Rundschau,* 268 (August 1941), 41–45.

Pecirka, Jan. "Aristophanes Ekklesiazusen und die Utopien in der Krise der Polis." *Wissenschaftliche Zeitschrift der Humboldt-Universität zu Berlin Gessellschafts- und Sprachwissenschaftsliche Reihe,* 12, No. 3 (1963), 215–220.

Peebles, H. P. "The Utopias of the Past Compared With the Theories of Bellamy." *Overland Monthly,* N.S. 15 (June 1890), pp. 574–577.

Percy, Walker. "Notes for a Novel About the End of the World," in his *The Message in the Bottle; How Queer Man Is, How Queer Language Is, and What One Has to Do with the Other* (New York: Farrar, Straus and Giroux, 1975), pp. 101–118.

Pereira, N.G.O. "Chernyshevsky's *What Is To Be Done?* as a Statement of Social Utopia." *Rocky Mountain Social Science Journal,* 9 (October 1972), 35–44.

Peretz, Martin. "Herbert Marcuse: Beyond Technological Reason." *Yale Review,* 57 (June 1968), 518–527.

"Perfection on Earth." *Times Literary Supplement,* 3133 (16 March 1962), 184.

Perkins, Merle L. "Voltaire and the Abbé de Saint-Pierre." *French Review,* 34 (December 1960), 152–163.

Perlini, Tito. "Metafisica e Utopia in Bloch," *Aut Aut,* No. 125 (1971), pp. 61–82.

Perrier, François. "En guise d'extroduction." *Topique,* Nos. 4–5 (October 1970), pp. 213–223.

Perrott, Roy. "Every guy's got his own utopia: five days' 'dynamic thinking' for a film scenario on the perfect society." *Observer* (August 3, 1969), p. 2.

Pesch, Ludwig. "Das Utopia der romantischen Kunstheorie und die Moderne," in *Wandlungen des Paradiesischen und Utopischen; Studien zum Bild eines Ideals,* Vol. 2 of *Probleme der Kunstwissenschaft* (Berlin: Walter de Gruyter, 1966), pp. 301–322.

Pěsić-Golubović, Zagorka. "La Culture en tant que pont entre l'utopie et la realité." *Praxis,* 8, Nos. 1–2 (1972), pp. 103–118.

Peters, Robert. "*Utopia* and More's Orthodoxy." *Moreana,* Nos. 31–32 (November 1971), pp. 147–155.

Petre, M. D. "Bolshevist Ideals and the 'Brave New World.'" *Hibbert Journal,* 31 (October 1932), 61–71.

Pfeiffer, Günter. "Utopie, Anti-Utopie und das Glück des Menschen; Gedanken über eine literarische Eigenart unserer Zeit." *Berichte und Informationen, Österreichischen Forschungs-Institut für Wirtschaft und Politik,* 18, No. 885 (1963), 12–13.

Pfeiffer-Belli, W. "Utopia — einst und heute." *Die Begegnung,* 5 (1950–1953), 75–76.

Pflaezer, Jean. "American Utopian Fiction 1888–1896: The Political Origins of Form." *Minnesota Review,* N.S. 6 (Spring 1976), pp. 114–117.

Philmus, Robert M. "The Language of Utopia." *Studies in the Literary Imagination,* 6 (Fall 1973), 61–78.

Philmus, Robert M. "Revisions of the Future: *The Time Machine.*" *Journal of General Education,* 28 (Spring 1976), 23–30.

Piccone, Paul. "Utopia and the Concrets [sic] Overcoming of Alienation." *Praxis,* 8, Nos. 1–2 (1972), 93–102.

Picton, J. A. "Sir Thomas More's 'Utopie' [Etymology of Utopia]." *Notes and Queries,* 7th series, 5 (February 11, 1888), 101–102; Replies: March 24, 1888, pp. 229–231 and May 12, 1888, p. 371.

Pieper, Annemarie. "Die Funktion von Utopien in der Philosophie." *Neues Hochland,* 4, No. 65 (1973), 351–363.

Pierce, John R. "Communications Technology and the Future," in *Utopias and Utopian Thought,* edited by Frank E. Manuel (Boston: Beacon Press, 1967), pp. 169–180.

Pierce, Roy. "Sociology and Utopia: The Early Writings of Simone Weil." *Political Science Quarterly,* 77 (December 1962), 505–525.

Pieterse, Jan Nederveen, "Het utopisch bewustzijn." *De nieuwe maand,* 15, No. 8 (October 1972), 417–486.

The Pilgrim (pseud.). "With Scrip, and Staff." *America,* 50 (November 4, 1933), 112.

Pilgrim, John. "Science Fiction and Anarchism," *Anarchy 34,* 3 (December 1963), 361–375.

Plank, Robert. "The Geography of Utopia: Psychosocial Factors Shaping the 'Ideal' Location." *Extrapolation,* 6 (May 1965), 39–49.

Plank, Robert. "Imaginary Voyages and Toy Novels." *Hartford Studies in Literature,* 6, No. 3 (1974), 221–242.

Plank, Robert. "Omnipotent Cannibals: Thoughts on Reading Robert Heinlein's 'Stranger in a Strange Land.' " *Riverside Quarterly,* 5, No. 1 (July 1971), 30–37.

Plank, Robert. "The Place of Evil in Science Fiction." *Extrapolation,* 14 (May 1972), 100–111.

Plank, Robert. "The Presidency in Science Fiction." *Extrapolation,* 16 (May 1975), 173–191.

Plank, Robert. "Quixote's Mills: The Man-machine Encounter in SF." *Science-Fiction Studies,* 1 (July 1973), 68–78.

Plattel, M. [G.]. "Utopia and Revolution." *Sociologia neerlandica,* No. 2 (1970), pp. 60–79. First published in *Sociale Wetenschappen,* 11, No. 4 (1968).

Plattel, M. G. "Wijsgerig-sociologische beschouwingen over der waarde van der utopie." *Tijdschrift voor filosofie,* 31, No. 1 (1969), 28–59.

Plummer, Kathleen Church. "The Streamlined Moderne." *Art in America,* 62 (January 1974), 46–54.

"A Poet's Vision of a Socialist Millennium." *Review of Reviews,* 3 (May 1891), 509–513.

Polak, Fred[erik] L. "Responsibility for the Future." *The Humanist,* (November/December 1973), pp. 14–16.

Polak, Frederik L. "Utopia and Cultural Renewal," in *Utopias and Utopian Thought,* edited by Frank E. Manuel (Boston: Beacon Press, 1967), pp. 281–295.

Polin, Raymond. "Economie et politique au xviiie siècle: L'*Oceana* de James Harrington." *Revue française de science politique,* 2 (January-March 1952), 24–41.

Poll, Max. "The Sources of Gulliver's Travels." University of Cincinnati *Bulletin,* No. 24, Series 2, Vol. 3 (November 1909).

Pollock, George H. "On Mourning, Immortality and Utopia." *Journal of the American Psychoanalytic Association,* 23, No. 2 (1975), 334–362.

Pomeau, René. "Voyage et lumières dans la littérature française du XVIIIe siècle." *Studies on Voltaire and the Eighteenth Century,* 57 (1967), 1269–1289.

Pompen, Aur. "Een nieuwe vertaling van Utopia." *Studia Catholica* (Nijmegan) 26, No. 2 (1951), 94–96.

Pons, Emile. "Les Langues Imaginaires dans le voyage utopique," "Un pré-

curseur: Thomas Morus,'' ''Les 'Jargons' de Panurge dans Rabelais,''
''Les Grammairiens: Vairesse et Foigny.'' *Revue de Littérature Comparée* (October-December 1930, April-June 1931, July-September 1932),
pp. 589–607, 185–218, 500–532.

Popper, Karl. ''The Erewhonians and the Open Society.'' *Etc.,* 20 (May 1963),
5–22.

Popper, Karl. ''Utopia and Violence.'' *Hibbert Journal,* 46 (January 1948),
109–116.

Porter, David L. ''The Politics of Le Guin's Opus,'' *Science-Fiction Studies,* 2
(November 1975), 243–248.

Porter, Philip W. and Fred E. Lukermann. ''The Geography of Utopia,'' in
*Geographies of the Mind: Essays in Historical Geography In Honor of
John Kirtland Wright,* edited by David Lowenthal and Martyn J.
Bowden (New York: Oxford University Press, 1975), pp. 197–223.

Portmann, Adolf. ''Utopisches in der Lebensforschung,'' in *Vom Sinn der
Utopie. Eranos Jahrbuch 1963* (Zürich: Rhein-Verlag, 1964), pp.
311–344.

Poster, Mark. ''Fourier's Concept of the Group.'' *Minnesota Review,* N.S. 6
(Spring 1976), pp. 76–87.

Poulat, Emile. ''Écritures et tradition fouriéristes.'' *Revue internationale de
philosophie,* No. 60 (1962), pp. 221–233.

Powell, J. M. ''Utopia, Millennium and the Cooperative Ideal: A Behavioral
Matrix in the Settlement Process.'' *Australian Geographer,* 11 (September 1971), 606–618.

''Premonizioni della parusia urbanistica: le visioni di dodici citta ideali.''
Casabeila, 361 (1972), 45–55.

Prescott, Henry W. ''Notes and Queries on Utopias in Plautus.'' *American
Journal of Philology,* 29 (January 1908), 55–68.

Presley, James T. ''Bibliography of Utopias and Imaginary Travels and Histories.'' *Notes and Queries,* 4th series, 11 (June 28, 1873), 519–521; 12
(July 5, July 12, 2 August 1873), 203, 22–23, 91; 5th series, 2 (September
1874), 252; 6 (July 8, 1876), 38; 7 (June 9, 1877), 458; Replies, 4th series,
12 (July 19, July 26, August 23, September 6, October 11, 1873), 41–42,
55, 62, 153, 199, 293; 5th series, 1 (January 24, March 1874), 78–79, 237;
6 (August 5, 1876), 118; 8 (July 7, 1877), 13–14; 6th series, 9 (February 2,
1884), 84.

Preston, John Hyde. ''Collective Living.'' *Harpers Magazine,* 176 (May
1938), 603–614.

Preu, James. ''Swift's Influence on Godwin's Doctrine of Anarchism.'' *Journal of the History of Ideas,* 15 (June 1954), 371–383.

Prevost, André. ''L'Utopie: Le Genre Littéraire.'' *Moreana,* Nos. 31–32
(November 1971), pp. 161–168.

Prince, J. F. T ''Nowhere Island: More's Utopia.'' *Blackfriars,* 16 (June
1935), 422–424.

Pritchett, V. S. "Books in General." *New Statesman and Nation,* 27 (April 15, 1944), 259.

Progoff, Ira. "The Dynamics of Hope and the Image of Utopia," in *Vom Sinn der Utopie. Eranos-Jahrbuch 1963* (Zürich: Rhein-Verlag, 1964), pp. 89–145.

"Prospective et utopie." *Esprit,* N.S. 34 (February 1966), pp. 178–281.

Pütz, Helmut. " 'Reale Utopien' als politische Integrationsfaktoren in der Bundesrepublik." *Aus Politik und Zeitgeschichte,* Appendix to the weekly "Das Parlament," of the Bundes Zentrale für Politische Bildung, 9 (1969), 27–32.

Quandt, Jean B. "Religion and Social Thought: The Secularization of Postmillennialism." *American Quarterly,* 25 (October 1973), 390–409.

Quattrocki, Ed. "Injustice, Not Councilorship: The Theme of Book One of *Utopia.*" *Moreana,* Nos. 31–32 (November 1971), pp. 19–28.

Quinzio, Sergio. "Utopia ed escatologia," in *L'Utopia nel mondo moderno* (Florence: Vallecchi, 1969), pp. 67–83.

R., J. K. "Walden and Walden 2." *Freedom,* 24 (February 23, 1963), 2.

Ragon, M. "Jules Verne, visionnaire de l'architecture, dépassé par la prospective architecturale d'aujourd'hui," *Oeil,* No. 227 (July 1974), pp. 44–49.

Rahner, Karl. "Marxistische Utopie und christliche Zukunft des Menschen," in his *Scriften zur Theologie,* 6 Vols. (Eiseiden: Benziger Verlag, 1965), Vol. 6, pp. 77–88.

Rahv, Philip. "The Unfuture of Utopia." *Partisan Review,* 16 (July 1949), 743–749.

Ranald, Ralph A. "George Orwell and the Mad World: The Anti-Universe of *1984.*" *South Atlantic Quarterly,* 66 (Autumn 1967), 544–553.

Randall, John Herman, Jr. "Plato's Treatment of the Theme of the Good Life and His Criticism of the Spartan Ideal." *Journal of the History of Ideas,* 27 (July-Septembre 1967), 307–324.

Rankin, H. D. "Plato and Bernard Shaw: Their Ideal Communities." *Hermathena* (Trinity College, Dublin), 93 (May 1959), 71–77.

Rasch, Heinz and Bodo Rasch. "Realisierte Utopie." *Bauen + Wohnen,* 22, No. 5 (May 1967), 198–200.

Rathmann, August. "Geist und Ungeist der Utopie." *Geist und Tat,* 20, No. 3 (March 1965), 81–88.

Raupach, Hans. "Utopia und Sowjetoikos," in *Gestaltungsprobleme der Weltwirtschaft; Andreas Predöhl aus Anlass seines 70. Geburtstages gewidmet,* edited by Harald Jürgensen (Göttingen: Vandenhoeck and Ruprecht, 1963), pp. 128–140. *Jahrbuch für Sozialwissenschaft,* Vol. 14, No. 3.

Raymond, Henri. "Utopia All-Inclusive: The Vacation World as World of the Future." *Landscape,* 13, No. 2 (Winter 1963–1964), 4–7.

"Recent Utopias." *Times Literary Supplement,* No. 1288 (October 7, 1926), pp. 661–662.

Reckford, K.H. "Some Appearances of the Golden Age." *Classical Journal,* 54 (November 1958), 79–87.

Reding, Marcel. "Utopie, Phantasie, Prophetie. Das Prinzip der Hoffnung im Marxismus." *Frankfurter Hefte,* 16 (1961), 8–13.

Reeve, Helen S. "Utopian Socialism in Russian Literature: 1840's-1860's." *American Slavic and East European Review,* 18 (October 1959), 374–393.

Reeves, W. P. "The Expansion of Utopia." *National Review,* 45 (July 1905), pp. 806–817.

Reichert, John F. "Plato, Swift, and the Houyhnhnmns." *Philosophy Review,* 47 (April 1968), 179–192.

Reichert, Karl. "Robinsonade, Utopie und Satire im *Joris Pines* (1726)." *Arcadia,* 1, No. 1 (1966), 50–69.

Reichert, Karl. "Utopie und Staatsroman, Ein Forschungsbericht." *Deutsche Vierteljahrsschrift für Literaturwissenschaft und Geistesgeschichte,* 39 (June 1965), 259–287.

Reigrotzki, Erich. "Die Utopialität als wissenschaftliche Kategorie," in *Sozialwissenschaft und Gesellschaftsgestaltung. Festschrift für Gerhard Weisser,* edited by Friedrich Karrenberg and Hans Albert (Berlin: Duncker and Humblot, 1963), pp. 103–119.

Reilly, Joseph J. "War and More's *Utopia.*" *Catholic World,* 154 (November 1941), 151–159.

Reinders, Robert C. "T. Wharton Collens and the Christian Labor Union." *Labor History,* 8 (Winter 1967), 53–70.

Reiss, Timothy J. "Structure and Mind in Two Seventeenth-Century Utopias: Campanella and Bacon." *Yale French Studies,* No. 49 (1973), pp. 82–95.

Renard, Georges. "Les cités imaginaires." *La grande Revue* (Paris), 35 (May 1931), 353–367.

Renard, Georges. "L'Utopie de Thomas Morus." *Revue Politique et Parlementaire.* 148, No. 442 (September 10, 1931), 381–393.

Renucci, Paul. "Deux étapes de l'utopisme humanita: la Château des Decameron et L'Abbaye de Thélème." *Bulletin of the John Rylands Library, Manchester,* 30 (May 1947), 330–346.

Rey, W. H. "The Destiny of Man in the Modern Utopian Novel." *Symposium,* 6 (May 1952), 140–156.

Reybaud, Louis, "Des Idées et des Sectes Communistes." *Revue des deux mondes,* 4th series, 31 (1842), 5–47.

Reybaud, Louis. "Socialistes Modernes. III. Robert Owen." *Revue des deux mondes,* 14 (1838), 5–39.

Reynolds, E. E. "Three Views of *Utopia.*" *Moreana,* Nos. 31–32 (November 1971), pp. 209–214.

Rhodes, Carolyn H. "Frederick Winslow Taylor's System of Scientific Management in Zamiatin's *We.*" *Journal of General Education,* 28 (Spring 1976), 31–42.

Rhodes, Carolyn H. "Tyranny By Computer: Automated Data Processing and Oppressive Government in Science Fiction," in *Many Futures Many Worlds: Theme and Form in Science Fiction,* edited by Thomas D. Clareson ([Kent, Ohio:] Kent State University Press, 1977), pp. 66–93.

Rhys, Rev. T. Tudor. "Man or Machine? Looking Back Upon the Future." *Expository Times,* 60 (April 1949), 186–190.

Riasnovsky, Alexander B. and Alvin Z. Rubinstein. "Russian Utopia and Soviet Communism." *Social Science,* 38 (June 1963), 151–167.

Richards, D. "Four Utopias." *Slavonic and East European Review,* 40 (December 1961), 220–228.

Richter, Peyton E. "Utopia/Dystopia? Threats of Hell or Hopes of Paradise," in *Utopia/Dystopia?* edited by Peyton E. Richter (Cambridge, Massachusetts: Schenkman Publishing Co., 1975), pp. 3–17.

Rideout, Walter B. "Introduction," in Ignatius Donnelly, *Caesar's Column: A Story of the 20th Century* (Cambridge, Massachusetts: Harvard University Press, 1960), pp. vii–xxxii.

Riegal, Robert E. "Edward Bellamy: Looking Backward 2000–1887." *Social Education,* 16 (January 1952), 11–13.

Riemer, Neal. "Some Reflections on 'The Grand Inquisitor' and Modern Democratic Theory." *Ethics,* 67 (1957), 249–256.

Riesman, David. "Some Observations on Community Plans and Utopia." *Yale Law Journal,* 57 (December 1947), 173–200.

Rihs, Charles. "Panorama de l'utopisme française au XVIIIe siècle." *Communautés Archives Internationales de Sociologie de la Coopération et du Développement,* No. 27 (January-June 1970), pp. 5–20.

Ringer, Alexander L. "J.-J. Barthelamy and Musical Utopia in Revolutionary France." *Journal of the History of Ideas,* 22 (July-September 1961), 355–368.

Ripepe, Eugenio. "Potere, società industriale e utopie." *Storia e Politica,* 6, No. 3 (July-September 1967), 445–458.

Rivers, John. "A French Utopia." *The Library,* 2nd Series, 6 (July 1905), 265–273.

Robertson, J. C. "The Social Ideals of Plato and Morris." in his *Mixed Company* (London: Dent, 1939), pp. 56–79.

Robertson, J[ohn] M[ackinnon]. "Utopia," in his *Spoken Essays* (London: Watts & Co., 1925), pp. 1–25.

Robinson, Lydia G. "A 'Lunatic's' Idea of Utopia." *Open Court,* 22 (November 1908), 686–694.

Roelens, Maurice. "Utopie, allégorie, roman dans *Le Monde Vrai* de Marivaux." *Revue des sciences humaines,* 39, No. 155 (July-September 1974), 410–423.

Roemer, Kenneth M. "American Utopian Literature (1888-1900): An Annotated Bibliography." *American Literary Realism,* 4 (Summer 1971), 227-254.

Roemer, Kenneth. M. "Edward Bellamy." *American Literary Realism,* 8 (Summer 1975), pp. 191-198.

Roemer, Kenneth M. "The Heavenly City of The Late 19th-Century Utopians." *Journal of The American Studies Association of Texas,* 4 (1973), 5-13.

Roemer, Kenneth M. "1984 in 1894: Harben's Land of The Changing Sun." *Mississippi Quarterly,* 26 (Winter 1972-1973), 29-42.

Roemer, Kenneth M. "Sex Roles, Utopia and Change: The Family in Late Nineteenth Century Utopian Literature." *American Studies,* 13 (Fall 1972), 33-47.

Roemer, Kenneth M. "Utopia and Methodology: Uses of Fiction in American Studies." *Rocky Mountain Social Science Journal,* 12 (January 1975), 21-28.

Roemer, Kenneth M. " 'Utopia Made Practical': Compulsive Realism." *American Literary Realism,* 7 (Summer 1974), 273-276.

Roemer, Kenneth M. "The Yankee(s) in Noahville." *American Literature,* 45 (November 1973), 434-437.

Rohde, Erwin. "Ethnographische Utopien, Fabeln und Romane," in his *Der Griechische Roman und siene Vorläuffer* (Leipzig: Breitkopf und Härtel, 1876), pp. 167-287.

Rohrmoser, Günter. "Geschichte und Utopie bei Shakespeare," in *Säkularisation und Utopie. Ebracher Studien. Ernst Forsthoff zum 65. Geburtstag* (Stuttgart: W. Kohlhammer Verlag, 1967), pp. 357-382.

Romeo, Rosario. "Jesuit Sources and the Italian Political Utopia in the Second Half of the Sixteenth Century," in *First Images of America: The Impact of the New World on the Old,* edited by Fredi Chiappeli, 2 Vols. (Berkeley: University of California Press, 1976), Vol. 1, pp. 165-184.

Rose, Lisle A. "A Bibliographical Survey of Economic and Political Writings, 1865-1900." *American Literature,* 15 (January 1944), 381-410. Unpublished Supplements, I (Houghton, Michigan) (April 28, 1944); II (Houghton, Michigan) (October 1, 1944); III (Urbana, Illinois) (October 5, 1949); IV (Urbana, Illinois) (1949-1951).

Rose, Steven. "The Fear of Utopia." *Essays in Criticism,* 24 (January 1974), 55-70.

Rosenbaum, Sidonia. "The Utopia of Lafcadio Hearn — Spanish America." *American Quarterly,* 6 (Spring 1954), 76-78.

Rosenberg, Adam. "Foregleams of the Fraternal State. II. Socialism in Ancient Israel." *Arena,* 28 (July 1902), 37-44.

Rosenberg, Aubrey. "Digressions in Imaginary Voyages," in *The Varied Pattern: Studies in the 18th Century,* edited by Peter Hughes and David Williams (Toronto: A. M. Hakkert, Ltd., 1971), pp. 21–37.

Roshwald, Mordecai. "The Idea of the Promised Land." *Diogenes,* No. 82 (Summer 1973), pp. 45–69.

Ross, J. Elliot. "On Rereading Bellamy." *Commonweal,* 23 (14 February 1936), 432–434.

Roth, Paul. "Utopien als Spiegebild ihrer Zeit." *Stimmen der Zeit,* 148 (April 1951), 43–53.

Rotstein, Abraham. "Robert Owen," in his *The Precarious Homestead: Essays on Economics, Technology and Nationalism* (Toronto: New Press, 1973), pp. 218–241.

Rottensteiner, Franz. "Kurd Lasswitz: A German Pioneer of Science Fiction." *Riverside Quarterly,* 4, No. 1 (August 1969), 4–18.

Rottensteiner, Franz, "Kurd Lasswitz: A German Pioneer of SF," in *SF: The Other Side of Realism,* edited by Thomas D. Clareson (Bowling Green, Ohio: Bowling Green University Popular Press, 1971), pp. 289–306.

Rötzer, Hans Gerd. "Utopie und Gegenutopie." *Stimmen der Zeit,* 174 (1964), 356–365.

Rude, Fernand. "Genèse et fin d'un mythe historique: Le préfouriérisme de l'ange." *Topique,* Nos. 4–5 (October 1970), pp. 175–189.

Rühle, Jürgen. "The Philosopher of Hope: Ernst Bloch," in *Revisionism: Essays on the History of Marxist Ideas,* edited by Leopold Labedz (New York: Frederick A. Praeger, 1962), pp. 166–178.

Russ, Joanna. "The Image of Women in Science Fiction," in *Images of Women in Fiction: Feminist Perspectives,* edited by Susan Koppelman Cornillon (Bowling Green, Ohio: Bowling Green University Popular Press, 1972), pp. 79–94.

Ruyer, Raymond. "Les Problèmes sociaux et les problèmes humaines d'après les utopies contemporains." (Nancy: Centre Européen Universitaire, Département Études des Civilisations, 1953), part 3.

Ryan, John K. " 'Scydromedia': Anthony Legrand's Ideal Commonwealth," *New Scholasticism,* 10 (January 1936), pp. 39–54.

S., M.E.W. "Possible Utopias." *Appleton's Journal,* 14 (August 21, 1875), 238–240.

Sacher, Hermann and R. Stein. "Utopie," in *Staatslexikon,* 5 Vols. (Freiburg im Breisgau: Herder, 1926–1932), Vol. 5, pp. 584–587.

Sackett, S. J. "The Utopia of Oz." *Georgia Review,* 14 (Fall 1960), 275–291.

Sadler, Elizabeth. "One Book's Influence: Edward Bellamy's *Looking Backward.*" *New England Quarterly,* 17 (December 1944), 538–555.

Sagar, Keith M. "Brecht in Neverneverland: *The Caucasian Chalk Circle.*" *Modern Drama,* 9 (May 1966), 11–17.

Sagerat, Jules. "Paradis laïques; Le Paradis d'Anatole France (Sur la pierre blanche)." *Mercure de France* (1908), pp. 215–228.

Saleebey, Dennis. "Pigeons, People, and Paradise: Skinnerian Technolgoy and the Coming of the Welfare Society." *Social Service Review,* 50 (September 1976), 388–401.

Salz, Arthur. "Bernard Bolzanos Utopie 'Vom besten Staate' " *Archiv für Sozialwissenschaft und Sozialpolitik,* 31, No. 2 (1910), 498–519.

Samaan, Angele Botros. "Bulwer Lytton and the Rise of the Utopian Novel." *Bulletin of the Faculty of Arts,* Cairo University, 27, Parts I and II (May, December 1964), pp. 1–32.

Samaan, Angele Botros. "Butler's *Erewhon:* A Centenary Tribute." *Moreana,* No. 36 (December 1972), pp. 97–102.

Samaan, Angele Botros "C. S. Lewis, The Utopist, and His Critics." Reprinted from *Cairo Studies in English 1964* (Cairo, U.A.R.: Costa Tsoumas and Co.).

Samaan, Angele Botros. " 'A Poet's Vision of the Socialist Millennium.' *News From Nowhere* and Its Critics." *Bulletin of the Faculty of Arts,* Cairo University, 24, No. 2 (December 1962). Reprinted: Cairo University Press, 1966.

Samuelson, David N. "Childhood's End: A Median Stage of Adolescence?" *Science-Fiction Studies,* 1 (Spring 1973), 4–17.

Samuelson, David N. "*Limbo:* The Great American Dystopia." *Extrapolation,* 19 (December 1977), 76–87.

Samuelson, David N. "The Lost Canticles of Walter M. Miller, Jr." *Science Fiction Studies,* 3 (March 1976), 3–26.

Sancton, Thomas A. "Looking Inward: Edward Bellamy's Spiritual Crisis." *American Quarterly,* 25 (December 1973), 538–557.

Sanford, Charles L. "Classics of American Reform Literature." *American Quarterly,* 10 (Fall 1958), 295–311.

Sargent, Lyman Tower. "An Ambiguous Legacy: The Role and Position of Women in the English Eutopia." *Extrapolation,* 19 (December 1977), 39–49.

Sargent, Lyman Tower. "An Anarchist Utopia." *Anarchy 104,* 9 (October 1969), 316–320.

Sargent, Lyman Tower. "English and American Utopias, Similarities and Differences" *Journal of General Education,* 28 (Spring 1976), 16–22.

Sargent, Lyman Tower "Existentialism and Utopianism: A Reply to Frederick L. Polak." *Minnesota Review,* 6, No. 1 (1966), 72–75.

Sargent, Lyman Tower. "Introduction," *Man Abroad* (Boston: Gregg Press, 1976), pp. v–viii.

Sargent, Lyman Tower. "A Note on the Other Side of Human Nature in the Utopian Novel." *Political Theory,* 3 (February 1975), 88–97.

Sargent, Lyman Tower. "Opportunities for Research on Utopian Literature to 1900." *Extrapolation,* 19 (December 1977), 16–26.

Sargent, Lyman Tower. "Themes in Utopian Fiction in English Before Wells." *Science-Fiction Studies,* 3 (November 1976), 275–282.

Sargent, Lyman Tower. "The Three Faces of Utopianism." *Minnesota Review,* 7, No. 3 (1967), 222–230.

Sargent, Lyman Tower. "A Twentieth-Century Jeremiah." *Minnesota Review,* 4 (Winter 1964), 286–288.

Sargent, Lyman Tower. "Utopia and Dystopia in Contemporary Science Fiction." *Futurist,* 6 (June 1972), 93–98.

Sargent, Lyman Tower. "Utopia: The Problem of Definition." *Extrapolation,* 16 (May 1975), 137–148.

Sargent, Lyman Tower. "Women in Utopia." *Comparative Literature Studies,* 10 (December 1973), 302–316.

Sargent, Pamela. "Women in Science Fiction." *Futures,* 7 (October 1975), 433–441.

Saulnier, V. L. "L'Utopie en France: Morus et Rabelais," in Université libre de Bruxelles. L'Institut pour l'étude de la Renaissance et de l'humanisme. *Les Utopies à la Renaissance* (Brussels: Presses Universitaire de Bruxelles, 1963), pp. 135–162.

Sauter, John. "Staat und Wirtschaft in den grossen Systemen des Idealismus," *Blätter für Deutsche Philosophie,* 2, Nos. 3-4 (October-January 1928–1929), 229–253.

Sawada, Paul Akio. "The Praise of Realpolitik? H. Oncken and More's *Utopia.*" *Moreana,* Nos. 15-16 (November 1967), pp. 145–164.

Sawada, Paul Akio. "Toward the Definition of *Utopia.*" *Moreana,* Nos. 31-32 (November 1971), pp. 135–146.

Saxton, Alexander. "*Caesar's Column:* The Dialogue of Utopia and Catastrophe." *American Quarterly,* 19 (Summer 1967), 224–238.

Sayre, R. F. "American Myths of Utopia." *College English,* 31 (March 1970), 613–623.

Schachterle, Lance and Jeanne Welcher. "A Checklist of Secondary Studies on Imaginary Voyages." *Bulletin of Bibliography,* 31 (July-September 1974), 99–100, 106, 110, 116, 121.

Scheck, Frank Rainer. "Augenschein und Zukunft. Die antiutopische Reaktion: Samjatins 'Wir,' Huxleys 'Schöne neue Welt,' Orwells '1984,' " in *Science Fiction: Theorie und Geschichte,* edited by Eike Barmeyer (Munich: Wilhelm Fink, 1972), pp. 259–275.

Schein, Ionel. "Frankreich: Utopische Realität." *Bauen + Wohnen,* 22, No. 5 (May 1967), 201–206.

Schiffman, Joseph. "Edward Bellamy's Altruistic Man." *American Quarterly,* 6 (Fall 1954), 195–209.

Schiffman, Joseph. "Edward Bellamy's Religious Thought." *PMLA,* 68 (September 1953), 716–732.

Schiffman, Joseph. "Introduction," in Edward Bellamy, in *The Duke of Stockbridge; A Romance of Shay's Rebellion* (Cambridge: Belknap Press, 1962), pp. vii–xxx.

Schiffman, Joseph. "Introduction," in Edward Bellamy, *Selected Writings on Religion and Society,* edited by Joseph Schiffman (New York: Liberal Arts Press, 1958), pp. ix–xiv.

Schlanger, Judith E. "Power and Weakness of the Utopian Imagination." *Diogenes,* No. 84 (Winter 1973), pp. 1–24.

Schleicker, Klaus. "Die pädogogische Funktion der Utopie und die Utopische Dimension in der Pädogogik." *Bildung und Erziehung,* 2, No. 23 (1970), 86–103.

Schlette, Heinz Robert. "Utopisches Denken und Konkrete Humanität." *Concilium, Internationale Zeitschrift für Theologie,* 5, No. 8 (1972), 355–362.

Schlosser, Alfred. "Von Utopia nach Ikaria." *Berliner Hefte,* 2 (February 1947), 131–138.

Schlösser, Anselm. "Der viktorianische Gulliver: Betrachtungen über Samuel Butlers *Erewhon* und *Erewhon Revisited." Zeitschrift für Anglistik und Amerikanistik,* 9, No. 2 (1961), 117–138.

Schmerl, Rudolph B. "The Two Future Worlds of Aldous Huxley." *PMLA,* 77 (June 1962), 328–334.

Schmidt, Burghard. "Gegen die gängige Verwechslung der Konkreten Utopie mit technischer Planung." *Werk,* 60 (September 1973), 1063–1072.

Schmidt, Erich. "Das Schlaraffenland." *Cosmopolis,* 6 (April 1897), 245–264.

Schmiele, Walter. "Zur Geschichte der Utopie." *Liberal,* 8, No. 12 (1966), 903–906.

Schmitt, Carl. "Die Tyrannei der Werte," in *Säkularisation und Utopie. Ebracher Studien. Ernst Forsthoff zum 65. Geburtstag* (Stuttgart: W. Kohlhammer Verlag, 1967), pp. 37–62.

Schoeck, R. J. "The Intellectual Milieu of More's Utopia." *Moreana,* No. 1 (September 1963), pp. 40–46.

Schoeck, R. J. "More, Plutarch, and King Agis: Spartan History and the Meaning of *Utopia." Philological Quarterly,* 35 (October 1956), 366–375.

Schoeck, R. J. " 'A Nursery of Correct and Useful Institutions': On Reading More's Utopia as Dialogue." *Moreana,* No. 22 (May 1969), pp. 19–32.

Scholl, Ralph. "Science Fiction: A Selected Checklist." *Bulletin of Bibliography,* 22 (January-April 1958), 114–115.

Schöllgen, Werner. "Das Prinzip Gegenwart: Natturrecht und Geschichte im Widerstreit menschlicher Grundhaltungen." *Wort und Wahrheit,* 18 (March 1963), 176–186.

Schomerus, Hans. "Irdische und utopische Gesellschaft bei Pascal," in

Säkularisation und Utopie. Ebracher Studien. Ernst Forsthoff zum 65. Geburtstag (Stuttgart: W. Kohlhammer Verlag, 1967), pp. 363–376.

Schonauer, Franz. "Prospekte auf die Welt von Morgen." *Eckart,* 25 (April-June 1956), 259–261.

Schotlaender, Rudolf. "Die Vermachtnisfreiheit als Ausdruck altrömischer Humanität." *Wissenschaftliche Zeitschrift der Humboldt-Universität zu Berlin. Gesellschafts- und Sprachwissenschaftsliche Reihe,* 12, No. 3 (1963), 273–284.

Schuster, Melvin M. "Skinner and the Morality of Melioration," in *Utopia/Dystopia?,* edited by Peyton E. Richter (Cambridge, Massachusetts: Schenkman Publishing Co., 1975), pp. 95–108.

Schwartz, Pedro. "El sueño de la razón: Argumentos económicos y filosóficos contra la utopia." *Anales de Ecónomia,* 3, No. 2 (May-June 1975), 133–145.

Schwedtke, Kurt. "Utopie und Ideal." *Deutsches Philologenblatt,* 41, No. 17 (April 26, 1933), 188–189.

Schwerdtfeger, Erich. "Der Begriff der Utopie in Blochs 'Abriss Sozial-Utopien.' " *Neue Zeitschrift für systematische Theologie und Religionsphilosophie,* 7 (1965), 316–338.

Schwonke, Martin. "Einbahnstrasse zum Ameisenstaat? Zur Kritik der negativen Utopien vom totalitären Endzustand." *Atomzeitalter: Information und Meinung,* Nos 7/8 (July-August 1962), pp. 199–201.

[Schwonke] Schwone [sic], Martin. "Heinleins Utopie." *Atomzeitalter: Information und Meinung,* 3 (March 1961), 67.

Schwonke, Martin. "Naturwissenschaft und Technik im utopischen Denken der Neuzeit." *Futurum,* 4, No. 3 (1971), 282–297. Also in *Science Fiction: Theorie und Geschichte,* edited by Eike Barmeyer (Munich: Wilhelm Fink, 1972), pp. 57–75.

"Science in Science Fiction." *Advancement of Science* (August 1965), pp. 195–207.

Scortia, Thomas N. "Science Fiction as the Imaginary Experiment." in *Science Fiction: Today and Tomorrow,* edited by Reginald Bretnor (New York: Harper & Row, 1974), pp. 135–147.

Scott, Samuel M. "The Prospects of Futurity." *Harvard Graduate's Magazine,* 32 (December 1923), 219–229.

Sears, Paul B. "Utopia and the Living Landscape," in *Utopias and Utopian Thought,* edited by Frank E. Manuel (Boston: Beacon Press, 1967), pp. 137–149.

Seeber, Edward D. "Ideal Languages in the French and English Imaginàry Voyage." *PMLA,* 60 (June 1945), 586–597.

Seeber, Hans Ulrich. "Bulwer-Lytton's Underworld: *The Coming Race* (1871)." *Moreana,* 30 (May 1971), 39–40.

Seeber, Hans Ulrich. "Hythloday as Preacher and a Possible Debt to Macrobius." *Moreana,* Nos. 31–32 (November 1971), 71–86.

Segal, Howard P. "*Young West:* The Psyche of Technological Utopianism." *Extrapolation,* 19 (December 1977), 50–58.

Séguy, Jean. "Une sociologie des sociétés imaginées; monachisme et utopie." *Annales,* 26 (March-April 1971), 328–354.

Seibt, Ferdinand. "Utopie im Mittelalter." *Historische Zeitschrift,* 208, No. 3 (June 1969), 555–594.

Seiden, Melvin. "Utopianism in the Tempest." *Modern Language Quarterly,* 31 (March 1970), 3–21.

Seitz, Franz. "Utopie-gewendet." *Welt der Schule,* 11, No. 12 (1958), 529–533.

Sempe, Pierre. "L'utopie triste." *Etudes,* 334 (Fall 1976), 231–237.

Sempers, C. T. "Utopian Dreams of Literary Men." *Harvard Monthly,* 3 (December 1886), 95–104.

Sen, Sri Chendra. "Utopias and Visions of the Future World." Calcutta University, *The Letter,* 30 (1939), 1–50.

Servier, Jean. "Il simbolismo onrico dell'utopia," in *L'Utopia nel mondo moderno* (Florence: Vallecchi, 1969), pp. 11–25.

Schaftel, Oscar. "The Social Content of Science Fiction." *Science and Society,* 17 (Spring 1953), 97–118.

Sheehan, Bernard W. "Paradise and the Noble Savage in Jeffersonian Thought." *William and Mary Quarterly,* 3rd series, 26 (July 1969), 327–359.

Shepard, Odell. "Utopia in America," in *American Story,* edited by Earl Schenck Miers (Great Neck, New York: Channel Press, 1956), pp. 154–158.

Sherman, Stuart. "The Utopian Naturalism of Wells," in his *On Contemporary Literature* (New York: Peter Smith, 1931), pp. 50–84.

Sherwin, Proctor Fenn. "Some Sources of More's *Utopia*." *Bulletin of the University of New Mexico,* No. 88. Language Series, 1, No. 3 (September 1917), 167–191.

Shinn, Roger L. "Realism, Radicalism, and Eschatology in Reinhold Neibuhr: A Reassessment." *Journal of Religion,* 54 (October 1974), 409–423.

Shklar, Judith [N.] "The Political Theory of Utopia: From Melancholy to Nostalgia," in *Utopias and Utopian Thought,* edited by Frank E. Manuel (Boston: Beacon Press, 1967), pp. 101–115.

Shklar, Judith N. "Rousseau's Two Models: Sparta and the Age of Gold." *Political Science Quarterly,* 81 (March 1966), 25–51.

Shurter, Robert L. "Introduction," Edward Bellamy, *Looking Backward 2000–1887* (New York: Modern Library, 1951), pp. v–xxi.

Shurter, Robert L. "The Literary Work of Edward Bellamy." *American Literature,* 5 (November 1933), 229–234.

Shurter, Robert L. "The Utopian Novel in America." *South Atlantic Quarterly,* 34 (April 1935), 137–144.

Shurter, Robert L. "The Writing of *Looking Backward.*" *South Atlantic Quarterly,* 38 (July 1939), 255–261.

Shuttleworth, H. C. "Utopias, Ancient and Modern." *Monthly Packet,* 90 (December 1895), 22–37, 174–178, 210–215, 401–406, 544–548, 655–660.

Sibley, Mulford Q. "Apology for Utopia: I. An Examination of Professor Sait's Excogitated Ideas." *Journal of Politics,* 2 (February 1940), 57–74.

Sibley, Mulford Q. "Apology for Utopia: II. Utopia and Politics." *Journal of Politics,* 2 (April 1940), 165–188.

Sibley, Mulford Q. "Nature, Civilization, and the Problem of Utopia," in his *Nature and Civilization: Some Implications for Politics* (Itasca, Illinois: F. E. Peacock Publishers, 1977), pp. 251–303.

Sills, Yole G. "Social Science Fiction," in *International Encyclopedia of the Social Sciences,* Vol. 14, pp. 473–481.

Silva Herzog, Jesús. "La 'Utopía' de Tomás Moro." *Cuadernos Americanos,* 141, No. 4 (July-August 1965), 123–129.

Silverstein, Henry. "The Utopia of Henry James." *New England Quarterly,* 35 (December 1962), 458–468.

Simmonds, James D. "More's Use of Names in Book II of *Utopia.*" *Die Neueren Sprachen,* N.S., No. 6 (June 1961), pp. 282–284.

Simon, Heinrich. "Arabische Utopien im Mittelalter." *Wissenschaftliche Zeitschrift der Humboldt-Universität zu Berlin. Gesellschafts- und Sprachwissenschaftsliche Reihe,* 12, No. 13 (1963), 245–252.

Simon, Marie. "Hellenistische Märchutopien." *Wissenschaftliche Zeitschrift der Humboldt-Universität zu Berlin. Gesellschafts- und Sprachwissenschaftliche Reihe,* 12, No. 3 (1963), 237–243.

Simon, Walter M. "History for Utopia: Saint-Simon and the Idea of Progress." *Journal of the History of Ideas,* 17 (June 1956), 311–331.

Simpson, Alan. "Saints in Arms: English Puritanism as Political Utopianism." *Church History,* 23 (June 1954), 119–125.

Skilton, David. "*The Fixed Period:* Anthony Trollope's Novel of 1980." *Studies in the Literary Imagination,* 6 (Fall 1973), 39–50.

Skinner, B. F. "Utopia and Human Behavior," in *Moral Problems in Contemporary Society,* edited by P. W. Kurtz (Englewood Cliffs, New Jersey: Prentice-Hall, 1969), pp. 96–115.

Skinner, B. F. "Utopia Through the Control of Human Behavior." *Listener,* 77 (January 12, 1967), 55–56.

Skinner, B. F. "Visions of Utopia." *Listener,* 77 (January 5, 1967), 22–23.

Skinner, Quentin. "More's *Utopia.*" *Past and Present,* No. 38 (December 1967), pp. 153–168.

Slater, Joseph. "The Fictional Values of 1984," in *Essays in Literary History Presented to Milton French,* edited by Rudolph Kirk and C.F. Main

(New Brunswick, New Jersey: Rutgers University Press, [1960]), pp. 249–264.

Slaughter, John Willis. "Bacon and the Ideal Commonwealth." *Rice Institute Pamphlets,* 13 (January 1926), 56–72.

Slaughter, J[ohn] W[illis]. "The Utopian Imagination and Social Progress." in *Utopian Papers: Being Addresses to "The Utopians",* edited by Dorothea Hollins (London: Masters, 1908), pp. 41–45.

Slee, J. C. van. "Simon Tyssot de Patot, professeur à l'École Illustre de Deventer (1690–1727)." *Revue du XVIIIᵉ siècle* (January-June 1917), pp. 200–219.

Slosson, Preston. "How to Build Utopias." *The Independent,* 105 (May 7, 1921), 480–481.

Smith, Curtis L. "The Books of Olaf Stapledon: A Chronological Survey." *Science-Fiction Studies,* 1 (Fall 1974), 297–299.

Smith, David E. "Millennarian Scholarship in America." *American Quarterly,* 17 (Fall 1965), 535–549.

Smith, G[eorge] C[harles] Moore. "The Date of the New Atlantis." *Athenaeum,* No. 3771 (February 3, 1900), pp. 146–148.

Smith, Goldwin. "Prophets of Unrest." *Forum,* 9 (August 1890), 599–614.

Smith, John Maynard. "Eugenics and Utopia," in *Utopias and Utopian Thought,* edited by Frank E. Manuel (Boston: Beacon Press, 1967), pp. 150–168.

Smith, Marcus. "The Wall of Blackness: A Psychological Approach to *1984.*" *Modern Fiction Studies,* 14 (Winter 1968–1969), 423–433.

Smith, R. E. F. "Note on the Sources of George Orwell's *1984.*" *Journal of Peasant Studies,* 4, No. 1 (October 1976), 9–10.

Smyer, Richard I. "*1984:* The Search for the Golden Country." *Arizona Quarterly,* 27 (Spring 1971), 41–52.

Snell, Bruno. "Arcadia: The Discovery of a Spiritual Landscape," in his *The Discovery of the Mind: The Greek Origins of European Thought,* translated by T. G. Rosenmeyer (New York: Harper & Row, 1960), pp. 281–309.

Snow, Thomas Collins. "Imagination in Utopia." *Hibbert Journal,* 11 (July 1913), 251–265.

"A Social Optimist [Sir Thomas More]." *Times Literary Supplement* (July 26, August 2, 9, 16, 23, 1917), pp. 349–350, 369, 381, 393, 405.

"Social Utopias." *Chambers's Papers for the People,* 3, No. 18 (1850), 37–68.

"Socialism in Literature." *The Bookman,* 27 (April 1908), 119–123.

Soleri, Paolo. "Utopia and/or Revolution. Utopie e o Revoluzione." *Perspecta,* No. 14, pp. 281–285.

Soloman, Maynard. "Marx and Bloch: Reflections on Utopia and Art." *Telos,* No. 13 (Fall 1972), pp. 68–85.

Sommer, Robert. "Planning 'Notplace' for Nobody." *Saturday Review,* 52 (April 5, 1969), 67–69.

Sorel, Georges. "Y a-t-il de l'utopie dans le marxisme?" *Revue de metaphysique et de morale,* 7 (1899), 152–175.

Sorenson, M. Susan. "An Existential Utopia." *Minnesota Review,* 4 (Spring 1964), 356–364.

Soulie, George. "The United States of the World." *Forum,* 47 (February 1912), 211–221.

Sparks, Edwin E. "Seeking Utopia in America." *Chautauquan,* 31 (May 1900), 151–161.

Spens, Willy de. "Les Royaumes d'Utopie." *La Table Ronde,* Nos. 168–170 (January-March 1962), pp. 60–68, 66–75, 59–65.

Spitz, David. "Bacon's 'New Atlantis': A Reinterpretation." *Midwest Journal of Political Science,* 4 (February 1960), 52–61.

Spriel, Stéphane and Boris Vian. "Un nouveau genre littéraire, la science fiction." *Les Temps modernes,* 7 (October 1951), 618–627.

Stafford, B.M. "Les deux édifices — the new Areopagus and a spiritual trophy: Humbert de Superville's vision of Utopia." *Art Quarterly,* 35, No. 1 (Spring 1972), 49–73.

Stallmach, Josef. "Das Heute dem Morgen geopfert. Vom Wert und der Gefährlichkeit alter und neuer Utopien." *Universitätszeitung,* 7, No. 3 (1952), 12–15.

Stammler, Heinrich A. "Das komfortable Zuchthaus: Zur Häresie des Utopismus im Denken der Gegenwart." *Wort und Wahrheit,* 22 (1967), 610–621.

Stammler, Rudolf. "Utopien." *Deutsche Rundschau,* 70 (January-March 1892), 281–296.

Stanley, Manfred. "Three Post Political Futures." *The Humanist* (November/December 1973), pp. 28–31.

Stanzel, Franz K. "Gulliver's Travels — Satire, Utopie, Dystopie." *Die Moderne Sprachen,* 7 (1963), 106–116.

Stegmeyer, Frank. "Zum Problem des Historischen Utopismus," in Immanuel Kant, *Zum ewigen Frieden* (Frankfurt am Main: Siegel-Verlag, 1946), pp. 5–46.

Stein, Robert. "Naturwissenschaft in Utopia." *Deutsche Geschichtsblätter,* 17 (January 1916), 48–59.

Steinhauer, H. "Hauptmann's Utopian Fantasy, *Die Insel der grossen Mutter.*" *Moderne Language Notes,* 53 (November 1938), 516–521.

Steininger, Alexander. "Scientists in Soviet Literature." *Survey,* No. 52 (July 1964), pp. 157–165.

Steintrager, James. "Plato and More's *Utopia.*" *Social Research,* 36 (Autumn 1969), 357–372.

Stemo, L. Johanne. "Utopias: The Geography of Dreams." *British Columbia Library Quarterly,* 35 (October 1971), 33–37.

Stern, Rev. Herman I. "Who Are the Utopians?" *The Nationalist,* 3 (October 1890), 165–171.

Sternberg, Kurt. "Über Campanellas 'Sonnenstaat.' " *Historische Zeitschrift,* 148, No. 3 (1933), 520–570.

Sternberg, Kurt. "Über die 'Utopia' des Thomas Morus." *Archiv für Rechts- und Wirtschaftsphilosophie,* 26, Nos. 4–27, No. 1 (1932–1934), 464–497, 232–297.

Steuert, Dom Hilary. "More's *Utopia.*" *Downside Review,* 56 (January 1938), 64–75.

Stevens, Irma Ned. "Aesthetic Distance in the *Utopia.*" *Moreana,* Nos. 43–44 (November 1974), pp. 13–24.

Stevick, Philip. "The Limits of Anti-Utopia." *Criticism,* 6 (Summer 1964), 233–245.

Stewart, Herbert L. "The Prophetic Office of Mr. H. G. Wells." *International Journal of Ethics,* 30 (1920), 172–189.

Stillwell, Robert L. "Literature and Utopia: B. F. Skinner's Walden Two." *Western Humanities Review,* 18 (Autumn 1964), 331–341.

Stock, A. G. "The Age of Nightmare." *Research Bulletin (Arts) of the University of the Punjab,* No. 7: *English Literature.* Whole issue.

Stöckl, Albert and Ernst M. Roloff. "Staatsromane," in *Staatslexikon,* 5 Vols. (Freiburg im Breisgau: Herdersche Verlagshandlung, 1912), Vol. 5, pp. 18–31.

Strauss, Sylvia. "Women in 'Utopia.' " *South Atlantic Quarterly,* 75 (Winter 1976), 115–131.

Stupple, A. James. "Towards a Definition of Anti-Utopian Literature," in *Science Fiction: The Academic Awakening,* edited by Willis E. McNelly. Special supplement to *CEA Critic,* 37 (November 1974), 24–30.

Sturgeon, Theodore. "Science Fiction, Morals, and Religion," in *Science Fiction: Today and Tomorrow,* edited by Reginald Bretnor (New York: Harper & Row, 1974), pp. 98–113.

Suchy, Viktor. "Zukunftsvisionen des 20. Jahrhunderts: die utopische Roman der Gegenwart als Diagnose der Zeit." *Wissenschaft und Weltbild,* 5 (1952), 18–29, 338–363.

Suits, Conrad. "The Role of the Horses in 'A Voyage to the Houyhnhnms.' " *University of Toronto Quarterly,* 34, No. 2 (January 1965), 118–132.

Supek, Rudi. "Utopie et réalité." *Praxis,* 8, Nos. 1–2 (1972), 3–7.

Surtz, Edward L., S.J. "Epicurus in Utopia." *ELH,* 16 (June 1949), 89–103.

Surtz, Edward L., S.J. "Interpretations of Utopia," *Catholic Historical Review,* 38 (July 1952), pp. 156–74.

Surtz, Edward L., S.J. "Link Between Pleasure and Communism in Utopia." *Modern Language Notes,* 70 (February 1955), 90–93.

Surtz, Edward L., S.J. "More's *Apologia Pro Utopia Sua.*" *Modern Language Quarterly,* 19 (November 1958), 319–324.

Surtz, Edward L., S.J. "The Setting for More's Plea for Greek in Utopia." *Philological Quarterly,* 35 (October 1956), 353–365.

Surtz, Edward L., S.J. "Sources, Parallels, and Influences," Introduction in *Utopia,* edited by Edward Surtz, S.J., and J.H. Hexter, Vol. 4 of *The Complete Works of St. Thomas More* (New Haven: Yale University Press, 1965), pp. cliii–clxxxi.

Surtz, Edward L., S.J. "Sources, Parallels, and Influences: Supplementary to the Yale Utopia." *Moreana,* No. 9 (February 1966), pp. 5–11.

Surtz, Edward L., S.J. "Thomas More and Communism." *PMLA,* 64 (June 1949), 549–564.

Surtz, Edward L., S.J. "*Utopia* as a Work of Literary Art," Introduction, in *Utopia,* edited by Edward Surtz, S.J., and J.H. Hexter, Vol. 4 of *The Complete Works of St. Thomas More* (New Haven: Yale University Press, 1965), pp. cxxv–cliii.

Susman, Margarete. "Geist der Utopie," in *Ernst Bloch zu ehren: Beiträge zu seinem Werk,* edited by Siegfried Unseld ([Frankfurt am Main:] Suhrkamp, [1965]), pp. 383–394. Reprinted from *Frankfurter Zeitung.*

Suvin, Darko. "Defining the Literary Genre of Utopia: Some Historical Semantics, Some Genology, A Proposal and A Plea." *Studies in the Literary Imagination,* 6 (Fall 1973), 121–145.

Suvin, Darko. "De la tradition utopique dans la science fiction russe." *Communautés Archives Internationales de Sociologie de la Coopération et du Développement,* No. 27 (January-June 1970), pp. 52–78.

Suvin, Darko. "On the Poetics of the Science Fiction Genre." *College English,* 34 (December 1972), 372–382.

Suvin, Darko. "Science Fiction and the Genological Jungle." *Genre,* 6 (September 1973), 251–273.

Suvin, Darko. "SF Theory: Internal and External Delimitations and Utopia (Summary)." *Extrapolation,* 19 (December 1977), 13–15.

Suvin, Darko. "*The Time Machine* versus *Utopia* as a Structural Model for Science Fiction." *Comparative Literature Studies,* 10 (December 1973), 334–352.

Suvin, Darko. " 'Utopian' and 'Scientific': Two Attributes for Socialism from Engels." *Minnesota Review,* N.S. 6 (Spring 1976), pp. 59–70.

Suvin, Darko. "Utopian Tradition of Russian Science Fiction." *Modern Language Review,* 66 (January 1971), 139–159.

Sweet, Paul R. "Young Wilhelm von Humboldt's writings (1789–1793) reconsidered." *Journal of the History of Ideas,* 34 (July 1973), 469–482.

Sweet, William Warren. "The Rise of Frontier Utopias," in his *Religion in the Development of American Culture 1765–1840* (Gloucester, Massachusetts: Peter Smith, 1963), pp. 282–311.

Swinney, S. H. "Comte's View of the Future of Society," in *Utopian Papers: Being Addresses to 'The Utopians'*, edited by Dorothea Hollins (London: Masters, 1908), pp. 102–120.

Sykes, W. J. "Is Wells Also Among the Prophets?" *Queen's Quarterly*, 49 (Autumn 1942), 233–245.

Sylvester, R. S. " 'Si Hythlodaeo Credimsus': Vision and Revision in Thomas More's *Utopia*." *Soundings*, 51 (Fall 1968), 272–289.

Szecsi, Maria. "Zur Pathologie der Utopie." *Neues Forum*, 15, No. 173 (May 1968), 325–328.

Tadić, Ljubomir. "Herbert Marcuse: Zwischen Wissenschaft und Utopie." *Praxis*, 8, Nos. 1–2 (1972), 141–168.

Taft, Philip. "First Utopians," in his *Movements for Economic Reform* (New York: Rinehart, 1950), pp. 6–24.

Talmon, J. L. "Utopianism and Politics: A Conservative View." *Commentary*, 28 (August 1959), 149–154.

Tarbell, Ida M. "New Dealers of the Seventies." *Forum*, 92 (September 1934), 133–139. Discussion 92 (October 1934), 257–260.

Taylor, A. E. "The Decline and Fall of the State in *Republic*, VIII." *Mind*, 48 (January 1939), 23–38.

Taylor, Angus M. "Science Fiction: The Evolutionary Context." *Journal of Popular Culture*, 5 (Spring 1972), 858–866.

Taylor, Walter Fuller. "On the Origin of Howells' Interest in Economic Reform." *American Literature*, 2 (March 1930), 3–14.

Teneti, Alberto. "L'Utopia nel Rinascimento (1450–1550)." *Studi Storici*, 7 (1966), 689–707.

Ten Hoor, Martin. "A City in the Skies." *Journal of Philosophy*, 49 (March 27, 1952), 226–232.

Theall, Donald F. "The Art of Social-Science Fiction: The Ambiguous Utopian Dialectics of Ursula K. LeGuin." *Science-Fiction Studies*, 2 (November 1975), 256–264.

Thieben, Ludwig. "Utopie und Ideal." *Goetheanum*, 13, No. 12 (March 25, 1934), 130–132.

Thier, Erich. "Der Wandel der technischen Utopie." *Kirche en der Zeit*, 9 (1954), 266–267.

Thomas, John L. "Introduction," Edward Bellamy, *Looking Backward 2000–1887* (Cambridge: Belknap Press, 1967), pp. 1–88.

Thomas, W. E. "In Defence of the Utopians." *Nation*, 139 (September 12, 1934), 299.

Thomas, W. K. "The Underside of Utopias." *College English*, 38 (December 1976), 356–372.

Thompson, E. P. "Romanticism, Utopianism, and Moralism: The Case of William Morris." *New Left Review*, 99 (September-October 1976), 83–111.

Tihany, L. C. "Utopia in Modern Western Thought: The Metamorphosis of an Idea," in *Ideas in History: Essays Presented to Louis Gottschalk by His Former Students,* edited by Richard Herr and Harold T. Parker (Durham, North Carolina: Duke University Press, 1965), pp. 20–38.

Tilley, Arthur. " 'Extraordinary' Voyages," in *Decline of the Age of Louis XIV, or, French Literature 1687–1715* (Cambridge: Cambridge University Press, 1929), pp. 169–183.

Tillich, Paul. "Critique and Justification of Utopia," in *Utopias and Utopian Thought,* edited by Frank E. Manuel (Boston: Beacon Press, 1967), pp. 296–309.

Tillich, Paul. "Kairos und Utopie." *Zeitschrift für evangelische Ethik,* 3 (November 1959), 325–331.

Tillich, Paul. "The Political Meaning of Utopia," translated by William J. Crout, Walter Bense, and James L. Adams, in his *Political Expectation* (New York: Harper & Row, 1971), pp. 125–180.

Tillotson, Geoffrey. "Morris and Machines." *Fortnightly Review,* 41 (April 1934), 464–471.

Tilman, Rick. "Ideology and Utopia in the Political Economy of Milton Friedman." *Polity,* 8 (Spring 1976), 422–442.

Tilman, Rick. "Thorstein Veblen: Incrementalist and Utopian." *American Journal of Economics and Sociology,* 32 (April 1973), 155–169.

Toldo, Pietro. "Les voyages merveilleux de Cyrano de Bergerac et de Swift, et leurs rapports avec l'oeuvre de Rabelais." *Revue des Études Rabelaisiennes,* 6 (1906), 295–334.

Töpfer, Bernard. "Die Entwicklung chiliastischer Zukunftserwartungen im Mittelalter." *Wissenschaftliche Zeitschrift der Humboldt-Universität zu Berlin. Gesellschafts- und Sprachwissenschaftsliche Reihe,* 12, No. 3 (1963), 253–262.

Topitsch, Ernst. "Die entzauberte Utopie." *Neue deutsche Hefte,* 4, No. 20 (1973), 3–25.

Towers, Tom H. "The Insomnia of Julian West." *American Literature,* 47 (March 1975), 52–63.

Townsend, S. R. "Modern Prophecy by Michael Jordan Conrad." *German Quarterly,* 31 (November 1958), 259–268.

Traugott, John. "A Voyage to Nowhere with Thomas More and Jonathan Swift: *Utopia* and the *Voyage to the Houyhnhnms.*" *Sewanee Review,* 69 (Autumn 1961), 534–565.

Trousson, Raymond. "Utopie et roman utopique." *Revue des sciences humaines,* 39, No. 155 (July-September 1974), 367–378.

Tuzinski, Ludwig. "Kultur- und Gesellschaftskritik im modernen englischen Zukunftsroman," in *Literatur — Kultur — Gesellschaft in England und Amerika. Aspekte und Forschungsbeiträge Friedrich Schubel zum 60 Geburtstag,* edited by Gerhard Müller-Schwefe und Konrad Tuzinski (Frankfurt am Main: Verlag Moritz Diesterweg, 1966), pp. 278–298.

Tyler, Alice Felt. "Cults and Utopias," in her *Freedom's Ferment: Phases of American Social History to 1860* (Minneapolis: University of Minnesota Press, 1944), pp. 46–224.

Tyng, Dudley. "The Confucian Utopia." *Journal of the American Oriental Society,* 54 (March 1934), 67–69.

Ulam, Adam. "Socialism and Utopia," in *Utopias and Utopian Thought,* edited by Frank E. Manuel (Boston: Beacon Press, 1967), pp. 116–134.

Underwood, John Curtis. "William Dean Howells and Altruria," in his *Literature and Insurgency* (New York: Biblo & Tannen, 1974), pp. 87–129.

Uscatescu, Giorgio. "L'Utopia sociale contemporanea," reprinted from Nos. 5–6 of *I Problemi Della Pedagogia* (September-December, 1963).

"Utopia." *The Golden Book Magazine,* 9 (January 1929), 36–39.

"Utopia." *The New Statesman,* 10 (January 5, 1918), 324–325.

"Utopia and Anti-Utopia." *Perspecta,* No. 14, pp. 209–285.

"Utopia Arraigned." *Freedom,* 23 (April 14, 1962), 2.

"Utopian Banquets." *National Review,* 9 (July 1859), 100–117.

"Utopian Urge: You Make the Future Today." *Harper's,* 246 (March 1973), 5–12, 101–103.

"Utopias." *Sociological Review,* 15 (July 1923), 241–245.

"Utopias." *Unpopular Review,* 10 (October-December 1918), 355–367.

"Utopias." *Yale Reports,* No. 366 (June 6, 1965), pp. 1–7.

"Utopie de Ville." *Werk,* 57, No. 8 (August 1970), 494.

"Utopien." *Materialdienst,* 18 (1955), 160–163.

"Utopische Funktion in Bildender Kunst und Architektur. Ein Interview mit Professor Ernst Bloch." *Werk,* 60 (September 1973), 1058–1062.

"Utopisten und Anti-Utopisten." *Der Monat,* 3, No. 32 (1951), 208–209.

Valkhoff, P. "De wonderbaarlike Reizen van Simon Tyssot de Patot." *De Gids* (February 1931), pp. 239–260.

Vandenberg, Stephen G. "Great Expectations, or the Future of Psychology (as seen in Science Fiction)." *American Psychologist,* 11 (1956), 287–298.

Van Loggem, Manuel. "Die amerikanische Zukunftsgeschichte oder die Science Fiction." *Akzente,* 4 (October 1957), 412–424.

Varwig, Roland. "Leibesübung und Körperliche Erziehung in Utopien." *Die Leibesübungen,* No. 10 (1931), pp. 259–262.

Vattimo, Gianni. "Sprache, Utopie, Musik." *Philosophische Perspektiven,* 4 (1972), 151–170.

Vedel, Georges. "L'Avenir politique de l'humanité à travers trois romans d'anticipation." *Revue des lettres modernes,* 1 (June-July 1954), 46–64.

Vida Najera, Fernando. "Estudios sobre el concepto y la organización del estado en las utopias." *Revista Ciencas Juridicas,* 11, No. 44 (July-September 1928), 315–368.

Vidler, Anthony. "The New Industrial World: The Reconstruction of Urban Utopia in Late Nineteenth Century France." *Perspecta,* No. 14, pp. 243–256.

Vincent, Bernard. "Paul Goodman et le paradigme perdu." *Esprit,* 42 (April 1974), 614–624.

Vincent, George E. "Utopia the Land of Nowhere." *Chautauquan,* 44 (September 1906), 90–97.

Virilio, Paul. "L'évangile nucléaire." *Esprit,* 42 (April 1974), 643–662.

Virnisch, M. "Die Erkenntnistheorie Campanellas und Fr. Bacons." No. 11 of *Renaissance und Philosophie. Beitrage zur Geschichte der Philosophie* (Bonn, 1920).

Visser, A. J. "Eerherstel der Utopie? iets naar aanleiding van een ergerlijk theologisch taalmisbruik." *Kerk en Theologie,* No. 25 (1974), pp. 1–11.

Viteles, Morris S. "The New Utopia." *Science,* 122 (December 16, 1955), 1167–1171.

Vlachos, Evan. "The Future in the Past: Towards a Utopian Syntax." Chapter III of 1972 American Anthropological Association Experimental Symposium on Cultural Futuristics: Pre-Conference Volume.

Vogelin, S. "Utopia des Thomas Morus." *Neue Gesellschaft, Monatsschrift für Sozialwissenschaft,* 1, Nos. 4, 12 (January, September 1878), 178–189, 617–635.

Vogt, Karl. "Utopisten," in *Die Religion im Geschichte und Gegenwart,* 5 Vols. (Tübingen: Mohr, 1909–1913), Vol. 5, pp. 1539–1546.

Voise, Waldemar. "Les Utopies et la pensée présociologique au XVIᵉ siècle," in *Italia, Venezia e Polonia; Tra Umanisimo e Rinascimento,* compiled by Mieczyclaw Braher (Wroclaw: Zaklad Narodowy imienia Ossolinskeisk, 1967), pp. 107–119.

Volkmann-Schluck, K.-H. "Wie die Idee zur Utopie Wurde." *Praxis,* 8, Nos. 1-2 (1972), 39–46.

"Voyage en Icarie." *Quarterly Review,* 83 (June 1848), 165–178.

"*A Voyage to the Moon: with Some Account of the Manners and Customs, Science and Philosophy, of the People of Morosofia and other Lunarians:* By Joseph Atterley. [Book review]." *American Quarterly Review,* 3, No. 5 (March 1828), 61–88.

Vuarnet, Jean-Noël. "Utopie et atopie." *Littérature,* No. 21 (February 1976), pp. 3–9.

Wagar, W. Warren. "H. G. Wells and the Radicalism of Despair." *Studies in the Literary Imagination,* 6 (Fall 1973), 1–10.

Wagar, W. Warren. "Utopian Studies and Utopian Thought: Definitions and Horizons." *Extrapolation,* 19 (December 1977), 4–12.

Wagener, Hans. "Faramonds *Glükseligste Insel:* eine pietistische Sozialutopie." *Symposium,* 26 (Spring 1972), 78–89.

Wagner, Friedrich. "Utopie und Wissenschaft," in his *Wissenschaft in unserer Zeit* (Cologne: Böhlau Verlag, 1957), pp. 37–50.

Walden, Daniel. "Edward Bellamy and William Dean Howells: The Infinity Beyond." *Journal of Human Relations,* 12 (1964), 325–334.

Walden, Daniel. "The Intellectual and the American Dream, Possibilities and Disillusionment From the Jacksonians to the Progressives," in Daniel Walden (ed.) *American Reform: The Ambiguous Legacy, Journal of Human Relations,* 15 (1967), 13–25.

Walker, Frances A. "Mr. Bellamy and the New Nationalist Party." *Atlantic Monthly,* 65 (February 1890), 248–262.

Walsh, Chad. "Attitudes Towards Science in the Modern 'Inverted Utopia.' " *Extrapolation,* 2 (May 1961), 23–26.

Walsh, Chad. "Pros and Cons of Paradise." *Saturday Review,* 49 (30 July 1966), 36–37.

Walsh, James. "George Orwell." *Marxist Quarterly,* 3 (January 1956), 25–39.

Walsh, James J. "Utopia: Where Men Were Happy." *American Catholic Quarterly Review,* 42 (July 1917), 435–453.

Walsh, William. "Utopia Lost: Satire." *Catholic World,* 122 (January-February 1926), 433–442, 600–607.

Walter, Nicolas. "Damned Fools in Utopia." *New Left Review,* Nos. 13–14 (January-April 1972), pp. 119–128.

Walter, Nicolas. "George Orwell: An Accident in Society." *Anarchy 8,* 1 (October 1961), 246–255.

Walters, Hellmut. "Das letzte Reich. Zum Wesen der Utopie." *Erdkreis,* No. 19 (1969), pp. 177–186.

Warner, Edwin. "A Voyage to Utopia in the Year 1971." *Time,* 97 (January 18, 1971), pp. 18–19.

Warrick, Patricia. "The Sources of Zamiatin's *We* in Dostoevsky's *Notes from Underground.*" *Extrapolation,* 17 (December 1975), 63–77.

Watson, Goodwin. "Utopia and Rebellion: The New College Experiment." *School and Society,* 92 (February 22, 1964), 72, 77–84.

Weber Eugen. "The Anti-Utopia of the Twentieth Century." *South Atlantic Quarterly,* 58 (Summer 1959), 440–447.

Weber, Katherina. "Staats- und Bildungsideale in den Utopien des 16. und 17. Jahrhunderts." *Historisches Jahrbuch,* 51, No. 3 (1931), 307–338.

Webster, Charles. "The Authorship and Significance of *Macaria.*" *Past and Present,* No. 56 (August 1972), pp. 34–48.

Webster, Charles. "*Macaria:* Samuel Hartlib and the Great Reformation." *Acta Comeniana,* 26 (1970), 147–164.

Wei, Tan Tai. "The Question of a Cosmomorphic Utopia." *Personalist,* 55 (Autumn 1974), 401–406.

Weinberger, J. "Science and Rule in Bacon's Utopia: An Introduction to the Reading of the *New Atlantis." American Political Science Review,* 70 (September 1976), 865–885.

Weinkauf, Mary S. "Edenic Motifs in Utopian Fiction." *Extrapolation,* 11 (December 1969), 15–22.

Weinkauf, Mary S. "Escape from the Garden." *Texas Quarterly,* 16 (Autumn 1973), 66–72.

Weinkauf, Mary S. "Five Spokesmen for Dystopia." *Midwest Quarterly,* 16 (January 1975), 175–186.

Weinkauf, Mary [S.] "The God Figure in Dystopian Fiction." *Riverside Quarterly,* 4 (March 1971), 266–271.

Weintrub, Stanley. "Homage to Utopia," in his *The Last Great Cause: The Intellectuals and the Spanish Civil War* (New York: Weybright and Talley, 1968), pp. 88–119.

Weiss, Joseph G. "Eine spatjudische Utopie religioser Freiheit." in *Vom Sinn der Utopia. Eranos-Jahrbuch 1963* (Zurich: Rhein-Verlag, 1964), pp. 235–280.

Weisskopf, Walter A. "The Psychology of Abundance," in *Looking Forward: The Abundant Society* (Santa Barbara: Center for the Study of Democratic Institutions, 1966), pp. 3–12.

Wellbank, Joseph H. "Utopia and the Constraints of Justice," in *Utopia/Dystopia?,* edited by Peyton E. Richter (Cambridge, Massachusetts: Schenkman Publishing Co., 1975), pp. 31–41.

Wells, H. G. "An Apology for a World Utopia," in *The Evolution of World Peace. The Unity Series. IV.,* edited by F.S. Marvin (London: Humphrey Milford, Oxford University Press, 1921), pp. 159–178.

Wells, H. G. "The So-called Science of Sociology." *Independent Review,* 6 (May 1905), 21–37.

Welskopf, Elisabeth Charlotte. "Entwicklungsstadien und Probleme: der Utopie im Altertum Einführung," *Wissenschaftliche Zeitschrift der Humboldt-Universtät zu Berlin. Gesellschafts- und Sprachwissenschaftsliche Reihe,* 12, No. 3 (1963), 195–202.

Welskopf, Elisabeth Charlotte. "Zur Entstehung der Utopie bei Platon." *Wissenschaftliche Zeitschrift der Humboldt-Universtät zu Berlin. Gesellschafts- und Sprachwissenschaftsliche Reihe,* 12, No. 3 (1963), pp. 229–235.

Wescott, Roger W. "Traditional Greek Conceptions of the Future," in 1972 American Anthropological Association Experimental Symposium - on Cultural Futurology, 1972.

West, R. H. "Science Fiction and Its Ideas." *Georgia Review,* 15 (Fall, 1961), 276–286.

Westlake, J. H. J. "Aldous Huxley's *Brave New World* and George Orwell's *1984:* A Comparative Study." *Neueren Sprachen,* 71 (N.S. 21), No. 2 (February 1972), 94–102.

Westmeyer, Russell E. "The Quest for Utopia," in his *Modern Economic and Social Systems* (New York: Farrar & Rinehart, 1940), pp. 3–96.

Wheatley, Richard. "Ideal Commonwealths." *Methodist Review,* 75 (July 1893), 581–597.

White, Howard B. "Political Faith and Francis Bacon." *Social Research,* 23 (Fall 1956), 343–366.

White, Thomas I. "Aristotle and Utopia." *Renaissance Quarterly,* 29, No. 4 (1976), 635–675.

Whittier, John Greenleaf. "Utopian Schemes and Political Theories," in *The Writings of John Greenleaf Whittier,* 7 Vols. (Boston: Houghton, Mifflin, 1889), Vol. 7, pp. 199–208.

Widmer, Kingsley. "Subterranean Universities? Reflections on Utopian Institutions." *AAUP Bulletin,* 57 (December 1971), 470–474.

Wieser, Wolfgang. "Die genetische Utopie," in *Club Voltaire, Jahrbuch für kritische Aufklarung I,* edited by Gerhard Szczesny (Munich: Szczesny Verlag, 1963), pp. 385–400.

Wijngarden, Nicholas Van. "Un double problème bibliographique et littéraire." *Bulletin du bibliophile et du bibliothécaire,* N.S. 12 (1934), pp. 439–446.

Wild, P. H. "Teaching Utopia: *Looking Backward* and *1984.*" *English Journal,* 55 (March 1966), 335–337.

Williams, C. H. "More's Utopia." *Open Court,* 31 (October 1917), 593–614.

Williams, C. H. "Sir Thomas More." *Open Court,* 31 (September 1917), 513–525.

Williams, Donald C. "The Social Scientist as Philosopher and King." *Philosophical Review,* 58 (July 1949), 345–359.

Williams, Kathleen M. "Gulliver's Voyage to the Houyhnhnms." *ELH,* 18 (December 1951), 275–286.

Williams, Preston N. "Black Perspectives on Utopia," in *Utopia/Dystopia?,* edited by Peyton E. Richter (Cambridge, Massachusetts: Schenkman Publishing Co., 1975), pp. 45–56.

Wills, Bernard. "Zur Dialektik der Planung: Fichte als Theoretiker einer geplanten Gesellschaft," in *Säkularisation und Utopie. Ebracher Studien. Ernst Forsthoff zum 65. Geburtstag* (Stuttgart: W. Kohlhammer Verlag, 1967), pp. 155–167.

Wilson, Bryan A. "Building Heaven on Earth." *Time and Tide,* 43 (January 4, 1972), 32–33.

Wilson, Bryan A. "Millennialism in Comparative Perspective." *Comparative Studies in Society and History,* 6 (1963), 93–114.

Wilson, John T. "Is Utopia possible," *English,* 20 (Summer 1971), 51–55.

Wimsatt, W. K. "In Praise of Rasselas: Four Notes (Converging)," in *Imagined Worlds: Essays on Some English Novels and Novelists in Honour of*

John Butt, edited by Maynard Mack and Ian Gregor (London: Methuen, 1968), pp. 111–136.

Winston, David. "Iambulus's *Islands of the Sun* and Hellenistic Literary Utopias." *Science-Fiction Studies,* 3 (November 1976), 219–227.

Winthrop, Henry. "Space Colonization and the Quest for Community." *Dalhousie Review,* 46 (Summer 1966), 233–248.

Winthrop, Henry. "Utopia Construction and Future Forecasting: Problems, Limitations, and Relevance," in *The Sociology of the Future,* edited by Wendell Bell and James A. Mau (New York: Russell Sage Foundation, 1971), pp. 78–105.

Wissel, Rudolf. "Zur Geschichte utopischer Staatsideen." *Archives für die Geschichte der Sozialismus und der Arbeiterwegismus,* 13 (1928), 65–79.

Wolfe, Don M. "Utopian Dissent and Affirmation: Howells, Bellamy and George," in his *The Image of Man in America,* 2nd edition (New York: Thomas Y. Crowell, 1970), pp. 169–198.

Wolfe, G. K. "Vonnegut and the Metaphor of Science Fiction: The Sirens of Titan." *Journal of Popular Culture,* 5 (Spring 1972), 964–969.

Wolfe, Peter. "*Walden Two* Twenty-five Years Later: A Retrospective Look." *Studies in the Literary Imagination,* 6 (Fall 1973), 11–26.

Wolff, Max J. "Englische Utopisten der Renaissance. Thomas More und Bacon." *Germanisch-Romanische Monatsschrift,* 16 (March/April 1928), 136–150.

Wolff, Max J. "Die Idee des Zukunftstaates in Altertum und Neuzeit." *Westermanns Monatshefte,* 142 (July 1927), 547–550.

Wolgin, W. P. [Volgin, Vyacheslav Petrovich]. "Campanellas Kommunistische Utopie," in Thomas Campanella, *Der Sonnenstaat: Idee eines philosophischen Gemeinwesens* (Berlin: Akademie-Verlag, 1955), pp. 5–13.

Wood, Joseph. "Some Utopias Past and Present," in *Utopian Papers: Being Addresses to 'The Utopians,'* edited by Dorothea Hollins (London: Masters, 1908), pp. 17–44.

Wood, Michael. "Freak Utopias." *New Society,* 24 (October 1968), 609.

Woodcock, George. "The Darkness Violated by Light: A Revisionist View of H. G. Wells." *Malahat Review,* No. 26 (April 1973), pp. 144–160.

Woodcock, George. "De Mille and the Utopian Vision." *Journal of Canadian Fiction,* 2, No. 3 (Summer 1973), 174–179.

Woodcock, George. "Utopias in Negative." *Sewanee Review,* 64 (Winter 1956), 81–97.

Woods, Katharine Pearson. "Edward Bellamy: Author and Economist." *The Bookman,* 7 (July 1898), 398–401.

Woody, Thomas. "In Utopia," in his *Life and Education in Early Societies* (New York: Macmillan, 1949), pp. 417–465.

Works, Austin M. "Utopias in Literature," *English Journal,* 22 (April 1933), 273-276.

Wrede, Friedrich Fürst von. "Die Entwicklung des Staatsromans." *Deutsche Révue,* 30, No. 1 (1905), 141-156.

Wright, John K. "Terrae Incognitae: The Place of the Imagination in Geography." *Annals of the Association of American Geographers,* 37 (March 1947), 1-15.

Wrinch, Dorothy Maud. "Bernard Bolzano." *Monist,* 27 (January 1917), 83-104.

Wynne-Tyson, Esme. "A Communist Utopia." *Contemporary Review,* 186 (December 1954), 368-370.

Youngblood, Gene. "World Game part two. The Ecological Revolution." *Chinook,* 2, No. 18 (May 14, 1970), 6, 14.

Zaehner, R. C. "Utopia and Beyond: Some Indian Views," in *Vom Sinn der Utopie. Eranos-Jahrbuch 1963* (Zürich: Rhein-Verlag, 1964), pp. 281-309.

Zaniello, Thomas. "Outopia in Jorge Luis Borges' Fiction." *Extrapolation,* 9 (December 1967), 3-17.

Zavala, Iris M. "Dreams of Reality: Enlightened Hopes for an Unattainable Spain." *Studies in the Eighteenth Century,* 6 (1977), 459-470.

Zavala, Silvio. "The American Utopia of the Sixteenth Century." *Huntington Library Quarterly,* 10 (August 1947), 337-347.

Zavala, Silvio. "Letras de Utopia Carta a Don Alfonso Reyes." *Cuadernos americanos,* 2 (1942), 146-162.

Zavala, Silvio. "La Utopia de America en el siglo XVI." *Revista nacional de cultura* (Caracas), No. 58 (September/October 1946), pp. 117-129. Also published in *Cuadernos Americanos,* 141, No. 4 (July-August 1965), 130-138.

Zemke, Kurt. "Der Bankerott des Utopismus." *Ludendorff's Volkswarte,* 3, No. 30 (July 6, 1931).

Zenkovsky, V. V. "Der Geist der Utopie im russischen Denken." *Orient und Occident,* No. 16 (1934), pp. 23-31.

Ziegler, Theobald. "Utopien und Staatsromane." *Die Wahrheit,* Vol. 7, pp. 377-382.

Zilberfarb, Johanson. "Les études sur Fourier et le fouriérisme vues par un historien." *Revue internationale de Philosophie,* No. 60 (1962), pp. 261-279.

Zipes, Jack. "Breaking the Magic Spell: Politics and the Fairy Tale." *New German Critique,* 6 (1975), 116-135.

Zuckerkandel, Victor. "Die Wahrheit des Traumes und der Traum der Wahrheit," in *Vom Sinn der Utopie. Eranos-Jahrbuch 1963* (Zürich: Rhein-Verlag, 1964), pp. 173-210.

UNPUBLISHED MATERIALS

Abensour, M. "Les Formes de l'utopie socialiste-communiste." Dissertation, Paris 1, 1973.

Ackermann, Elfriede Maria. "*Das Schlaraffenland* in German Literature and Folksong. Social Aspects of an Earthly Paradise, with an Inquiry into its History in European Literature." Dissertation, University of Chicago, 1944.

Adams, Robert Pardee, "The Philosophical Unity of More's Utopia." Unpublished doctoral dissertation, University of Chiago, 1937.

Aiken, John. "Utopianism and the Emergence of the Colonial Legal Profession, New York, 1664–1710, A Test Case." Unpublished doctoral dissertation, University of Rochester, 1966.

Anderton, Elizabeth Anne. "Utopian Ideas and their Effects in English Fiction, 1890–1955." Unpublished M.A. thesis, London University, 1958.

Arnquist, James Dennis. "Images of Catholic Utopianism and Radicalism in Industrial America." Unpublished doctoral dissertation, University of Minnesota, 1968.

Bailey, James Osler. "The Scientific Novels of H. G. Wells." Unpublished M.A. thesis, University of North Carolina, 1927.

Bailey, John Osler. "Scientific Fiction in English 1817–1914. A Study of Trends and Forms." University of North Carolina, 1934.

Barber, Otto. "H. G. Wells' Verhältnis zum Darwinismus." Dissertation, Munich, 1934.

Bendemann, Oswald, "Studie zur Staats- und Sozialauffassung der Thomas Morus," Dissertation, Berlin, 1928.

Berger, Harold L. "Anti-Utopian Science Fiction of the Mid-Twentieth Century." Unpublished doctoral dissertation, University of Tennessee, 1970.

Bikle, George Brown. "The New Jerusalem: Aspects of Utopianism in the Thought of Kagawa Toyohiko." Unpublished doctoral dissertation, University of California, Berkeley, 1968.

Bleich, David. "Utopia: The Psychology of a Cultural Fantasy." Unpublished doctoral dissertation, New York University, 1968.

Bliesener, Erich. "Zum Begriff der Utopie." Dissertation, Frankfurt am Main, 1950.

Blum, Irving D. "Avarice in English Utopias and Satires from 1551 to 1714." Unpublished doctoral dissertation, Rutgers University, 1953.

Boggs, W. Arthur. "The Literary Sources of Edward Bellamy's *Looking Backward*." Unpublished M.A. thesis, University of Southern California, 1941.

Böttger, Heinz. "Samuel Butlers satirische Romane und ihre literarische Bedeutung." Dissertation, Marburg, 1936.

Bowen, Roger. "Isolation, Utopia, and Anti-Utopia: The Island Motif in the

Literary Imagination. A Selective History of the Archetype and Its Characteristics, with Special Studies in H. G. Wells, Joseph Conrad, and William Golding." Unpublished doctoral dissertation, Harvard University, 1972.

Brostowin, Patrick R. "John Adolphus Etzler: Scientific — Utopian during the 1830's and 1840's." Unpublished doctoral dissertation, New York University, 1969.

Browning, William Gordon. "Anti-Utopian Fiction: Definition and Standards for Evaluation." Unpublished doctoral dissertation, Louisiana State University, 1966.

Burt, Donald C. "Utopia and the Agrarian Tradition in America, 1865–1900." Unpublished doctoral dissertation, University of New Mexico, 1973.

Carlock, Nancy. "An Analysis of Utopian Concepts in Selected Nineteenth Century Fiction." Unpublished doctoral dissertation, Occidental University, 1964.

Cary, Francine Curro. "Shaping the Future in the Golden Age: A Study of Utopian Thought, 1888–1900." Unpublished doctoral dissertation, University of Wisconsin, 1975.

Christensen, John Michael. "Utopia and the Late Victorians: A Study of Popular Literature, 1970–1900." Dissertation, Northwestern University, 1974.

Cole, Susan Ablon. "The Utopian Plays of George Bernard Shaw: A Study of the Plays and their Relationship to the Fictional Utopias of the Period from the Early 1870's to the Early 1920's." Unpublished doctoral dissertation, Brandeis University, 1972.

Cruse, Hans. "Die Utopia des Thomas Morus und die soziale Frage." Dissertation Erlangen, 1904.

Curzon, Gordon Anthony. "Paradise Sought: A Study of the Religious Motivation in Representative British and American Literary Utopias, 1850–1950." Unpublished doctoral dissertation, University of California, Riverside, 1969.

Däubler, Alfred. "Die Utopie als Denkform." Dissertation, Tübingen, 1951.

Decoo, Wilfried L. J. "Utopie et transcendence: Essai sur la signification de la religion dans les utopies littéraires." Unpublished doctoral dissertation, Brigham Young University, 1974.

Dege, Charlotte. "Utopie und Satire in Swifts Gulliver's Travels," Dissertation, Jena, 1934.

De Maria, Robert. "From Bulwer-Lytton to George Orwell: The Utopian Novel in England 1870–1950." Unpublished doctoral dissertation, Columbia University, 1959.

Diaconu, Emil I. "Utopia in Literatura Engleza." Dissertation, Cluj, 1936.

Durán, Juan Guillermo. "Literatura y Utopia en Hispanoamerica." Unpublished doctoral dissertation, Cornell University, 1972.

Ekstrom, William F. "The Social Idealism of William Morris and William Dean Howells: A Study of Four Utopian Novels." Unpublished doctoral dissertation, University of Illinois, 1947.

Emkes, Max Adolf. "Das Erziehungsideal bei Sir Thomas More, Sir Thomas Elyot, Roger Ascham und John Lyly." Dissertation, Marburg, 1904.

Ewbank, David Robert. "The Role of Woman in Victorian Society: A Controversy Explored in Six Utopias, 1871–1895." Unpublished doctoral dissertation, University of Illinois, 1968.

Falke, Rita. "Persönliche Freiheit und die Utopien." Dissertation, Hamburg, 1954.

Fink, Teresina. "Die deutsche Utopie in der neueren deutschen Dichtung." Dissertation, Vienna, 1939.

Fisher, Robert Thaddeus. "A Historical Study of the Educational Theories Contained in the Classical Utopias." Unpublished doctoral dissertation, Michigan State University, 1959.

Fox, Vivian Carol. "Deviance in English Utopias in the 16th, 17th and 18th Centuries." Unpublished doctoral dissertation, Boston University Graduate School, 1969.

Fulweiler, Howard Wells. "Heaven Versus Utopia: A Study of the *Tracts for the Times,* 1883–1841." Unpublished doctoral dissertation, University of North Carolina, 1960.

Gelbart, Nina Rattner. " 'Science' in Enlightenment Utopias: Power and Purpose in Eighteenth-Century French 'Voyages imaginaires.' " Unpublished doctoral dissertation, University of Chicago, 1974.

Grant, Lawrence Vernon. "The Utopian Novel as Political Theory: The Utopian Thought of Edward Bellamy and B. F. Skinner." M.A. thesis, University of Illinois, 1968.

Guenther, Paul F. "A Survey of Utopia Before 1800." Unpublished doctoral dissertation, University of North Carolina, 1955.

Günther, Max. "Entstehungsgeschichte von Defoes Robinson Crusoe." Dissertation, Greifswald, 1909.

Gutter, Agnes. "Freie und Staatliche Fürsorge. Sozialtheoretische Untersuchung mit besonderer Berücksichtigung der Staatsutopien." Dissertation, Freiburg, 1948.

Hallgren, I. "Changes in Conceptions of English Literary Utopias." Unpublished B. Phil. thesis, St. Andrews University, 1958.

Hardt, Maria Agnelies, S.A.C. "Die Anthropologie H. G. Wells' Darstellung und Kritik seines Utopischen Menschenbildes." Dissertation, Bonn. 1949.

Hearn, Betty Holland. "An Interpretative Study of the Relationship Between Political and Educational Theory in Four Literary Utopias." Unpublished doctoral dissertation, University of Mississippi, 1972.

Heckel, Joseph. "Das Bevölkerungsproblem und die Staatsromane." Dissertation, Breslau, 1923.

Hercourt, Raymond. "L'Utopie de Thomas Morus." Thesis, Poitiers, 1911.

Herzog, Arthur, III. "Revolt in Utopia. A Study of Utopian Writings in Modern British and American Literature." Unpublished M.A. thesis, Columbia University, [1956].

Highland, Harry Joseph. "Utopian Education: A Study of the Ideal Worlds from Sir Thomas More to H.G. Wells." 2 Vols., unpublished doctoral dissertation, New York University, 1943.

Hill, David R. "Creative Eutopia: The Political Thought of Lewis Mumford." Unpublished doctoral dissertation, University of Minnesota, 1972.

Hillegas, Mark Robert. "The Cosmic Voyage and the Doctrine of Inhabited Worlds in Nineteenth-Century Literature." Dissertation, Columbia University, 1957.

Hoover, Ernest L. "The Christian Utopia." Unpublished doctoral dissertation, Dallas Theological Seminary, 1952.

Hoyenga, Betty Ritchie. "Samuel Butler's *Erewhon:* A Critical and Annotated Edition." Dissertation, University of Nebraska-Lincoln, 1967.

Hubner, Herbert. "Die soziale Utopie des Bauhauses. Ein Beitrag zur Wissenssoziologie der Bildenden Kunst." Dissertation, Munster, 1962.

Huntemann, Georg H. "Utopische Menschenbild und utopische Bewusstsein im 19. und 20. Jahrhundert. Geschichte der Utopien von Etienne Cabet bis George Orwell als geschichte utopishen Selbstverständnisses." Dissertation, Erlangen, 1953.

Hutchinson, Mary Louise. "The Influence of Science Upon H. G. Wells." Unpublished thesis, University of Chicago, 1927.

Huttenhower, Helen Graham. "Utopian Conceptions of Education as a Social Force." Master's essay, Johns Hopkins University, School of Higher Studies in Education, 1936.

Iles, Robert L. "Limitations on Individualism in the Utopias of Bellamy and Morris." M.A. thesis, Bowling Green State University Press, 1960.

Jackson, Alan Stewart. "George Orwell's Utopian Vision." Unpublished doctoral dissertation, University of Southern California, 1965.

Kaiser, Helmut Horst. "Subjekt und Gesellschaft. Studie zum Begriff der Utopie." Dissertation, Frankfurt am Main, 1961.

Kateb, George. "Anti-Utopianism." Dissertation, Columbia University, 1960.

Keeler, Clinton Clarence. "The Grass Roots of Utopia: A Study of the Literature of the Agrarian Revolt in America, 1880–1900." Unpublished doctoral dissertation, University of Minnesota, 1953.

Kern, Helmut. "Staatsutopie und allgemeine Staatslehre: ein Beitrag zur allgemeinen Staatslehre unter besonderer Berücksichtigung von Thomas Morus und H. G. Wells." Dissertation, Mainz, 1951.

Kerr, Stephen Thomas. "Future Perfect? The Image of the Coming Society in

Soviet Science Fiction, 1957-1968." Unpublished M.A. thesis, Columbia University, [1969].

Kessler, Meta. "Weltanschauung und Kulturideale bei Thomas More. Ein Beitrag zur Geschichte des Humanismus." Dissertation, Munster, 1926.

Kesting, Hanno. "Utopie und Eschatologie. Ein Beitrag zur Geistesgeschichte des 19. Jahrhunderts." Dissertation, Heidelberg, 1952.

Kirchmann, George H. "Utopia and Reality: The Life and Social Theories of Victor Considerant." Unpublished doctoral dissertation, City University of New York, 1973.

Klein, Mary Ann. "Conceptual and Artistic Limits of Eight Nineteenth-Century British Literary Utopias." Unpublished doctoral dissertation, Marquette University, 1973.

Klemm, Heinrich. "Die beiden liberalen Utopien bei Franz Oppenheimer und in der Freiburger Schule: Eine vergleichsweise und kritische Betrachtung." Dissertation, Tübingen, 1950.

Knepper, Bill Garton. "*Back to Methuselah* and the Utopian Tradition." Unpublished doctoral dissertation, University of Nebraska, 1967.

Knight, J. Richard. "Political Scepticism in Robert Burton's *Anatomy of Melancholy:* Prolegomenon to 'An Utopia of Mine Own.'" Dissertation, Washington University, 1969.

Koch, Fritz. "Bellamys Zukunftsstaat (Analyse und Kritik)." Dissertation, Bonn, 1924.

Koerner, James David. "Triumph of the Dinosaurs: A Study of the Politico-Economic Novel of Protest in America, 1888-1906." Unpublished doctoral dissertation, Washington University, 1952.

Kolar, Heinz. "Das Problem der sozialen Gerechtigkeit in den deutschen Staatsroman und Utopien mit Berücksichtigung der englischen." Dissertation, Vienna, 1936.

Kritzman, Edwin M.J. "The Pre-War German Utopian Novel." Unpublished doctoral dissertation, Brown University, 1936.

Lang, W[ilbert] J[ason]. "Utopias: [A Chronological List, 395 B.C. — 1920 A.D.]." Manuscript, Harvard University Library, nd.

Leary, Paul M. "The Romantic Reaction: Politics and Utopia in Contemporary Social Criticism." Unpublished doctoral dissertation, Rutgers - The State University, 1966.

Leitenberg, Barbara. "The New Utopias." Unpublished doctoral dissertation, Indiana University, 1975.

Leo, Robert Joseph. "Tommaso Campanella: Rhetorician and Utopian." Unpublished doctoral dissertation, University of Washington, 1968.

Leibich, André Leonard. Between Ideology and Utopia: The Politics and Philosophy of August Cieszkowski." Unpublished doctoral dissertation, Harvard University, 1974.

Lettau, Reinhard Adolf. "Utopie und Roman. Untersuchungen zur Form des deutschen utopischen romans im Zwanzigste Jahrhundert.'' Unpublished doctoral dissertation, Harvard University, 1960.

Lipow, Arthur Sherman. ''The Technocratic Utopians: Social and Historical Roots of Authoritarian Anti-Capitalism.'' Unpublished doctoral dissertation, University of California, Berkeley, 1969.

Lipscomb, Winifred Lawrence. ''Status and Structure of the Family in Idealistic Communities: A Study of Selected Utopias, Literary, Religious and Secular.'' Unpublished doctoral dissertation, University of North Carolina, 1947.

Louvancour, Henri. ''De Henri de Saint-Simon à Charles Fourier: Étude sur le socialisme romantique français de 1830.'' Thesis, Paris, 1913.

Lyon, Laurence Gill. ''German Literary Utopias of the Eighteenth Century with Emphasis on the Period 1700–1740.'' Unpublished doctoral dissertation, Harvard University, 1974.

McClintock, Michael William. ''Utopias and Dystopias.'' Unpublished doctoral dissertation, Cornell University, 1970.

McHugh, Christine. ''Edward Bellamy and the Populists: The Agrarian Response to Utopia, 1888–1898.'' Unpublished doctoral dissertation, University of Illinois at Chicago Circle, 1976.

Mann, William-Edward. ''Robinson Crusoé en France. Étude sur l'influence de cette oeuvre dans la littérature française.'' Thesis, Paris, 1916.

Martin, Harry Stratton. ''A Posthumous Work of Fontenelle.'' Unpublished M.A. thesis, University of Minnesota, 1948.

Mattes, William Ward. ''Aldous Huxley and the Utopian Tradition.'' Unpublished doctoral dissertation, Texas Technological University, 1971.

Mazer, Charles Litten. ''Orwell's *1984,* Zamyatin's *We,* and the Sociology of Knowledge.'' Unpublished M.A. thesis, Texas Technological College, 1968.

Meyers, Carolyn Hodgson. ''Psychotechnology in Fiction about Imaginary Societies, 1923–1962.'' Unpublished doctoral dissertation, University of Kentucky, 1965.

Minkowski, Helmut. ''Die Neu-Atlantis des Francis Bacon. Ein Beitrag zur Geistesgeschichte des 17. Jahrhunderts.'' Dissertation, Berlin, 1936.

Moran, Kathryn. ''Utopias, Subtopias, Dystopias in the Novels of Anthony Burgess.'' Unpublished doctoral dissertation, Notre Dame University, 1974.

Müller, Wolf Dietrich. ''Die Geschichte der Utopia-Romane der Weltliteratur.'' Dissertation, Münster, 1938.

Nergert, Heinz. ''Der Einfluss der Utopisten auf Marx.'' Dissertation, Tübingen, 1952.

Nydahl, Joel Mellin. ''Utopia Americana: Early American Utopian Fiction, 1790–1864.'' Unpublished doctoral dissertation, University of Michigan, 1974.

Odegard, Holtan P. "Administrative Democracy: A Creative Utopia," Unpublished doctoral dissertation, University of Wisconsin, 1959.

Olexa, Joseph Stephen. "Search for Utopia." Unpublished doctoral dissertation, University of Oregon, 1972.

Panage, John H. "Representative Late Nineteenth Century Utopias." Unpublished doctoral dissertation, University of Minnesota, 1939.

Park, Mary C. "Joseph Priestley and the Problem of Pantisocracy." Unpublished doctoral dissertation, University of Pennsylvania, 1947.

Parrington, Vernon Louis, Jr. "The Utopian Novel in America." Unpublished doctoral dissertation, Brown University, 1943.

Parssinen, Terry Mitchell. "Thomas Spence and the Spenceans: A Study of Revolutionary Utopianism in the England of George III." Unpublished doctoral dissertation, Brandeis University, 1968.

Pfaelzer, Mary Jean. "Utopian Fiction in America, 1880–1900: The Impact of Political Theory on Literary Form." Unpublished doctoral dissertation, University College, London University, 1976.

Piotrowski, Sylvester Anthony. "Etienne Cabet and the Voyage en Icarie, a Study in the History of Social Thought." Dissertation, The Catholic University, 1935.

Pomerance, Irwin. "The Moral Utopianism of Georges Sorel." Unpublished doctoral dissertation, Columbia University, 1950.

Pratter, Frederick Earl. "The Uses of Utopia: An Analysis of American Speculative Fiction, 1880–1960." Unpublished doctoral dissertation, University of Iowa, 1973.

Quissell, Barbara Carolyn. "The Sentimental and Utopian Novels of 19th Century America: Romance and Social Issues." Unpublished doctoral dissertation, Univrsity of Utah, 1973.

Ransom, Ellene. "Utopus Discovers America or Critical Realism in American Utopian Fiction, 1798–1900." Unpublished doctoral dissertation, Vanderbilt University, 1946.

Rauschenbusch, H. "Utopische Ideen, inbesondere in ihren wirtschaftlichen Auswirkungen." Dissertation, Frankfurt, 1922.

Rawson, Graham Stanhope. "William Morris's political romance 'News from Nowhere'. Its sources and its relationship to 'John Ball' and Bellamy's political romance 'Looking Backward.'" Dissertation, Jena, 1914.

Reich, Erna. "Der deutsche utopistische Roman von 1850 bis zur Gegenwart." Dissertation, Vienna, 1927.

Rensenbrink, John C. "Technology and Utopia: Political Claims of Moral Freedom." Unpublished doctoral dissertation, University of Chicago, 1956.

Rhodes, Harold V. "The Methodology of Utopian Political Theory." Unpublished doctoral dissertation, University of Arizona, 1964.

Richter, Helene. "Neure englische Utopien seit 1870 in ihrer Beziehung zur Thomas More und Francis Bacon." Dissertation, Vienna, 1956.

Robinovitch, Sidney Paul. "Information and Utopia: The Aesthetic Transformation of Man's Symbolic Environment." Unpublished doctoral dissertation, University of Illinois at Champaign, Urbana, 1970.

Roemer, Kenneth M. "America as Utopia, 1888–1900: New Visions, Old Dreams." Unpublished doctoral dissertation, University of Pennsylvania, 1971.

Rooney, Charles J. "Utopian Literature as a Reflection of Social Forces in America, 1865–1917." Unpublished doctoral dissertation, George Washington University, 1968.

Rubenstein, William C. "English Utopias of the 19th Century." Master's thesis, New York University, 1947. Discarded.

Russel, Margaret. "The Utopian Motif in the English Romance of the Seventeenth Century." Unpublished doctoral dissertation, Yale University, 1923.

Saine, Ute Miller. "Bernadin de Saint-Pierre's Paul et Virginie: From Social Utopia to Escape Novel." Unpublished doctoral dissertation, Yale University, 1971.

Samaan, Angele Botros. "The Novel of Utopianism and Prophecy. From Lytton (1871) to Orwell (1949). With Special Reference Its Reception." Unpublished doctoral dissertation, London University, 1962 [1963 on binding].

Samuelson, David Norman. "Studies in the Contemporary American and British Science Fiction Novel." Unpublished doctoral dissertation, University of Southern California, 1969.

Sargent, Lyman Tower. "The Relationship Between Political Philosophy and Political Ideology: A Study of Étienne Cabet and His Communitarian Experiments." Unpublished doctoral dissertation, University of Minnesota, 1965.

Schaeffer, Kurt. "Die sozialistischen Systeme Theodor Hertzkas und Anton Mengers mit besonderer Berücksichtigung ihrer Entwicklung aus dem ökonomischen Individualismus." Dissertation, Halle, 1907.

Schectman, Aaron Henry. "Education in Selected American Utopian Literature 1900–1950." Master's thesis, Rutgers- The State University, 1954.

Schectman, Aaron Henry. "The Uses of Utopia in Selected American Educational Proposals." Unpublished doctoral dissertation, Rutgers - The State University, 1971.

Schepelmann, Wolfgang. "Die englische Utopie im Übergang: von Bulwer-Lytton bis H. G. Wells. Strukturanalysen an ausgewählten Beispielen der ersten evolutionistischen Periode." Dissertation, Vienna, 1973.

Schick, Selma. "Ideas of Educational Reform in Certain Utopias in the Sixteenth and Seventeenth Centuries," Master's thesis, New York University, 1939. Discarded.

Schiffman, Joseph. "The Genesis of Edward Bellamy's Thought." Unpublished doctoral dissertation, New York University, 1951.

Schmid, Josef. "Die englischen Utopisten des 16. und 17. Jahrhunderts und die religiöse Frage. Ein Beitrag zur Geschichte der religiösen Aufklärung in England." Dissertation, Freiburg im Breisgau, 1933.

Schmidlin, Dorothy Ruth. "American Literary Utopias Before the Civil War." Unpublished Masters thesis, University of Colorado, 1942.

Schmückle, Karl. "Logisch-historische Elemente der Utopie." Dissertation, Jena, 1923.

Schoenfeldt, Eberhard. "Ideologie und Utopie als Probleme der politischen Bildung." Thesis, Hamburg, 1971.

Schumpp, Mechthild. "Städtebau und Utopie: soziologische Überlegungen zum Verhältnis von Städtebaulichen Utopien und Gesellschaft." Dissertation, Göttingen, 1970.

Segal, Howard. "Technological Utopianism and American Culture, 1830–1940." Unpublished doctoral dissertation, Princeton University, 1975.

Seitz, Sister M. Agnes (Luise). "Thomas Morus und seine Utopia im Urteil der Renaissance." Dissertation, Freiburg, 1924.

Sengfelder, Carl. "Utopische Erziehungsideale und praktische Schulreformversuche der neuesten Zeit." Dissertation, Erlangen, 1929.

Shaw, Nonna Dolodarenko. "The Soviet State in Twentieth Century Utopian Imaginative Literature." Unpublished doctoral dissertation, Indiana University, 1961.

Sherman, Shirley. "Postwar Soviet Science Fiction." Unpublished Master's thesis, Columbia University, [1956].

Shurter, Robert L. "The Utopian Novel in America 1865–1900." Unpublished doctoral dissertation, Western Reserve University, 1936.

Smith, Lewis Conrad, Jr. "The Decline of Utopian Literature in the Seventeenth Century." Unpublished doctoral dissertation, State University of Iowa, 1950.

Smith, Walter A. "The Religion of Edward Bellamy." Unpublished Master's thesis, Columbia University, 1937.

Solberg, Victor. "A Source Book of English and American Utopias." Unpublished doctoral dissertation, Ohio State University, 1932.

Spangenberg, Kurt. "Die Funktion der Utopie in der anglo-amerikanischen Prosa der 19. und 20. Jahrhunderts." Dissertation, Berlin, 1945.

Sterling, Sybil Stewart. "Ideas Persisting Through Utopias in English Literature." Unpublished Master's thesis, University of Colorado, 1922.

Stokes, Ella Harrison. "The Conception of a Kingdom of Ends in Augustine, Aquinas, and Leibnitz." Unpublished doctoral dissertation, University of Chicago, 1912.

Stupple, A. James. "Utopian Humanism in American Fiction, 1888-1900." Unpublished doctoral dissertation, Northwestern University, 1971.

Sweetland, James Harvey. "American Utopian Fiction, 1798-1926." Unpublished doctoral dissertation, University of Notre Dame, 1976.

Taylor, Walter Fuller. "Economic Unrest in American Fiction 1880-1901." Unpublished doctoral dissertation, University of North Carolina, 1929.

Thal-Larsen, Margaret. "Political and Economic Ideas of American Utopian Fiction." Unpublished doctoral dissertation, University of California, 1941.

Theim, Jon Edgar. "The Artist in the Ideal State: A Study of the Troubled Relations Between the Arts and Society in Utopian Fiction." Unpublished doctoral dissertation, Indiana University, 1975.

Thomas, George Boyd. "Blueprints for Tomorrow: American Novels of Future Change, 1869-1900." Unpublished doctoral dissertation, Harvard University, 1970.

Tieje, Ralph E. "The Prose Voyage Imaginaire Before 1800." Unpublished doctoral dissertation, University of Illinois, 1917.

Tihany, Leslie Charles. "French Utopian Thought, 1676-1790." Unpublished doctoral dissertation, University of Chicago, 1943.

Topik, Fred S. "Utopische Gedanken in modernen deutschen Romanen, 1930 bis 1951." Unpublished doctoral dissertation, University of Southern California, 1956.

Travis, James Richard. "An Analysis of the English Utopian Literature of the Nineteenth Century." Unpublished Master's thesis, Columbia University, 1940.

Volk, Winfried. "Die Entdeckung Tahitis und das Wunschbild der seligen Insel in der deutschen Literatur." Dissertation, Heidelberg, 1934.

Wackwitz, Friedrich. "Entstehungsgeschichte von D. Defoes 'Robinson Crusoe.'" Dissertation, Berlin, 1909.

Wahlke, John. "Charles Fourier and Henri Saint-Simon: Two Theorists of the Reaction." Unpublished doctoral dissertation, Harvard University, 1952.

Walter, Helmut. "Grenzen der Utopie. Die Bedingungen des utopischen Romans, dargelegt an Franz Werfels Stern der Ungeborenen." Dissertation, Erlangen, 1958.

Welsh, Charles Whitefield. "From Plato to Wells. An Analysis of the Doctrines of Justice, Property, Government, Education and Religion as Contained in the Utopias from 'The Republic' to 'The Outline of History.'" Unpublished doctoral dissertation, Southern Baptist Theological Seminary, 1922.

Wijngaarden, Nicolaas van. "Les Odyssées philosophiques en France entre 1616 et 1789." Dissertation, Amsterdam, 1932.

Winning, Charles Del Norte. "The Ideal Society in Nineteenth-Century

English Literature: A Study of Utopian Phantasies." Unpublished doctoral dissertation, New York University, 1932. Lost.

Winston, David. "Iambulus: A Literary Study in Greek Utopianism." Unpublished doctoral dissertation, Columbia University, 1956.

Wolf, Hans. "Utopismus und politische Wirklichkeit zur Zeit der Commonwealths." Dissertation, Hamburg, 1937.

Wolff, Emil. "Francis Bacons Verhaltnis zu Platon." Dissertation, Munich, 1908.

Wooden, Warren Walter. "Sir Thomas More, Satirist: A Study of the *Utopia* as Menippean Satire." Unpublished doctoral dissertation, Vanderbilt University, 1971.

Ziegler, Rudolf. "Utopien und Vorschläge zu sozialen Reformen bei Victor Hugo." Dissertation, Munich, 1924.

Author Index to the Chronological List

NOTE: The Addendum is not indexed.

Acworth, Andrew, 1896
Adams, Frederick Upham, 1897
Adams, Jack, 1900
Addison, Hugh, 1923
Adlard, Mark, 1971, 1972, 1975
Adolph, Mrs. Anna, 1899
Aermont, Paul, 1873
Agricola, 1908
Aiken, John, 1970
Aikin, Charles, 1895
Alban, Antony, 1968
Albertson, Garrett V., nd.
Aldiss, Brian W., 1955, 1957, 1960, 1961, 1965, 1968, 1975
Alerial, 1887
Alexander, James B., 1909
Alington, Adrian Richard, 1941
Allen, Charles G. B., 1884
Allen, Henry Francis, 1886, 1891
Allen, Henry Ware, 1936
Allighan, Garry, 1961
Allott, Kenneth, 1937
Alterego, 1937
American Society of Martians, Providence, 1924
Anderson, Colin, 1970
Anderson, Poul, 1952, 1953, 1955(2), 1957, 1959, 1963, 1967, 1973(2)
Andrew, J. O., 1892
Andrews, Lewis M., 1974
Andrews, William S., 1860
Andrusius, *Pantarch*, 1860
Anson, August, 1938
Anthony, Piers, 1968
Anvil, Christopher, 1962
Appel, Benjamin, 1959
Appleton, Jane Sophia, 1848
Aratus, 1793
Ardrey, Robert, 1944

Arlen, Michael, 1933
Armour, John P., 1905
Armstrong, Charles Wicksteed, 1892, 1936
Arnason, Eleanor, 1974
Arozin, 1920
Ascher, Isidore Gordon, 1898
Ashbee, Charles Robert, 1910
Asimov, Isaac, 1950, 1951, 1954, 1955, 1957(2), 1970, 1975
Astor, John Jacob, 1894
Athey, Henry, 1898
Atterley, Joseph, 1827
Auden, W. H., 1940
Augustinus, 1898, 1899
The Author of Miss Molly, 1911
The Author of "Our Neighborhood", 1836
Author of "Theodore", 1848
Authwise, Eugene, 1872-73
Aycock, Roger Dee, 1954
Babcock, George, 1922
Bacas, Paul Edmond, 1954
Bachelder, John, 1890
Bacon, Francis, 1626
Bailey, Hilary, 1965
Bair, Patrick, 1950
Baker, William Elliott Smith, 1883
Balch, William S., 1881
Ball, F. N., 1961
Ball, Frank P., 1923
Ballard, J. G., 1960, 1961(2), 1975
Balsdon, John Percy Vyvian, 1936
Balscopo, Giovanni Battista, or Jose, 1825
Banim, John, 1824
Barber, Elsie Oakes, 1950
Barbor, Herbert R., 1922
Barker, Arthur W., 1927
Barlow, James William, 1891
Barlow, Jane, 1891
Barnaby, Hugo, 1895

Fulton, James A., 1915
Galier, W. H., 1896
Gallego, Serapio Gonzalez, 1944
Galloway, James M., 1897
Gaskell, Jane, 1957
Gaston, Henry A., 1880
Gazella, Edith Virginia, 1928
Gazlay, Allen W., 1856
Geissler, Ludwig A., 1891
Geister, Carl, 1864
Genone, Hudor, 1886, 1887
A Gentleman On His Travels, 1762
Gentlemen, Francis, 1765
George, W. L., 1926
Gerrare, Wirt, 1898
Geston, Mark S., 1967
Gibbs, Barbara, 1975
Gibbs, Lewis, 1951
Gieske, Herman Everett, 1940
Gilbert, John Wilmer, 1940
Gildon, Charles, 1720
Giles, Fayette Stratton, 1894, 1896
Gillette, King Camp, 1894, 1910, 1924
Gillon, Diana, 1961
Gillon, Meir, 1961
Gilman, Bradley, 1901
Gilman, Charlotte Perkins, 1911, 1915, 1916
Gilpin, William, 1890
Girad, Dian, 1974
Glass, L. A., 1970
Glenn, Goerge Alan, M. D., 1940
Gloag, John, 1933, 1940
Glossop, Reginald, 1926
Glyn, Alice Coralie, 1896
Glynn-Ward, Hilda, 1921
Godwin, Francis, 1638
Golding, William, 1954
Goldsmith, John Francis, 1935
Goldsmith, Oliver, 1765
Golfing, Francis, 1975
Gonsalez, Domingo, 1635
Good, Charles H., 1963
Goodrich, Charles H., 1963
Goodwyn, Burmby, 1840's
Gordon, Rex, 1955, 1966
Gorer, Geoffrey, 1936
Gotschalk, Felix C., 1975
Gott, Samuel, 1648
Gotthelf, Ezra Gerson, 1935
Goulart, Ron, 1970
Gould, F. J., 1891
Graham, Peter Anderson, 1923
Grant, Isabell Francis, 1926
Gratacap, Louis Pope, 1903, 1910
Graves, Charles L., 1898
Graves, Robert, 1949

Gray, Curme, 1951
Gray, John, 1831
Green, A. Romney, 1937
Green, Henry, 1948
Green, Nunsowe, 1882
Green, Robert, 1968
Greener, William O., 1898
Greg, Percy, 1880
Gregory, Owen, 1918
Gresswell, Elsie Kay, 1935
Grey, Charles, 1954
Grierson, Francis D., 1928
Griesser, Wilhelm, 1923
Griffin, C. S., 1889
Griffith, George, 1895, 1903, 1906
Griffith, Mary, 1836
Griffiths, Isabel, 1922
Griggs, Sutton Elbert, 1899
Grigsby, Alcanoan O., 1900
Grimshaw, Robert, 1892
Grip, 1882
Gronlund, Lawrence, 1884
Groom, Arthur John Pelham, 1948
Gross, Werter Livingston, 1946
Grove, W., 1890
Groves, John William, 1968
Gubbins, Herbert, 1914
Guérard, Albert, 1930
Guest, Ernest, 1929
Gull, Cyril Arthur Edward Ranger, 1906
Gulliver, Lemuel, 1726, 1969
Gulliver, Lemuel, Junior, 1796, 1830
Gunn, James E., 1955, 1961, 1962
Gunn, Neil M., 1944
Guthrie, Kenneth Sylvan, 1919
H., R., Esquire, 1660
Hadley, Arthur T., 1958
Haedicke, Paul, 1895
Hahn, Charles Curtz, 1899
Hake, William Augustus Gordon, 1840
Haldane, J. B. S., 1950's
Hale, Edward Everett, 1867, 1871
Hale, John, 1969
Hall, Austin, 1921
Hall, Granville Stanley, 1920
Hall, Harold Curtis, 1942
Hall, Joseph, 1605
Halle, Louis J., 1963
Hamada, Nobuya, 1922
Hamilton, Mary Cicely, 1909, 1922
Hamilton, Patrick, 1939
Hanvey, Robert, 1903
Harben, William Nathaniel, 1892, 1894
Harding, Ellison, 1907
Harness, Charles Leonard, 1953
Harney, Gilbert Lane, 1900

Title Index to the Chronological List

The Cosmopolitan Railway, 1890
Cost of Living, 1952
The Council of Seven, 1921
Counter Clock World, 1967
The Countesse of Pembrokes Arcadia, 1590
The Coup D'Etat of 1961, 1908
The Crater, 1847
Crimson Courage, 1940
Crisis! 1992, 1936
Critical Mass, 1961
Cromwell the Third, 1886
Crossroads to Nowhere, 1956
Crucible Island, 1919
A Crystal Age, 1887
The Crystal Button, 1891
The Curious Culture of the Planet Loretta, 1968
The Curious Republic of Gondour, 1875
The Curve of the Snowflake, 1956
The Cybernetic Brains, 1962
Cynia: An Original Utopia, 1965
Dalleszona and the Seventh Treasure, 1922
Dark Boundaries, 1953
Darkening Island, 1972
Darkness and Dawn, 1884
Darkness and the Light, 1942
The Day Before Forever, 1967
The Day of Faith, 1921
The Day of Judgment, 1923
The Day of Prosperity, 1902
The Day of the Coastwatch, 1968
The Day of the Drones, 1969
Day of the Republic, 1968
The Day of the Women, 1969
Daybreak, 1896
Days After Tomorrow, 1944
Deadly Image, 1958
The Death Master, 1959
Death Rocks the Cradle, 1933
Deathworld 2, 1964
The Decadence, 1929
Declaration of Principles, 1887
The Decline and Fall of the British Empire, 1890
Deep Freeze, 1955
The Demetrian, 1907
Democracy - False or True?, 1920
Depopulation, 1899
The Description of a New World, 1666
A Description of Millenium Hall, 1762
A Description of New Athens in Terra Australis Incognita, 1720
Description of Spensonia, 1795
A Description of the Famous Kingdom of Macaria, 1641
A Description of the South Indies, 1605

Desirable Lakeside Residence, 1973
The Devil's Advocate, 1952
The Devil's Altar Boy, 1945
Dewey Outlines Utopian Schools, 1933
Dialogue on Etzler's Paradise, 1843
The Diothas, 1883
The Disappearance, 1951
The Discovered Country, 1899
The Discovery of a New World, 1605
The Discovery of Altruria, 1895
A Discovery of Fonseca, 1682
The Dispossessed, 1974
Doctor Crosby's Strange Experience, 1935
Dr. Leete's Letter to Julian West, 1890
Dr. Silex, 1904
The Dome, 1968
Domesday Village, 1948
The Dominion in 1983, 1883
Don't Hold Your Breath, 1973
Doomed, 1920
The Doomsday Gene, 1974
The Doomsday Men, 1968
Doomsday Morning, 1957
Doppelgangers, 1947
Double Illusion, 1966
Doubting Thomas, 1956
The Dream, 1924
The Dream City, 1920
Dream of a Free-Trade Paradise, 1872
A Dream of a Modest Prophet, 1890
The Dream of a Warringtonian, 1900
The Dream of an Englishman, 1892
A Dream of an Ideal City, 1897
A Dream of John Ball, 1886–87
A Dream of Reform, 1848
A Dream of the Twenty-First Century, 1902
The Dreamer, 1754
Drumble, 1975
Dry Bread, 1891
Dune, 1965
Dune Messiah, 1969
The Dust Which is God, 1907
The Dwellers in Vale Sunrise, 1904
Early Christians of the 21st Century, 1949
Earth Abides, 1949
An Earth Gone Mad, 1954
Earth Revisited, 1893
Earthjacket, 1970
Earthman, Come Home, 1955
The Earthquake, 1892
Eastward Ho, 1958
Easy Millions, 1925
Eat, Drink, and be Merry, 1974
Ecodeath, 1972
Ecotopia, 1975
The Ecumen of Nations, 1961

Inside Straight, 1955
Interface, 1971
Intermere, 1901
The Interpreter, 1960
The Interpretors, 1954
Interworld, 1932
Into the Dawn, 1945
Into the Tenth Millenium, 1956
Intrigue on the Upper Level, 1934
An Introduction to Islandia, 1942
Invaded by Love, 1966
Invaders from Earth, 1956
The Inventory of Judgements
  Commonwealth, 1655
Ionia, 1898
Irish Rose, 1975
The Iron Heel, 1907
Is This Utopia?, 1942
Island, 1962
The Island Forbidden to Man, 1946
The Island of Anarchy, 1887
The Island of Eugenia, 1921
The Island of Fantasy, 1892
The Island of Liberty, 1848
The Island of Not-Me, 1935
The Island of Progress, 1893
Islandia, 1942
The Islar, 1969
The Isle of Pines, 1668
It Can't Happen Here, 1935
It Could Never Happen, 1932
It Might Be, 1896
It Was the Day of the Robot, 1964
The Jagged Orbit, 1969
James Ingleton, 1893
A Japanese Utopia, 1905
Jim McWhirter, 1933
John Bull: Socialist, 1909
John Harvey, 1897
John Innocent at Oxford, 1939
John Sagur, 1921
John Smith, Emperor, 1944
The Journal of David Q. Little, 1967
Journey Beyond Tomorrow, 1962
A Journey in Other Worlds, 1894
A Journey Lately Performed Through the
  Air, 1784
Journey of Joenes, 1962
Journey to Mars, 1894
A Journey to the Sun, 1866
Journey to Utopia, 1970
My Journeys with Astargo, 1952
The Joy Makers, 1961
The Joy Wagon, 1958
June, 1993, 1893
Kalomera, 1911

Kalos, 1970
Kark, 1969
The Karma Machine, 1975
The Keeper, 1968
The Key of Industrial Co-operative
  Government, 1886
King of Kulturia, 1915
The Kingdom of Heaven is at Hand, 1898
The Kingdom Within, 1934
The Kite Trust, 1900
Kronk, 1970
Kurrajong, 1954
Ladies Day, 1968
Lady Ermyntrude and the Plumber, 1912
The Lake of Gold, 1903
The Land of Nison, 1906
The Land of the Changing Sun, 1894
Land Under England, 1935
Landslide, 1934
The Language of Pao, 1957
The Lani People, 1962
Laputa Revisited by Gulliver Redivivus in
  1905, 1905
Last and First, 1930
The Last Days of the American Empire, 1975
The Last Inca, 1874
Last Days of the Republic, 1880
The Last Generation, 1908
Last Men in London, 1932
The Last Millionaire, 1923
The Last of My Race, 1924
The Last Persecution, 1909
The Last Refuge, 1966
The Last Spaceship, 1949
The Last Starship from Earth, 1968
The Last Voyage of Lemuel Gulliver, 1883
The Last War, 1898
L...A...T... to His Fellow Citizens, 1836
Late Final, 1951
The Law of Freedom in a Platform, 1652
The Laws of Leflo, 1911
A League of Justice, 1893
A Leap Into the Future, 1900
The Left Hand of Darkness, 1969
Left On!, 1973
The Legal Revolution of 1902, 1898
The Legend of Cougar Lou Landis, 1973
Legions of the Dawn, 1908
Lesbia Newman, 1889
Lest Ye Die, 1922
Let There Be Light, 1900
Let's Triumverate, 1943
Letters from New America, 1900
Letters from the Planets, 1887
Level 7, 1959
Libellus Vere Aureus Nec Munius Salutaris

The Marriage Lease, 1907
Mars Revealed, 1880
The Marshall Duke of Denver, 1895
The Marsian, 1940
Martha Brown M. P., 1935
The Marvelous Isles of the Western Sea, nd.
Mary's Country, 1957
The Masculinist Revolt, 1965
The Master Beast, 1907
The Master Plan, 1936
Masters of Evolution, 1959
The Mathematics of Labor, 1899
The Mayor of New York, 1910
Meccania, 1918
Meda, 1891
Melbourne and Mars, 1889
Meleager, 1916
Mellonta Tauta, 1849
The Melting Pot, 1932
Memoirs of Planetes, 1795
The Memoirs of Sigr Guadentio Di Lucca, 1737
Memories of the Future, 1923
The Men in the Jungle, 1967
Men Like Gods, 1922
Mental Travels in Imagined Lands, 1878
Me-Phi Bo-Sheth, 1934
Mercia, 1895
The Message, 1907
Message Ends, 1969
A Message from "Mars", 1924
A Message from the Stars, 1893
A Message to Thee, 1926
Messages from Mars, 1892
The Messiah, 1927
Messiah, 1954
The Messiah of the Cylinder, 1917
Messiah on the Horizon, 1940
Metatopia, 1961
Methods from Mars, 1913
The Midas Plague, 1954
Migrants of the Stars, 1931
Mildred Carver, U.S.A., 1919
Military Socialism, 1911
The Millenium, 1927
The Millenium, 1929
Millenium 1, 1945
The Milltillionaire, 1895
Minimum Man, 1938
The Missing Man, 1971
Mr. Jonnemacher's Machine, 1898
Mr. Oseba's Last Discovery, 1904
Mr. Podd, 1923
Mr. Stranger's Sealed Packet, 1889
The Mistriss of Virialis, 1955
Mizora, 1889

The Model Town, 1869
Moderan, 1971
A Modern Coöperative Colony, 1898
Modern Gulliver's Travels, 1796
Modern Lilliput, 1924
Modern Paradise, 1915
A Modern Utopia, 1905
The Moment of Truth, 1949
Monadelphia, 1832
The Monarch Billionaire, 1903
The Monarchy of Millions, 1900
The Monikins, 1835
The Monk of the Mountains, 1866
My Monks of Vagabondia, 1913
The Monster Municipality, 1882
Monument, 1961
Moonblight, 1892
Morgan Rockefeller's Will, 1909
Morrow's Ants, 1975
Moscow 1979, 1940
The Mossback Correspondence, 1889
Moth Race, 1972
Mother of Necessity, 1955
Moving the Mountain, 1911
Multiface, 1975
The Mummy!, 1827
Mundus Alter et Idem, 1605
Mural, 1945
Murder in Milleniun VI 1951
My Lady Green Sleeves, 1956
My Own Utopia, 1963
My Petition for More Space, 1974
My Sovereign Guide, 1898
My Vacation, 1891
My Visit to Sybaris, 1867
My Wondrous Dream, 1923
Myora, 1903
Mystery of the North Pole, 1908
Mystery-Wisdom from Mars, 1961
The Napolean of Notting Hill, 1904
A Narrative of the Travels and Adventures of Paul Aermont, 1873
National Evils and Practical Remedies, 1849
National Life and Character, 1893
Nationalism, 1889
Negrolana, 1924
Neocracy, 1968
Nephelococcygia or Letters from Paradise, 1929
Nequa, 1900
Neuroomia, 1894
Neutopia, 1925
A New Adventure of Telemachus, 1731
New Amazonia, 1889
A New and Further Discovery of the Isle of Pines, 1669

The Wind Trust, 1903
Windmills; A Book of Fables, 1915
With Gyves of Gold, 1898
With Her in Ourland, 1916
With the Bentfin Boomer Boys on Little Old New Alabama, 1972
With the Lid Off, 1935
With the Night Mail, 1909
Wolfbane, 1959
A Woman of Tomorrow, 1896
A Woman's Utopia, 1931
The Women Who Vowed, 1907
Wooden Centauri, 1975
Work For All, 1914
The World A Department Store, 1900
The World As I Want It, 1934
The World As I Want It, 1935
The World Below, 1929
A World Beyond, 1967
World-Birth, 1938
World Corporation, 1910
World D, 1935
The World Grown Young, 1892
The World in 1931, 1921
The World Inside, 1971
The World Jones Made, 1956
World of Chance, 1955

World of Tomorrow, 1919
A World of Women, 1919
World Out of Mind, 1953
The World Set Free, 1914
The World the World Wants, 1947
A World To Be, 1963
World Well Lost, 1970
A World Without a Child, 1905
World Without Women, 1960
World Without Raiment, 1943
Worlds Beginning, 1944
The World's Crisis, 1890
Worlds To Watch and Ward, 1947
The Wreck of the South Pole, 1899
The Wreck of a World, 1890
The Writing on the Wall, 1921
The Wrong End of Time, 1971
Year of Consent, 1954
The Year of Regeneration, 1932
The Year of the Comet, 1955
The Year of the Sex Olympics, 1969
Year 2018, 1956
Yezad, 1922
The Yorl of the Northmen, 1892
You'll See, 1957
Young West, 1894